P9-DZN-759

Tooth and Nail

A Novel Approach
to the New SAT

Charles Harrington Elster
& Joseph Elliot

A Harvest Test Preparation Book
Harcourt, Inc.
San Diego   New York   London

Text copyright © 1994 by Charles Harrington Elster and Joseph Elliot
Glossary copyright © 1994 by Charles Harrington Elster, Joseph Elliot,
and Harcourt Brace & Company

All rights reserved. No part of this publication may be reproduced or
transmitted in any form or by any means, electronic or mechanical,
including photocopy, recording, or any information storage and retrieval
system, without permission in writing from the publisher.

Requests for permission to make copies of any part of the work
should be mailed to the following address: Permissions Department,
Harcourt, Inc., 6277 Sea Harbor Drive, Orlando, Florida 32887-6777.

SAT is a registered trademark of the College Entrance Examination Board.

"The Brain—is wider than the Sky—," by Emily Dickinson, is reprinted
by permission of the publishers and the Trustees of Amherst College
from The Poems of Emily Dickinson, Thomas H. Johnson, ed., Cambridge,
Mass.: The Belknap Press of Harvard University Press, Copyright © 1951,
1955, 1979. 1983 by the President and Fellows of Harvard College.

Library of Congress Cataloging-in-Publication Data
Elster, Charles Harrington.
    Tooth and nail: a novel approach to the new SAT/Charles
Harrington Elster & Joseph Elliot.
        p.   cm.—(A Harvest test preparation book)
    ISBN 0-15-601382-7
    1. Scholastic aptitude test—Study guides.   I. Elliot, Joseph,
1960–.   II. Title.   III. Series.
LB2353.57E47   1994
378.1'662—dc20   93-30958

Designed by Lydia D'moch
Printed in the United States of America

First edition
V U T S R

Harcourt Trade Publishing books may be purchased for educational, business, or
sales promotional use. For information please write: Harcourt Trade Publishing,
attn: Director of Special Sales, 525 B Street, Suite 1900, San Diego, CA 92101.

For Myrna and Anne:
indefatigable partners, beneficent wives.

But thou art all my art and dost advance
As high as learning my rude ignorance.
—Shakespeare, Sonnet 78

Contents

Acknowledgments

The authors wish to thank the following persons for their assistance: Chuck Valverde of Wahrenbrock's Book House in San Diego, for sharing his esoteric knowledge of rare books; Steve Hayes, for help in the early stages; Philip Williams, for sage advice; Philip Turner, for a good tip; Cory Meacham; John Uphouse; Norman Storer and Mary Hiatt; and Nancy and Reinhardt Elster, for putting us up and putting up with us.

Preface

Congratulations. You have just done something very smart—something **commendable** and **meritorious,** as the people who write the SAT would probably put it.

Why are you so smart? Because in picking up this book you've just taken the first step toward preparing yourself for the verbal sections of the SAT in a refreshing, creative way.

You also might have some fun in the process.

Studying for the SAT, fun? Give me a break, you're thinking. Well, that's just what we intend to give you.

The book you're holding in your hands represents a complete break from the SAT preparation methods of the past. It's a break from boring lessons. It's a break from trying to memorize **tedious** lists of unrelated words. It's a break from sharpening No. 2 pencils and filling in multiple-choice ovals. It is unlike any other SAT preparation book or program available today.

That's because *Tooth and Nail* takes an **innovative** approach—as the subtitle says, "a **novel** approach." It offers you a way to build your vocabulary, improve your reading comprehension skills, and enjoy a good story all at the same time.

If that sounds like a better way to go, read on.

The "**Novel** Approach" and How It Works

You've probably already realized there's a double meaning in the phrase "a **novel** approach." We chose it, of course, to show that *Tooth and Nail* is unusual in two ways.

First, this book represents an entirely new way to build your vocabulary for the SAT. Second, it's *not* a text book. It's an actual novel that contains words you're likely to see on the test. In short, our "**novel** approach" says good-bye to word lists and lessons and lets you read your way toward a stronger SAT vocabulary.

Here's how it works:

Every boldfaced word in this book (boldface is **dark type, like this**) is an SAT word. Boldfacing is our **subtle** way of calling words to your attention without interrupting the flow of your reading. Think of it as a little flag that says, "Hey, here's one that may come up on the test!"

For example, of the four hundred words you've just read, six were boldfaced: ***commendable, meritorious, tedious, innovative, novel,*** and ***subtle.*** ("**Dark type, like this**" doesn't count because it was just an example.) These six and the hundreds of other boldfaced SAT words in *Tooth and Nail* are defined in the glossary at the back of the book. To quickly find out what a boldfaced word means, just flip to the glossary and look it up. Then reread the passage in which the word occurs to reinforce your understanding of the meaning.

Besides giving definitions, the glossary has two other useful features:

1. *Cross-referencing of SAT synonyms.* Look up ***adept*** in the glossary and you'll find a definition followed by cross-references to four SAT synonyms: ***adroit, deft, dexterous,*** and ***proficient.*** Checking the definitions of these and all the other cross-referenced synonyms in the glossary will help you build your vocabulary faster by associating groups of related SAT words.

2. *Page references showing where each SAT word occurs in the*

book. Many SAT words come up several times in *Tooth and Nail.* When you begin using the glossary, you'll see that each entry lists the page numbers where you can find that word. If you're trying to master a particular SAT word, you can easily study every passage where it appears in the book.

For further review and reinforcement, we've also included a section of exercises. There you'll find SAT-style analogies, sentence completions, and reading comprehension questions based on passages in the novel.

We're convinced that if you **peruse** *Tooth and Nail,* make **diligent** use of the glossary, and do all the exercises **conscientiously,** your brain will be in excellent shape for the SAT.

So, what do you think? Does our "**novel** approach" sound better than sweating over lessons and lists? Maybe even a little bit fun? If you're thinking yes, then you know exactly why we wrote *Tooth and Nail*: to provide you with an effective *and* enjoyable method of building your vocabulary for the SAT.

What Exactly Is an "SAT Word"?

You may be wondering how we determined which words were "SAT words," the ones we've boldfaced in this book. Here's what we did:

We **analyzed** the verbal sections of thirty-five published SATs. With the aid of a computer, we **compiled** a list of all the words that appeared two or more times on the test. Then, with the help of references teachers use to determine vocabulary grade level, we pared down our big list, eliminating simple words below the eighth-grade level until we were left with all the high school- and college-level words—the most challenging portion of the SAT vocabulary. Our final list contained more than twelve hundred upper-level words, many of which showed up on numerous SATs. These are the words you will find in the pages of *Tooth and Nail.*

Now, lets face facts. Because English has more than a million

words, and because the particular SAT you take will be different from the tests we examined, we can't guarantee that our
list contains every tough word you'll encounter on your test.
Based on our breakdown, however, we can **assert** that all the
words in our list have a better-than-average chance of appearing on the SAT. So it stands to reason that learning as many of
them as you can will improve your chances of doing well on
the test.

But that's enough about word lists, because—we'll say it
again—this book is *not* about lists. Lists are **insipid.** They have
no **vitality.** To quote a spokesperson for the SAT, "Word lists
are out; reading is in."

The Key to the SAT: Read, Read, Read

Reading is what *Tooth and Nail* is all about. It's also what the
SAT is all about. The SAT has always emphasized reading comprehension, and even the College Entrance Examination
Board (the people responsible for making you miserable for
several hours on a Saturday morning) admits that the best way
you can learn the words you need to know for the test is to
"read and read widely."

Since 1994, when SAT I was introduced, about half of all
the questions in the verbal sections have been based on the
reading comprehension passages. Overall there have been
more questions that test "verbal reasoning skills and knowledge of vocabulary in **context.**"

You don't have to be an Einstein to figure out that there's
only one way to build your knowledge of vocabulary in **context**: by reading. And that, as we said before, is what *Tooth and
Nail* is all about.

*Learning Vocabulary in **Context***

Think of **context** (it's in the glossary—check it out) as a word's
environment. **Context** is where words dwell.

Studying a word in a vocabulary list is like studying an animal in a cage. You can't **discern** its true nature because it's been removed from its environment. When you study a word in **context**—in the phrases and sentences and paragraphs where it lives—you learn far more than its definition. You see the word in action, affirming its existence in the language and **exerting** its special influence on its surroundings. You watch how it behaves and pick up clues about its personality. And as you come to understand how it **clarifies** or **enhances** what you're reading, you discover not only what the word means but also how it works.

Studying a word in **context** involves two things: (1) **scrutinizing** all its dictionary definitions to determine which one is applicable and why; and (2) asking yourself some **astute** questions: What precisely does this word **imply**, and how does it flavor the passage? Is it positive or negative, **abstract** or concrete, **explicit** or **obscure**? Does it suggest a state of mind or indicate how to interpret an action? Does it tell you something about a person or the quality of a thing? How do the words surrounding it provide clues to its meaning? Every earnest attempt to answer these questions as you read this book will help you develop your ability to **ascertain** meaning from **context** and improve your chances of doing well on the new SAT.

We could write a lengthy **treatise** on learning vocabulary in **context,** but don't worry, we won't. Instead we'll be **concise:** Other SAT preparation books present words out of context. *Tooth and Nail* puts SAT words in **context** and helps you befriend them.

Now that's about as **succinct** as you can get.

A Few Words to the Wise

You probably will already know some of the boldfaced SAT words you see in this book. (If you know them well, that's great; you're on your way to a better score.) Many other boldfaced words may seem familiar and you may think you know what they mean, but when it comes to filling in those little ovals on exam day, *thinking* you know the meaning of a word may not be good enough.

We know you'll check the definitions of unfamiliar words, but it's also important to look up the words you only *think* you know. Remember, many words can be used in more than one way, and the SAT specializes in verbal surprises, so don't take the meaning of any boldfaced word in this book for granted. Combing the **context** for clues, then checking the word's definition, and then rereading the sentence or paragraph in which it occurs is the most effective way to reinforce your knowledge.

Also, be careful not to guess the meaning of a word. For example, many people think that *enervated* means "filled with energy," because it looks and sounds like *energized.* In fact, *enervated* means just the opposite: "weakened, drained of energy." The point is, your **subjective assessment** of what a word means may not be reliable. So be sure to check the definition in the glossary and in your dictionary, and then reread the **context.**

In short, be honest with yourself. If you're only fifty-percent sure what a word means, or even if you're ninety-nine percent sure, look it up. It's painless, and no one's peering over your shoulder in judgment. There's also an added benefit to checking and rechecking the definitions of words you come across in your reading. Not only will it help you prepare for the SAT, it will also help you build a strong and permanent vocabulary, one that will serve you well through college and beyond.

Extra Credit for the Extra-Serious Reader

Now that we've gotten that **admonition** out of the way, let's talk about how you can do even more to score high on the test.

In addition to the hundreds of boldfaced SAT words in *Tooth and Nail,* we have incorporated numerous "extra-credit" words in the book. Most of them are at or above the eleventh-grade level. Many appeared only once in our **analysis** of SAT materials; others we have included because our story required them. For example, *decrepit, sodden, cumbersome, interject, amorous, tenuous, circumscribed, redoubtable, conundrum, jocular,* and *delectation* are just a few of the dozens of challenging extra-credit words in *Tooth and Nail.* They're all over the book, waiting for you to discover them.

Keep in mind that these extra-credit words are not printed in boldface, which means they're not defined in the glossary. As you read and look up the boldfaced SAT words in the glossary, also keep an eye out for anything unfamiliar that isn't printed in boldface. By keeping your dictionary close by while reading, you can look up the extra-credit words right away. You can also highlight them with a marker and look them up later, after finishing each chapter. (Highlighting is a good idea because it gives you an easy way to find these words again just by flipping through the book.)

We have included these extra-credit words to give you, as a **motivated** student, more chances to build your vocabulary and prepare for whatever may come your way on the SAT. Consider it a further opportunity for **edification** and **enlightenment.** (Go on, check the glossary!)

Two Tips for SAT Success

When studying vocabulary for the SAT, you will learn more, learn faster, and be more likely to retain what you've learned if you follow these two **precepts:**

1. *Get a partner (or two).* Working with a partner—a "study buddy"—is an excellent way to solidify your knowledge of the words you learn from reading *Tooth and Nail* (especially if your partner is reading it too).

2. *Make it fun.* Preparing for the SAT doesn't have to be torture. (That's why we wrote this book, remember?) Though taking the test may not be one of life's most pleasurable experiences, learning SAT vocabulary can be both enjoyable and productive.

Here are some ideas that may help:

✎ Read *Tooth and Nail* with a friend. When you have someone to help you, and someone you can help, it's a lot easier to stick to a studying schedule and accomplish your goals. Try giving each other a weekly reading assignment, and get together regularly to discuss the book and review the SAT words you've learned.

✎ Ask your friend to select a passage at **random** from *Tooth and Nail,* one that has several boldfaced SAT words, and read it aloud. Listen, and then define the words. (Use the glossary to check your answers, and use your dictionary to check pronunciation or to research other definitions.) Discuss how the SAT words influence the meaning of the passage. Then reverse the procedure and quiz your friend.

✎ Try learning the vocabulary in reverse—from the definition to the word. Give your friend a list of the words you want to study and ask him or her to read you the definition, either from the glossary or from a dictionary. Then try to come up with the word that matches the definition.

✎ Find a handy place to record your "target words," the ones you find most difficult and the ones you most want to learn. The classic method (which really works!) is to create flashcards on three-by-five index cards, writing the word on one side and the definition on the other. Carry the cards with you and test yourself by flipping through them between classes, at lunch, on the bus, or wherever. You can also keep your words and definitions in a pocket-sized notebook that's easy to carry around. If you have access to a computer, you can create a special database of SAT words you want to learn or of all the challenging words you find in your reading. However you decide to set up your list, be sure to review it at least once or twice a day. Remember also that reviewing involves more than just skimming. For best results, quiz yourself regularly and keep track of your score.

✎ Each time you open this book, review the words that you learned in the last section you read. Look them up again in the glossary, and also keep a dictionary close by so you can check other definitions and also pronunciation. As they say, practice makes perfect, and review is the key to building a **tenacious** (as opposed to an **evanescent**) vocabulary.

✎ Remember that SAT words don't just appear on the SAT—they can pop up anywhere. Keep *Tooth and Nail* and a dictionary nearby while you're doing your reading for classes. When you come across a challenging word, see if it's in the glossary. If not, look it up in your dictionary. Also, try to read a newspaper or magazine for a few minutes every day with the goal of finding one or two words you *don't* know.

✎ Finally, challenge yourself every few days to use two or three of your newly acquired SAT words in a **pertinent** way, either in conversation or in writing.

As you can see, *Tooth and Nail* will expose you to lots of SAT words in **context**, but the responsibility for mastering them **ultimately** lies with you. We hope our "**novel** approach" will inspire you to **assiduously** build your word knowledge and fight tooth and nail to ace the SAT.

Charles Harrington Elster   Joseph Elliot
San Diego, California   Brooklyn, New York

Tooth and Nail

Chapter 1

Off to College

A Saturday in early September

Caitlin Ciccone knew what was coming and she dreaded it. They were standing by the gate waiting for the call to board the plane.

"Don't say it, Dad. Please."

But he said it anyway.

"'Parting is such sweet sorrow,' my dear."

Caitlin rolled her eyes. "Dad, I swear!"

"Don't swear, Caitlin. Remember what Juliet told Romeo? 'Do not swear at all; or if thou wilt, swear by thy gracious self.'"

"Yes, I know, but—"

"But nothing. I'm sending my daughter—my only child—off to college. Can't I be a little **sentimental**?"

Caitlin stuffed her hands in the pockets of her faded jeans and prepared for the **inevitable**. Her father was an English professor who loved to quote Shakespeare. Sometimes he couldn't help being a bit **pretentious** and **verbose**.

"My little scholar, off to 'suck the sweets of sweet philosophy' as the **eloquent** Shakespeare put it so **aptly** in *The Taming of the Shrew*. Now, I want you to keep in mind Tranio's advice: 'No profit grows where is no pleasure taken.'"

Caitlin listened **stoically** as her father delivered his

grandiloquent valedictory address. When the flight was announced, he held out his arms and they hugged for a long time.

"I'll miss you, sweetheart. Be **assiduous.** Work hard."

"I will. And I'll write—a lot."

"You'd better. I don't want you racking up the **exorbitant** phone bills you do at home."

"I won't."

"But call if you need anything."

Caitlin kissed her father's cheek. "Thanks, Dad. Don't worry. I'll be fine." She brushed back her long black hair, picked up her bags, and strode through the gate.

Caitlin had said goodbye to her mother on the phone the night before, and her mother had cried. Her parents had been divorced for six years, since she was twelve. Throughout her four years at the High School for Literature and the Performing Arts in Manhattan, she had lived with her mother one month and her father the next.

On the plane to Chicago, Caitlin thought about how all the moving back and forth had **wreaked** havoc on her social life. Perhaps to **compensate** for that disruption, she had applied herself to her schoolwork, earning straight A's in English and scoring high on her SATs. In her senior year she was elected editor of the school newspaper and at graduation she was salutatorian, ranking second in her class behind a nerd who wound up going to Harvard. The reward for all her **diligence** was a generous scholarship to Holyfield College, one of the most **prestigious** schools in the Midwest, with excellent programs in her primary interests, English and journalism.

In Chicago she changed planes for Des Moines, Iowa, where she boarded a bus for Holyfield, a small city another two hours away.

Caitlin stared out the window as the bus plowed down straight two-lane roads through the rich **abundance** of the flat midwestern farmland. Acres and acres of tall, tasseled corn rolled by, along with rippling fields of hay and a lovely, golden sort of grass that she thought might be wheat. **Quiescent** cows looked up as the bus passed. **Garrulous** birds **congregated** on power lines and circled over fields and barns. It was beautiful country, **wholesome** and **salutary**, she thought, but so alien compared with the familiar concrete and congestion of New York City.

A sign for the City of Holyfield flashed by the window, rousing Caitlin from her **contemplative** mood. Within minutes the bus arrived at the terminal downtown. Caitlin quickly gathered her belongings and made her way to the taxi stand outside.

The young cab driver tipped back the brim of her Minnesota Twins baseball cap and slung her arm over the front seat.

"Hi. You must be going up to the college, huh?"

"That's right," Caitlin answered cheerfully.

"Are you a freshman?"

"Does it show?"

"Maybe just a little," the driver said with a smile. "My name's Annie. I go to Holyfield too. I'm a junior."

"Really? Glad to meet you, Annie. I'm Caitlin."

"You sound like you're from back East, Caitlin."

"Yeah, from New York City."

"I grew up right here in Holyfield. It's a great place. The air's clean and the people are friendly."

Caitlin laughed. "That'll be a nice change from New York."

Annie turned around and started the engine. "So where can I take you?"

"Ummm, East Quad, Prospero Gate, I think."

"Which dorm are you in?"

"LaSalle Hall."

"That's in West Quad, on the opposite side of campus."

"I thought I'd walk across and get familiar with things."

"Are you sure? That's a long walk with luggage."

"Don't worry. My bags aren't too heavy. I like to travel light. My folks are shipping the rest of my stuff."

"Okay, Prospero Gate it is," Annie said, pulling away from the curb.

As the cab glided through the downtown traffic, Caitlin dug out her campus map and opened it on her lap. Holyfield College, with its nineteen hundred students, lay not in the center but on the **periphery** of town. The seventy-five-acre **urban** campus had a **symmetrical** layout that reminded Caitlin of a baseball diamond. Cedar, Chickasaw, State, and Madison streets defined the perimeter, and College and Holyfield streets bisected its sides into four large quads. At the corners, where the bases would be, were four main gates.

Caitlin smiled when she saw the X she had written in the block indicating the Student Center in South Quad. From reading the college catalogue she had gleaned that the center housed the office of the *Holyfield Herald*, the campus daily.

The cab stopped at a red light and Annie looked at Caitlin in the rearview mirror. "I think you'll like Holyfield. There's always something interesting going on."

"Oh yeah? Like what?"

The light turned green and Annie stepped on the accelerator. "Movies, plays, concerts, sports—whatever you're into. The mixers are pretty good, especially when you're just getting to know people. Then there are some **traditional** campus-wide blowouts, like the Spring Fling."

"What happens then?"

"On the day the dogwood trees bloom in Olsen Garden, everybody puts on shorts and T-shirts or bathing suits and goes to the garden for a big water-balloon fight. Last year there was still snow on the ground and we froze our buns off. But it's great because it's totally **impulsive** and **spontaneous**."

Annie chuckled. "The most incredible event, though, is

the Halloween **masquerade**. Every year a bunch of seniors from Jefferson Hall dress up in gorilla outfits and run around **instigating** whatever trouble they can get away with. At five o'clock they crash Guild Hall and jump around the president's office for a while, until they're officially crowned kings and queens of the **masquerade**. Then after dinner they lead a parade up to Steinbach Commons, where there's a huge costume party."

"That sounds wild," Caitlin said. Down the tree-lined street she could see the buildings at the edge of campus.

Annie braked for a stoplight. "Here's Spenser Gate. Most of the off-campus action is up there on Chickasaw. You can shop there, and there are good places to eat too. You like pizza?"

"'Like' is an **understatement**. I practically live on it."

Annie turned right onto State Street. "Then you should check out Salerno's. A lot of people hang out at Pesto Palace, but it's rowdy and kind of tacky and definitely not for the **frugal** person on a tight budget, like me. In my opinion, Salerno's is the best in town."

Caitlin could taste the pizza already.

A minute later Annie maneuvered the cab through a maze of vehicles and double-parked in front of a massive stone archway. Caitlin paid the tab and gave Annie a twenty-five percent tip.

"Hey, thanks a lot!" Annie said. "If everybody tipped like that, I'd have no trouble paying my way through medical school."

"You want to be a doctor?"

Annie laughed. "I don't plan on driving a cab forever, and I'm certainly not double-majoring in chemistry and biology for the fun of it. Look," she added, scribbling on the back of a receipt, "here's my phone number. You need anything—a ride, someone to talk to, whatever—just give me a call, okay?"

"Sure, Annie. Thanks." Caitlin took the paper and put it in her purse. "See you around."

She grabbed her bags, climbed out of the cab, and plunged into the mass of people passing through Prospero Gate.

Phil McKnight set down his two **ponderous** suitcases and camera bag on the sidewalk outside Prospero Gate. All around him a bustling crowd of students and families and friends unloaded sedans, station wagons, vans, and Jeeps.

Two days ago Phil had left his neighborhood and high school friends and brother and sister and parents in San Diego, California, and boarded a train that had taken him to Las Vegas, then Salt Lake City, then through the Rocky Mountains to Denver, then over the plains to Omaha, and finally to Osceola, Iowa. From there he had taken a bus to the City of Holyfield. Others might have been impatient with such a **protracted** trip, but Phil had no regrets about his choice of transportation. The train had been much less expensive than flying, and he had enjoyed seeing the country.

As he watched the taxi **dwindle** to the size of a matchbox, Phil remembered how worried and **vulnerable** his mother had looked when she had said goodbye and how as he got on the train his dad had told him it was okay to be scared because everyone else going off to college was probably scared too. Now, standing before the entrance to his home for the next four years, Phil had to admit he was nervous, but he wasn't scared. Something told him everything was going to be fine.

Phil took a deep breath, enjoying the **novel** feeling of complete **autonomy**. It's great being on your own, he thought, especially when you've got a chunk of money saved up from working all summer caddying for the **prosperous** golfers at Mission Trails Country Club.

It was a mild day, but the crisp smell of fall already filled the air. Dead leaves scraped along the sidewalk, blown by light gusts of wind. Phil zipped up his red-and-white Hoover High School varsity jacket. Shading his eyes from the mid-afternoon sun, he surveyed the scene.

So this is Holyfield College, he thought.

Facing the street were two **monolithic** buildings of roughly hewn **masonry**. Ivy, with thick vines at the base, crawled up the sides, and the stone, dark and damp and stained, seemed ancient. Phil's sense of architecture was defined chiefly by the graceful Spanish stucco, squat bungalow, and **prosaic** post–World War II ranch styles common in San Diego, and he had difficulty placing these **staid** buildings. They were of a different order altogether.

As he looked at them he could hear Mr. Alvarez, his eighth-grade earth science teacher, describing the vast glacier that had come down out of Canada, flattened the **antediluvian** Midwest, and melted, leaving a sea that stretched out over what became the prairies and **fertile** plains of the American frontier. Phil pictured this glacier plowing through Iowa, leveling the earth and wearing itself down to the point where it dropped these two impressive **edifices** in its path, and here they stood.

A **grandiose** arch spanned the gap between the buildings. Squinting, Phil noticed that the elaborately carved stone contained two sculpted faces: William Shakespeare and Edgar Allan Poe, one of his favorite writers. Under the arch an **imposing** iron gate stood open to the flood of arriving students hustling in and out of the passageway.

Phil reached into his camera bag and pulled out the map that had been sent to him in August. He located Prospero Gate and saw that the **adjacent** buildings were Fogborn, which housed the Philosophy Department, and Wright, home of the African-American Studies Department. Let's see, he thought, to get to Ericson Hall—

"Heads up, dude!"

Phil turned and saw two **brawny** students carrying an overstuffed sofa. They were coming at a slow trot directly at him. Evidently, they didn't intend to slow down.

He quickly moved his bags, narrowly avoiding a collision. Marveling at the **breadth** of both the sofa and the burly pair who were lugging it so **industriously,** Phil **mused** that perhaps these were football players assigned to help new arrivals, or perhaps moving furniture was part of their conditioning program.

Phil stuck the map in his pocket, picked up his luggage, and joined the crowd under the arch. Up ahead he noticed an attractive young woman in a sleek leather jacket. Her long, raven-black hair flipped and bobbed in the wind as she maneuvered through the press like an **erratic** driver on the freeway.

Chapter 2

Entrance Examination

Growing up in New York City, Caitlin had learned that walking was a lot like driving—a **complex** skill whose **subtleties** were too often taken for granted, sometimes with **catastrophic consequences**. She knew that to become **proficient** at either activity, you must follow four fundamental rules: First, **assert** yourself, but don't be aggressive; there is a big difference between **exploiting** an opportunity and asking for trouble. Second, keep moving or you'll be eaten alive. Third, keep your distance. And last, keep a **wary** eye out for the unpredictable; never overestimate the **competence** of those around you.

With these **precepts** in mind, Caitlin weaved through the **sluggish** human traffic in the East Quad courtyard like a veteran. The way to West Quad and LaSalle Hall would take her by several **prominent** buildings on campus, and she was eager to see how Holyfield looked up close. She charted a diagonal route across the quad, heading for Holyfield Street.

"Hey, Leather Lady! Want some help with those bags?" called a gruff voice behind her.

Leather Lady? Must be my jacket, Caitlin thought. She glanced over her shoulder. Two husky young men in sweatsuits, probably football players, were jogging toward her carrying a large, somewhat **dilapidated** couch.

"You'll need to grow another set of arms, guys."

"Just toss your stuff on the couch. We're headed for Larraby. What's your destination?"

For a moment Caitlin toyed with the idea of accepting the offer of help. But what if her new roommates saw her arrive with a couple of sweaty jocks in tow? She decided she was better off on her own for now.

"I'm going to LaSalle. It's out of your way. I'll make it all right, thanks."

The two bruisers smiled and resumed trotting with the sofa down the path.

Caitlin studied the people she passed along the way. She had read **innumerable** catalogues in her quest for the right college, and all had claimed to "encourage cultural **diversity**" and "**nurture** individual expression." She was **gratified** that the school she had chosen appeared to live up to those **commendable egalitarian** claims, for all around her she saw a hodgepodge of humanity—all shapes, sizes, and colors, in all manner of dress, from the formal and **conventional** to the most **eccentric** and **bizarre**.

The notion of bright and talented women and men of every ethnic and socioeconomic background and from all parts of the country coming together in the heartland of America to broaden their horizons **kindled** Caitlin's interest and **stimulated** her imagination. In such a **heterogeneous** environment, she felt sure she'd fit in.

When she reached Holyfield Street she saw the campus art gallery, which bore a colorful sign for an exhibit called "Shakespeare's Colleagues: Artists and **Artisans** of Elizabethan England." Further on she saw the quaint, ivy-covered red brick campus chapel with its adjoining bell tower, a **dominant** landmark that she recognized from the photograph on the cover of the college catalogue.

Beside the tower was an odd structure not included in the photograph—an **austere** building that Caitlin didn't remember being identified on the map. She looked at the heavy wooden door and **somber** stone walls and wondered how such a **discordant** element had come to exist among the otherwise **harmonious** and **benign** buildings on campus. There was something eerie about the place, she thought.

She continued walking and a minute later reached the corner of College and Holyfield streets—the center of campus. Across the way, rising high like a cathedral of **enlightenment**, stood Tillinghast Library. Its Gothic **eminence eclipsed** everything else on the street. Caitlin imagined generations of **pensive** scholars **perusing** stacks of old brown books filled with the wisdom of the ages.

Students and professors bustled under the tall, pointed arch leading into the vast building while a band of Renaissance musicians, a juggler, and a pantomimist, all dressed in **archaic** costumes, entertained the passersby. Two large signs framed the library entrance: "Welcome, Shakespearean Scholars," read one; the other, "Opening Soon: The Prospero Memorial Library of Rare Books and Manuscripts."

Caitlin crossed the street. She picked up a copy of the *Holyfield Herald* from a newspaper stand on the corner. Tucking it under her arm, she continued toward West Quad. The theater should be coming up next, she thought.

The Edwin Mountford Fincke Theater, Caitlin had learned in the afternoon she'd spent researching Holyfield in New York's 42nd Street Library, had received its unfortunate name from an otherwise distinguished Holyfield alumnus who became a wealthy industrialist and patron of the arts in the late 1800s. Except in formal **contexts**, however, no one used the theater's real name. Years ago the students had affectionately dubbed it "the Stink," and that's what everyone had called it for as long as anyone could remember.

The Stink was a **formidable** red brick building with a graceful rose window **adorning** the center of the steep triangle created by its gable roof. A wide flight of steps led up to three sets of broad double doors. Above these stretched a long banner announcing a production of Shakespeare's *Romeo and Juliet*. The first performance was that night.

The banner reminded Caitlin of her father. He had taken her to many plays on and off Broadway and to the **renowned** Shakespeare series every summer in Central Park. Although her primary interest was writing, in high school Caitlin had participated in a few productions as stage manager or assistant director, and one time she had played Hippolyta, a small role in Shakespeare's *Midsummer Night's Dream*. Theater at Holyfield might be worth checking out as an **extracurricular** activity, she thought, and decided to attend the opening to find out more about it. Maybe she could persuade her roommates to come along.

Caitlin shifted both her bags to one hand and opened the newspaper with the other. She began reading as she walked. Under the banner headline "Welcome, Freshmen!" were two articles surrounding a photo of a young woman in Shakespearean garb. Caitlin looked at the piece on the left: "Freshmen and Elizabethans arrive on campus," by Bill Berkowitz, *Herald* editor.

"Holyfield College," read the lead, "opens its **venerable** doors to yet another crop of promising freshmen today, as it has done for more than 120 years. That, in itself, is **noteworthy**. This fall, however, something special will make their arrival even more memorable." The article went on:

> To honor the most famous writer in the English language and celebrate the upcoming dedication of the Prospero Memorial Library, the college is sponsoring an academic conference called "Shakespeare: 400 Years of Scholarship," in conjunction with an Elizabethan Festival that will include plays, concerts, exhibits, and other forms of **edifying** entertainment.
>
> Scholars and experts from all over the nation, including some from abroad, have traveled to Holy-

field to participate in an **ambitious** two-week program of lectures and symposia.

The fortnight of festivities—as the Bard might have put it—officially began last night at Guild Hall with a reception for visiting dignitaries hosted by President Harriet O'Donnell and Dean Arthur Calvin Herbert.

So that explains all this Shakespearean stuff I've been seeing, Caitlin thought. She stopped walking. The hand holding both bags was screaming for a rest. She looked around. Several dozen students sprawled on a wide lawn, reading and talking and soaking up the afternoon sun. She hauled her bags to a nearby tree and set them down. Then she sat, leaning against the trunk, and continued reading.

The article in the right-hand column, also written by Bill Berkowitz, was titled "Prospero library wing to open soon; executors named to manage rare collection." It said:

When Edward Anthony Prospero, class of '22 and Harcourt Professor of English emeritus, died last month at 93, he left his large and valuable collection of rare books and manuscripts to Holyfield College. In preparation for this **bequest,** two years ago Prospero donated $3.5 million to expand Tillinghast Library. The nearly completed wing, bearing his name, will house the collection.

"This priceless gift will be a perpetual **asset** to the college," said Professor Harold Hargrave, library curator, adding that no one knows precisely what the collection contains. "I suspect we may find some extremely unusual items of **profound** importance to scholars worldwide," he said.

In his will, the late Professor Prospero designated five literary executors to oversee the collection: Professor Hargrave, who will lead the group; Professor

Bartholomew Martext, artistic director of the Fincke Theater; Professor Theophilus Bibb of the Renaissance Studies Department, an expert on rare books; Associate Professor Carmen Torres of the English Department; and Leo Kabnis, a senior honors student who worked for Prospero as a research assistant.

The executors will meet tomorrow to discuss how to manage the **voluminous** collection. Although the **arduous** task of cataloguing the material is expected to continue into next year, the Prospero Memorial Library will be officially dedicated in two weeks, at the close of the Shakespeare Symposium and Elizabethan Festival.

Caitlin folded the paper and leaned her head against the tree. A rich old professor donates his collection of rare books and manuscripts to the college and nobody knows precisely what it contains? There must be a newsworthy secret or two hidden in there, she thought. Writing an article about this Professor Prospero and the new library would be a good way to start with the *Herald*. She resolved to track down Bill Berkowitz and propose the idea to him as soon as she got settled.

The decision renewed Caitlin's strength. She picked up her bags and within a few minutes reached LaSalle Hall. After checking in and receiving her key and registration packet, she found her room on the fourth floor.

This is it, she thought. College really starts now. She took a deep breath and put her key in the lock.

"Hi, there! You must be Caitlin, right?" said a voice behind her.

Chapter 3

Go Fish

The door to Ericson 5-M, in East Quad, was wide open. Phil stood on the threshold inspecting his new home.

He could see immediately that the woman at the folding table who had given him his room assignment and key had not been joking when she told him his roommates had already moved in.

"Jessica," the Allman Brothers' endless anthem, thundered from the **colossal** sound system set up on the left side of the living room. Three cases of CDs and a crate of old LPs were stacked beside the stereo. Someone must be a classic rock buff, Phil thought. He looked to the right. Between two windows, a large flag with bright horizontal bands of blue, black, and white was tacked to the wall. Other decorative objects—a poster of Michael Jordan flying toward the hoop, a mobile of miniature military aircraft, a throw rug **depicting** five dogs around a poker table—lay on the floor, awaiting their appointed places.

Phil set down his suitcases and camera bag and closed the door. Then he made his way around several partially unpacked boxes to the open door on the opposite side of the room. Poking his head in, he saw a tall, barefoot guy in shorts and a Pittsburgh Pirates T-shirt leap from a desk and—

fiercely strumming a tennis racket to the final, drawn-out chord changes of the song—land squarely on an unmade bed. As the coda ended, he jumped down from the mattress.

"Hiya. I'm Chris. Chris Bednarski. You must be Phil McKnight. Nice to meet you."

"Likewise."

The roommates shook hands.

"Hey, let me go turn down the stereo. Hang on a second, okay?"

Phil looked around the room, which was not much larger than the one he had had to himself back in San Diego. Apparently, unpacking hadn't been limited to the living room. Besides the three sets of beds, bureaus, desks, and chairs issued by the college, several clumps of unorganized belongings were strewn around half the room. It was going to be a tough fit.

Chris returned from the living room. "Sorry about the mess," he said. "I had to get my equipment set up and put some music on before I could do anything." He shrugged and smiled at Phil. "What can I say? It's a **priority**."

"No problem. I know what you mean," Phil said. He looked around the room. "Where should I dump my stuff?"

"All my junk's on that side," Chris said, motioning to an **amorphous** heap on an unmade bed and piles of books and supplies on a nearby bureau and desk.

"And that's Jimmy's." Chris pointed to another unmade bed on which lay a green daypack and leather briefcase. A blue blazer hung from the chair of the **adjacent** desk.

Phil retrieved his bags from the living room and set them down on the mattress Chris had just jumped on.

"Jimmy and I got here yesterday," Chris said. "Have you met him yet?"

"Not yet."

"He should be back soon. Went out to get the paper. He's from Charleston, South Carolina."

"Is that his flag on the wall in the other room?"

"No, it's mine. You like it?"

"Sure. What country is it from?"

"Estonia. It's a former republic of the old Soviet Union."

"Yeah, I know. On the Baltic Sea in Eastern Europe, right?"

Chris nodded.

"Did your parents come from there?"

"My grandparents on my mother's side came over during World War II. I'm from Pittsburgh. See?" Chris pointed to his Pirates T-shirt. "And you?"

"San Diego."

"No kidding. Do you surf?"

"I try, but I'm not very good. My main sport is soccer. I was cocaptain of my school team."

Chris jumped up on his bed and pretended to surf on the mattress. "Man, I'd love to learn how to ride a wave!"

Phil laughed. "I don't think they surf much here in Iowa—unless it's on snowdrifts."

"Yeah, seriously," Chris said. He jumped down from the bed, walked to the window, and looked out. "In a few months there's going to be so much snow out there we'll have to wear snowshoes to get to class."

"Actually, that sounds like fun," Phil said. He zipped open one of his suitcases and began to unpack. "You're not going to believe this, but I've seen snow only twice in my life."

"Get out of here!" Chris snorted.

"No kidding. It never snows in Southern California, except in the mountains. I'm looking forward to the change in climate."

On one of the bureaus rested a small fishbowl, in which a single guppy swam. As he unpacked, Phil watched the guppy swim frantically round and round the bowl. He wondered how long it could keep up such a **manic** pace.

"I don't think your fish likes its new home."

"It's not mine. It's Jimmy's."

"That's right, it's mine," said a voice with a Southern accent behind them. Phil turned and saw a short guy with blond hair standing in the doorway, a newspaper folded under his arm. He was dressed in a button-down pinstripe shirt, khaki chinos, and penny loafers.

"His name's Siggy, short for Sigmund—as in Freud. I'm Jimmy Thomas, short for Jimmy Thomas. And you must be Phil."

"Hi. Nice to meet you, Jimmy," Phil said.

Jimmy walked across the room and held out his hand. His **affable** face seemed on the verge of a sly smile or wink, suggesting that the present circumstances, whatever they were, were hilarious, and that if one only knew how to look under the surface and see things for what they were, one would barely be able to **suppress** laughter. Phil felt as if the hand extended to him was offering not only the promise of friendship but also membership in a club whose **skeptical** and **discerning** members saw the world in a special way. They shook.

"What's this about old Siggy?" Jimmy asked Phil.

"Does he always swim around like that?"

"I don't know. I picked him up at a pet store on Chickasaw Street this morning, so we're just barely getting acquainted."

The two studied the poor fish, who continued to swim in a frantic circle. The water looked cloudy and Siggy's eyes seemed to bulge with a fishy kind of desperation.

"Poor Siggy," Jimmy said. "He does look a bit **overwrought**, doesn't he? What's your **diagnosis**, doc? You don't think it's a terminal case, do you?"

"Maybe he needs some other fish to keep him company," Phil suggested. "Or at least some pink and blue pebbles in his bowl. Every fishbowl needs pebbles."

"They were extra. Besides, you don't want to give these

creatures everything all at once. It spoils them."

"You have a point."

As they discussed Siggy's **prognosis** and the merits of different treatments, the guppy's **erratic** circumnavigations increased to the point where water began to splash up from the surface.

"Maybe he's hungry again," Chris said, picking up a small box of fish food next to the bowl.

"What do you mean, 'again'?" Jimmy asked. He took the box from Chris and looked inside. "No wonder he's going bonkers. You gave him enough food to feed a whale! Haven't you ever heard the word *moderation*?"

"I'm sorry. He seemed hungry. He was hardly moving."

"Well, he's moving now," Jimmy said. He picked up the fishbowl and ran out of the room as fast as he could without spilling the water. Phil and Chris followed him down the hall to the **communal** bathroom.

"Get the door!" Jimmy cried.

Phil pushed it open and a cloud of steam billowed out.

"Everything's going to be okay, Sig," Jimmy muttered to his ailing fish as they rushed inside.

They crowded around the nearest of the several sinks that lined one wall. Through the mist Phil saw another student standing in front of a sink at the end of the row. He was tall, black, and trim, and he looked older, probably a senior. With his strong jawline and close-cropped hair, Phil thought he resembled Denzel Washington in Spike Lee's movie *Malcolm X*, only without Malcolm's **distinctive** glasses. Even wearing only a towel wrapped around his waist, he seemed serious, almost formal, as he **meticulously** shaved the last few whiskers from his chin and washed the stray bits of lather off his face.

He glanced over at the commotion the three new roommates were making. "What seems to be the problem?" he asked in a deep, **authoritative** voice.

As Phil explained the situation, Jimmy began to pour the

water from the bowl, **painstakingly** using his fingers to keep Siggy from going down the drain.

"Stop! You're going to lose him!" Chris warned.

The older student put down his razor and came over to **assess** the situation. "Don't panic," he said. "I'll be right back."

His self-assured tone soothed them, loosening the knot they had tied themselves into around the sink. They looked up and saw themselves in the mirror—three guys standing in a bathroom getting all worked up over a guppy in a bowl. They laughed at the **absurdity** of the image.

"I guess we look pretty silly," Phil said.

"I don't know if the word *silly* is strong enough," Chris **countered**. "How about *inane*?"

"No, that still strikes me as a **euphemism**," Jimmy said. "I'd say *ludicrous* sums up the situation pretty well."

The door swung open and the older student stepped in.

"See if this helps," he said, handing Jimmy a tennis racket. "It should keep the fish in while you change the water."

"How **pragmatic** of you," Jimmy said. "Thanks."

"Gee, I should've thought of that," Chris mumbled.

Phil poked Chris in the ribs. "What, and get your air guitar all wet?"

"By the way," said the older student, "I'm Leo Kabnis. You guys are in 5-M, right?"

The three freshmen nodded.

"Then I'm your freshman counselor," Leo said.

As they made their introductions, the door to the bathroom opened and a scruffy-faced young man in a rumpled bathrobe entered. His long brown hair was tied back in a ponytail. "Hey, Leo, how ya doing?" he grunted as he passed the group.

"Max, my man, what's up?" Leo said.

"Not much. Just getting cleaned up for dinner."

"How's Irwin?"

"He's taking an after-dinner nap." Max hung his bathrobe on a hook and stepped into the shower stall.

"I won't ask what he ate," Leo said with a laugh.

"Who's Irwin?" Chris asked.

"Max's pet."

"What kind of pet?" Phil asked.

Leo flashed an **evasive** grin. "You'll find out soon enough."

"What does this mysterious pet eat?" Jimmy pressed.

"Let's just say you'd be wise to keep your little fish away from Max's room," Leo answered **enigmatically**. He retrieved his shaving kit from the end of the row of sinks. "I'd like to talk to you guys some more, get to know you better. How about if we all have dinner together tonight?"

The three freshmen said they'd like that.

"Then let's meet in my room in half an hour," Leo said, opening the bathroom door. "I'm in 5-A, right by the stairway."

The freshmen returned to their room and busied themselves without feeling the need to talk. Jimmy put bowl and Siggy, now **quiescent**, on the window sill, no doubt for its excellent view, and with nothing to unpack—his luggage having taken a wrong turn at the airport in Charleston—he settled down with the *Holyfield Herald*. Chris, wearing a pair of headphones attached to a tape player on his belt, hummed to himself as he worked **doggedly** but, it seemed to Phil, unproductively through his disorganized belongings. Phil quickly found places for the contents of his suitcases. The rest of his things, his parents had assured him, would arrive by freight in a few days.

Phil lay on his bed daydreaming for a while, then got up and looked out the open window. **Stately** trees graced the courtyard and shaded the flagstone pathways that cut across a wide ribbon of green lawn to the limestone dorms and classroom buildings lining all sides of the quad. To his left, Phil could just make out Prospero Gate. To his right was the campus art gallery, beyond which rose the bell tower. Across the quad he saw the main dining hall, Steinbach Commons, and behind that, just across College Street, loomed the grandest building on campus.

An awesome structure, Tillinghast Library inspired in Phil a mixture of admiration and **apprehension**. He tried to imagine the one million volumes of which the college catalogue boasted. How could you fit that many books in a single building? Phil wondered which ones he'd be required to read and what he'd be expected to know. Would his classes be too **arduous**? Would he be able to keep up? What would it be like, this school he'd worked so hard to get into? Now that he was finally here, what exactly it was he had wanted out of college seemed **obscure**, an **enigma** the key to which perhaps lay behind the walls of the magnificent **edifice** that **dominated** the roofline across the quad.

He took his 35mm camera out of its case, focused carefully on the library, and pressed the shutter release.

Chapter 4

First Impressions

It certainly was an impressive view. From the window of her room in LaSalle Hall, on the top floor of the building, Caitlin could see the **expanse** of the West Quad compound, with its quaint Victorian buildings and majestic old oaks, maples, and elms. Straight ahead, **prominent** above the treetops and roofs, were three of the campus landmarks she had passed on the way to her dorm. In the foreground was the Stink, where *Romeo and Juliet* would open tonight; in the background, the **ornate** steeple of the Holyfield bell tower. Between them, at the center of campus, rose the **aloof grandeur** of Tillinghast Library.

Caitlin could just make out the upper part of the new wing, which lay snuggled against the back of the main building. It was surrounded by scaffolding that she assumed would be **dismantled** before the dedication ceremony at the end of the Elizabethan Festival. She remembered what she had read in the *Herald* about the distinguished collection of rare books the new wing would house and wondered if she'd be able to see any of them. Perhaps Bill Berkowitz could use his authority as editor of the *Herald* to arrange access to the collection for her. But that was putting the cart before the horse, she thought. First she would have to persuade him to let her write the story.

Caitlin turned from the window and looked around the room. The moment she'd entered, she could tell she was in good company. Both her roommates had preceded her and had wasted no time transforming their cold quarters into a cozy home. Already fuzzy throw rugs dotted the floor of the living room, which was furnished with a small floral-print sofa, a coffee table, and an armchair. A print of Monet's water lilies and a colorful Native-American tapestry **adorned** the walls above a thriving pair of indoor plants. A Bach Brandenburg Concerto softly **exerted** its elegant magic from a stereo-CD unit that had been set up between the two large windows in the far wall.

Juliet Jacques had greeted Caitlin in the hall, then ushered her in to meet their other suitemate, Lucy Kwon. The two helped Caitlin get settled, and as she unpacked her bags they talked. Being **inquisitive** by nature, Caitlin soon found herself playing the familiar role of **impartial** journalist, plying her new roommates with questions and **eliciting** information about their backgrounds.

The **loquacious** Juliet was only too eager to talk. She came from a small town outside St. Paul, Minnesota, she said. Her father, who was French Canadian, repaired trucks and farm equipment. Her mother, who worked at a day-care center, was Native American, a Blackfoot Sioux from South Dakota. (She had made the tapestry in the living room, Caitlin found out.) Juliet said she'd like to go into a career where she could help other people. She thought she might major in psychology or sociology and maybe become a teacher or a social worker.

In her T-shirt, leggings, and running shoes, Juliet looked lean and strong and full of **vitality**. She must be an athlete, Caitlin thought. "Do you play any sports?" she asked.

"You bet," said Juliet. "I lettered in cross-country running and basketball. I'm also into cross-country skiing and tennis, and I'm an **avid** ice hockey fan."

"Ice hockey?"

"In Minnesota we practically grow up on skates. When I was a kid I used to play hockey with my brother. He's now on the varsity at the University of Minnesota."

"Isn't it a violent sport?" Caitlin asked, deciding to move the conversation away from facts for the moment and into opinion.

"A lot of people think so, and sometimes the pro teams get out of control," Juliet said. "But in high school and college it's not such a big macho free-for-all. It's just incredibly fast and exciting to watch. And really, when you think about it, it's nowhere near as aggressive as football."

Baseball, Caitlin told Juliet, was her favorite spectator sport, and she had always despised football, which seemed like hand-to-hand combat between vicious packs of padded **pugilists**. It was a **biased** view, she admitted. But then, when it came to sports, not many people were **indifferent**.

In Lucy Kwon, Caitlin saw a marked contrast to the hardy, **spontaneous** Juliet. Lucy was petite, with earnest, **captivating** eyes and delicate hands—the hands of a musician, Caitlin thought. She was extremely **articulate**, but there was a **tentative**, almost **fastidious** quality to her speech, as though she were carefully crafting her words to **convey** a precise meaning.

Lucy explained that she was first-generation Korean-American, from Seattle, Washington. Her parents had come to America in the early '70s. She had two older brothers—one a lawyer back in Seattle, one in medical school in California—and a younger sister in tenth grade.

Lucy enjoyed doing volunteer work and was proud to have **initiated** a recycling program at her high school. For recreation she liked to go backpacking and cycling, but more than anything, she confessed with a sheepish grin, she loved to curl up on the couch on a rainy day, eat chocolate-chip cookies, and watch reruns of old TV shows. Her favorite subjects were history, math, and—Caitlin and Juliet were impressed—Latin, but now, with so many **diverse** courses to

choose from, Lucy was considering trying something different, perhaps majoring in philosophy, art history, or music.

"Do you play an instrument?" Caitlin asked.

"Yes, the piano," Lucy said. "Mostly classical, and a little
jazz. Do you play something?"

"The flute, but I'm not very good at it. My mom's a
music teacher, and she pushed me pretty hard, but I hate
practicing."

"Who doesn't?" Lucy said, flashing a knowing smile.

That was an hour ago. Now, as Caitlin stood by the window, Juliet was poring over the Holyfield course catalogue
while Lucy sat at her desk writing a letter on her computer.
When Caitlin had remarked how nice it must be to have a
computer, Lucy had told her and Juliet they were welcome to
use it any time. This generous offer made Caitlin silently **ecstatic**. She had had access to her father's computer and to the
ones at school, but she had never had one of her own. Some-
day, she thought, when I'm a professional writer—

"It's almost time for dinner," Lucy said, looking at her
watch. "Should we get ready to go?"

"I'd like to go to the opening of *Romeo and Juliet* afterward," Caitlin said. "You guys want to come along?"

"I'll see anything I'm starring in," Juliet said with a
histrionic toss of her hair. "No, seriously, I love that play. We
read it in sophomore English."

"I love it too," Lucy said. "It's so romantic and
poignant."

"Yeah, 'Parting is such sweet sorrow' and all that," Juliet
said.

Caitlin **grimaced**, remembering her father's **florid**
farewell at the airport. Poor Dad. She'd have to call—no,
write—and tell him about the production. He'd like that.

While Caitlin brushed her hair, Juliet went down the
hall to the bathroom to wash up and Lucy changed into a
skirt and blouse and put on a little makeup. Fifteen minutes

later the three roommates were strolling together up Holy-field Street toward Steinbach Commons.

The door to Ericson 5-A opened in response to Phil's knock.

"Hi, I'm Bill Berkowitz," said a gangly, bespectacled guy with an **unkempt** mass of curly brown hair. He was wearing a Holyfield sweatshirt and jeans with holes in the knees. "Leo told me you'd be coming over. He went down to the basement to put some stuff in the storage room, but he'll be right back. Why don't you guys come on in and make yourselves comfortable."

Phil and his roommates introduced themselves and Bill waved them inside. The freshmen looked at the two arm-chairs and couch and remained standing, unable to decide where to sit.

"Have a seat," Bill said **cordially**, motioning toward the couch. The freshmen obeyed. Bill plopped down in an arm-chair and draped a long, skinny leg over the arm. He squinted at them through his thick glasses. "So, where do you all come from?"

Jimmy and Chris made small talk about their respective hometowns and high schools. Bill explained that he was from Chicago and Leo from St. Louis; they'd met as fresh-men and had roomed together ever since.

While the others chatted, Phil looked around. Compared with their own living room, Bill's and Leo's was **immaculate**. There was no clutter, no sense of **chaos**. Things were tidy. Late-afternoon sunlight poured through the windows.

Standing bookcases lined two of the walls, and as Phil looked more closely at them he noticed that their contents were arranged **meticulously**, both alphabetically and by sub-ject—the **manifestation** of considerable academic **endeavor** and interest.

Phil had been in many private homes in which a wall in the family room or den was devoted to a set of encyclopedias, a dictionary, a thesaurus, a Bible, a photograph album, a few books on American history and pop psychology, and a **profusion** of **trivial** bestsellers. Often these libraries seemed either **randomly** or **arbitrarily compiled**. There was no telling why some books had been bought nor how long some of them had **languished** on the shelf. And there was no telling why certain people had books in their homes at all, except to **embellish** their walls.

There was nothing **haphazard** or **indifferent** about the selections in Bill and Leo's library. Phil had the impression that each volume had been thoughtfully chosen, read, discussed, written about, and then carefully placed on the shelf, where it stood, not useless and forgotten, but **vital** and always ready to be of use.

"Those are mostly Leo's," Bill said, looking at Phil. "I'm a **voracious** reader, but he's a real **bibliophile**."

Phil was about to ask what a **bibliophile** was when the door opened and Leo entered.

"Hi, you guys," he said. "Hope you haven't been waiting long. Are we ready to go?"

In his plaid flannel shirt, loose-fitting jeans, and black high-top sneakers, Leo managed to appear both collegiate and casual. For a moment Phil worried that his colorful Hawaiian shirt would make him stick out at dinner, and he wondered why he'd decided to wear it—to make a statement of geographical identity and let everybody know he was a laid-back dude from California? Perhaps, he thought. But the last thing he wanted on the first day of college was to appear **conspicuous** or foolish. He zipped his varsity jacket halfway up as they left the dorm.

Chapter 5

Study What
You Most Affect

Caitlin, Juliet, and Lucy sat at a round table in a corner of
Steinbach Commons. The **capacious** hall, easily the size of a
football field, rumbled with the **din** of several hundred excited students, freshmen and upperclassmen alike. The
vaulted ceiling **augmented** their **jovial** laughter and **garrulous** conversation.

Caitlin looked at the food on her plate (if it could properly be called food) and one word came to mind: *repugnant.*
For the past five minutes she had **grappled** with a piece of
meat smothered in an **insipid** greenish brown sauce that apparently was gravy. It was an exercise in **futility**, she thought.
No matter how she attacked it, the meat (if indeed it was
meat) refused to submit to her knife. Perhaps some **drastic**
measure was necessary—a hatchet or a chain saw might do
the job.

Her battle with the meat brought back a **vivid** memory of
the **petrified** pot roast her sweet but **senile** Irish grandmother
used to serve years ago when Caitlin was little and she and
her folks would visit on Sundays after church. She remembered how she'd tried so hard to be polite, chewing and
chewing until her jaws ached. But she never swallowed, for
fear of choking. Instead she would wait until no one was

looking, then deposit the gristly glob in the napkin in her lap, quietly wrapping up and discarding the evidence when the meal was done. Unfortunately, she reflected, that particular **stratagem** was not an option for a young woman sharing dinner with her peers.

Caitlin sighed, set down her knife and fork, and took a long drink of soda. "Maybe we should go for pizza after the play."

"That's a great idea," Lucy said. Caitlin noticed her roommate had barely touched her dinner and was now nibbling at her dessert—chocolate cake, a delectation Caitlin had eschewed. One had to give up certain other temptations to accommodate a passion for pizza, she reasoned.

"Boy, there sure are some weird classes in here," Juliet said. She had brought the course catalogue along and was browsing through it while munching away at a mixture of raw vegetables she'd **concocted** at the salad bar. "Listen to this: 'Multivariate Data **Analysis** with **Latent** Variables.'"

"What kind of **jargon** is that?" Lucy asked.

"It's a psych course," Juliet said. "I think I'll skip that one." She flipped a few pages. "How about 'History of the Israelite **Monarchy**'?"

"I never knew there *was* an Israelite **monarchy**," Caitlin said.

"Well, you learn something new every day. That's what college is all about, right?" Juliet looked up, expecting a laugh, but Lucy and Caitlin just rolled their eyes. "Okay, okay," she said, opening to another page. "Let's see. Hey, Caitlin, this one looks perfect for you: 'Bohemians, Bachelors, the New Woman, and the Novel.'"

"Everything I'm interested in, all wrapped up in one class," Caitlin said. "Just add pizza to the list and you've got the complete college experience." She looked at Juliet. "Mind if I take a look at that catalogue?"

"Go ahead," Juliet said, handing it over.

"I saw one in here before that cracked me up," Caitlin said. "Here it is: 'The Biology of Evil.' Can you believe that?"

"Sounds like an interdisciplinary course," Lucy said.

"What, for biology majors and evil studies majors?" Caitlin said. They all laughed. "Here's another **prerequisite** for evil studies: '**Deviant** Behavior and Social Control.'"

An unfamiliar voice broke into their conversation. "Only the first night at college and already we're discussing **deviant** behavior?"

They looked up. Standing beside Caitlin, holding a tray of food, was a tall, attractive woman with short, dark, curly hair. A stylish pair of round-rimmed glasses rested on her **prominent, regal** nose. Gleaming silver and turquoise bracelets and earrings and a squash-blossom necklace **enhanced** her black blouse and flowing, multicolored skirt. The effect was striking and **sophisticated** without being **ostentatious**, Caitlin thought.

"You guys look a bit lonely over here in the corner," the woman said. "I'm Carmen Torres. I teach in the English Department. Mind if I join you?"

"Please do," Caitlin said. She proceeded to introduce her roommates, who seemed surprised that a faculty member would eat in a student dining hall, much less eat with students.

"A pleasure to meet you all," Torres said. She set down her tray and slid into the empty seat next to Caitlin. "I presume you're freshmen—or perhaps I should say fresh*women*? Or do you prefer fresh*persons*?" She smiled broadly.

"We're so fresh we don't know *what* we are yet," Caitlin said.

Torres chuckled. "Now, tell me, if you don't mind," she said, settling down to eat. "What was all that laughter about **deviant** behavior?"

"We were looking through the course catalogue," Juliet said, "and we found a couple of classes with silly titles."

"There was one on **deviant** behavior we thought might be a requirement for the evil studies major," Lucy said.

Torres laughed. "'Evil studies.' That's funny. Maybe at the next faculty meeting I'll suggest starting a program in it. But you know, you're right. A lot of course titles in the catalogue sound **implausible**. In fact, one of my seminars, 'The Politics of Sexuality in Renaissance Literature,' raised a few eyebrows the first time I taught it. I suppose because of the word *sexuality* some people assumed the content would be **prurient**. Apparently they overlooked the fact that social roles and human relationships are at the heart of great literature. Take Shakespeare, for example: Sexuality is an essential element in his work; it **pervades** the plays. *The Taming of the Shrew, A Midsummer Night's Dream, Antony and Cleopatra, Hamlet, Othello*, and of course *Romeo and Juliet*—almost anywhere you look there's a **profound** inquiry into the nature of love, **fidelity**, passion, or the power struggle between the sexes."

The professor paused and took a drink of water. Caitlin noticed her roommates were listening as intently as she was.

"You should go to the opening of *Romeo and Juliet* tonight," Torres went on. "You'll see what I mean. I hear it's a good production, too. Bartholomew Martext, the professor who runs the theater, is directing. He's quite **eccentric**. It should be a **novel** interpretation."

"Funny you should bring it up, professor," Caitlin said. "We've already agreed to go together after dinner."

"That's terrific, Caitlin. But please, call me Carmen. I don't see any point in erecting artificial barriers between students and teachers. Besides," she added with a warm smile, "I've been teaching a long time. I don't need to be constantly reminded that I've earned a Ph.D."

"How long have you been teaching at Holyfield?" Lucy asked.

"Nine years—long enough to become thoroughly **hidebound** and **cynical**," Torres replied. She looked around the table at the three young women, her eyes twinkling with mischievous **irony**. "I suppose I should warn you. I've got a reputation to maintain. The students call me the Dragon Lady. If you take one of my classes, you'll see what they mean."

"Boy, I'm sure glad I wasn't planning to major in English," Juliet said. Everyone laughed.

Caitlin decided she liked the professor's **feisty** and **forthright** attitude. "What did you do before coming here?" she asked, wanting to know more about this **intriguing** woman.

"I taught at Middlebury College in Vermont for three years," Torres said, "and at UCLA for two. That's where I got my doctorate. I got my B.A. at the University of Arizona. I'm from Tucson, originally—the seventh and youngest child of wonderful, loving, hardworking parents." She took a bite of food, then wiped her mouth carefully with her napkin. "My parents never had the benefit of a college education, but they managed to provide that opportunity for five of their children. I'll never forget the proud look on their faces the day I received my B.A."

Professor Torres fell silent, as if remembering the moment. Then she looked around the table and smiled. "Well, that's enough talk about me. Now I'd like to know more about you three. Caitlin, your accent tells me you're from New York. Am I right?"

As Leo and Bill led Phil and his roommates across the East Quad courtyard and onto a tree-lined pathway, the conversation turned toward the three freshmen's plans. Leo asked about their majors.

"Economics," Chris replied matter-of-factly. "I'd like to get into the the five-year B.A.–M.B.A. program."

"That's very competitive," Leo said. "But if you stay focused, I'm sure you'll do all right."

Phil wondered how anyone could be so certain about what he wanted to do with his life. Economics—he had al-

ways assumed it was a **tedious** subject, filled with graphs and
statistics, but now that he'd heard this field of study declared
so **emphatically** by Chris, he thought he might have been
too hasty in his judgment. Perhaps he'd try an econ course
second semester.

"You want to go into business after college?" Leo asked
Chris.

"Yup."

"And make a lot of money?"

"Uh huh."

"Can't argue with that. You have to promise me one
thing though, Chris."

"Sure. What's that?"

"Ten years from now," Leo said, "when you've made
your first million, promise me you won't forget your old
freshman counselor. It doesn't have to be a lot, just a small,
round, memorable figure—say, an even ten grand, okay? You
won't forget?"

"Don't listen to him, Chris," Bill said. "Leo'll never need
anything from you or me. The guy got 1590 on the SAT, and
the one question he got wrong he proved was **ambiguous**,
but they wouldn't change his score. Leo's **exceptional**—
summa cum everything. He's won every prize there is to win.
It's more likely we'll be asking him for a handout."

"And you," Leo said, ignoring his roommate and turning
to Jimmy. "What are you planning to study?"

"Literature, I think," Jimmy said. "Right now I'm most interested in Elizabethan England. I love Marlowe and Jonson
and Kyd. And Shakespeare, of course. He's the greatest of all."

Who were Marlowe, Jonson, and Kyd? Phil wondered.
Members of a law firm? He began to suspect that his room-
mates had prepared their answers. They sounded so certain.
And now it seemed **inevitable** that Leo would pose this same
question to him. Maybe he should prepare an answer as well.
Engineering? History? Pre-law? Art? Phil tried to picture

these different versions of his future self, but the picture failed to **clarify**.

"Well, this is the time and place for it," Leo told Jimmy. "Holyfield is hosting an Elizabethan Festival for the next two weeks. Did you see Bill's article on it in the *Herald*? There'll be all sorts of things going on. The festivities kick off tonight with a production of *Romeo and Juliet*. You should go."

Jimmy said he'd love to, and Chris and Phil agreed to go along.

Leo patted Phil's shoulder. "And what are you planning to study, Phil? Got any ideas yet?"

"I'm not sure. Maybe engineering. Or maybe history— I'm pretty good at that. Pre-law is also a possibility. Or maybe art, because I like drawing and photography."

"Excellent," Leo said, to Phil's surprise. "You should try as many different subjects as you can before settling on anything. Let curiosity and instinct be your guide. 'In brief, sir, study what you most affect.'"

"Isn't that line from Shakespeare?" Jimmy asked.

"*The Taming of the Shrew*, my man," Leo said. He turned to Phil. "The point is, don't feel pressured to fit yourself into some **predetermined** category that doesn't suit you. You have to follow your own **predilections**. I changed my major twice, and I'm glad I did."

"I agree," said Bill. "I'm putting my plans to go to law school on hold for a year so I can run the *Herald*. It was too interesting an opportunity to pass up. And you never know. Maybe I'll decide to go to journalism school instead."

Phil was **gratified** by their generous response. He breathed a quick sigh of relief and looked across Holyfield Street. **Adjacent** to the commanding bell tower stood a **grave**, windowless building about three stories high. **Symmetrical turrets** rose from the front corners of the flat roof. A massive door made of planks fastened together with black iron hinges was shut tight.

"That building over there," Phil said. "What's it used for? It looks like a miniature castle."

"Seems more like a **grandiose mausoleum** to me," Jimmy said.

Bill laughed. "In a way it is. That's Tooth and Nail. It's a secret society."

"A what?" Chris asked.

"A secret society, like those famous ones at Yale—Skull and Bones, Scroll and Key, Book and Snake, and a bunch of others. It's basically just a **glorified** fraternity, but no one's supposed to know who its members are."

"If it's supposed to be such a secret," Jimmy said, "how come you know about it?"

Bill laughed again. "I'm a journalist. It's my business to dig up information. Back in the '30s and '40s and '50s, secret societies were a big deal at Holyfield. There were four or five of them and secrecy was strict. But today they're practically **obsolete**. In fact, Tooth and Nail is the last one on campus. No one really takes it seriously anymore."

Phil was puzzled. "What did these societies have to hide? Were they involved in **illicit** activities or something?"

"Not exactly," Bill said. "**Elitism** may be **deplorable**, but it's usually not illegal. In general, Holyfield's secret societies—like Yale's—functioned as highly **exclusive** networks for the rich and powerful. They weren't necessarily **corrupt**, but membership had its benefits, as they say, and ensured a **prosperous** career.

"It's said that Tooth and Nail was founded by Edward Anthony Prospero himself back in 1919 as a literary club," Bill went on. "But by the late '30s it had become an **elitist** secret society. That's when they built that **ostentatious** building. Later, during the '60s and '70s, there were rumors it had turned into a kind of neo-Nazi brotherhood that **allegedly** practiced some strange **rituals**.

"The society's not as intensely secretive as it once was.

It's common knowledge now that Prospero's grandson, Teddy, has the run of the place—and apparently he's been running it into the ground. There's been talk of financial problems, and in the past couple of years the college administration has been quietly considering trying to **rescind** its charter and shut it down. These days I doubt membership in Tooth and Nail could further anyone's career."

"This Prospero character," Phil said. "Is the gate to East Quad named after him?"

"Right."

"Who was he?" Phil asked as they arrived at Steinbach Commons. From the huge dining hall inside a hubbub of excited chatter and laughter and shouts and the clinking of glasses and silverware reached their ears. The question was forgotten for the moment.

Caitlin took a sip of coffee, then turned to Carmen Torres. "I think I saw your name in the *Herald* today," she said. "Aren't you one of the literary executors for the Prospero collection of rare books and manuscripts?"

"Yes, that's right," Torres said.

"I'm hoping to become a staff writer for the paper, so I'm looking for some good story ideas. Would you mind if I proposed something on your involvement with the collection?"

"I don't know if my involvement will be all that exciting, but you're certainly welcome to interview me, and I'd be happy to introduce you to the other executors."

Caitlin smiled. "Oh, that'd be great . . . Carmen."

"The first thing you need to do, though," Torres said, pointing across the dining hall, "is talk to that guy standing in line over there. His name's Bill Berkowitz, and he's the editor of the *Herald*. He's also an **exemplary** student."

Caitlin looked across the wide room at the crowded line of students waiting to enter the kitchen. "Which one is he? The dark-haired guy in the red-and-white varsity jacket?"

"No, Bill's the tall skinny guy with curly hair and glasses standing in front of him. He's wearing a Holyfield sweatshirt."

"Okay, thanks," Caitlin said. She stood up. "I think I'll get some more coffee. Anybody want anything?"

Chapter 6

The Prospero **Enigma**

As Phil stood in line, his stomach growled in response to the smell of food, reminding him that he hadn't eaten anything since that morning.

It was warm inside the dining hall. Phil took off his jacket and slung it over his shoulder. If somebody wants to comment on my shirt, fine, he thought. I'm not going to let it bother me.

Leo poked Phil's arm. "Hey, I have to check something on the bulletin board. I'll be back in a minute."

As Bill and Chris and Jimmy cracked jokes and took in the **boisterous** atmosphere, Phil watched Leo walk back through the dining hall doors into the common room, where he was **accosted** by an **impeccably** dressed student whose pretty-boy face was twisted in an angry scowl. The encounter looked anything but **amiable**. The pretty boy was shaking his fist and seemed to be yelling at Leo, who stood listening with his arms crossed, apparently **indifferent** to this display of **animosity**.

Phil looked at Bill and saw that he was **oblivious** to what was going on with Leo. He was still talking enthusiastically with Chris and Jimmy and was right in the middle of describing some summer **exploit** when a young student in a stylish leather jacket interrupted him. She had striking blue eyes and long, wavy black hair. The girl from Prospero Gate, Phil thought.

"Excuse me. Are you Bill Berkowitz?" she asked.

Bill turned. "Yes?"

"Hi. I'm Caitlin Ciccone," she announced briskly, stepping forward and extending her hand.

Phil found her face **alluring**. Her expression was **placid** and **poised**, but her **beguiling** eyes sparkled with **vitality**.

"Nice to meet you, Caitlin," Bill said, shaking her hand.

"I hear you're the editor of the *Holyfield Herald*."

"That's right. What can I do for you?"

"I want to be a reporter."

"Well, you don't waste any time, do you?"

"I try not to."

"You're a freshman?"

"Yes."

Bill paused and **scrutinized** Caitlin for a moment. "Now look," he said, scratching the back of his head, "I can't promise you anything. But come by the *Herald* tomorrow and we'll see what we can do, okay?"

"What time?"

"Usually I'm down there bright and early, but tomorrow's Sunday—my one day to sleep in. How does eleven o'clock sound?"

"That's fine."

"Do you have some writing samples you can show me?"

Caitlin nodded. "Absolutely."

"Good. Do you know where the office is?"

"Yes, in the Student Center."

"Right," Bill said. "Next to the rear entrance to the building there's a flight of steps to the basement." He smiled. "It's a **subterranean** office. Very cozy."

Caitlin flashed a smile in return. "Thanks, Bill. See you tomorrow." As she turned to leave, her eyes met Phil's for an instant. She hesitated.

"Nice shirt," she said coolly, then walked away.

Phil watched her disappear into the crowd. He wondered if she was serious or just making fun of him.

Jimmy's voice interrupted his thoughts. "Hey, Bill. Who's that guy arguing with Leo over there?"

Bill looked to where Jimmy pointed. Phil turned and saw Leo and Pretty Boy now engaged in a **hostile** exchange, both talking angrily at once.

Bill snorted with **derision**. "That's Teddy Prospero."

"The guy from Tooth and Nail?" Phil asked.

"Yeah. He's a royal pain in the neck."

They watched as Teddy stuck his finger in Leo's face, growled a few final words, and then stomped off. Leo shook his head, then walked away in the opposite direction.

"They don't seem to like each other much," Chris said.

Bill chuckled. "It's a mutually **antagonistic** relationship."

The line advanced and they entered the kitchen. As they picked up trays, silverware, and napkins from a row of dispensers at the end of the counter, Phil looked over his shoulder.

"Shouldn't we wait for Leo?" he asked.

"Don't worry," Bill said. "He'll find somebody to cut in with and join us in a couple of minutes."

Phil watched **perfunctory** servers scoop up unappetizing portions of meat, potatoes, gravy, and cooked vegetables from trays on steam tables and plop identical mounds on their plates. Oh well, he thought, I can always fill up on salad if the food is really as bad as it looks.

"So what's this guy Teddy's beef with Leo?" Chris asked as Bill led the freshmen to an empty table. They settled down to eat and Bill began **expounding** on the origin of the **hostility** between the two students.

"All last year," Bill explained, "Leo worked part-time as an assistant to Edward Anthony Prospero. He did research for him, handled his correspondence, and helped him revise some of his scholarly writings, in particular his Shakespeare

concordance. Well, as I said, Leo's a star pupil, and the old man took a shine to him, began to think of him as his grandson in spirit if not in name. For when Prospero died last month, at the ripe old age of 93, in his will he named Leo one of the executors of this **voluminous** and incredibly valuable private library that he donated to the college. They've just finished building a new wing to hold it, which they're going to dedicate at the end of the Elizabethan Festival."

"Ah, yes," Jimmy said. "I read your excellent article about that in the paper. It was quite **enlightening**."

"Thanks, pal, but there's no need to stroke my ego," Bill said, patting Jimmy on the back. "Unless, of course, you're hoping to land a spot on the *Herald* masthead," he added with a wink at Phil and Chris.

Jimmy showed no **perturbation** at being the butt of Bill's joke. "I hadn't planned on becoming a journalist," he said with perfect **equanimity**, "but it never hurts to have an **illustrious** senior as an ally."

Bill grinned. "I can tell you're going to do just fine in college, Jimmy."

"Bill, isn't being an executor a great honor?" Phil asked.

"Yeah," Chris said, "isn't Leo a little young for that kind of responsibility?"

Bill nodded. "That's just the point. Prospero took Leo into his confidence, like a trusted colleague or a close relative. Of course that **alienated** Teddy, especially when he found out his grandpa had left him zip and had made Leo an executor of the collection."

"So envy is the source of Teddy's **enmity** toward Leo then?" Jimmy asked.

"In a nutshell, yes." Bill took a bite of food and continued. "I have to admit, it cracks me up every time I imagine what Teddy's face must've looked like when they read his grandfather's will. Leo was there, and he told me the will said something like 'And to my grandson, Edward, I leave the wish that one day he'll read a play by Shakespeare instead of a pornographic magazine or a junk-bond prospectus.'" Bill burst out laughing and slapped the table. "What a joke! Can you believe that?" he said, looking around at the three freshmen.

"Do you know why Prospero cut Teddy out of his will?" Phil asked between mouthfuls. He was making some headway with his dinner, which wasn't as bad as it looked after all.

Bill took a sip of soda. "No one really knows. Some people think Prospero **disowned** Teddy when Teddy took over Tooth and Nail. Others say he didn't approve of some of his grandson's **dubious** pastimes. Another theory is that the old man simply decided to spread his wealth around. You see, Teddy's father, who was Prospero's only child, made a lot of money in the stock market. When he died of a heart attack a few years ago, Teddy reportedly got a fat inheritance in the form of a trust fund. So maybe Old Man Prospero thought, why give Teddy more money when he already seems spoiled by what he has?"

Leo appeared at the table wearing a **somber** expression. "Sorry I took so long," he said, setting down his tray of food and taking the empty chair next to Phil.

"Hey, Leo. These guys saw you and Teddy arguing and they want to know something," Bill said. "Is Edward Anthony Prospero III an **arrogant boor**, a **malicious** lunatic, or what?"

The muscles around Leo's mouth tightened. Then he sighed. "Teddy's just going through a **covetous** phase brought on by his grandfather's death. He's got that 'lean and hungry look,' like Cassius in Shakespeare's *Julius Caesar*." Leo looked at his roommate. "You know, Bill, you should stop talking so much. Everybody else is half-finished and you've hardly touched your plate."

Something in his freshman counselor's tone told Phil it

would be a good idea to change the subject. "What about Old Man Prospero?" he asked Leo. "Can you tell us what he was like?"

Phil's choice of topic must have been the right one, for Leo, after a thoughtful pause, launched into a **mesmerizing** tale about his late mentor.

"Edward Anthony Prospero was the most unusual person I've ever known," he began. "Nothing **conventional** about him, that's for sure. He was a gentleman and a scholar, a bit of a poet, and a little bit of a nut, too. He was also deeply mysterious."

Phil and his roommates listened as Leo told how Prospero had been a man of **eclectic** interests and **formidable** accomplishments. He had escaped the **impoverished** streets of New York City's Lower East Side by winning a scholarship to Holyfield, but the First World War soon **intervened**. After serving in France as a reconnaissance balloonist and in the Intelligence Corps as a cryptanalyst, cracking German codes, he returned to Holyfield to study French, Italian, and English literature.

After college, in the **flourishing** economy of the 1920s, Prospero proved himself a **resourceful** businessman by building a hugely successful import-export company. That was when he developed his **penchant** for rare books and objets d'art. In his late twenties, however, Prospero came to the realization that he was extremely **affluent** but unfulfilled. So one day he left the office and never went back. Just before the crash of '29 and the Great Depression, he sold his company for a small fortune, which he invested wisely. Then he changed course utterly.

First he tried the literary life. He directed a couple of plays off Broadway, acted a little, wrote poetry, and published a novel that was reasonably well received. Then, yearning for adventure, he toured Europe, Africa, and Asia. He climbed mountains in the Canadian Rockies and led expeditions into the South American jungle. He supervised archaeological excavations at Palenque, Mexico, and Giza in Egypt. Finally, after almost a decade of wandering, he enrolled at Yale, earned his **doctorate**, and eventually returned to Holyfield College to focus his **prodigious** energies on teaching and scholarship.

Always a great collector of facts and **artifacts** and books, Prospero was often called on to **appraise** or **authenticate** rare manuscripts, and in the 1940s he **compiled** a **comprehensive annotated concordance** to Shakespeare, a work that made his academic reputation. Some say he even did a little **espionage** for the army during World War II, and helped them **decipher** a number of enemy codes.

Prospero had always had a **predilection** for creating and solving puzzles. From time to time he would offer rewards for the solution of riddles he had devised or the discovery of a treasure he had planted, and for nearly thirty years he ran an annual literary scavenger hunt on campus that was very popular.

Throughout his **tenure** at Holyfield, Prospero was also known as an **ingenious** but **incorrigible** practical joker. One time, at a swanky fundraiser for the campus theater, he appeared from a swirling cloud of mist dressed as the ghost of Hamlet's father. Bartholomew Martext, the theater's artistic director, nearly fainted when Prospero told all the guests to swear upon his sword that they would make generous donations. But they did!

Then there was the strange case of Professor Theophilus Bibb's disappearing desk. Every year the poor fellow would arrive one day at his office to find that his desk—a Louis XVI escritoire of some value—had vanished. It would turn up safely a day or so later in some outrageous place, **ensconced** in the faculty washroom or in the middle of the old cemetery behind the college chapel. Usually there was a note attached, something to the effect of "A restless desk is a sign of a **stagnant** mind."

The first time it happened, Professor Bibb was outraged

and wanted Prospero **censured**. The college administrators acknowledged the incident was regrettable, but they said Prospero was too beloved a member of Holyfield to receive an official **reprimand** for an essentially **innocuous** prank, and they advised Bibb to take Prospero's antics in stride. Eventually he did, fighting fire with fire by occasionally playing a trick of his own on the old man.

Sometimes Prospero's jokes were too cunning and they backfired. In addition to his other talents, Prospero was also a skilled amateur calligrapher, and he once fooled Professor Harold Hargrave, now the chief curator of Tillinghast Library, with an **illuminated** manuscript he had **forged**. As the story goes, Hargrave, who back then was just coming into his own as an expert, was so **duped** by the fake that he wrote a scholarly **treatise** on it, hoping to advance his career.

By the time Prospero got wind of what Hargrave was up to, it was too late; the article had been published. Prospero apologized publicly, but as far as Hargrave was concerned, the damage had been done. Apparently it was a sore point between the two men for a long time, until Prospero offered to bankroll the new library wing and donate his collection to it after his death.

Though he was rich, Prospero was no miser. His lifestyle was **modest**, never **lavish** or **extravagant**, and he was widely hailed as a great **philanthropist** and a man of **staunch** principles and **integrity**. He gave generously to many worthy causes and of course donated a great deal to the college, including money for a much-needed **renovation** of the theater and a substantial gift to establish an endowment for scholarships in the humanities.

Some, however, thought Prospero **eccentric**, for although he could be **gregarious** when the occasion warranted, he enjoyed **solitude** and carefully guarded his privacy. And while he **abhorred** dishonesty, he delighted in secrecy. Indeed, this was a man who, **paradoxically**, seemed to have found life's meaning in its mystery.

When Leo finished his story, nearly an hour had passed and the dining hall was almost empty. As they got up to dispose of their trays, he looked at his watch.

"If you guys are still planning to see *Romeo and Juliet* tonight, you'd better get a move on. It starts in ten minutes."

Chapter 7

Fair Play or Foul?

Phil, Jimmy, and Chris ran up the steps to the balcony, taking them three at a time. Phil led the charge. "C'mon guys. Hurry up! We can make it."

They reached the top. Chris's watch **emitted** several piercing beeps. Eight o'clock.

"Great," Jimmy said. "We're going to miss the curtain, and then they won't let us in till intermission."

"Don't worry," Chris said. "My watch is three minutes fast."

Jimmy made a face. "I hope that obnoxious piece of hardware isn't going to beep and squawk through the whole play."

Chris shrugged. "Sorry, but I think it is."

"Can't you turn it off?" Phil asked.

"I lost the instruction manual, and now I can't figure out how to program it. The thing's incredibly **complex**. It's got a calculator, a stopwatch, a calendar—"

"I don't care what it has," Jimmy said. "That idiotic beeping is distracting. Can't you stick the thing in your pocket?"

"Okay, okay, chill out," Chris said.

The usher looked at their ticket stubs and waved them

inside. "You're just in time. Curtain in two minutes. To the left, row P, seats 4, 5, and 6."

"I can't believe we got the last seats in the house," Phil said. "It's amazing. What a lucky break."

Jimmy frowned. "The last and worst seats, I might add. Look. We're in the back row, stuffed in the corner."

He pointed. There were six seats in the row. Three young women occupied the ones nearest the aisle.

"Those seats are terrible," Jimmy complained. "We won't be able to see or hear anything."

"Hey, why don't we just forget it and go to the Student Center and shoot some pool," Chris suggested. "We could come back tomorrow night or maybe find some dates to take on Friday."

"That's not a bad idea," Jimmy said. "The play's running all week."

Phil held up his hands in protest. "Wait a minute. We just ran our butts off to get here and now you guys want to leave?"

"I didn't say I wanted to leave," Jimmy said. "I'd just rather not sit in those crummy seats."

"Excuse me," said the young woman in seat P-3. "The play's about to start. Would you mind sitting down, please?"

Caitlin's polite request fell on deaf ears.

"Listen," Phil told his roommates. "We made it on time and the tickets are paid for. There's no point in wasting money."

"Excuse me. The play's about to start," Caitlin said again.

The three young men continued to disregard the interruption.

"What's a few bucks lost when we can all go somewhere else and have a good time?" Chris said with a shrug.

"You might not mind **squandering** your money," Phil said, "but I certainly do."

Jimmy nodded. "Phil's not only **frugal**, Chris. He's right.

It's stupid to be a **spendthrift**. I suppose we'll just have to accept the **consequences** of our actions."

Chris was **persistent**. "I still think we should play pool."

"C'mon, man," Phil said. "Let's just sit down and try to
enjoy it, okay?"

The house lights dimmed slightly.

Caitlin decided it was time for serious action. "Hey," she
called out in a **strident** voice. "Are you bozos going to sit
down, or are you going to stand there blabbing in the aisle
all night?"

"Pardon me, mademoiselle," Jimmy replied, bowing **obsequiously**. "We'll be there in a moment." He turned and
whispered to Phil. "Since you're the one who persuaded us to
stay, I think you should sit next to the **querulous** shrew.
Maybe you can tame her," he added with a grin.

"Yeah, and next week you can go to *The Taming of the
Shrew* and pick up a few dating tips," Chris teased.

Phil glanced at the young woman who had **upbraided**
them. She was casting **malicious** looks in their direction. He
couldn't believe it. She was the same one with the dark hair
he'd seen at Prospero Gate, the one who'd come up to Bill
Berkowitz while they were in line at Steinbach Commons,
the one who'd commented on his shirt. What had she told
Bill her name was? Cathy? Kate? No, Caitlin. That was it.
Maybe these seats wouldn't be so bad after all, he thought.

The house lights faded, flickered momentarily, and then
went out. The theater was completely dark.

Caitlin felt a chill run down her spine, and a lump began
forming in her throat. She had been to the theater many
times, but no matter how often she went, she was always
overcome with a **profound** excitement when the play began.
It was like the time she'd stayed up all night finishing an
English paper and gone up to the roof of her father's apartment building to watch the dawn. The huge city, so frantic

and filthy in the hard light of day, had seemed strangely hushed and **serene**, like an empty cathedral.

A brassy **flourish** of music swelled from powerful speakers hidden offstage. A cymbal crashed, and there was a long, low drum roll. Caitlin's heart pounded with expectation. She swallowed hard and clutched the armrests.

"Oh my God, excuse me," she mumbled, releasing her grip on Phil's arm.

"Hey, no problem. You can have the armrest."

"That's okay, really," she whispered. "You take it. I've got the one on the other side."

She was so close Phil could smell her breath—a faint scent of licorice, or was it peppermint? Suddenly the theater felt like a boiler room and Phil wished he had taken off his jacket before sitting down. He could feel the sweat breaking out on his forehead. He tried to ignore it and focus on the stage, which was still dark.

A man's deep, **resonant** voice came over the sound system, filling the theater. As he spoke, the lights came up slightly and the curtain rose, revealing a dozen or so shadowy, **obscure** figures scattered around the stage. They seemed frozen in various awkward positions. The **sonorous** voice went on:

From forth the fatal loins of these two foes
A pair of star-crossed lovers take their life

Phil leaned toward Caitlin and whispered, "So that's where that phrase comes from."

Caitlin looked at him out of the corner of her eye. "What phrase?"

"'Star-crossed lovers.'"

"Oh, sure. A lot of common expressions come from Shakespeare."

"Like what?"

"I don't know. I'll tell you later. The first scene's about to start."

"Okay. Sorry."

The voice finished speaking and the lights came up quickly, fully **illuminating** the stage. The frozen figures all suddenly began to move as though nothing had ever interrupted their actions. It was a strange scene, Phil thought. Though the actors were dressed in modern clothing and the set looked like a modern city street, something about the whole thing seemed faintly **archaic**. Phil couldn't quite put his finger on it.

Two large, scruffy-looking men wearing overalls, hardhats, and heavy leather tool belts swaggered downstage and began talking to each other. Phil had expected the actors to speak with British accents, but the men's gruff voices sounded American. In fact, they sounded just like the carpenters and drywall hangers Phil had worked with the summer after eleventh grade, when his father, who was a field supervisor for a big construction company, got him a job as a laborer with a crew building tract homes in a new development. Except the actors weren't talking like the guys he'd worked with, saying things he could never have repeated to his mother or his English teacher. They were speaking **florid** Elizabethan English. Was this how they did Shakespeare's plays now? Phil was perplexed.

He tapped Caitlin's arm. "What's going on?"

"What do you mean?"

"Why are they dressed in **contemporary** clothes and speaking with American accents?"

"Haven't you ever seen a modern interpretation before?"

Phil was about to say no, he hadn't, but decided against it. He slumped back in his seat and listened to the two men.

SAMPSON: I will take the wall of any man or maid of Montague's.

GREGORY: That shows thee a weak slave; for the weakest goes to the wall.

SAMPSON: 'Tis true; and therefore women, being the weaker vessels, are ever thrust to the wall. Therefore I will push Montague's men from the wall and thrust his maids to the wall.

GREGORY: The quarrel is between our masters and us their men.

SAMPSON: 'Tis all one. I will show myself a tyrant. When I have fought with the men, I will be civil with the maids—I will cut off their heads.

GREGORY: The heads of the maids?

SAMPSON: Ay, the heads of the maids or their maidenheads. Take it in what sense thou wilt.

What sense *should* he take that in? Phil wondered. It was Shakespeare's **flamboyant** English, but it sounded like a dirty joke. Maybe Elizabethan construction workers were just as **ribald** and **belligerent** as the ones he'd worked with—the same sort of coarseness and **vulgarity**, only in a different **dialect**, time, and place. Was that the message the director was trying to get across by using **contemporary** clothing and sets?

The play continued and Phil tried hard to find deeper meanings, but after concentrating for several scenes he grew tired and more confused than ever. From reading the play in tenth-grade English he knew that Romeo and Juliet were from feuding families and that against all odds they would fall in love and die tragically. He also knew that their deaths would be **precipitated** by Romeo's killing Tybalt, Juliet's cousin, in revenge for Tybalt's killing Mercutio, Romeo's friend. Beyond that **meager synopsis**, Phil's recollection ceased.

Phil leaned toward Caitlin again. "Can you understand what they're saying?"

"Most of it, but it's hard to hear way back here. Why?"

"I was trying to figure out what Romeo and Juliet meant by all that stuff about prayer and sin—you know, when they first met and he kissed her in that last scene?"

"Look, can we talk about it at intermission? I can't explain now. I'm trying to watch the play."

"I was just wondering what Shakespeare meant by that."

Caitlin gave him a **reproachful** look. "I guess you'll just have to learn to read between the lines."

Phil felt stupid, like a little kid **chastised** by his mother. He bit his lip and stewed in his **resentment** for a few minutes. Then he decided that was stupid too, so he gave up feeling **morose** and tried to focus on the play again.

As the scenery changed for the second act, Phil stole a **furtive** look at Caitlin. She was watching the play intently and scowling, not unattractively but in a way that made her look serious and intelligent.

A **clamor** of voices rose from the stage. Phil saw Caitlin's lips part as if to speak, then come together in a **reflective** pout. After a while she sighed, put her elbow on the armrest, and rested her cheek on her palm.

Suddenly she looked at him. "What are you doing?"

"Nothing. What do you mean?"

"You're staring at me."

"No I'm not. I was just stretching my neck."

"Well cut it out," she snapped. "It's distracting."

"Yeah, sure, fine," Phil mumbled. Jimmy was right, he thought. The woman was a shrew. He crossed his arms and stared **glumly** at the stage.

There he saw Juliet leaning on the railing of a small balcony, her dark, flowing hair bathed in soft light. Romeo stood in semidarkness on the other side of the stage. Turning toward the audience, he began to speak:

> But soft! What light through yonder window breaks?
> It is the East, and Juliet is the sun! . . .

It is my lady! O, it is my love!
O, that she knew she were!
She speaks, yet she says nothing. What of that?
Her eye **discourses**; I will answer it.
I am too bold; 'tis not to me she speaks. . . .

See how she leans her cheek upon her hand!
O, that I were a glove upon that hand,
That I might touch that cheek!

Chapter 8

A **Shrewd** Conversation

At the intermission, Jimmy surprised Phil by playing the **suave** social director. After the lights had come up and they'd all stepped into the aisle, Jimmy introduced himself and his roommates to the three young women, then offered to buy refreshments. Now the six freshmen stood in the main lobby, sipping soft drinks amid the buzz of **animated** conversation.

Phil looked at Caitlin, who was studying some posters of past theatrical productions on a nearby wall. She had blasted him with **condescension**, making him feel like a fourth grader by telling him to learn to read between the lines. Then she had caught him staring at her and had squashed him like a bug. Was it worth attempting another conversation with someone who seemed so **haughty** and **supercilious**? Probably not, he thought, but what the heck. He had nothing to lose except his pride.

"You have an interesting face. Would you mind if I sketched you sometime?"

Caitlin turned. "What?"

"I like to draw, and I'm pretty good at it, I guess, and I was just wondering if you'd be willing to let me draw your face. You've got a very interesting face."

"What's so interesting about it?"

"I don't know. It's just unusual . . . different."

Caitlin laughed. "Different, huh? What's different about it? Is it especially ugly or something?"

"No, of course not. It's just the opposite."

Caitlin smiled.

Good, Phil thought. All is not lost. Feeling more confident, he went on. "It's not your average, everyday face. It's got a lot of character. It's kind of . . . **exotic**."

Caitlin looked at Phil for a long moment. Is he for real, she wondered, or is this just another **impudent** come-on? All through high school she had encountered guys who for some inexplicable reason had thought that saying something **inane** or **offensive** was the best way to gain her attention or her affection. Most of them had treated her as if she were a brainless sponge, ready and waiting to soak up their every word. How could they have expected her to take them seriously?

Caitlin studied Phil's face. His hair was dark and wavy and combed neatly. His eyes were also dark and quite **vivid**. His nose curved down slightly—an aquiline nose, like an eagle's beak, that was strong but stopped short of **arrogance**. His mouth was strong and full too, but there was something gentle about it that matched the **tentative** way he spoke. It was a friendly face, she decided, full of **integrity**.

"Thanks. That's a nice compliment," she said finally.

"You know," Phil said, changing the subject, "I saw you earlier tonight, at Steinbach Commons. You were talking to Bill Berkowitz, the editor of the *Herald*." He decided not to mention her comment about his shirt. Let her bring it up, he thought.

"That's right," Caitlin said. "I remember seeing you there too. I told you I liked your Hawaiian shirt," she added with a **winsome** smile.

Phil swallowed quickly. "Yes, I remember."

"Anyway, it was sort of a lucky break. I was telling Carmen Torres—this English professor who ate dinner with us tonight—that I wanted to be a reporter for the paper, and she pointed out Bill to me."

"That's interesting. I'll be taking an intro class with Professor Torres."

"Really? That's great. But watch out—she told us her students call her the Dragon Lady."

Phil laughed.

"So how do you know Bill Berkowitz?" asked Caitlin.

Phil told her about Bill and Leo, and when he mentioned Leo's involvement with Edward Anthony Prospero, she said that would make a great article because of the new Prospero Library.

"It would be perfect if I had a story idea ready to hand Bill tomorrow," she said. "Do you think you could introduce me to Leo so I could interview him about the Prospero collection?"

"Sure, I'll do anything to help an **aspiring** journalist."

"Anything?"

"Anything within my power—that is, if you let me draw you."

"Phil, you have no **ethics**," Caitlin said. Then she smiled. "Okay, it's a deal."

Before Phil could think of what to say next, he felt a hand thump down on his shoulder.

"I see you two are getting along famously," Jimmy said. With a **droll**, sidelong glance at Phil, he added, "Have we been discussing *Romeo and Juliet* or *The Taming of the Shrew*?"

"Neither, actually," Phil said, giving Jimmy his best you'd-better-shut-up-or-I'll-pound-you look.

"Why would we be discussing *The Taming of the Shrew*?" Caitlin asked.

"Because I thought you might be looking ahead to next week's offering," Jimmy said. "Maybe we all can come earlier and get better seats together."

Phil marveled at how **shrewdly** his roommate **manipulated** the conversation. He seemed to have a clever answer for everything. Maybe too clever for his own good, Phil thought, as he saw Jimmy wink at him and then turn to Caitlin.

"How do you like the production?" he asked her.

"I think it's exciting. The acting's good and the interpretation is original."

"Original?" Jimmy's expression was a **melodramatic** combination of astonishment and **indignation**. "Anyone can do something **radical** or **absurd**. That doesn't make it original."

"You've got a point there. But don't you agree it's refreshing when artists take risks like that?"

"Maybe about as refreshing as watching summer reruns of 'Wheel of Fortune.'" Jimmy leaned forward, put his hand next to his mouth, and spoke in a stage whisper. "You know what? I've heard this place is called the Stink. Maybe that's because it's **infamous** for rotten productions."

Caitlin laughed. "C'mon, you know that's not why it's called the Stink. It's just a **facetious** nickname, because *stink* rhymes with *Fincke*."

Jimmy shrugged. "Whatever. All I can say is, every time the actors open their mouths they drive another stake into the heart of some of the most **eloquent** language ever written. If I were the Bard, I'd be turning over in my grave watching this."

"That's because you just crawled out of one yourself," Caitlin quipped. "Jimmy, who says a production has to be **conventional** to be good? If you were Shakespeare, wouldn't you be **gratified** to know that after four hundred years not only is your work still being produced and enjoyed but people are taking an **innovative** and **contemporary** approach to it?"

Jimmy snorted. "**Gratified**? Why, I'd be **mortified**!"

By now the **animated** debate had attracted the attention of the others.

"Hey, Jimmy," Chris cut in. "Get a life, will you? Since

when did you become the college drama critic?"

"Your idea of how Shakespeare should be produced just reflects your own **bias**," said Juliet.

"I agree," Lucy said. "You can't **prescribe** what a work of art should or shouldn't be. You have to judge it in **context**."

"All right, all right, everybody," Jimmy said, throwing up his hands. "The next time the Stink stages a production of *Julius Caesar*, I promise I'll try out for the title role. Or would you prefer to assassinate me right now and get it over with?"

"Now that sounds like a plan," Chris said.

Jimmy sighed. "*Et tu*, Bednarski?"

Everyone laughed, and a moment later a voice came over the P.A. announcing the end of the intermission.

Long after her roommates had gone to sleep, Caitlin lay awake in her bed in LaSalle Hall, **ruminating.**

It had been a full day, a good day. She had traveled halfway across the country to a new place where, if everything worked out right, she would spend the next four years of her life gaining knowledge and experience and making new friends. She had been lucky to get nice roommates, and she had met an interesting professor and the editor of the *Holyfield Herald*. She had also seen a good play and eaten some delicious pizza afterward.

Caitlin was grateful to Annie, the cab driver, for suggesting Salerno's. The others had wanted to go to Pesto Palace because it was the biggest restaurant on Chickasaw Street and it was teeming with rowdy students. But she had persuaded them that there was a better place further on. And they weren't disappointed. Salerno's was lively but not so loud that you couldn't have a normal conversation. They all sat around a big table with a red-checkered tablecloth, gobbling down thin-crusted pizza with the meat on top, just as it should be. It took only a couple of bites before everyone was praising Caitlin's choice.

When they had finished eating they talked for a long

time, sharing stories about their respective high schools and their **aspirations** for college. The discussion was **convivial** and **stimulating**, full of jokes and laughter. Shortly after midnight the boys walked the girls back to LaSalle and said goodnight.

If so much could happen in just one day in college, Caitlin wondered, then what lay ahead?

A **plethora** of possibilities crowded her mind, and the more she pondered her future, the more awake she became. Finally she decided that if she wasn't going to sleep, she might as well get up. She slipped out of bed and into her robe and stole quietly out of the room.

She made for the stairwell, climbed the steps to the top, and found the door to the roof unlocked. When she stepped outside, the cool night air enveloped her and she pulled the collar of her robe tight around her neck and throat. Bits of gravel crunched under her slippered feet as she crossed to the parapet and looked out.

Holyfield College lay **shrouded** in shadowy sleep. Hooded lamps dotted the empty flagstone pathways of West Quad, and here and there a light glimmered in a window, but most of what she could see of the campus was dark. Above the grim silhouette of Tillinghast Library the moon hovered like a **wizened** old professor lost in thought.

Caitlin listened to the night's **tranquil** sounds—the soothing, rhythmic call of crickets and the trees creaking as they swayed. Somewhere, something **exquisite** was blooming, probably in Olsen Garden, she thought. She breathed deeply, drinking in the rich aroma, then gazed up into the night.

The silvery cloud of the Milky Way streamed across the wide sky. **Myriad** stars dimpled the darkness with light—more stars than she had ever seen anywhere before. Caitlin felt as if she were gazing into a distant mirror that reflected the whole world. Was she one of the **minuscule** stars in that **scintillating** sky? she wondered.

The bell in the Holyfield tower struck twice. Two o'clock.

Caitlin sighed and leaned against the cold stone wall. No use trying to resolve all my feelings tonight, she thought. I'd better get some rest so I'll be ready for my appointment at the *Herald* in the morning.

She blew a goodnight kiss to the pale, **pensive** moon and hurried back to bed.

Chapter 9

Don't Judge a Book
by Its Cover

Sunday

Leo Kabnis tucked in his shirt, knotted his tie, slipped on a blazer, and, after a quick look in the mirror, dashed out the door and down the stairs.

Hurrying along the flagstone pathway, he glanced at his watch: 9:45 A.M. No problem making the ten o'clock meeting on time, he thought, but too late to grab some breakfast beforehand. He'd just have to hang on until lunch.

Leo looked up and saw it was a cloudy morning. As he strode past students on their way to the dining halls or church, he wondered about the awesome responsibility Professor Prospero had given him. What would being a literary executor **entail**? Would it require much of his time? Would he get paid?

The aromas of baked dough and frying bacon **pervaded** the air around Steinbach Commons. Leo had to resist the urge to go in and **satiate** his hunger. At the corner of College and Holyfield streets he waited impatiently for the light to change, then trotted across and bounded up the well-worn stairs to the vaulted entrance of Tillinghast Library.

It was the Sunday before the first day of classes, and the library was officially closed. Leo showed the security guard the special access permit he had been issued for the executors' meeting, and the man ushered him in. He briskly crossed the dim, empty lobby, entered the rosewood-paneled elevator, and pressed the button for the third floor.

As he walked down the hall toward the Bohring Conference Room, the bell in Holyfield Tower began tolling the hour. Listening to the familiar sound that had measured all the days and nights of his college years, Leo smiled. The **imposing** tower and its massive bell were an **integral** part of the atmosphere on campus. Leo remembered how as a freshman he had found the constant clanging **unsettling**, at times even **ominous**. Now he rarely noticed it, and whenever he did it served to remind him of who he was and where he was going, and he found that reassuring.

The last peal of the bell trailed off as Leo entered the conference room. At the end of a mahogany table that **dominated** the **stately** wood-paneled and red-carpeted room, Professors Carmen Torres and Bartholomew Martext sat conversing quietly.

Torres looked up. "Leo, how are you? How was your summer?" she asked, rising and giving him a hug.

"Fine, Carmen. How was yours? Did you get to England?"

"Indeed I did. It was wonderful. I dug up loads of material for my book in London and Oxford. Which reminds me, Leo. You haven't forgotten what I told you about your essay on Chaucer, have you?"

"Oh, no, I haven't forgotten. But I have a whole list of questions I'd like to talk to you about."

Since taking an advanced composition class with Torres his freshman year, Leo had been an appreciative **beneficiary** of her support and concern. Last spring he had taken her seminar on English **epic** poetry, and she had liked his term paper so much that she had urged him to make some revisions and submit it for publication. Over the summer Leo had broadened his research and pondered her suggestions. Now he needed a sounding board for his ideas.

"You had such an interesting **thesis**," Torres said. "What was your title again?"

"'Virtue, Necessity, and the **Paradox** of Chivalry in *The Knight's Tale*.'"

"Ah, yes. Excellent. We could discuss it Friday afternoon during my office hours if you like."

"That sounds great. Thanks a lot."

"So, Carmen, is this the wunderkind you've been telling me so much about?" Martext asked. His **urbane** baritone voice was carefully modulated.

"A **felicitous** word, *wunderkind*," Torres said with a chuckle. "Bart, allow me to introduce Holyfield College's **preeminent** undergraduate scholar, Leo Kabnis. Leo, this is Bartholomew Martext, artistic director of the Fincke Theater and professor of theater studies."

"Pleased to meet you, Professor Martext," Leo said.

"The pleasure's mine," Martext said, getting up to shake Leo's hand. "But call me Bart. Like Carmen, I'm not one to insist on the **traditional** forms of academic address."

Leo had often seen Martext around campus but had never met him. His friends in the theater program had told him that the man was a brilliant but **capricious** director, **affable** and agreeable one day then **aloof** and **obstinate** the next. Martext's striking appearance gave **credence** to these accounts. He had a stern mouth, a chiseled jaw and nose, and **fervid**, deep-set eyes that seemed to smolder with barely **suppressed** emotion. Those features, coupled with his long, wavy salt-and-pepper hair and sideburns, made him look like some grim pioneer or **fanatical** preacher who had just stepped out of a daguerreotype from the nineteenth century.

Leo knew many professors who might be described as **idiosyncratic**, but Martext struck him as a few degrees beyond that. He seemed to be the kind of person who self-consciously cultivates an **unorthodox** image the way a **shrewd** actor might **exploit** the **inherent** peculiarities of a character to amuse or stir or shock an audience.

There was a muffled noise at the door. Leo turned to see the squat, **rotund** frame of Theophilus Bibb, the Stanley B. Prattle Professor of Intellectual History and chair of the Renaissance Studies Department, waddle into the conference room.

Bibb was dressed in his customary **attire**: a **lackluster** old pair of wingtip shoes, a baggy, somewhat **threadbare** gray wool suit, a rumpled white shirt, and a faded red bow tie. In one hand he held an ivory-tipped cane, in the other a battered leather briefcase. Bibb's **salient** facial features were almost **ludicrous**, Leo thought. The tip of his bulbous nose was raspberry red, his bushy gray eyebrows seemed permanently raised in an expression of arch amusement, and his crown was as smooth and hairless as a tired-out tennis ball.

"Good morning, Professor Torres, Professor Martext," Bibb said in the orotund voice of a seasoned lecturer, nodding to his colleagues. "Leo," he continued, lumbering into the room and setting his briefcase and cane on the table, "so good to see you again. I must say I was delighted when I heard you'd been selected one of the executors. It's precisely what we **obdurate** old academics need—a **vivacious** representative from the undergraduate ranks to arouse our **phlegmatic** blood."

There was something **ambiguous** about the way Professor Bibb said the word *ranks* that made Leo think he was putting a double spin on the word, as though he associated a foul, or rank, odor with the Holyfield student body. He searched the professor's face but couldn't detect any trace of **irony** or **condescension**. Bibb's **benign** expression was **inscrutable**.

In his sophomore year, as one of the electives for his double major in English and humanities, Leo had taken an upper-level seminar with Bibb entitled "Authority, Authorship, and the **Evolution** of the Printed Word," in which they had studied various reproductions and translations of works by a **diverse** selection of authors from Dante to Dryden.

Leo had found Bibb a devilishly demanding but superbly entertaining teacher, learned and witty and brimming with **obscure** facts and lively **anecdotes**. With **inimitable** style, Bibb had expertly **elucidated** the **esoteric** mysteries of textual **analysis**, and under his tutelage Leo had worked so hard that toward the end of the semester he could almost feel his brain growing, pumping up like a muscle disciplined on the bench press of knowledge. As a result, Leo had earned an A from a man **notorious** for **dispensing** them about as often as Halley's comet makes a flyby past the earth.

Leo was considering how to respond to the **corpulent** professor's **bombastic** greeting when the conference room door closed abruptly. He looked over and saw that the fifth and final member of the executors' committee had entered the room.

Professor Harold Hargrave, chief curator of Tillinghast Library, was a man of medium build. He was dressed in a conservative gray business suit and **staid** tie. His thinning hair was parted low on one side and plastered across the top of his head in a **futile** attempt to cover a **conspicuous** bald spot. His nose was sharp and pointed and his lips were slim. There was a **furtive** quality about his expression that reminded Leo of the drawings of Templeton the rat in E. B. White's *Charlotte's Web.*

"Welcome, everyone," Hargrave said crisply, saluting his fellow professors and exchanging a formal handshake with Leo. He walked to the far end of the conference table and set down his oversized briefcase. "I apologize for my **tardiness**. It couldn't be helped. Let's get down to work, shall we?"

The five executors took their seats. Hargrave removed a file from his briefcase, laid it open before him, and drummed the tips of his long, bony fingers on the tabletop for a moment.

"To begin with, I apologize for calling you together on a Sunday morning. I know it's an unusual time for a meeting, especially with classes beginning tomorrow, but we all have busy schedules, and certain matters need to be addressed before the dedication of the new Prospero wing.

"The first matter before us," Hargrave continued, "is the **disposition** and role of the executors. I have here the codicil to Prospero's will that establishes this committee and sets forth its bylaws. I received it last week from Merrilee Shylock, Prospero's attorney and legal executor. For your convenience, I have made photocopies for each of you."

The chief curator paused to pass out the copies. When Leo received his, he began reading the document:

Codicil A
Last Will & Testament of
Edward Anthony Prospero

I hereby declare that my literary estate, by which is meant the books, manuscripts, and all other written or printed materials now owned by me or in my possession, shall be given separate consideration from the rest of my estate and shall become, upon my death, wholly and entirely the property of Tillinghast Library at Holyfield College, in **accordance** with the terms and conditions set forth in my prior agreement with the trustees and officers of the college, which provides for the establishment of Prospero Memorial Library as an **adjunct** to Tillinghast Library, to be used to good purpose and made available to the faculty and students of the college, and the general public, for their benefit and **edification**.

What a **complex, convoluted** sentence, Leo thought. Legal writing is like philosophical writing: the more precise the intention, the more **ponderous** the prose. He read on:

In light of the foregoing, I hereby appoint the following persons as executors of my literary estate, to assure its safekeeping, and, in all other matters, to exercise full authority over its contents as they see fit:

Harold Hargrave, who shall be principal executor, in recognition of his academic achievement and **estimable** position as chief curator of Tillinghast Library;

Theophilus Bibb, the **proficient** scholar and **bibliophile** upon whose **expertise** in evaluation and **authentication** I have many times relied, in recognition of our long and **provocative** intellectual association;

Bartholomew Martext, the **innovative** artistic director who **revitalized** theatrical production at Holyfield College, in recognition of his creative talent and his willingness to heed the advice of an **officious** old man;

Carmen Torres, whose career I have watched with great interest since she first came to the college, and whose **collaboration** on *De Gustibus: An Inquiry into Modern Literary Style* was invaluable, in recognition of her devotion to the pursuit of knowledge and her **surpassing** ability as a teacher; and

Leo Kabnis, who without doubt or reservation is the most able and promising student I have ever had the pleasure of knowing, in recognition of his superior intelligence, good character, and wit.

Leo smiled. Wit, he thought. That's nice.

"As you will see on page three," Hargrave was saying, "Prospero stipulates that all five executors must be present to conduct any business concerning the collection, and a minimum of four votes is required to sell or transfer or otherwise dispose of any of its contents. Beyond that we are free to

adopt rules, determine **priorities**, and proceed in this enterprise as we deem appropriate. Are there any questions?"

"Yes," Carmen Torres said. "I must confess I'm sitting
here on pins and needles wondering what sort of literary material we'll be responsible for superintending. Can you give
us an idea of what Prospero's collection contains?"

"That is the second matter on my agenda," Hargrave
said. "When I met with Ms. Shylock, she also briefed me on
the **status** of the collection. As you know, Prospero was an
extraordinarily **affluent** man. He built his literary estate over
many decades, often **augmenting** his holdings by purchasing
whole collections from book dealers and fellow **connoisseurs**.
Thus, because of its **magnitude** and **scope**, it is difficult to
say with any **specificity** what the Prospero collection contains. I can, however, provide a few details that may prove
enlightening."

"Please do. We're all ears," Martext said.

Hargrave cleared his throat and went on. "According to
Ms. Shylock and a Mr. Augustus H. Murray, an independent
book specialist assigned by the probate court, Prospero's literary estate comprises about fifty thousand books and manuscripts, of which roughly fifteen thousand items may be
classified as fine or rare. The value of these fine pieces varies
considerably, from as little as a hundred to as much as a
hundred thousand dollars. There are also a number of **exceptional** pieces—most **notably** certain incunabula, or books
printed before 1500 A.D.—that are worth up to half a million
dollars or more."

Hargrave paused, as if for dramatic effect. The muscles
around his mouth tightened, and his thin lips grew thinner
still. "Shortly before his death, Prospero estimated the worth
of his entire collection at fourteen to fifteen million dollars.
Mr. Murray's estimate adjusts that figure to seventeen to
twenty million dollars."

An **audible** and **collective** gasp of astonishment issued from Leo, Torres, and Martext. Bibb sat calmly, hands folded on the table, looking at Hargrave.

"At my request, Professor Bibb has consulted with Mr. Murray and has been attempting to **corroborate** these estimates and **compile** more information on the collection," Hargrave continued. "He's spent a good deal of time cataloguing and **appraising** material that has been moved into Tillinghast in preparation for the opening of the new wing. He has also been studying Prospero's notes on his holdings, which unfortunately are sketchy and incomplete."

"What have you **ascertained** so far, Theo?" Torres asked. "May we expect a report from you?"

Bibb nodded. "At present there's not much to add to Harold's summary. My **preliminary** report will be ready for your inspection at our next meeting."

"Excuse me, Harold," said Martext, "but what I'd like to know is where are all the books right now? And when are we going to be able to have a look at them?"

"If any executor wishes to examine the collection, he is welcome to do so at any time," Hargrave said. "Or she is," he added with an apologetic nod to Torres.

"Thank you, Harold," Torres said stiffly.

"Professor Bibb has informed me that he will make himself available as a docent, should you wish to avail yourselves of his expert services," Hargrave continued. "As to your other query, Bart, regarding the location of the books and manuscripts, I'm afraid that's a more complicated matter.

"About half the material is already here at Tillinghast, being held temporarily in the special collections archive. Another substantial portion is still at Inverness, the Prospero mansion, waiting to be properly packed and transported. Two other smaller portions are at Prospero's summer house on Martha's Vineyard and his villa in northern Italy. That accounts for about ninety percent of the collection. The remaining ten percent is at present **diffused**, on loan to various museums and libraries around the world, and will be recovered in due time."

The chief curator leaned back in his chair and touched the tips of his spidery fingers together. "And now, if there are no further questions, I would like to move on to the third item on the agenda, which is a matter of **grave** concern."

The executors shuffled their feet, shifted in their chairs, and gave Hargrave their full attention.

"As principal executor, it is my duty to **apprise** you of all news **germane** to the collection or to the **endeavors** of this committee. I regret to inform you that recently we received some very bad news indeed."

Leo, suddenly **prescient,** sat up straight in his chair. Some beta wave was sending him warnings about what was coming next.

"On Friday," Hargrave said, "I received a letter from an attorney representing Edward Anthony Prospero III—otherwise known as Teddy Prospero, the grandson of Old Man Prospero and a senior here at Holyfield College. Some of you, I am sure, are well aware of the reputation Teddy has for flouting authority and causing all kinds of **malicious** mischief."

Leo's beta wave pulsed like a **garish** neon sign: *I told you it was Teddy! I told you it was Teddy! I told you it was Teddy!*

Bibb sighed loudly. "What is the young rascal up to now, Harold?"

Hargrave leaned forward and cleared his throat. "He's planning to contest the will and file suit against the college for a share of his grandfather's literary estate."

"How much of a share?" asked Martext.

"The attorney's letter didn't **specify**," Hargrave said, checking one of the papers in his file. "It simply said, and I quote, 'significant damages commensurate with the pain and suffering my client has undergone as a result of the **collusion** between the late Edward Anthony Prospero and Holyfield College to defraud him of his rightful inheritance.'"

"Poppycock!" sputtered Bibb. "The old man could dispose of his estate however he wished. Teddy has no more right to his grandfather's money—or his books—than I do."

"Quite true, Theo," Hargrave said calmly, "but listen to what the letter says next: 'My client further states, and I am prepared to prove his **assertion** in court if necessary, that each and every one of the appointed literary executors had a selfish interest in seeing him stripped of his **legacy**, an interest prompted by **cupidity** and a warped desire for self-advancement. To this end they fostered a **sycophantic** association with the senior Prospero, which, like Iago's **insidious corruption** of Othello or the **undermining** of King Lear's innocent daughter Cordelia by her **callous** and wicked sisters, turned the grandfather unfairly against his defenseless grandson.'"

Listening to the **ostentatious allusions** in the lawyer's letter, Leo wondered if Teddy Prospero had hired someone who had cut as many English classes in college as Teddy had and who was now trying to pass off a **paltry** knowledge of Shakespeare as a badge of intellectual achievement.

While Leo **ruminated** on this point, the rest of the table erupted in protest.

"This is **preposterous**!" bellowed Bibb.

"It's **farcical**!" raged Martext.

"It *is* **appalling**," Torres **concurred**.

Hargrave frowned and stroked his chin. "Whether the charge has merit is of little import. What matters is that it's a nuisance suit—call it legal blackmail, if you will. It presents us with a classic **dilemma**. On the one hand, it would be **imprudent** to **capitulate** and settle with Teddy and his **mercenary** attorney simply because they **categorically** demand it. On the other hand, the **exorbitant** expense and **adverse** publicity that might attend a **protracted** court proceeding could have **dire consequences**, not only for the future of the Prospero Memorial Library but for each of us as well."

"That's right, Harold," said Martext. He leaned forward and looked around the table. His eyes were like two smoking

coals. "No one is **immune** to **frivolous** lawsuits, and the innocent are the most **vulnerable**. That's because people like
Teddy Prospero enjoy making others' lives miserable and
watching them squirm. They crave the sadistic thrill of it!"

Bibb slammed his plump fist down on the table. "I agree
most **emphatically**. Teddy Prospero was the most **incorrigible**
student I've ever had—when he came to class, that is."

Torres looked at Hargrave. "Harold, the suit seems so
outrageous and **ill-conceived**. Obviously Teddy Prospero and
his attorney have **fabricated** these charges to scare us into a
settlement. Can't we just call their bluff?"

Torres's question went unanswered, for at that moment
the door to the conference room opened and a big man in a
smartly tailored blue suit stepped inside. His sturdy build,
erect posture, and stiffly waxed handlebar mustache lent him
an air of self-contained **sophistication**. A stranger might have
guessed his age at forty-five, but he was actually closer to
sixty.

"Is this an appropriate time, Harold?" the man asked in a
crisp English accent.

Leo jumped up from his seat. "Reggie, what a nice surprise! I didn't know you were coming."

"Hullo, Leo. It's good to see you too," the man said with
a gracious smile. "Professor Hargrave asked me to come at
ten-thirty, and it's ten-thirty on the button, so here I am."

Hargrave stood up. "I presume all of you know Mr. Reginald Burton-Jones, Prospero's manservant?"

"*Valet*, if you don't mind, old chap," Burton-Jones said.

"Yes, of course."

Burton-Jones and the other executors exchanged greet-
ings and began chatting **amiably**.

Hargrave rapped his knuckles sharply on the table. "Excuse me, everyone, but if you would please take your seats
again, Reggie is here to preside over the final piece of business on our agenda today."

The committee came to order. Burton-Jones stood at the

head of the table opposite Hargrave, who gestured for him to proceed.

"Of course you know that Prospero thought highly of you all," Burton-Jones said. "But what you may not know, because it was not part of his formal will, is that he provided a special gift for each of you, in consideration of your services as executors of his collection and as a token of his **esteem**. It is my pleasure to be here today as the emissary of his **largess**. Harold, would you do me the honor, please?"

Hargrave nodded and stepped to a closet door in the corner of the conference room. He produced a set of keys from his jacket pocket and unlocked the door. From a shelf within he retrieved several packages wrapped in brown paper and placed them, one at a time, on the table in front of Burton-Jones.

When the librarian had finished and returned to his seat, Burton-Jones handed him one of the packages and said, "Let's begin with the principal executor, shall we?"

"Thank you, Reggie," Hargrave said. He unwrapped his gift slowly and carefully. "My lord," he muttered when he saw what he had received.

It was an original edition of the Authorized Version of the Bible, commonly known as the King James Version, published by Robert Barker in London in 1611. Unfortunately, it was not in good condition. As Hargrave delicately examined the fragile old book, Leo could see that the binding was decayed and many of the deeply yellowed pages were nicked or torn.

"I'm honored," Hargrave said at last, setting the book down on the table in front of him. "This is an extraordinary thing to bestow."

Bibb leaned back in his chair and sighed. "It's too bad it's so damaged, Harold. As you know, a fine copy would easily fetch anywhere from $125,000 to $150,000 in the open market. In that **tattered** condition it's probably worth between $5,000 and $10,000."

"Its monetary value doesn't concern me, Theo," Hargrave said in an edgy voice. "As the saying goes, it's the thought that counts." He opened a small white envelope that had been included with the package and removed the card it contained. As he read it, he frowned.

"What does it say?" Torres asked.

"It's just a well-known passage from the New Testament, Matthew 5:38–41." Hargrave cleared his throat and read it aloud.

> Ye have heard that it hath been said, An eye for an eye, and a tooth for a tooth:
> But I say unto you, That ye resist not evil: but whosoever shall smite thee on thy right cheek, turn to him the other also.
> And if any man will sue thee at the law, and take away thy coat, let him have thy cloak also.
> And whosoever shall **compel** thee to go a mile, go with him twain.

Martext snorted. "That's it? No other words of wisdom from the old man?"

Hargrave shook his head. "Just 'Best wishes, Prospero.'"

"How odd," Torres said. "What do think he meant by selecting that quotation?"

Hargrave's face was blank. "I honestly have no idea. He could be a very strange bird at times."

"Something about it seems **prophetic**," Torres said, shaking her head thoughtfully.

Martext chuckled. "Probably because it's a quotation from the Bible, Carmen. Jesus was a prophet, you'll recall."

"Let us move on now to Theophilus Bibb," said Burton-Jones, handing the stout professor his package.

Bibb tore off the plain brown wrapping paper with glee,

revealing a large, uncut volume: Sir Thomas Malory's *Le Morte d'Arthur*, illustrated by Aubrey Beardsley, J. M. Dent's first limited edition, 1893—one of a run of only three hundred copies, Bibb informed the group. The accompanying card, which Torres urged Bibb to read aloud, said, "You should find **salutary** recreation in these pages if you rarefy your **magnanimous propensities** at the side of the noble King Arthur and cultivate your **hedonistic** ones at the feet of the **decadent** Beardsley."

"A most flattering gift indeed," Bibb remarked coolly when everyone's laughter had **subsided**, "valued as it is at about six thousand dollars. I shudder, however, to think what it would be worth had Beardsley signed it."

Martext's package contained a rare, early-nineteenth-century translation of the great Spanish author Miguel de Cervantes's **epic** romance *Don Quixote*, with a card that read, "To Bart, whose **iconoclastic** genius **revels** in slaying windmills. May you always dream your impossible dreams and never wake up."

"I suppose I should follow my **prestigious** colleague's high moral example and take that as a backhanded compliment," Martext said with a grin, eyeing Bibb.

"As you wish," Bibb replied, "but I should think that the seventy-five-hundred-dollar price tag on the book makes the compliment more of an openhanded one."

Next came Carmen Torres, and when she saw her gift she could barely contain her delight. "It's the Bristol edition of *Lyrical Ballads*," she cried, proudly displaying the cover to the group. Printed in 1798, the book contained poems by the great English Romantics William Wordsworth and Samuel Taylor Coleridge, most notably Wordsworth's "Tintern Abbey" and Coleridge's "Rime of the Ancient Mariner." Bibb, who was clearly relishing his self-appointed role of **assessor**, calmly **apprised** Torres that this new addition to her library was worth no less than fifteen thousand dollars.

"Maybe I'll use it as collateral on a loan for a snazzy foreign sports car," Torres quipped.

Finally it was Leo's turn. Carefully he unwrapped the small package that Burton-Jones handed him. Inside was a paperbound volume entitled *The Prose Romances of Edgar A. Poe*, so slender that it seemed more like a pamphlet than a book. The cover was stained, the binding was chipped, and not a few of the forty pages were foxed.

Tucked inside the front cover was a sealed envelope with Leo's name typed on it. Parting words from Prospero, he presumed. He decided to read the letter later, in private.

Leo couldn't help feeling disappointed that the other executors had received more valuable books than he had, for even Hargrave's Bible, despite its defects, was an awesome literary **artifact**. Was it because they were all professors, colleagues of Prospero's, and he was only a student?

He wondered if perhaps the old man hadn't had such a high opinion of him after all and had simply regarded him as a **resourceful** helper, nothing more. Try as he might, though, Leo couldn't bring himself to accept that conclusion. Prospero had always treated him like a trusted friend, almost a **confidant**, and in turn he had always regarded the old man with the utmost respect. Then another possibility struck him. Could this gift, or something about it, be part of yet another one of Prospero's **infamous** practical jokes, played out **posthumously** at the expense of an unsuspecting student?

Seeing the **ambivalent** expression on Leo's face, Torres leaned over and patted his shoulder. "You look worried. Is something wrong?"

"No, it's nothing," Leo said. "I was just thinking about Professor Prospero, about how he gives—gave so much."

"May I have a look at your book, young man?" asked Bibb. Leo nodded and passed it across the table. Bibb examined the cover, thumbed gently through the pages with his pudgy fingers, and **scrutinized** the information printed on the title page. Then he handed the book back to Leo.

"That text is extremely valuable, you know," he said, stressing the word *extremely*. "From what I've read, there are only fourteen **extant** copies of it. It was published **obscurely** in Philadelphia, by William H. Graham, in 1843, and its original selling price was just twelve and a half cents. Today it is the rarest and most **coveted** of all Poeiana."

"Even in this condition?" Leo asked.

"Even in that condition. Of course, if you have it professionally repaired—and I can recommend some fine **artisans**—it'll be worth a pretty penny indeed. In 1990 a restored copy sold at auction for sixty thousand dollars. As is, it's still probably worth at least half that sum."

"You're kidding me!" Leo practically shouted. Beyond those three words, he was dumbstruck. What a fool he was! He had allowed his disappointment to **deceive** him into doubting Prospero, only to feel **chastened** when he learned that the old man had given him a gift worth more than all the others combined. Suddenly it hit him.

"Of course!" he cried, and burst out laughing.

Hargrave frowned. "What on earth is so funny?"

"I just got the joke."

"Whose joke?" asked Torres.

"Professor Prospero's."

Martext **smirked**. "How can a dead man play a joke on you?"

"I wouldn't put it past the old codger," Bibb mumbled.

"It was as if he could read my mind somehow," Leo explained. "I think he wanted to teach me a lesson."

"And what lesson is that?" Torres asked.

Leo studied his book for a moment and then looked up at Reggie, who was smiling from ear to ear. "It's a familiar **adage:** Don't judge a book by its cover."

Hargrave stood up, looking at his watch. "Well, I'm afraid our time is up. At our next meeting we need to discuss preparations for the Prospero Library dedication ceremony and form subcommittees to handle the various aspects of

managing the collection. I will also update you on any devel-
opments concerning the **imminent** lawsuit. Any objections
to meeting next Saturday at noon over lunch at the faculty
club?"

Martext, Torres, and Leo voiced their **assent** and began
rising from the table. Bibb was already scurrying toward the
door.

"Hear, hear!" he cried, clutching his briefcase and cane
in one hand and his precious Beardsley in the other.

Chapter 10

Opportunity Knocks

Caitlin stood outside the South Quad entrance to the Student Center, a **nondescript** sandstone **edifice** that housed the college bookstore, post office, canteen, game room, coffee shop, and various other recreational facilities. To her right, a steep flight of concrete steps led to a basement. At the bottom of the steps was a heavy steel door on which the words *Holyfield Herald* were stenciled in faded black letters.

Caitlin had expected something more **distinctive**, or at least more **conspicuous**. After all, the *Herald* was one of the few college newspapers that still operated on a daily basis, and the opportunity to work for a quasi-professional paper was one of the factors that had led her to apply to Holyfield College.

Somewhat disappointed, she descended the steps and tried the door. Locked. She looked for a buzzer, but there was none, so she rapped on the gray metal and waited. No answer. She checked her watch: 10:50 A.M. Ten minutes to kill.

Caitlin sat down on the steps and opened her portfolio, wishing she had a magazine or something to keep her from worrying about the interview. As she looked at the articles she had written for the *Spotlight*, her high school's biweekly newspaper, she wondered if she had picked the best ones to show Bill.

There were three profiles of influential professionals who had visited her school—a novelist, a Broadway director, and a reporter for *The New York Times*. These were followed by an editorial and two reviews of theatrical productions that she felt were **articulate** examples of her ability to write a formal, **objective critique**.

Then there was a report from her early days with the paper on a stunning victory over Peter Cooper High in boys' basketball. The writing was **vivid**, though maybe a bit **verbose**. At least it would help show her **diversity**, she thought.

Finally there was the feature on the challenges that Tim Owens, one of her classmates, had faced trying to set up a soup kitchen for the homeless. Caitlin had been quite taken by Tim's **altruistic zeal**, and they had gone out together for most of her junior year. She knew the tone was somewhat **biased** and preachy, but overall it was a **poignant** story and she was proud of it.

A cheery voice called out from the top of the stairs. "Good morning! Beautiful day, isn't it?"

Caitlin turned and saw an **ebullient** Bill Berkowitz descending the stairs with an **unwieldy** set of keys in his hand. With each step he took, the keys jangled in accompaniment to the bouncy movements of his lanky frame. Caitlin glanced at the sky. It was overcast and the air felt cool—much cooler than September in New York. The day didn't look so beautiful to her, but Bill's sunny manner was reassuring.

"It should be all right," she replied cautiously, putting her articles away and standing up to give him room to get by.

"I hope you haven't been waiting long," Bill said, fumbling for the key to the door.

"No, not at all. I just got here."

"Caitlin Ciccone, right?"

"Right."

Bill unlocked the door, gripped the knob, and pulled

hard. The metal grated harshly against the concrete.

"Well, come on in, Caitlin," Bill said over his shoulder.

He reached to his left and switched on a row of fluorescent ceiling lights that ran down the center of the room.

"Shall I give you the twenty-five-cent tour?"

"Sounds great."

"This is the newsroom. Mornings are generally pretty light in here—a few phone calls, some copyediting, maybe a meeting or two. After lunch it gets busy, and most of the work gets done from the late afternoon, after classes, to midnight—or later."

Caitlin looked around the room. Stacks of back issues of the *Herald* were piled against the far wall between several file cabinets and a makeshift bookcase with sagging shelves. In the middle of the room, two long worktables sat end to end. On their surfaces lay the paraphernalia of graphic design: pencils, markers, scissors, tape, razor blades, rulers, protractors, erasers, glue, correction fluid, and bits and pieces of galley proofs and newsprint. An empty pizza box and four abandoned cans of soda indicated a hasty repast at a late hour.

Two workstations with computers and laser printers occupied the left side of the room. On the right side sat two metal desks, one practically bare except for a typewriter and a telephone, the other burdened with a computer, telephone, fax machine, vertical file, and several piles of paper. The wastebasket beside the desk was overflowing.

"The messy desk's mine, of course," Bill said with a grin. "The assistant editors and reporters share the other one."

Caitlin looked around at the walls. Nearly every inch of space was taped, glued, and tacked with clippings, photos, cartoons, and headlines. She **scrutinized** one particularly dense section. Many of the items were old and yellowed, with new ones simply pasted over them, giving the effect of a **burgeoning** mural or collage.

"It's a kind of tradition," Bill said, seeing Caitlin pause to study the wall. "When you find something interesting in a newspaper or magazine, you're welcome to tack it up. That way we're surrounded by examples to **emulate**."

"How do people know where to look?" Caitlin asked, wondering how one would find anything in such a **chaotic array**. "Is there any system to it?"

Bill laughed. "No, it's totally **random**. But you'd be surprised. After a while you absorb a lot of it."

"What happens when you run out of room?"

"That's happened only once since I've been working here, when I was a freshman. There wasn't an inch of wall left, and the clippings were seven or eight layers deep. Francine Kendall, the editor that year, was sick of it. She said it was like some kind of **noxious** fuzz growing on the inside of a cave. Anyway, one night we took it all down. There'd been stuff up there for ten years."

Bill led Caitlin to the end of the newsroom, where a set of swinging doors opened into the print shop. The *Spotlight* had always sent its copy out, so the sight of printing equipment and the **pungent** smell of ink and solvents were new to Caitlin.

The two offset machines in the middle of the room could crank out the eight tabloid pages of the *Herald* in a couple of hours, Bill explained. To the right was a binding machine that could collate, staple, fold, and trim eighteen hundred items an hour. Metal shelving units for inks, papers, tools, and whatnots lined the walls. A large, pneumatic guillotine for cutting down stock and a bulky photocopier **dominated** the back of the shop. And to their left, crowded in the corner, stood two **archaic** letterpress machines—a Washington and a Heidelberg, Bill noted.

Caitlin marveled at these **relics** from a bygone era, with their **ornate** iron legs and feet and their heavy bolts, levers, and gears. "They're beautiful," she said.

"Sure, they're beautiful. They're also in the way. I wish I

could get them out of here, but they weigh a ton, **literally**."

"You don't use them?"

"No way. It takes forever to set type. Once in a while somebody comes down here and fools around with one—maybe an art major doing something creative or someone printing invitations to a poetry reading. Other than that, they just collect dust."

Bill led Caitlin back to the newsroom. He placed a folding chair beside his desk and then sat down in his own chair behind the desk. "Well, let's get the show on the road," he said. "Have a seat, Caitlin, and tell me why you want to be a writer."

Caitlin had anticipated the question, but as she sat down the smooth answer she had carefully prepared suddenly **eluded** her. She realized she would have to wing it.

"I guess it's what I've always wanted to do," she began. "In ninth grade we read *All the President's Men* in American history, and for a while Woodward and Bernstein were my heroes. I wanted to do something that would have a **beneficial** effect on society, so I decided I'd become an investigative reporter and expose lies and **corruption**. I'm still interested in journalism, but I also want to study other kinds of writing. I'd like to write poetry, plays, novels—stuff in which I express my **insight** and **perception** of things and not just the facts." Caitlin paused. "I'm sorry. I guess that sounds kind of **pretentious**."

"No, not at all," Bill said. "Your attitude is refreshing. Most people are afraid to admit what they're serious about, or else they pretend they're serious because they want to make a good impression. Do you write every day?"

"I try to. I keep a journal."

"What kind of journalism experience do you have?"

"I've written lots of reviews and features, and senior year I was editor of my school paper."

"That's good."

"I have some clips here if you'd like to see them."

"You bet."

Caitlin reached into her portfolio and handed Bill the neatly bound set of photocopied articles. He leaned back in his chair and took his time **perusing** them, now and then raising his eyebrows or chuckling to himself.

Caitlin couldn't help interpreting every change in his expression as a sign of disapproval. She tried to look at the walls instead, preparing herself for the worst.

"Well, I tell you what," Bill said finally. "Would you like to start right away?"

"What? I mean, yes, of course. I'd love to."

"Okay. There's a panel discussion on Shakespeare at KHCR, the college radio station, today at two o'clock. It's part of the Elizabethan Festival. The station's in the Calhoun Humanities Complex. You know where that is?"

"If it's on the campus map, I can find it. No problem."

"Good. Then check it out and give me five hundred words. We'll run the article in tomorrow's edition."

"Are you sure?" Caitlin asked, immediately aware of the stupidity of the question.

Bill laughed. "Of course I'm sure, Caitlin. I'm the editor, remember? Now, do you have a computer?"

"I don't, but my roommate does. I could probably—"

"Don't bug your roommate. You hardly know each other yet. Just get the story down—either typewritten or in longhand, it doesn't matter—and I'll show you how to use our software, okay?"

"Okay, but—"

"But what?"

"Don't I need an angle?"

"I don't usually tell my writers how to approach a story. Just follow the fundamental rules—who, what, where, when, why—and then report what seems **noteworthy** to you. If it interests you, it'll be interesting to your reader. But make sure you get everyone's name and title, and I'll want some quotations." Bill paused and waved a bony hand at Caitlin. "Ah, forget it. I don't have to tell you how to write a story. It's obvious from your clips you know what you're doing. I'll see you back here after dinner. Around seven, okay?"

"Okay," Caitlin said, rising and extending her hand. "This is great. Thank you so much. You don't know how grateful I am."

"No, thank *you*, Caitlin," Bill insisted. "I'm not going to write the article. You are."

They shook hands and Bill walked her to the door. Halfway up the steps she turned and looked back at him.

"By the way," she said, "I saw your piece on the Prospero Library in yesterday's paper."

"Yes?"

"I thought it was really good. I was thinking maybe I could do a follow-up on it."

"Did you have something specific in mind?

"Yes. At dinner last night I met Carmen Torres, who said you were one of her best students."

"That's nice, but hardly worthy of an article."

Caitlin laughed. "I also met a guy last night, a freshman, Phil McKnight."

"I know Phil."

"You do?"

"Yes, my roommate is his freshman counselor."

"Leo Kabnis, right?"

"That's right."

"Well, Phil told me that Leo used to work for Professor Prospero, and Professor Torres told me she'd be willing to let me interview her. She also said she'd introduce me to the other executors of the collection. From what you wrote and what Phil told me I gathered that Prospero must have been a really interesting man. I thought I could write a profile of him—sort of a man-behind-the-books piece—that might tie in with the dedication of the new library. How does that sound?"

"Interesting," Bill said. "But let's talk about it after you do this piece, okay?"

"Okay," Caitlin said. "Thanks again," she added, smiling.

"Don't mention it."

Bill watched Caitlin climb the rest of the stairs and disappear from sight. Something tells me that young woman's going to be one heck of a good reporter, he thought.

Chapter 11

The **Telltale** Spelling

Always **prudent** where time was concerned, Caitlin arrived at the Calhoun Humanities Complex twenty-two minutes early. Three minutes later she stood in the corridor outside the KHCR studios studying the notices on the station's bulletin board.

A hand lightly tapped her shoulder. "Hi there," said a familiar voice.

She spun around. "Hey, Phil. What are you doing here?"

"I work here."

"At KHCR? You're kidding."

"Nope. I just got hired this morning—as a volunteer. The station's run by student volunteers. I'm going to be the board operator for the live panel on Shakespeare at one o'clock."

"Really? I'm here to cover it for the *Herald*."

"Hey, that's great. You got an assignment already."

"Yeah, my interview this morning went well. So how did you manage to finagle a job here so fast, Phil?"

"After we got back to the dorm last night, Chris and I were listening to KHCR and talking about what music we liked. Chris said he knew Nancy Kenneally, the station manager, because she went to his high school and had gone out with his brother for a while. He said he was going to ask her for a job as a DJ, and I said I'd be interested in working as an audio engineer.

"So this morning we came over to check things out and Nancy was here. She said there was plenty to do if we wanted to get involved. She told Chris she'd apprentice him to one of the senior DJs, and she asked me to fill in today because the scheduled board operator was sick. So here I am: Mr. College Radio Audio Engineer. Not bad, huh?"

"Not bad at all. But do you know what you're doing?"

"Oh, sure. A friend of mine on my high school soccer team—his older brother was a junior at the University of California in San Diego and worked Saturday nights at the radio station there. We used to go up and hang out with him, help him out. Sometimes he'd let us arrange and even announce a few sets. I started bugging him to teach me how to set up the equipment and run the board, and eventually he did. So I know the **rudiments**, anyway."

Phil looked at the clock. "We'd better get going. The panelists will be here in a couple of minutes. Come on. I'll show you the studio."

At the end of the corridor Phil pushed open a swinging door. "This is the reception area and lounge," he said **ironically**. "Not bad for lounging, I guess—if you're a serious couch potato—but not much of a place for a reception, is it?"

Caitlin looked around. A **haphazard** assortment of battered furniture cluttered the room. Bare cement was visible through several spots in the **threadbare** shag carpeting.

Caitlin laughed. "It's an interior decorator's nightmare."

They crossed the room and turned left into a narrow hallway. From a speaker in the ceiling came a smooth tenor voice.

"A couple more tunes and I'm outta here, guys. But don't go away, 'cause we've got a totally awesome segment coming up at two o'clock—a live panel on Bad Billy Shakespeare, featuring hair-raising **rhetoric**, **heretical hypotheses**, and totally outrageous **oratory** from some of Holyfield's most popular pundits. That's right here at two on your standing ovation station, KHCR!"

Phil chuckled. "That's Randy 'The Maniac' Malone, assistant station manager and DJ extraordinaire. He's intense. You'll meet him in a minute."

They turned right into another narrow hallway with doors on both sides.

"Here's Nancy's office," Phil said, pointing to the first room on the left, "and this is a kitchenette that makes the lounge look like something out of *Good Housekeeping* magazine." He pointed to the right. "Over here are the production rooms. They put together news spots and music tracks in there."

Above one of the doors the "on-air" light was **illuminated**.

"Take a look," Phil said.

Caitlin peered through a small square of heavy glass reinforced with chicken wire and saw a young woman in a Grateful Dead T-shirt bending over a recording machine, **deftly** splicing a section of tape.

They walked to the end of the hall to a heavy door marked "Authorized Access Only."

"This is the main studio," Phil said. "We'll be doing the panel in here."

Suddenly the door burst open and a wiry young man with curly red hair emerged.

"Hey, man. You're on in ten," he said. "You all set?"

"Sure, Randy. Don't sweat it," Phil said. "Nancy showed me where everything is."

"What about the panelists?"

"They should be here any minute, I guess."

"Okay. As soon as they get here, get 'em in the studio and get some levels on 'em. I've left some notes on the board to help you through the segues."

"Thanks, Randy." Phil turned to Caitlin. "Why don't you

get settled while I see if the panelists are here." He started to leave but stopped when he heard voices coming toward them.

Caitlin looked down the hall and saw Carmen Torres and three other professors rounding the corner—a slender woman with straight, shoulder-length hair and glasses, a casually dressed man with long gray hair and sideburns, and a bald, **portly** man wearing a bow tie and carrying a briefcase and a cane.

"Oh, no," Randy whispered. "If it isn't the redoubtable **misanthrope** himself."

"Who's that?" Caitlin whispered back.

"The **pompous** baboon with the bow tie and cane—Professor Theophilus Bibb. He gave me a D last year because I got my final paper in one lousy day late. Hey, Phil. You got it under control, right?"

Phil nodded.

"Good, 'cause I'd better get out of here before the Bibbster bites off my lips or something."

With that, Randy "The Maniac" Malone shielded his face with his hands, bolted past the four professors, and disappeared around the corner, heading for the safety of the lounge.

Harold Hargrave's office was all dark woods and Persian rugs and soft, scholarly light. An antique maple desk and an **ornate** credenza occupied one end of the room. Three walls were covered with floor-to-ceiling bookcases. On the fourth wall a delicate Japanese textile print hung between stained-glass lancet windows.

The first thing Leo noticed was the room's **distinctive** smell. From his many hours working in Professor Prospero's personal library, he had grown to love the musty aroma of old books. He also was struck by how orderly the room appeared. Everything spoke of elegance and grace and the **fastidious** taste of the **connoisseur**. In the kingdom of books that was Tillinghast Library, Hargrave clearly had set himself up as **monarch**.

As Leo entered, the chief curator and Reginald Burton-Jones rose from wing chairs positioned at each end of an oxblood leather couch.

"Hello, Leo," Hargrave said. He gestured toward the couch. "Please have a seat."

"Thank you, sir." Leo crossed the large room, shook hands with Hargrave, then turned to Burton-Jones. "I didn't expect to find you here, Reggie."

The Englishman gave Leo's hand a friendly, **vigorous** shake and the three men sat down.

"After the executors' meeting," Burton-Jones explained, "Harold invited me out to the faculty club for a bite to eat, and I wasn't about to forgo an opportunity to enjoy their **sumptuous** Sunday brunch. The bill of fare is absolutely **superlative**." He chuckled and patted his firm belly. "At any rate, Harold was just **expounding** on this distressing business of Teddy's lawsuit. Did you come to offer your suggestions on how to deal with that **haughty, avaricious** young **malcontent**?"

Leo smiled and shook his head. "Sorry, Reggie, but Teddy's machinations are a mystery to me."

"Perhaps you're wondering what to do with that valuable Edgar Allan Poe book the old man gave you," Hargrave said. "We could keep it for you here in special collections, if you like."

"Thank you. I'll consider that, sir," Leo said. "Actually, I came about something else."

"And what might that be?"

"I wanted to discuss the letter."

"The letter?"

"The letter that accompanied my gift from Prospero."

"I see," Hargrave said, clearing his throat. "And what did you want to discuss about it?"

"There's something wrong with it, I think."

"Something wrong?"

"Yes. I'm not sure what, exactly. But my **intuition** tells me it wasn't written by Professor Prospero."

Burton-Jones raised his eyebrows. "Is that so?"

"Yes. Something about it doesn't seem right."

"And what is that?" Hargrave asked, frowning.

Leo reached into the pocket of his sports jacket and removed the letter. He unfolded it carefully and looked at it for a moment. "The handwriting looks like Prospero's, but right here, in the third-to-last line, the word *theater* is spelled *t-h-e-a-t-r-e*, the British way, with *-re* at the end instead of *-er*."

Leo shifted position on the couch and showed the letter to Hargrave, pointing to the line in question.

The librarian glanced at it, then shrugged. "That spelling's common enough, Leo. What's troubling you about it?"

"What's troubling me is that Professor Prospero never would have used it. He was **adamant**, perhaps even **fanatical**, in his preference for American spellings and **idioms**. He often told me that he felt it was our duty, as citizens of a republic that had won its independence from Great Britain, to safeguard our linguistic freedom as well. He loved Shakespeare and the other great British writers, but he was always a **zealous** defender of what he called 'the American language.'"

"That's right, Leo," said Burton-Jones. "The professor used to badger me mercilessly about my Briticisms—saying 'call box' for 'telephone booth,' 'to hand' for 'at hand,' 'lift' for 'elevator,' and the like. It was all in good fun, of course, but he did love to **harass** me about it. In fact, I think for a while he was working on a manuscript about British versus American English. I wonder what became of it."

Hargrave cleared his throat. "So what are we getting at here, then?"

Burton-Jones looked at Leo. "May I see the letter?"

"Of course," Leo said, handing it over.

Burton-Jones removed a pair of glasses from his inside breast pocket and slipped them on. When he finished reading, he passed the letter back to Leo.

"Well, what do you think, Reggie?" Hargrave asked.

A muscle twitched in the **stalwart** Englishman's jaw. "Leo's right, Harold. The professor couldn't have written this. I'm certain of it."

After Leo and Burton-Jones left his office, Harold Hargrave went to his bookshelf and removed a **ponderous tome** on wills, trusts, and estate law. Then he took off his jacket, loosened his tie, and settled down in a wing chair to study the book. After a few minutes, however, he grew tired and found he couldn't concentrate. There was so much to do, he thought. Managing the Prospero collection would be **formidable** enough without the added inconvenience of Teddy's **impending** lawsuit. And now the surfacing of Leo's **apocryphal** letter presented a new **impediment**.

Hargrave yawned and set the heavy book on his lap. Suddenly the office door burst open.

"Harry, you old bookworm! I knew I'd find you hiding in here—even on Sunday. Don't you ever take a lousy break?"

Hargrave looked up and saw a slender, fashionably dressed young man leaning **nonchalantly** in the doorway, an **insolent smirk** on his face.

The librarian scowled and rose stiffly from his chair. "What the devil—"

"No, not the devil, Harry," Teddy Prospero said, **sauntering** into the room, "but the devil's grandson, perhaps."

Chapter 12

To Be or Not to Be
Shakespeare

At precisely five seconds before two o'clock, Phil flicked on the station ID tape. He glanced at Caitlin, who was seated comfortably in the corner of the small control room, notebook at the ready, and then back at the panelists in the studio. At fifteen seconds after one, he shut off the tape, adjusted the knobs for the panelists' microphones to the appropriate level, and signaled through the double-glass window.

Inside the studio, the professor at the head of the table leaned toward her microphone. "Good afternoon," she said in a mellow voice. "This is Professor Enid Davies, your moderator for this week's KHCR round table. Our topic for today's panel discussion is 'Shakespeare: A Question of Identity.' It has been specially scheduled to **coincide** with Holyfield's ongoing Elizabethan Festival.

"As you may know, many details about William Shakespeare's life and work are still an **enigma** to us, and for generations a debate has raged over what constitutes the truth about this remarkable—and remarkably **obscure**—English playwright and poet. In the next hour we will explore several theories about who Shakespeare really was, or may have been, and why.

"I am joined by three of my **esteemed** colleagues on the Holyfield College faculty: Professor Bartholomew Martext, artistic director of the Fincke Theater; Associate Professor Carmen Torres of the English Department; and Professor Theophilus Bibb of the Renaissance Studies Department. We will each give a presentation, after which time will be **allotted** for discussion, questions, or **rebuttal**. Professor Martext, would you care to **initiate** the colloquy?"

"Thank you, Professor Davies," Martext said. "Before I begin, I would like to ask our listeners to abandon for a moment the **tedious** insistence on **objective** fact and **impartial analysis** that **tyrannizes** so much scholarship and to **indulge** instead their powers of **speculation**. For today, by way of Shakespeare, I would like to call into question one of our culture's most **rudimentary** and enduring assumptions, and such an **endeavor** requires that we cast off all intellectual **inhibitions** and engage in a free interplay of the imagination and the possible."

In the control room, Phil looked at Caitlin. "Geez, will you listen to the way this guy talks? He's totally **verbose**."

"He seems brilliant to me. He directed *Romeo and Juliet*, you know."

Phil raised his eyebrows. "Oh, so that explains it."

Caitlin looked up. "Explains what?"

"Why he sounds so **pretentious**."

"What do you mean?"

"He's an artiste. Therefore, he has a license to bore."

Caitlin made a face. "Oh, stuff it, Phil, will you? I'm trying to take notes for an article here, all right?"

Phil chuckled and leaned back in his chair, getting set for the long haul. As Martext launched into the body of his **discourse**, however, Phil found himself gradually being drawn in, and he leaned forward and listened more carefully. The director's **thesis**, although delivered in a **convoluted** and **circumlocutory** manner, was as simple as it was **radical**. In a nutshell, Martext was arguing that the creator of the plays **attributed** to Shakespeare was not an individual but a **collective**.

"No one person could have single-handedly written so many plays of such high quality in such a short period of time," Martext said. "It is far more **plausible** that they were produced through a **collaborative** process in which the writer, the director, and the actors worked together on an **impromptu** basis to amend or **abridge** scenes and improvise new ones.

"Also, I am sure you all are well aware that many scholars agree that a number of the plays, specifically *Henry IV: Part I*, *Timon of Athens*, and *Pericles*, were the result of **collaboration**. Others believe that John Fletcher was the coauthor of *Henry VIII*, and some **speculate** that Philip Massinger assisted the elderly Shakespeare in writing *The Winter's Tale* and *The Tempest*. Indeed, **collaboration** was so **prevalent** in the Elizabethan theater that today it is impossible, in many cases, to determine precisely who wrote what.

"Thus, there is a good deal of evidence to **corroborate** the view that Shakespeare, like many playwrights of his day, was in fact a so-called stage editor or play doctor, **adept** at revising and polishing existing material and adapting old plays and poems by **obscure** authors for the audiences of his day.

"In *Hamlet*, for example, arguably his greatest play, we are given a portrait of this **collaborative** process: The traveling tragedians, to please their host, insert a scene into the play at the last minute. Thus, we see that a script was not **immutable**, something carved in stone by a lone authority and meant to be followed **scrupulously** by **servile**, **subordinate** players. In other words, for Shakespeare and his **contemporaries** in the Elizabethan theater, the **conventional** division of labor between writer, director, and actor was less binding than it is today.

"Moreover," Martext continued, "the **diversity** of versions in which many of the plays survive **underscores** the notion of a Shakespeare who was flexible and willing to **integrate** others' suggestions and revisions. Thus, the **petty** academic **squabbles** over which version is most **authentic** are beside the point because Shakespeare clearly did not work in isolation. Instead, as a member of various tight-knit theatrical **troupes**, he was **stimulated** by and able to thrive in the company of his fellow professionals.

"And so," Martext concluded in his most **histrionic** voice, "it might be said that Shakespeare's work demonstrates that the essence of theater is **collaboration**, that in a **comprehensive** sense all playwrights function not as **autonomous** artists who stand **aloof** and create, like God, out of **chaos**, but as conduits **facilitating** the **divergent** flow of **communal** forces of which they are only a part."

A moment of silence followed this earnest peroration. Then Enid Davies spoke.

"Thank you, Professor Martext," she said. "Are there any comments or questions from the other panelists?"

Throughout Martext's presentation, Bibb had rolled his eyes and fidgeted in his seat, impatient for the opportunity to express his disagreement. "I have only one question," he said, his bass voice booming into the microphone.

Phil quickly adjusted the level to prevent feedback.

"My dear Professor Martext, let's say I want to administer an English exam. Aside from essay questions, I need a section of IDs. How would I put it together?"

"It's a standard procedure," Martext replied **warily**, uncertain about the direction the **interrogation** was taking. "I'm sure you're familiar with it."

"Yes?"

"Well, one could give the students a list of quotations taken either from books that were assigned in class or from books that were unassigned but by the same authors who wrote the books that were assigned."

"Why would you want to test your students on material for which they weren't strictly responsible?" Bibb queried.

"Wouldn't this latter method be unfair?"

"Not at all. The idea is to test the students' sense of an author's voice and style."

A **haughty** smile spread across Bibb's face. "So may I take it that you believe different authors have different styles and voices and that these differences can be taught and tested?"

"Obviously."

"And do you think that Shakespeare has a voice different from that of his **contemporaries**?"

"Yes—more or less," Martext waffled, beginning to feel the walls of the corner he had backed himself into.

"Well then, sir," Bibb said, moving in for the kill, "don't you find it difficult to **reconcile** your own admission that Shakespeare has a distinct, identifiable voice with your **thesis** that he is some kind of **collective entity**?"

"I see your point," Martext answered. "However, I see no reason to believe that a group cannot have an identity. Look at music, with its orchestrations and arrangements, or politics, with its party platforms **bolstering** the vision of a single candidate. Or take, for example, the Brooklyn Bridge. It was built by a great many people, yet it has its own architectural personality."

This Socratic game of cat and mouse continued for several minutes with Bibb playing the crafty Greek philosopher, asking questions and trying to catch Martext in a **contradiction**, and Martext unwillingly playing the straight man, answering **obliquely** and trying to **evade** each trap Bibb set for him. Phil and Caitlin were relieved when Professor Davies, **citing** time **constraints**, finally interrupted this verbal fencing match and introduced Professor Torres.

"I'm glad to be following Professor Martext today," Torres began in a **poised**, **sophisticated** voice, "because my view on Shakespeare's identity also assumes that the plays arose from a **collaborative** and not an individual effort—a **collaboration**, however, of a **singular** nature. And unlike Professor

Martext's **thesis**, my view is not widely entertained or even widely known. In fact, on the rare occasions when it has been **promulgated**, scholars generally have **castigated** and **vilified** its **advocates**, summarily dismissing them with **ridicule** and **contempt**."

In the control room, Caitlin nudged Phil. "What do you think she's going to propose?"

"I haven't a clue," Phil said, folding his arms. "Maybe that Shakespeare never existed at all and was just the **fabrication** of a bunch of **pompous** professors sitting around a table."

Caitlin rolled her eyes.

"My theory," Torres was saying, "depends on a document whose existence has always been much disputed. It is referred to only once in the notes for a study of literature by an **obscure** seventeenth-century monk and scholar, a **recluse** about whom we know **virtually** nothing. Apparently much of the **dissertation** has been lost, and what little is left is **abstruse** and often **ambiguous**. At one point, however, the text **alludes** to a letter, **allegedly** in Shakespeare's own hand, addressed to a woman. In it the playwright supposedly **chastises** her for demanding **compensation** for a manuscript she had delivered to him.

"When I came upon this bookish monk's **treatise** in a remote abbey in Scotland several years ago, I must confess I was astonished and had no idea what to do. I decided to share my discovery with our late colleague, Professor Edward Anthony Prospero, and was delighted when he encouraged me to pursue the investigation. With his help, I have researched the **authenticity** of this document for some time, but so far I have come up empty-handed. If in fact it exists and if what the monk **purports** is true, then without doubt it will alter our **perception** of Shakespeare **radically** in the following way:

"Shakespeare must have been **acutely** aware of his creative limitations and frustrated by the constant pressure to produce successful plays. He also knew that women were denied access to the Elizabethan stage and therefore could not threaten or **usurp** his reputation. These circumstances may have led him to **exploit** a woman of equal or greater talent to further his considerable literary ambitions. In short," Torres concluded, "I believe it is possible that William Shakespeare may have hired a woman to ghostwrite some or perhaps even all of his plays."

A ripple of what could only be called intellectual shock passed over the table. The other members of the panel cleared their throats and squirmed in their chairs. Phil saw that Caitlin had stopped writing and was sitting up straight, her pen **poised** in the air, nibbling nervously on her lower lip.

Torres waited until everyone had settled down and then went on. "The notion that Shakespeare hired a woman to write for him is not as **outlandish** as one might think. Throughout history, because of their secondary **status**, women writers have resorted to **pseudonyms** and masks. Mary Ann Evans took the pen name George Eliot, Hilda Doolittle preferred the **anonymity** of initials, and Emily Dickinson led a **secluded** life to veil her literary activities. The Brontë sisters also concealed their identities, even from their publishers, for most of their careers.

"Furthermore, had this **alleged** ghostwriter been male, then the **chroniclers, predominantly** male, would have had little or nothing to lose in reporting the true author. The issue of gender would not have been a **hindrance. Pseudonyms** and ghostwriting were common in the Elizabethan period, and it would have been simply a case of moving the mantle of genius from one male to another. The **traditional** assumption that intellectual ability and creative power are male and not female **attributes** would have remained unchallenged.

"On the other hand, it is easy to imagine how the discovery of a female ghostwriter would be considered an **affront** to certain **orthodox** beliefs about creativity and might have been **censored**. Certain historians might have tried to **suppress** whatever evidence existed in the interest of preserving the patriarchy. For as we all know," Torres said with a sly look at Professor Bibb, "historians are not always **objective**. They are neither **immune** to **intolerance** nor **impervious** to prejudice, and some might even be called **dogmatic**.

"However, because of this **enigmatic** monk's **peripheral** life and **relative insignificance** as a scholar, his **contemporaries** were not aware of him and therefore could not **sabotage** his work. Had he been less **obscure**, it is likely that the evidence I have presented today would have been unavailable."

"Thank you, Professor Torres," said Enid Davies. "Despite your **dearth** of evidence, you **ingeniously** transform your argument's weaknesses into strengths. Yet I wonder if that **alchemical** process is possible in real, sociological terms."

"How do you mean?"

"Though I sympathize with your **sentiments**, I'm afraid I do not find your **analysis plausible**. You **portray** Elizabethan society as so thoroughly patriarchal, so **repressive** toward women, that the only way a woman could seek artistic expression was in the **guise** of a man. Yet, isn't this **repression** more **profound** than the clothes one wears or the name one adopts?"

"Of course," Torres responded. "If it weren't, women would never have had so much difficulty **circumventing** it."

"Precisely," Davies **concurred**. "Now, I presume you remember that Virginia Woolf, not exactly a male apologist, argues in *A Room of One's Own* that a woman in Shakespeare's day, because of the harsh and **onerous** yoke she had to bear, could never have achieved what Shakespeare did. She would never have had enough education, privacy, freedom, confidence, and, above all, money to attempt the creative enterprise on such a grand scale."

"The kind of woman you describe would probably fail in her efforts to write," Torres replied. "Yet there must have been at least a few women, perhaps among the **aristocracy** or nouveau riche—the merchants and landowners—who lived in more favorable circumstances. An **affluent** widow, an heiress who remained unmarried, or a gifted child who was taken under a scholar's wing—all are possible. Remember, the English **monarch** herself, Queen Elizabeth I, was a woman and a first-rate scholar."

"That's interesting," said Davies. "Shakespeare as Queen Elizabeth. Hmmm. I believe we have now officially crossed the boundary that separates the **plausible** from the **absurd**."

Professor Torres laughed.

"Before we venture any further into this uncharted territory," Davies continued, "I believe we should pause, admit that our peregrinations have led us astray, and ask for help. Professor Bibb, would you like to point our discussion in a new direction?"

"I most certainly would, Professor Davies," Bibb said, rubbing his palms together with barely contained glee. He was **savoring** his approaching moment in the limelight the way a **fervent** preacher, convinced of the **efficacy** his sermon will have on his **wayward** congregation, might approach the pulpit.

Bibb proceeded to spend several minutes **rebutting** Martext's and Torres's **theses** in **painstaking** detail. "And so," he said when he had completed his **dissection**, "although the opinions of my colleagues at first appear to be merely amusing **novelties**, it is precisely this **facade** of playful innocence, this **charade** of **naive speculation**, that makes them so **insidious**. Why? Because if they cannot be **substantiated**, then they cannot be **refuted**, and therein lies the rub. Unfortunately, the **impressionable** young student, who should be struggling to comprehend the **subtle** art of **documentation**, is fatally **seduced** by this **perniciously** cavalier style of **analysis** and, once bit, seldom recovers. A teacher can only shake his head."

Bibb shook his own head **ruefully** and took a sip of water.

"Now," he went on, "when **propounding** theories on the identity of Shakespeare, we must not stray from the realm of fact and common sense. Whoever penned the plays clearly was an individual; however, that individual was probably not the man known as William Shakespeare. It is **inconceivable** that the son of a humble provincial could have **procured** for himself the **erudition**—the knowledge of history, law, languages, and the classics—the **breadth** of culture, **sophistication**, and nobility of spirit that his greatest plays **manifest**. In his youth, Shakespeare was an **obscure**, struggling actor and playwright, and despite his later success he was never more than an **aspiring** middle-class landholder. There is no evidence that he ever left England, nor is there any proof that he ever attended university.

"That the records of so great a writer's life are **sparse**, that so little was written about him by his **contemporaries**, and that none of his manuscripts have survived—these facts strongly suggest a **surreptitiousness** on Shakespeare's part that is **dubious**, to say the least. In short, he was probably a front for a member of the **aristocracy**, a class that **shunned** association with the theater, which was considered a **vulgar** pastime. In my opinion, he could have been working for one of several noblemen, most likely the famous **rationalist**, Francis Bacon, Viscount St. Albans.

"To begin with, as a man of breeding, Bacon traveled widely and had a **comprehensive** education. He knew foreign and classical languages, and his writings show a familiarity with nearly all of the more specialized subjects **alluded** to in Shakespeare's plays. Furthermore, a number of **cryptic** messages indicating Bacon's authorship can be found **embedded** in several Shakespearean texts. For instance, there is the famous 'long word' in *Love's Labour's Lost: honorificabilitudini-*

tatibus. This *hapax legomenon*—a Greek term meaning 'something said or used only once, a single **citation** of a verbal form'—has been shown to be an anagram for the Latin *hi ludi F Baconis nati tuiti orbi*, meaning 'these plays, born of Francis Bacon, are preserved for the world.'"

At the sound of Professor Bibb's **reverent** pronunciation of *honorificabilitudinitatibus*, Caitlin and Phil looked at each other in amazement.

"*Honorifi*-what?" Phil gasped.

Caitlin laughed. "Beats me. I'll have to ask him to spell that one for me."

"It is also possible," Bibb continued, "that Edward de Vere, seventeenth earl of Oxford, may have been the creator of the oeuvre **attributed** to Shakespeare. His early poems display a remarkable **affinity** to Shakespeare's immature **lyric** work. Some of these are said to be in his own hand, yet are signed 'W. S.' Moreover, de Vere is supposed to have given up writing only half a year before the first record of Shakespeare as a playwright emerges. It is also believed that the earl chose the **pseudonym** Shakespeare because his coat of arms was a lion shaking a spear. Are all these circumstances merely **coincidental**? I think not.

"Now, these are the two most likely candidates; however, not a few respected scholars have also proposed Roger Manners, Earl of Rutland, and William Stanley, Earl of Derby, as possible foils for the slippery, **elusive** Shakespeare. But the evidence to support these claims is at best tenuous and circumstantial. *Hamlet*, for example, is said to mirror Lord Rutland's childhood—and I shudder to think what a **traumatic** childhood that must have been. As for William Stanley—" Bibb paused and grinned at his colleagues. "Well, his initials are W. S., and if that bit of cryptographic coincidence doesn't persuade you that he was Shakespeare, I suppose nothing will."

The panelists all laughed, after which Bibb resumed.

"One last possibility, which I find **intriguing** although

hardly **credible**, is that Christopher Marlowe, the playwright to whom Shakespeare has been shown to be so much in debt, did not die in a tavern brawl in 1593, as is commonly thought, but, because of pressing financial **adversity**, **feigned** his death and fled to Italy. From there, he continued to write plays, using Shakespeare as his contact in England.

"A host of other historical personages," Bibb concluded, smoothing the rumpled lapel of his jacket with a plump hand, "have been nominated for the job of being the true Shakespeare, but, as in politics, the wide field of candidates at the outset of a campaign quickly narrows itself down to an **elite** few from which one man of **integrity** must be chosen. That man, I propose, is most probably Francis Bacon."

"Thank you, Professor Bibb," said Enid Davies, "for your, as always, **provocative** views. Questions?"

Martext and Torres, who had had great difficulty keeping quiet through Bibb's presentation, wincing at the **implication** behind such words as *elite, nobility*, and *breeding*, did not spare Bibb now that he had finished.

"Professor Bibb," Torres said, "your argument was quite **lucid** and **sagacious**. It showed a **perspicacious** grasp of the facts. You are certainly a very learned man."

"Why thank you, Professor Torres."

"Don't mention it. Were you always that way?"

"What do you mean, *that way*?"

"Were you always so **erudite**?"

"Of course not. No one's born a scholar. It takes a great deal of dedication and **diligent** labor."

"Well," Martext said, cutting in and picking up the thread, "if knowledge is not **innate**, but something one must cultivate, then any person, regardless of the class into which he was born, as long as his physical and mental **faculties** were **intact**, could have acquired the learning needed to write these plays. **Theoretically,** Shakespeare could have been from the lowest **stratum** of society."

"**Theoretically**, of course, Professor Martext, all men are created equal," Bibb replied. "And that theory is especially applicable to today's society. But one must remember that in Elizabethan times the lot of the lower classes was unfortunate in the extreme. Had Shakespeare been from the lowest **stratum**, living in **penury**, he would have been so preoccupied with the struggle to survive, his day-to-day life would have been such an **unremitting ordeal**, that he wouldn't have had the leisure to pursue formal education, let alone artistic creation."

Martext and Torres rigorously cross-examined Bibb until the **corpulent** don finally began to break down. He granted it was true that many of the foremost writers of the Elizabethan period were commoners, lacking in university education, who used their pens and their wits to make a living and about whose lives and affairs little information had survived. Pressed even further, Bibb admitted that, although it was highly **improbable**, it was nevertheless possible that someone from the lower classes could have been a **zealous** autodidact, borrowing or scrimping or starving to obtain the books and experience that would broaden his sphere of knowledge and **nurture** his talent.

"Yet," Bibb **asserted obstinately**, "it would be **rash** to suppose such a **metamorphosis** in a man of such **singular** achievement. What Shakespeare—or perhaps I should say Francis Bacon—did was **unprecedented**, and no one since has matched his accomplishment. It is **ludicrous** to entertain the notion that someone so lacking in **refinement** could have transformed himself into the greatest writer of English who ever lived."

"However," Torres **countered**, "isn't it also **rash** to assume that a person is incapable of transforming himself simply because one has never heard of its happening before? Besides, Shakespeare is commonly regarded as a genius, am I right?"

"Of course, but—"

"And if we look at geniuses of Shakespeare's **stature** in the world of music, for example," Torres continued, ignoring the interruption, "we see that Bach and Mozart and Beethoven—arguably Shakespeare's equals in their own field—were also of the common people. Surely, Professor Bibb, you will agree that genius is not a birthright, but a **random** and perhaps divine gift. Surely you wouldn't argue that one's class, one's standing in the **hierarchy** of money and power, is the sole, **immutable** determinant of one's level of achievement, would you?"

"Certainly not!" Bibb fumed. "But I must protest that your misleading analogies and **convoluted** logic have entirely **perverted** my point, which is that—"

"Thank you very much, professors," said Enid Davies, deciding it was time to **mediate** before the debate **digressed** any further and flew out of control. "Our discussion thus far has been **enlightening**. Following the path of 'the possible,' as you say, Professor Martext, can lead one to the most astonishing places. These last few minutes of the program will be devoted to my own more **traditional** and, alas, less glamorous and **exotic** view of the matter."

There was nothing unusual about Davies's argument: She held that Shakespeare was simply Shakespeare. "I do not find his **copious** output **problematic**," she said. "Nature is **prolific**. Her **permutations** are endless, and everywhere there can be found examples of rare and gifted variations from the norm.

"Although Professor Martext is correct in pointing out that Shakespeare was not fussy about authority and may even have encouraged input from his actors—after all, the records show they were extremely devoted to him—nevertheless, I cannot see how that flexibility necessarily indicates **collaboration**. And though there is an **array** of voices in Shakespeare's work, they are the natural and fully realized voices of different characters, all springing from the same authorial imagination.

"As for your theory, Professor Bibb, I'm afraid I don't agree that Shakespeare would have needed any specialized education or upbringing to write what he did. One must keep in mind that The Globe—Burbage's theater, where many of Shakespeare's plays were produced—was designed to accommodate the unlettered commoners, and that for the most part Shakespeare's plays deal with **universal** experience and our most fundamental concerns at the **visceral,** or gut, level.

"Therefore, whatever facts Shakespeare may have needed to know he probably acquired by the age of twelve through the **rudimentary** education available to anyone of his station. All the rest is the polish and craft of the professional, which he surely learned as an apprentice to the stage. Thus, although scholarship may help us **elucidate** certain **idiosyncrasies** of Shakespeare's **diction** and **syntax,** we don't have to be geniuses to read and enjoy him, nor did Shakespeare the man have to be a **prodigious** scholar to be Shakespeare the writer.

"In fact, though it may seem **paradoxical,** Shakespeare's language was both **novel** and **vernacular,** highly **innovative** and yet thoroughly accessible. Linguists have shown that Shakespeare made up more than 8.5 percent of his vocabulary, and many of the words and phrases he coined or recorded have proved **tenacious** enough to stand the test of time. Some are among the most **ubiquitous** in our vocabulary today. Consider where we would be, for example, without such basic words as *generous, lonely,* and *hurry* or such **audaciously** highfalutin words as *auspicious, multitudinous,* and *sanctimonious.* Shakespeare invented those and hundreds more. Indeed," Davies added with a mischievous smile, "where would we college professors be had Shakespeare not given us the word *critic?*"

The panelists all roared with laughter and Phil frantically adjusted the levels on their microphones. When the **tumult**

subsided, Davies continued.

"I think it's fair to say that Shakespeare almost single-handedly transformed English from the tongue of roughnecks and barbarians into a **sophisticated** language full of beauty and **vitality**. As one scholar wrote, 'Reading his works is like witnessing the birth of language itself.' Who but a single genius, with one ear trained on the common speech and the other tuned to his **muse**, could have done such a remarkable thing?

"Yet," she concluded, "perhaps the most **compelling** evidence that Shakespeare was Shakespeare is the simple fact that none of his **contemporaries** ever suspected him of being anyone else. On the contrary, in his lifetime some fifty plays were falsely **attributed** to him, which **attests** to his great popularity and **renown**. Apparently, his name alone could draw an audience, and of course it still does. As Ben Jonson put it, 'He was not of an age, but for all time.'

"And so I ask you, how could a man so much in the public eye, working in a medium, as Professor Martext so rightly pointed out, that requires constant interaction and emotional exposure, have kept secret an enormous literary **hoax** for so many years? That would be not only **improbable** but impossible. I must conclude, therefore, that despite a **paucity** of **conclusive** evidence to prove it, Shakespeare was indeed the author of his work."

Through the studio window, Davies saw Phil waving at her and pointing to his watch. "And now," she said, acknowledging him with a nod, "I'm afraid our time is up. It has been an exciting and **illuminating** discussion. Thank you all for sharing your views." The three other panelists gave Davies a polite round of applause. "Until next week's round table, this is Professor Enid Davies wishing you good day."

"And you're listening to KHCR, your standing ovation station," Phil said into his board mike, right on cue. As he shut off the studio mikes, he glanced at the schedule Randy

Malone had left for him. "Stay tuned for the news at two o'clock, followed by a special program of Elizabethan folk music hosted by Professor Thomas Arne."

Phil activated a tape of transitional music, then leaned back in his chair and breathed a sigh of relief.

"Nice job," Caitlin said, flashing him a thumbs-up sign.

Chapter 13

The Gentleman Doth Protest Too Much

Shortly after the professors departed, the two freshmen made their way out of the radio station to the lawn in the court-yard of the Calhoun Humanities Complex. Phil lay down on the grass and basked in the Sunday midafternoon sun while Caitlin sat cross-legged, poring over her notes.

"So, what did you think of the discussion?" he asked when she seemed close to finishing.

"Just a sec," she said, flipping quickly through the pages again to make sure she had recorded everything she needed. Finally she looked up. "I'm sorry. What did you say?"

"I was just wondering what you thought of the panel. Obviously you had a lot of thoughts about it," he added, in-dicating her notepad. "You want to know what I think?"

"Sure."

"I agree with Professor Davies's **analysis**. Shakespeare was a man, no doubt about it. And he was probably just good old Willy Shakespeare, although Professor Bibb's **hypothesis** about Francis Bacon was interesting. Martext's and Torres's theories were just plain crazy. Shakespeare a **collective**? No way. And Shakespeare a woman? Give me a break!"

Caitlin set her notebook on the grass. "Actually, I thought Carmen's presentation was the most interesting one."

Phil chuckled. "It figures."

"What do you mean 'it figures'?"

"It figures that a woman would be attracted to the notion that Shakespeare was a woman."

Caitlin **grimaced**. "Look, just because I'm a woman doesn't mean I'm **biased** if I entertain the idea that Shakespeare was a woman—or, to be more precise, that a woman may have ghostwritten some of Shakespeare's work. It's simply a matter of liking Carmen's views on the subject. She made some **insightful** comments that really opened up the debate."

"Maybe. Or perhaps you're just so **enamored** of *Carmen*," Phil stressed the name in a mocking tone, "that you're inclined to accept her opinion, even if it's totally **implausible**."

"**Implausible**? What's so **implausible** about it?"

"It's an **innovative** idea and nothing more. You can accept it, but you can't prove it. Look, I don't mean to **disparage** Professor Torres, who obviously knows a lot more about literature than I do, but where's the beef? I heard a lot of **speculation**, but I didn't hear anything **conclusive**, did you?"

Caitlin sighed. "No, I didn't, but Carmen wasn't the only one who couldn't prove her theory. Frankly, I thought Professor Bibb's case for Francis Bacon was pretty **dubious**, and although Professor Davies's argument for Shakespeare as Shakespeare was reasonable and **articulate**, it was **commonplace**—she just told us the same old stuff with no new proof. I did like a lot of what Professor Martext said about **collaboration**, but I thought he went off the deep end a couple of times."

"Tell me about it," Phil said.

"But all that's beside the point," Caitlin went on, "which is that there's precious little **conclusive** evidence about Shakespeare at all—especially concerning his identity, which is why people are still arguing about it today. I'm not saying you have to **endorse** everything Carmen said, but you should at least give her theory some **impartial** consideration before you go around **implying** that she's a **charlatan** and I'm prejudiced."

"I'm not **implying** that at all," Phil protested. "That's what you **inferred**."

"Oh c'mon, Phil. Why don't you just admit it? You were making **subjective** judgments, dismissing anything that didn't fit your **preconceived** opinions about Shakespeare. Tell me, what do you really know about him—or her—anyway?"

"Look, just because I may not know as much about Shakespeare as Professor Torres or you or anybody else doesn't mean I can't have my own opinion on the subject. Besides, there's plenty of evidence to show that Shakespeare was a man."

"Such as?"

"Such as . . . such as his picture, his name, what everybody says he is. Well, almost everybody. Oh, the heck with it, Caitlin. You win, all right? If you want to believe Shakespeare was a woman, or hired a woman to write for him, fine. All I know is you don't have to be a Renaissance scholar to see that *you're* the one who's **distorting** the facts to suit your opinion."

"I'm not **distorting** any facts, Phil. I'm just considering possibilities. Why are you being so **obstinate**?"

"If you think I'm being stubborn, fine. I don't care. The real issue here is, whose opinion has more **credibility**?"

"I guess we'll see," Caitlin said **cryptically**. She looked at her watch. "Hey, I'd really like to talk more, but I don't have time right now. Nothing personal, but I've got a seven o'clock deadline on this article. Gotta go. See you soon, I hope." She stood up. "No hard feelings, right?"

"Yeah, sure," Phil grumbled.

Caitlin smiled. "Great. See you later!"

Phil watched as she took off down the path. At one point

she turned and waved, and he waved back halfheartedly. When she rounded a corner and disappeared from sight, he put his hands behind his head and stared at the sky. He tried to **eradicate** their conversation from his mind, but her question—what did he really know about Shakespeare anyway?—kept nagging him. He had to admit that he didn't know much at all, and the admission made him feel **incompetent** and foolish.

Phil knew that if he expected to be a serious, **diligent** student and not just cruise through the next four years for the sake of a diploma, he would have to take some **initiative** and cultivate his interests. His education was his responsibility. He had known it before, but he had never felt it as **keenly**.

He also knew that when one's knowledge of a subject was insufficient, there was only one way to **rectify** the situation: read more about it. He resolved to go to the library first thing in the morning and get a good book on Shakespeare—or maybe a couple of good books.

After that he'd see what Caitlin Ciccone had to say.

Chapter 14

Fortune Favors
the Hungry

Monday

At the corner of College and Holyfield streets, a **colossal** tractor-trailer had double-parked to make a delivery at Steinbach Commons, **impeding** the flow of traffic down to State Street and beyond.

Caitlin was amazed. She did not hear the usual **incessant** honking of **irascible** hacks. Nor did she see an **exasperated** driver step out of his car to give the owner of the offending vehicle a few **strident** tips on driving. Instead, here in the city of Holyfield, the **placid** motorists waved to each other in neighborly fashion as they patiently took turns using the narrow lane around the tractor-trailer.

The sight of this unexpected civility had a soothing effect on Caitlin's nerves, which had been wound tightly on this first day of classes. She took a deep breath of the **invigorating** morning air, and as she exhaled she felt her shoulders relax.

"I can't believe it!" Juliet exclaimed as she and Lucy and Caitlin joined the **throng** at the crosswalk. "I'm *so* nervous."

"Don't worry," Lucy said, trying to **assuage** Juliet's fears. "No one's going to give you a test or anything on the first day of class."

"Don't bet on it," Caitlin said. "My father's an English

professor, and he always gives a vocabulary and reading comprehension test the first day. He calls it a '**competence assessment** test,' says he's trying to '**ascertain** the students'
propensity for **apprehension** and **misapprehension**.'"

"How horrible," said Juliet. "I mean the test, not your
dad."

Caitlin laughed. "Yeah, I took it last spring, just to see
how I'd do, and it was **arduous**, a real killer. Sort of like taking the SAT verbal all over again."

As they waited for the light to change, Caitlin looked
down College Street toward the Student Center. Maybe the
Herald had come out, she thought. Last night she had typed
her story on the Shakespeare radio panel into the computer,
but she hadn't seen any galley proofs or mechanicals.

"Hey, guys?" she said as the "walk" sign appeared and
the crowd of students surged into the street. "I'm going to
drop in at the *Herald* for a second. Will you save me a seat at
breakfast?"

"You're going over there at seven-thirty in the morning?" Juliet asked **incredulously**.

"Sure, why not? If I check in early, maybe I can pick up a
lead or get another assignment."

Juliet shook her head. "Wow, that's **diligence**."

"I hope you catch the worm, early bird," Lucy said. "But
we'll save you a seat just in case."

"Thanks," Caitlin said and hurried off.

As she weaved through the **pedestrian** traffic, Caitlin
wondered if the *Herald* would be open this early. If anyone
was there it would be Bill. He had been pleased with her
story. Although he had cut a few lines that he described as
digressions and a few phrases that he called **verbose**, he had
pronounced the finished product "a solid piece of work." She
liked the sound of those words.

The door to the office was open and there was a meeting
taking place in the newsroom. When Caitlin entered, Bill

Berkowitz looked up from the head of one of the long layout tables and waved her over.

"Hey, Caitlin. Come join us. We just started."

Bill introduced her to the rest of the staff. Tanesha Jackson was art director and production manager. Tony Scolari was assistant editor for campus affairs. Gina Prescott handled the financial end of operations. Caitlin hadn't expected to get involved in any editorial decisions, but she was glad Bill had invited her to join. She took a seat at the table.

"Look at this, you guys," Bill said, holding up a copy of *The Plains*, the City of Holyfield's daily newspaper. He pointed to a **salient** headline in the left-hand column: "Tillinghast Library chief attacked."

"Whoa, this looks big," Tony Scolari said. "What happened?"

"Someone, for reasons still **obscure**, assaulted Harold Hargrave, the chief curator, while he was working last night in his office," Bill said.

"Is he all right?" Tanesha asked.

"Apparently. But he was knocked out cold and it appears the place was searched. The security guard found him at about eight o'clock and radioed campus security, who brought in the Holyfield police. Listen, here are the details." Bill read the story aloud. When he was done he folded the paper and laid it on the table. "Can you believe it?" he asked no one in particular. "If something this **deplorable** happens on the first day of classes, what's the rest of the semester going to be like?"

Caitlin listened intently as Bill explained that he had called the meeting to decide whether to put out a special two-page edition of the *Herald* that afternoon. He noted that this could be one of the most significant campus stories ever and it would look bad if *The Plains* scooped the *Herald* on its own turf.

Tanesha said that as far as she was concerned an extra

edition was no problem. If her help was needed, she'd be glad to give it; she wasn't going to miss much on the first day of classes. Gina warned that money was tight and that an extra would be costly. Tony suggested that they wait until they had enough information to put together a **scrupulous** in-depth report.

A short discussion followed, a vote was taken, and a compromise was reached. They all agreed there was no sense in going to the trouble of publishing an extra if their story was not substantially different from the one in *The Plains*. Instead, they would lead with the story in tomorrow's edition. This would give them time to come up with some new information for a front-page feature. Then they could follow up on all the angles later in the week. Although Bill had not gotten his way on the issue, Caitlin noticed that his enthusiasm did not **wane** once the decision had been reached. It was a good trait in a boss.

Bill decided they needed a team to cover different aspects of the story. Tony would contact Walter Chang, the public relations officer for the college, and the Holyfield Police. Bill would talk to campus security and track down the security guard who had found Hargrave. "And you," he said, turning toward Caitlin, "I want you to go to CHS and see if you can speak with Hargrave himself. He was being treated last night and *The Plains* reporter couldn't get to him for a statement. It's **imperative** that we talk to him first."

"What's CHS?" Caitlin asked.

"Oh, sorry. I forgot you're still new around here. It's College Health Services—right up Holyfield Street, two blocks past Madison. You can make it in ten minutes if you leave now."

Caitlin frowned.

"What's the matter?" Bill asked.

"I've got classes from nine to noon, and I haven't had breakfast yet."

"I see," Bill said, scratching his head. "All right, you have to make your classes and we have to have the story. So I guess you'll have to skip breakfast."

Caitlin laughed nervously. "You're kidding, right?"

Bill pulled off his glasses and looked her dead in the eye. "No, I'm not. I could put Steve Rosenblum on this—he's got a lot of experience with hard news—but you're the one who wanted to do something on the Prospero collection, and this is a great place to start. Don't you see, Caitlin? This could be a big story, really big, and I'm putting you on the team because I'm confident you're **inquisitive** and **astute** enough to be a good investigative reporter. So what's it going to be? I need something on my desk by five o'clock. What's more important, your education and your writing career or your stomach?"

Caitlin did some quick mental calculations. The clock on the newsroom wall said 7:55. If she hustled she'd have forty-five minutes to interview Hargrave and ten to make it back for her nine o'clock class. She had another morning class and afternoon classes from one to three, but she was free after that. Two hours should be enough time to get a draft together and meet the deadline, she thought.

"Well?" Bill said.

"Forget about Steve Rosenblum. I'm on my way."

Caitlin hurried up Holyfield Street to Madison, crossed and headed up a long, tree-lined block of **grandiose** Victorian houses set back from the street.

Walking past the lush lawns and **meticulously** kept gardens filled with **luxuriant** shrubs and plots of **vivid** flowers, she thought of all the questions she could ask Hargrave. Did he usually work late in his office on Sunday nights? How might the **assailant** have entered? Had he heard the person approach?

As her lines of inquiry multiplied, Caitlin began to feel as if she were a character in a story she had rehearsed in her mind a thousand times before. She had always wanted to be the **vigilant**, **tenacious** reporter hot on the investigative trail, and often she had imagined herself asking the **crucial** question that would **elicit** the **telltale** fact and make the perpetrator crack and confess. Now, here she was, a real reporter investigating a real crime. It was almost too real to be true.

At the end of the next block Caitlin reached her destination. She paused at the entrance and looked up at the four stories of the College Health Services building. The exterior was **austere** and functional. The windows were simply windows, without any architectural **embellishment**, and the dreary walls showed the wavy marks of the plywood forms into which the gray concrete had been poured. The **edifice** seemed **somber** and out of place on this boulevard of green lawns and **winsome** old houses.

When Caitlin reached out to open the glass doors, they parted with an effortless whoosh. Inside the reception area a few people sat in molded plastic chairs reading copies of *Newsweek, Cosmopolitan*, and *Sports Illustrated*. To the left was a long white counter. Behind it a young man sat at a desk, working at a computer terminal.

Caitlin walked to the counter and set down her tote bag. "Good morning," she said **amiably**.

The young man glanced up from the screen. "I'll be right with you, okay?" He rattled off something on the keyboard, then stood up and came to the counter. He was a good foot taller than Caitlin, and his **ponderous** frame was **imposing**. He leaned forward on his hands and studied her from behind wire-rimmed glasses. "May I help you?" he asked in a deep voice.

"Yes, please. I'm Caitlin Ciccone from the *Holyfield Herald*." She extended her hand.

"Hello, Caitlin Ciccone from the *Holyfield Herald*," the young man said, smiling as he shook her hand. "I'm Ben Schofield from College Health Services."

"Pleased to meet you, Ben Schofield from College Health Services," Caitlin said, acknowledging the joke.

"Well," Ben said, "what's an enterprising young reporter like you doing at CHS so early in the morning on the first day of classes? Got a bad case of writer's cramp already?"

Caitlin laughed. "No, I'm here on an assignment. Can you tell me where I can find Professor Harold Hargrave? He's a patient here. He was brought in last night."

"I see. Let me check the computer." Ben sat down at his desk and typed in a command. "Let's see. Hargrave . . . Hargrave," he muttered, scrolling his monitor. "I'm sorry," he said after a minute, "but there's no Hargrave here."

"Really?"

"Really."

"But that's impossible." Caitlin took out the copy of *The Plains* from her bag and pointed to the front page. "It says right here that Harold Hargrave was admitted to CHS last night."

Ben returned to the counter and examined the article. "Yes, it sure does. I guess you can't believe everything you read nowadays."

Caitlin felt **deflated** by Ben's **terse** dismissal of the report. The **insinuation** that what was printed in the newspaper might not be entirely trustworthy was **disconcerting** to her. "Are you sure he's not here?" she pressed.

Ben nodded. "Positive. Maybe he checked out earlier this morning." He walked back to the computer. "Let's take a look. What was the name again?"

"Hargrave. Harold Hargrave."

Caitlin leaned over the counter and tried to **decipher** the data on the screen.

"Here we go," Ben said. "You just missed him. He left at seven-thirty, right after first rounds. I guess he couldn't wait."

"You mean he's okay?"

"I suppose so. But you'll have to ask him for the details."

Ben smiled. "Sorry. Is there anything else I can do for you?"

Caitlin thought for moment. She didn't want to waste the trip up here if she could help it. "Well, maybe. Perhaps I could speak with his doctor?"

Ben checked the computer again. "That would be Dr. Abigail Benson. She was on the night shift in emergency. She went off duty a few minutes ago, at eight o'clock. Sorry."

"Is there anyone else here now who might know something about his case?"

Ben leaned back in his chair and rubbed his chin. "Well, I don't think so. But there's something else that might help you."

"Anything would be great, Ben."

"Okay, wait a minute. I'll be right back."

Ben disappeared through a pair of swinging doors, then emerged a moment later with a manila folder. "Here's his file," he said, placing it on the counter.

"Are you allowed to show me this?" Caitlin asked.

Ben shrugged. "Not really."

Caitlin gave him a **skeptical** look. "'Not really' means 'no,' right?"

Ben leaned over the counter. "Actually, they could probably fire me for showing you this," he whispered, "but I must confess, I've got a soft spot in my heart for reporters. My mom writes for the *Washington Post,* so I've heard all her war stories about how hard it is to get people to cooperate and release important information for a breaking story."

Caitlin frowned. "I don't want to get you in trouble."

"Don't worry. They need me too much around here, anyway. I'm the only one who knows the **intricacies** of their computer system. If anybody finds out, I'll probably just get one of those official **reprimands**, in triplicate like everything else around this place. Besides, it's not as though I'm **divulging** government secrets or **disclosing** the Pentagon Papers or something. There's nothing in that file that Dr. Benson wouldn't tell you if she were here."

Caitlin felt caught in an **ethical dilemma**. She didn't want to **coerce** Ben into doing something wrong, but at the same time she didn't want to **dissuade** him from showing her something that probably would help her investigation.

"Are you sure?" she asked. "If anything happens, I can say it was my fault."

Ben smiled. "That's sweet but unnecessary. Just consider this a leak from a sympathetic **anonymous** source, all right?"

"Well, all right."

Tentatively, Caitlin opened the file. Inside were several forms, each in triplicate. They seemed to have been scrawled on by a child whose language was not English and whose penmanship was particularly **inscrutable**. Caitlin couldn't make head or tail of it. She looked up at Ben. "Do you understand any of this medical **jargon**?"

Ben leaned over and studied the forms for a minute, then squinted at Caitlin through his glasses. *"Blessé à la tête trépané sous le chloroforme."*

"What?"

"That's from 'La Jolie Russe' by Apollinaire."

"The French poet?"

"Yes. It's from a poem in which he takes a sort of survey of the **ordeals** he's gone through and then measures the sum of those experiences against love."

"I don't get it," Caitlin said. "How is the poem **pertinent** to Hargrave's medical report?"

"The line refers to Apollinaire's head injury in World War I and his operation. They put him under with chloroform. You see this?" Ben pointed to a notation on one of the forms. "$CHCl_3$. That's the chemical formula for chloroform," he explained. "In the old days it was used as an anesthetic. Apparently, someone knocked the poor guy out with it. The stuff is pretty **toxic**. It can be **lethal** if the person administering it doesn't know what he's doing. Your man's lucky to be alive."

"Wow, that's really interesting," Caitlin said, closing the

folder. "Thanks for all your help, Ben. I'd better get going or I'll miss my first class of the semester."

"Hey, Caitlin," Ben said, flashing her a smile. "You won't forget me when you win the Pulitzer Prize, will you?"

Caitlin laughed. "No way. You'll be the first person I thank in my acceptance speech."

The heavy glass doors quietly slid open and Caitlin took a deep, **rejuvenating** breath of the **wholesome** morning air. She had done it. She had hung in there and uncovered an important fact: chloroform. On the other hand, she had failed to find Hargrave, and Bill had said it was **imperative** that she interview him.

As she strode back along the tree-lined sidewalk toward Madison Street, Caitlin realized that if she were going to make it to all her classes *and* meet the deadline, she would have to track down Hargrave between noon and one—her lunch hour.

She frowned and kicked a pile of dead leaves. When you're an investigative reporter, I guess you don't eat, she thought.

Chapter 15

Something Ventured, Something Gained

The Indian summer air was clear and the sun already warm when Phil strolled out onto the broad steps of Steinbach Commons. After a **fitful** night's sleep he had awakened early, well before his roommates, and headed off alone to satisfy his **voracious** appetite with a huge breakfast—two fried eggs, bacon, hash browns, an English muffin, a cheese blintz, half a grapefruit, orange juice, and two cups of coffee. This was hardly a low-fat, low-cholesterol menu, but at five feet, eleven inches and a trim, muscular 175 pounds, Phil figured he could handle it. Not a bad way to begin the first day of classes, he **mused**, patting his **surfeited** belly.

Phil gazed across East Quad, which was alive with **spontaneous** activity on this first morning of school. Scores of students were hurrying off to class or breakfast or sitting on the stone benches in the courtyard, chatting or reading. Someone had put stereo speakers in an open window, and music floated over the entire scene.

Phil took a deep breath of the **salubrious** air, then pulled off his varsity jacket and tied the sleeves around his waist. He looked at his watch: 8:52 A.M. Plenty of time before his first class at ten o'clock. No sense **procrastinating**, he thought, remembering the resolution he had made yesterday. Might as well get a head start on the semester.

He trotted down the steps and rounded the corner of the dining hall. Then he jogged across College Street and took the steps up to Tillinghast Library two at a time.

The arched entryway was empty except for a beefy security guard sitting behind a desk to one side of the entrance. Phil approached.

"Excuse me, sir. Where can I find the information desk?"

"You want a map?"

"Sure, thanks."

The guard handed him a brochure from a pile on his desk.

Phil wandered into the lobby, studying the map. Main reading room and periodicals to the right; computers, reference room, and information to the left. He headed left.

Five huge stained-glass windows lined one side of the hallway, each **depicting** a scene from American history. Phil walked by them slowly, admiring the way they **diffused** the morning light into bands of color that projected the scenes partly on the far wall and partly on the stone floor.

The first window showed Thomas Jefferson, Benjamin Franklin, and several other Founding Fathers signing the Declaration of Independence. In the next, George Washington stood in a boat full of soldiers crossing the Delaware River. The third pictured Abraham Lincoln holding a copy of the Emancipation Proclamation and manumitting a group of slaves. The fourth **portrayed** Robert E. Lee surrendering his Confederate Army of Northern Virginia to Ulysses S. Grant at Appomattox.

Phil paused by the last stained-glass window, not recognizing the **grave** face of the man it **depicted**. He wore an academic gown and a mortarboard on his head. One hand held a feather pen, raised as though to write in the air; the other hand held a large book with the words *Holy Bible* on the spine. On a rolling banner above the man's head was the Latin *Homo doctus in se semper divitias habet.* Below the man's feet another banner read, "*Nil desperandum, 1878.*"

In the first phrase, Phil knew that *homo* meant "man" and *semper* meant "always," as in *semper fidelis*, "always faithful," the motto of the U.S. Marine Corps. The meaning of the whole, however, was **obscure**. From reading the college catalogues, Phil recognized the second phrase as the Holyfield motto, "Never say die."

Beneath the window was a small plaque, which Phil examined. "The Rev. Ephraim Elijah Harper (1828–1900)," it read, "founder and first president of Holyfield College." Phil **surmised** 1878 must have been the year the man had established the college.

Taking several steps back, he looked at all five stained-glass windows again. That's interesting, he thought. All the people in the scenes are men. Even the slaves surrounding Lincoln are all men. Where are the women? he wondered.

As he **pensively** rubbed his jaw, it occurred to him that when Tillinghast Library was built, back in the 1920s, it was common for the **endeavors** of men to **eclipse** the contributions of women. That was the social norm, the **prevailing bias** of the time.

Phil remembered the honors seminar in American history he had taken last year in which several of the assignments had focused on important women. His teacher, Mrs. Fernandez, had impressed on them that although **conventional** American history books might make it seem that all women had led **servile**, **commonplace** lives, one only had to look a bit more **diligently** to see that men weren't the only ones who had had a **profound** and lasting influence on the nation's course.

Much had changed for the better in the relationship between the sexes since these windows were designed, Phil reflected. Yet the **ultimate** democratic goal—equality not only between men and women but among all people—still seemed remote. How do you go about solving a problem when its nature is so **elusive** and its causes so difficult to **ascertain**?

Phil turned, continued down the long hall, and entered a vast room lined with reference books, computer stalls, and **antiquated** wooden card catalogues. The center of the room was filled with rows of long desks at which a handful of people sat reading or writing.

Phil looked up. On an elaborate frieze that ran around the room at the edge of the ceiling, the names of dozens of **renowned** writers and thinkers were painted in **ornate** Gothic lettering. They were in alphabetical order: Aeschylus, Aristotle, St. Augustine, Balzac, Bentham, Blake, Cervantes, Chaucer, Cicero, Copernicus, Dante, Descartes, Donne, Emerson, Euripides—the list of intellectual heavyweights went on and on. Phil read every name; then, astounded, he **scrutinized** them again, counting carefully this time. Out of seventy-seven names, he recognized only two that belonged to women. The history of man was everywhere, he thought, but where was the history of woman?

On the right side of the room stood the information desk, behind which sat a librarian of **indeterminate** age.

"May I help you, young man?"

"Yes. I'd like to take out a book."

"Well, you're in the right place. Do you have an ID?"

Phil reached into his wallet and pulled out the card that had been sent in the mail a month before. It was the same photograph he had used for his yearbook.

The librarian examined his card. "Where's your **validation** sticker?"

"**Validation** sticker?"

"You should have been sent a blue **validation** sticker when you paid your fees. The sticker goes here, on the bottom of your card," she explained. "Are you a freshman?"

"Yes."

"What's your Social Security number?"

Phil recited his number. The librarian entered it into a computer, then spent a few moments studying the information on the screen.

"Okay, Mr. McKnight, it looks as if your fees have been paid. Go down to the bursar's office tomorrow and get a sticker. In the meantime, fill out this form. It gives you temporary borrowing privileges. You can take out up to six books for a maximum of twenty-one days. That doesn't include books on overnight reserve. To check those out, you need your sticker."

Phil completed the form and gave it to the librarian. A minute later she handed him his temporary card and a brochure explaining how to use the computerized catalogue. "Good luck," she said with a smile.

Phil walked to one of the computer stalls and settled in, map and brochure in hand.

"Title, subject, or author?" the prompt on the screen asked. Phil moved the highlight bar to "author," pressed the "enter" key, then typed in "Shakespeare" at the prompt for "name." The computer searched, then displayed the message "41 items found. Press 'F1' to search a title. Press 'enter' to view list."

Only forty-one items? This should be fairly easy, Phil thought. He pressed "enter" to view the list.

"Whoops," he muttered. On the screen was a list of Shakespeare's works. Phil realized he should have selected "subject" instead of "author." He wanted a book *about* Shakespeare, not one *by* him.

He returned to the main menu and instructed the computer to search again. In a moment the machine informed him that it had found 842 **relevant** items.

Undaunted, Phil pressed "enter" and began scrolling **industriously** through the list. *Emblems of Uncertainty in the Late Tragedies, The Hawk and the Handsaw: A Study in **Rhetorical** Strategies*, and *Much Ado about Nothing: **Desultory** Delights and Other **Aesthetic Digressions*** were just three of the long inventory of **esoteric** titles **enumerated** on the screen.

Which book should he choose? And how could he decide on one if he couldn't even **fathom** its title? Clearly the task of finding something appropriate was going to take longer than he had at first envisioned. He decided to come back the next day when he would have more time.

On his way out, Phil tried to be **inconspicuous** as he passed the information desk. He hoped to **evade** the librarian, who was **engrossed** in a book. He didn't want her to see him leaving so soon after going to the trouble of getting a temporary card.

"Couldn't find what you wanted?" she asked, not looking up from her book.

Geez, thought Phil, stopping in his tracks, that woman must have some kind of extrasensory **perception**. "I'm going to come back and try to find it tomorrow," he told her.

"What are you looking for? Maybe I can save you a trip."

"That's okay. I don't want to trouble you again."

"It's no trouble," she said, putting her book down **decisively**. "It's my job, after all."

"Well, I'm looking for something on Shakespeare. Nothing fancy, just a book."

"That shouldn't be a problem. There are lots of them."

"That's just it," Phil agreed. "There are a whole lot— more than eight hundred—with **abstruse** titles I can't understand. I don't know which one to pick."

"It's like trying to find a needle in a haystack?"

"More like starving at a banquet table."

The librarian chuckled. "I know the feeling. I've worked here for eighteen years and I haven't read even one-half of one percent of the books in this library. We have more than a million volumes here, not including the books in our **archives** and special collections. Plus we subscribe to nearly two thousand periodicals."

"Yes, I read that in the catalogue."

"A college library has so many resources. It can be a little overwhelming when you're not used to it."

Phil nodded **abjectly**.

"But don't worry," the librarian went on, giving him a

cordial smile. "I can help you. You said you wanted something on Shakespeare—an introduction to his work, perhaps?"

"Yes, that'd be great."

"Give me a moment." The librarian entered a few commands into her computer and looked at the screen. Then she scribbled on a slip of paper and handed it to Phil. "This book should fill the bill. It's an **engaging** volume by a woman who taught Shakespeare here for many years. You'll find it up in the stacks, on the seventh floor. I jotted down the call number for you. The elevator's around the corner, at the end of the hall."

"Thanks a lot," Phil said. He looked at the slip of paper and saw that the librarian had recommended *A Garden of Words: The Life and Work of William Shakespeare*, by Margaret Hargrave.

Fifteen minutes later the elevator doors opened and Phil walked to the checkout counter feeling **competent** and **resourceful**. Armed with the call number, he had navigated the dense stacks and found the book nestled on a shelf near the floor at the end of a long, dim row. He checked it out and left the building, whistling softly. Next time Caitlin Ciccone wants to talk about Shakespeare, he thought, I'll be ready.

The sign on the door read, "Central Administration: Library Personnel Only." Caitlin knocked and waited. When no one answered, she opened the door **tentatively** and peeked inside.

"Hello. Anybody there?" she called out in a soft voice. She hesitated, then stepped in and closed the door behind her.

The office was empty. Hargrave's secretary must be at lunch, she thought, trying to ignore the rumbling in her stomach and feeling envious of anyone who might be eating at the moment.

At the end of the room was a door marked "Chief Curator: Private." Caitlin approached and rapped on it lightly. Someone inside stirred and mumbled something, which she **inferred** was an invitation to enter. She opened the door.

The lights were dim. In the center of the **commodious** room, a man lay perfectly still on a dark leather sofa. His face was **pallid** and his eyes were closed. With one hand he held his forehead as if he had a bad headache. The long, spidery fingers spread across the thinning hair on his scalp.

"Mary, you can leave whatever it is on my desk," he said. "I'm not feeling well right now. I probably should have heeded the doctor's **admonishment** and **recuperated** at CHS for another night. Ah, well. Please, no calls or visitors for the next hour or so, all right?"

"Sir," Caitlin began, taking a step into the room, "I'm very sorry to disturb you but—"

"Who are you?" he asked, opening his eyes. For a moment he stared at her, **disoriented**. Then he struggled to sit up straight and smooth his disheveled hair.

"Please don't get up," she said, feeling guilty for disturbing him. "May I get you a glass of water or something?"

"No, thank you. But perhaps you would be so kind as to tell me who you are and why you're in my office?"

Caitlin felt herself blush. "Oh, of course. It was impolite of me to barge in. I'm sorry. My name's Caitlin Ciccone and I'm from the *Holyfield Herald*. I'm looking for Professor Harold Hargrave. That's you, right?"

"Ah-ha! I expected some kind of media circus," Hargrave grumbled **cantankerously**. He looked up at Caitlin. "Well, I'm the man you're looking for. You're here, no doubt, to ask me about last night's mugging."

"Yes, but I could come back some other time."

"Now that you're here, you might as well stay. I suppose I can spare a few minutes." Hargrave took out a handkerchief and wiped his brow. "They say that suffering sells newspapers. Do you think that's an accurate **assessment** of the fourth estate, Ms. Ciccone?"

"I don't know," Caitlin said nervously. She felt she was being tested, but she wasn't sure how or why. "What's the fourth estate?"

"Ah, I see that like so many journalists today, you are woefully **unenlightened** about your profession. By the end of the Middle Ages," the librarian explained in a **listless** voice, "power was divided among three classes, or estates: the clergy, the nobility, and the commons, which included the lower class and the emerging **bourgeoisie**. The fourth estate came along after the invention of printing; it refers to those in your line of work, the public press. The term has also been variously applied to the army and to *mobile vulgus*—a Latin phrase meaning the **fickle** crowd, the **frivolous** and **capricious** masses, from which comes our word *mob.*"

Hargrave paused and squinted at her. It seemed to Caitlin that he was trying to gauge something—perhaps the level of **compassion** or **empathy** or maybe plain stupidity—in her face.

"But you didn't come to hear a lecture," he said finally. "I understand you're just trying to do your job. Please have a seat."

"Thank you, sir." Caitlin crossed the room and sat down in a plump wing chair. From her bag she removed a notebook and pen.

"You don't mind if I lie down while we do this, do you?" Hargrave asked.

"Of course not."

"Do you have enough light?"

"Plenty, thank you."

The chief curator stretched out wearily on the couch, closed his eyes, and released a long sigh. An **enigmatic** smile flickered at the corners of his mouth. "Now then. Where would you like to begin?"

Caitlin was relieved that Hargrave was being so **amenable** and **compliant**, but some **intuitive** voice told her to remain **vigilant**. "Let's start with **motives**. Is there any reason to believe that someone is angry with you?"

"Well, perhaps. But the last thing the college needs is for the *Herald* to start linking Teddy Prospero's lawsuit and this regrettable assault. But I suppose paranoid **conspiracy** theories sell newspapers too."

"I wouldn't know about that," Caitlin said. "When was the last time you saw this Teddy Prospero?"

Chapter 16

Poetry, Philosophy, and Pizza

In Room 217 of Iowa Hall, in South Quad, Carmen Torres stood at the end of a Formica-topped seminar table, facing her students in English 112: An Introduction to Literature and Composition. The clock on the dreary beige wall read 4:32.

On the blackboard behind her, written in a flowing, cursive hand, was a summary of the lecture she had just delivered: "The Well-Tempered Essay: (1) state your **hypothesis**; (2) **substantiate** your argument by **citing** evidence from the text; (3) strive for **continuity** and build toward **synthesis**; (4) refine and **underscore** your points in your conclusion." To one side of these **succinct directives** were the phrases **"subjectivity = bias + speculation"** and **"objectivity = impartiality + analysis."**

Torres closed her eyes and breathed deeply. Then she slowly spread her arms and spoke:

> The Brain — is wider than the Sky —
> For — put them side by side
> The one the other will contain
> With ease — and You — beside —

Each word of Emily Dickinson's poem came out of Torres's mouth fully energized, like a tongue of fire, and her students, their imaginations **kindled**, listened earnestly. Phil was **mesmerized** and guessed that this **fervent eloquence** was part of the reason the professor had earned the nickname Dragon Lady.

> The Brain is deeper than the sea —
> For — hold them — Blue to Blue
> The one the other will absorb —
> As Sponges — Buckets — do —
>
> The Brain is just the weight of God —
> For — Heft them — Pound for Pound —
> And they will differ — if they do —
> As Syllable from Sound —

A **protracted** silence settled on the room as the twenty-odd freshmen—some sitting around the table, others occupying lecture chairs scattered along the walls—tried to comprehend what they had just heard. A student in the back of the room coughed. Another tapped the eraser end of a pencil on the seminar table.

Phil fidgeted in his chair and stared at his handout. The poem seemed **incoherent**. How could a brain contain "the weight of God"? And how does a "syllable" differ from "sound"? What was Dickinson getting at?

Phil glanced around the room. His **timorous** classmates were all **diligently** studying their handouts, **studiously** avoiding eye contact with Professor Torres, who had seen Phil look up. She smiled at him.

"Phil?"

Now the other students looked up, and Phil could feel their eyes on him. The entire class was waiting for his response.

"Yes?"

"Is that furrowed brow evidence of some **profound insight** into this perplexing poem, or are you just feeling **ambivalent** about speaking in class?"

"Pardon me?"

The class laughed. Phil **perused** the professor's face. There was nothing **malicious** in her expression; on the contrary, her **benign** smile was full of encouragement. He realized she was just making a joke, trying to get him to loosen up.

"Did anything in the poem strike you?" Torres asked.

"Strike me? What do you mean?"

"What do you think is the focus of the poem?"

"Well, I'm not sure, really. It seems like a riddle to me."

"An **astute** observation. I couldn't agree with you more. The riddle is a **venerable** form that many writers have **exploited**. Dickinson was especially fond of it."

Phil was relieved that Professor Torres had chosen to be so **magnanimous** in her interpretation of his admission of ignorance.

"Does anyone else find this poem **enigmatic**?" she asked, trying to **stimulate** discussion.

The class's attention shifted toward the door. Phil looked over his shoulder.

"Yes, Heather?"

Heather had three silver earrings in each ear and **flamboyant** streaks of blue and orange **meandering** through her long, strawberry blond hair. A walking neon sign, Phil thought.

"There's a lot in this poem that puzzles me," she said. "The 'you' in line four, especially the way you read it, seems to be referring to us. But how are we contained by a brain? Whose brain? And don't we usually think of the brain as being inside the skull rather than outside?"

"All **pertinent** questions," replied Torres. "Can anyone respond to them?"

Next to Phil, a wiry guy with curly hair raised his hand.

"Basically, I would **concur** with Phil and Heather," he began, squinting at his handout as if to look up would **hamper** his concentration. "But maybe what Dickinson is saying is that the brain is the power of the imagination or the power of poetry, and imagining something like the sea or the sky and putting it in a poem is a way of putting it in a container and containing it. And so when she tells us the brain contains the sea and the sky, she's telling us her poem contains these things—and us as well, whenever we read it. And it comes alive even though she's dead. We're contained in it, trapped in it, like a coffin. It's like she's reaching out from the grave with her brain and—"

The student's **burgeoning exegesis** was cut short by two sharp, **disconcerting** buzzes from the speaker below the clock on the wall. The class, which had been **seduced** by this **torrid,** passionate train of thought, was now abruptly brought back to the present. Phil rubbed his eyes and yawned. It had been a long day of classes and orientation and errands.

"What a nuisance!" exclaimed Torres, scowling at the buzzer. "God knows why we need to have our brains rattled at the end of every class. Jake," she said, turning to the student who'd been interrupted, "that's an interesting **hypothesis** you're developing."

"Thanks, professor."

"How many of you think it could be developed further?"

A few hands shot up around the room. Torres gauged the response and then continued. "Okay. Listen, everybody. This is the suggested topic for your first essay: Does the poem contain the reader or the reader contain the poem? I'd like three to four double-spaced pages. No novels, please—and no haikus, either. Remember, there are no correct answers, only **articulate, coherent**, well-**substantiated** ones. Your papers are due Friday. If you don't like the topic, see me in my office tomorrow morning and we'll come up with something else. If you have any questions, I'll be here for a few more minutes."

Phil carried his full tray of food toward the round table in the middle of Steinbach Commons where Jimmy, Chris,

Lucy, and Juliet were sitting. They were **engrossed** in conversation and seemed to be in high spirits.

"Why, Mr. McKnight, so glad you could join us," Jimmy said with characteristic **mock** formality.

"Phil," said Juliet, patting the table at the place next to her, "we saved you a seat."

"Thanks, Juliet. Hi, everybody."

Phil parked himself next to Juliet. Chris—without a word of warning, but continuing to chew a mouthful of spaghetti—raised a hand above his head, ready for a high five. Phil raised his hand to **reciprocate**. Their palms met with a **robust** thwack.

"Juliet was just regaling us with an **anecdote** about her day," Jimmy told Phil. He turned to Juliet. "Would you care to finish your story?"

As Juliet picked up where she had left off, Phil began eating with **alacrity** the plentiful helping of spaghetti and meatballs on his plate.

"And to make matters worse," Juliet was saying, "I'm running around fifteen minutes late. When I finally find the Calhoun Humanities Complex, it turns out 201 is a lecture hall. The professor hasn't shown up yet. There must be almost two hundred rowdy students packed into the place, and I'm thinking, 'This is supposed to be an introductory philosophy course? There can't be that many people interested in Plato, Socrates, and Aristotle. I must be in the wrong place.'

"But just then this funny-looking white-haired man comes hobbling into the hall, and I think, 'This guy is the professor?' He's short and shabbily dressed and kind of hunched over. He looks as if he's carrying around this great invisible weight on his back. He makes his way slowly through the crowd and up to the **podium**, and then he just stands at the lectern for a couple of minutes, wiping his glasses with his handkerchief, patiently waiting for everybody to calm down.

"Finally he starts speaking and it wasn't at all what I expected. I thought he would have this timid, **inaudible** voice and be **incoherent**, and I'd be struggling to take notes on all these **complex metaphysical** theories that I couldn't even hear. But instead he was totally **comprehensible** and his voice was incredibly **resonant**. It was **mesmerizing**. The entire hall was silent. He lectured for forty-five minutes straight, without any notes and without a bit of **ambiguity**. Everything he said was **lucid**. And he was intense, as though he were bearing witness to some **ordeal** he had survived. I never really thought ideas could have so much significance and be so **relevant**."

"Sounds like your classic **eccentric** professor," Chris said.

"Or some kind of ancient **oracle**," Lucy said. "What's the guy's name?"

"Professor Schwartz."

"Does this Professor Schwartz have opinions or is he just an **illustrious orator**?" Jimmy asked.

Juliet ignored Jimmy's **facetious** tone. "There were two main points to his lecture. He opened with the **contention** that the unexamined life isn't worth living, that if you don't really look at and choose what you do, then you're just reacting slavishly to circumstance."

"Some people," Chris interjected, "believe it's the other way around—that it's precisely when you examine your life and see emptiness and failure that you decide to jump out a window. To **paraphrase** T. S. Eliot, people can't take too much reality. It's better for them not to think, just to do."

"Ah, yes," Jimmy cried, "to be or to do—that is the **vexatious** question that has plagued philosophers forever. Sartre said, 'To do is to be.' Camus said, 'To be is to do.' But I think Frank Sinatra had it right when he sang, 'Do be do be do.'"

Everyone laughed. Then Lucy turned to Chris. "Maybe not thinking is all right for you and T. S. Eliot, but not for me. As Allen Ginsberg said, 'We eat reality sandwiches,' **implying** that reality confronts us all the time, whether we like it or not. So why not develop an appetite for it?"

"Yeah, Chris," Phil chimed in, "if reality's a sandwich that's always in your face, you might as well take a bite. Otherwise you'll just become **emaciated** and then die, right?"

"Which brings me to Professor Schwartz's second point," Juliet said. "According to Socrates, if you care for your soul and live your life according to philosophical principles, there's no reason to fear death."

"I agree that fear of the unknown is **irrational**," Jimmy said. "If there is another life, there's no reason to believe it won't be a better life, and you might as well look forward to it. But if there isn't one and you're simply dead, then you won't be able to feel whatever pain you imagine death **entails**. In the end, if you've led a philosophical life, fulfilling your inner self as well as your **overt** responsibilities, then you'll have nothing to regret. You'll be able to face death with **serenity**."

"That depends," Phil **countered**. "If you're like Chris and believe that people can't face life, then what makes you think they can face death? But if, like Lucy, you look forward to growth and change, then—who knows—death, the most **profound** change, might be the thing you look forward to the most."

"Speaking of death, I thought I saw a dead man today, and let me tell you, it wasn't pretty."

The five freshman looked up to see Caitlin holding her tray. Phil noticed that she looked **enervated**, her normally **vibrant** eyes dulled by fatigue.

"Hi, everyone," she said. "I haven't had anything to eat all day and I'm **voracious**. Mind if I join you?"

"Sorry, Caitlin," Juliet said. "We were so involved in our conversation that we didn't notice you. Have a seat."

"Thanks." Caitlin set down her tray between Phil and Chris.

"So," Phil said, picking up on Caitlin's entrance line, "you said you saw a dead man today?"

"Or so it seemed."

Caitlin described in **vivid** detail how she'd seen Harold Hargrave lying on his couch, **pallid** and **inert**.

"Wow!" Juliet gasped. "Did you scream? I would've."

Jimmy chuckled. "Are you kidding? Caitlin Ciccone, ace reporter for the *Holyfield Herald*, scream? Impossible."

"I'm flattered by your high opinion of my professional **demeanor**, Jimmy," Caitlin said. "But I must confess that screaming was an option that crossed my mind."

"Why is the *Herald* interested in this guy?" Chris asked.

"A whole list of reasons," Caitlin said. "Last night someone broke into the library, knocked him out with chloroform, and rummaged through his office."

"Sounds nasty. Who do they think did it?"

"Hargrave seems to think it was a student—some guy named Teddy Prospero."

"Hey, Jimmy, remember him?" Phil said. "Bill talked about the **antagonism** between him and Leo. I guess this Teddy has a little trouble making friends."

Jimmy nodded. "Yeah, I remember. He's the **unsavory** grandson of the guy whose name is all over campus. Head of some kind of fraternal organization called Arm and Hammer, or Hammer and Tongs, or Tongue in Cheek, or—"

"Tooth and Nail," Caitlin corrected him, laughing.

"Tooth and Nail! That's it!" Jimmy said, **gratified** that he'd made her laugh.

"I don't see anything logical in this attack," Chris said. "It seems to me that if Teddy wants to get a piece of his grandfather's pie, he wouldn't want to do something **irrational,** like commit a felony, and jeopardize his chances."

"Crimes don't have to be **rationally motivated**," Lucy said. "Some are just **random**, and a lot of others are passionate, triggered by a **complex** set of emotions."

"If Teddy's such a **hostile, malicious** character, maybe he's got some screwed-up reason to hate Hargrave," Jimmy suggested.

"Or maybe it wasn't anything personal," Juliet said. "Maybe he was looking for something and Hargrave happened to show up."

"Yeah, but you don't just happen to have chloroform," Caitlin pointed out.

Phil set down his utensils and wiped his mouth. "Any idea what the perpetrator was looking for?"

"Most likely some valuable item in the Prospero collection," Caitlin replied, "but no one's certain."

Phil and Lucy fetched coffee for the table, and the group continued to discuss the case, raising various **hypotheses** concerning **motivation** and **assessing** the evidence for and against Teddy Prospero as the culprit.

"But if it's not Teddy," Juliet asked finally, "then who else could it be?"

"Someone who knows the value of books," Jimmy answered.

"I think you're right," Phil said. "It's probably someone who has an idea of what's in the collection and wants something specific." He looked at his watch and frowned. "Well, whoever it is, we'll never find out unless we return to the scene of the crime and investigate."

"What's that supposed to mean?" Chris asked.

"That it's time to hit the books, pal."

"What, go to the library? Right now?"

"That's right. Life is short and my assignments are not. Anyone care to join me?"

Groaning in **feigned** agony, the others picked up their trays and followed Phil to the busing station.

"Phil, are you sure you don't want to come out for pizza?" Lucy asked. The two sets of roommates stood at the foot of the stone steps leading down from Tillinghast Library.

Phil was glad to be outside. After three hours of stale library air and the dull hum of fluorescent light, the night was cool and **invigorating**. Although he didn't want to seem antisocial, a hot pizzeria didn't appeal to him. Besides, he had promised to give his parents a call.

"No, thanks," he replied, shouldering his backpack. "I need to get back to the dorm and take care of a few things."

Jimmy gave Phil a **skeptical** look. "'Things,' huh?"

"Sounds pretty slippery and **evasive** to me," Chris said.

Phil laughed at his roommates' jocular **prodding**. "You guys make everything sound so **surreptitious**. I just promised I'd call my folks tonight to let them know how everything's going."

"Oh my God, I forgot!" Juliet exclaimed. "I'm supposed to call home too."

"Sure," Jimmy said in a **dubious** tone. "The earth is flat, zebras don't have stripes, and Phil and Juliet have to call their parents." Phil tried to interrupt, but Jimmy raised an index finger in playful **admonition**. "Phil, don't **perjure** yourself. I respect every individual's right to privacy. If you need to do something you don't want to talk about, that's okay by me. I won't pry. But do me a favor. When you're done with your 'things,' would you check up on Siggy for me? I'm worried that Irwin might be on the loose, looking for a snack."

Phil chuckled. "Don't worry. Your fish is in **competent** hands. See you guys later."

As the others began to leave, Caitlin hesitated for a moment. The thought of a **luscious** slice of pizza at Salerno's was **tantalizing**, but duty called.

She turned to Phil. "Do you mind if I come along with you? I was thinking that if Leo was around, you could introduce me and I could interview him about the Prospero business."

"Sure," Phil said. "I'll show you where his room is."

"This pizza expedition is **dwindling** by the second," Lucy said. "Let's get out of here before there's no one left."

"Yeah, let's go," Juliet said. "I'm starving. I'll call my folks tomorrow."

Chris chuckled. "That's right. Spend their money tonight; call them for more tomorrow."

"Hey, that's not true!" Juliet protested. "It's my own money that I saved from my summer job."

"Pay no attention to the **cynical** cry of **disaffected** youth, sweet Juliet," Jimmy said **melodramatically**, leading the foursome down the pathway.

"Don't worry, Juliet," said Lucy. "We all know you're a **frugal, prudent** young woman."

"Except perhaps where pizza is involved," Chris teased.

As their friendly **banter** faded into the night, Phil looked at Caitlin. "Ready to get on the case, Ms. Lane?"

Caitlin laughed. "Sure, Mr. Kent, ready when you are. Just promise me one thing, okay?"

"What's that?"

"Don't drag me into any phone booths for your next **metamorphosis** into Super-Freshman."

They crossed College Street and made their way across East Quad. When they reached Ericson Hall, Phil shouldered his backpack and led the way upstairs. At the fifth-floor landing he held the fire door open for Caitlin, who flashed him a smile in return for the courtesy.

"Leo and Bill's room is on the right," Phil said, following her into the hallway.

The door to Ericson 5-A was slightly ajar and the room was dark.

"That's odd," Phil muttered.

"You think he's home?" Caitlin asked.

"I don't know. Maybe he just forgot to lock his door."

"Maybe he's asleep already."

Phil checked his watch. "It's not that late, only a little after ten." He rapped lightly on the door. There was no response. He rapped again, harder this time. Still no response. He called out softly, "Leo? You there?"

There was no answer.

"It's no big deal," Caitlin said. "I can talk to him tomorrow."

Phil was perplexed. "I don't understand why the door
would be open if he's not in. Leo wouldn't do that."

"Look, why don't we just shut the door and go join the
others at Salerno's?"

"No, wait a minute. Something seems weird here. I'm
going to take a look around."

Caitlin was about to say she didn't think that was a good
idea when Phil pushed the door open and stepped inside. Instinctively, she followed him.

"Anybody home?" Phil said into the darkness. He turned
to Caitlin. "Can you get the light?"

Caitlin groped along the wall, found the switch, and
flicked it on. Then she gasped.

Chapter 17

Blood Is Thicker
Than Ink

Leo Kabnis lay **prone** in the middle of the room, his glazed
eyes half-open, his arms splayed above his head. Blood oozed
from an ugly **laceration** in his scalp, trickling down his tem-
ple and staining the rug. Books and papers lay scattered on
the floor.

Phil let go of his backpack and rushed to his counselor's
side. He dropped to his knees and checked Leo's wrist for a
pulse. It was **sluggish** but **tangible** enough to **impart** hope.

"He's okay," Phil said. "Out cold, but alive at least. I'll
get something to put on this cut and stop the bleeding."

"And I'll call the campus police and tell them we need
an ambulance," Caitlin said, looking around for the phone.

Immediately after talking with the police, she dialed the
Herald and asked for Bill Berkowitz.

Twenty minutes later they stood on the steps outside Ericson
Hall answering **terse** questions from a campus police officer.
Leo had just been wheeled out and taken to CHS, accompanied by Bill, and the crowd that had gathered to gawk and
gossip was beginning to **disperse**.

"Just before you and the paramedics arrived," Phil was
explaining, "Leo came to for a minute. He said he was caught

by surprise and didn't see who attacked him. Then he lost consciousness again."

"I see," said the officer, making a notation in his book. "The room appears to have been searched. Do you have any idea what the **assailant** was looking for?"

"No, we don't," Caitlin said.

The officer looked at Phil.

"Sorry, sir. No idea."

"And you're sure you didn't hear an altercation or see anyone suspicious?" the officer asked.

They shook their heads.

"Did Mr. Kabnis have any enemies or **adversaries**? Do you know anyone who was angry with him or who might have wanted to hurt him?"

Phil glanced at Caitlin, who shrugged her shoulders. "Well, officer," he said, "Saturday at dinner I saw him get into a **vehement** argument with a guy named Teddy Prospero."

"This was a good idea, Caitlin. It really hits the spot. Thanks for buying."

"You're welcome."

They sat at a corner table in Java Jones, the cafe in the Student Center, sipping cappuccino and staring gloomily around the **sparsely** occupied room.

"Are you sure Leo's going to be all right?" Caitlin asked.

"The paramedics told me he'll need stitches, and he probably has a concussion, but he should be okay in a couple of days."

"You know, I think I'm still in shock. I just can't believe this happened."

"Neither can I. Leo's such a nice guy. Why would anyone want to attack him?"

"I don't know. All I know is that this makes two people assaulted in two days."

"What do you mean?"

Caitlin sighed. "It's weird," she said, pushing her hair back from her forehead, "but I can't help thinking that what happened to Leo is somehow connected to last night's incident with Harold Hargrave. Do you think Teddy Prospero's behind it?"

Phil rubbed his chin **pensively**. "I'm no detective, but if I were, I'd be talking to that guy."

There was a long, **melancholy** pause as they finished their cappuccinos.

"I think I'd like another one of these," Phil said. "How about you—my treat this time?"

"Sure. Thanks."

While Phil placed his order at the counter, Caitlin anxiously drummed her fingers on the table. The **vivid, unsettling** image of Leo unconscious and bleeding on the floor kept invading her mind's eye. Violence, she thought, was not even remotely among her expectations for college. But there was no denying it now. The **insulated, harmonious** world of study and recreation she had envisioned had been shattered, **decisively**, by the assaults on Hargrave and Leo. And it seemed that she too, in an indirect way, had been **violated**— she and everyone else who had come to Holyfield College **blithely** assuming it would be safe. If people were being attacked in their offices and dorm rooms, anyone and everyone was **vulnerable**, and who could predict what might happen next?

Caitlin's gaze fell on the pile of books spilling out of Phil's backpack. There were three paperback textbooks, two spiral notebooks, and a hardcover bound in heavy blue library buckram. Curious to know what Phil had taken out of the library, she **scrutinized** the title printed on the spine: *A Garden of Words: The Life and Work of William Shakespeare.* Aha, she thought, our discussion after the radio panel must have really **stimulated** him.

She removed the book from the pile, then almost dropped it when she saw the name of the author on the title page: Margaret Hargrave. What a strange coincidence, she thought. Could Margaret be related to Harold? As she began thumbing through the pages, she was surprised again when a thin envelope suddenly slipped out of the book into her lap. She looked down at the name written on the front of the envelope and her mouth fell open.

"Here's your cappuccino," Phil said.

Caitlin almost jumped out of her chair. "Phil, don't scare me like that!"

"I'm sorry. Hey, you still seem pretty shaken up. Maybe you shouldn't have any more coffee."

"No, I'm okay," she said hoarsely. "I was spacing out and you startled me, that's all." She clutched her cup and took a quick sip.

"What were you spacing out about?" he asked.

"I—you're not going to believe this."

"Believe what?"

"I found something in your book."

"You what?"

"In your Shakespeare book—something fell out of it."

"What are you talking about?"

"Look," she said, retrieving the envelope from her lap and holding it up so he could see the handwriting. "It's a letter addressed to Leo."

"I still don't see why you're in such a rush," Phil said as they sipped their cappuccinos. "Why can't we just hang onto it until Leo gets out of CHS or give it to Bill for safekeeping?"

Caitlin released an **exasperated** sigh. "Okay, I'll explain it again. It's a matter of **ethics**, Phil. This letter may contain **vital** information—perhaps a clue to the identity of Leo's **assailant** or maybe even something that poses a further threat to him. Do you really want to risk the potential **consequences** of failing to **divulge** something like that?"

"Of course not, it's just that—"

"I'm glad you agree. Then we'll deliver the letter to Leo tonight," Caitlin said **decisively**.

Phil was **skeptical**. "But it's almost midnight, and we don't know what room he's in or if he's in any condition to read it."

"Don't be so **intractable**, Phil. I've got a strong hunch there may be something **crucial** in that letter. If you don't want to take it to Leo, then I will. Are you going to trust me on this or am I going alone?"

The threat was enough to **dispel** Phil's **reluctance**. He **acquiesced** without further complaint.

Caitlin's plan worked like a charm. From a pay phone at the cafe she called CHS and asked for Leo's room number, explaining that she was a concerned friend who wanted to check on his condition and see if she could visit him in the morning. Then they hurried over to the building, slipped up the back stairs to the third floor, and tiptoed down the hall. The only **impediment** was the nurses' station, which to their great relief they found momentarily unoccupied.

Minutes later, Leo sat up in his bed in room 312, awake and alert. His injured head was wrapped neatly in a white gauze bandage.

"This is incredible," he said, staring at the unopened letter in his hand. "It's from Prospero. I can tell from the handwriting on the envelope."

Caitlin nudged Phil with her elbow. "You see? I told you it was important."

"I bet this is the real letter I was supposed to get with my book," Leo said. "Somebody must have stolen it and replaced it with the other one."

"What do you mean 'the real letter'?" Phil asked.

"Reggie—Reginald Burton-Jones, Prospero's valet—came to the executors' meeting at the library yesterday morning and handed out gifts from Prospero. There was a letter similar to this one in the Edgar Allan Poe book I got, but it didn't look right to me. There were some **dubious** things about it that made me suspect it might be a **forgery**. So I showed it to Reggie and Professor Hargrave later, and Reggie agreed. Phil, do you have any idea how the letter got in your book?"

Phil shrugged. "Not the foggiest notion. I checked the book out of the library this morning. I hadn't even cracked the binding yet when Caitlin found the letter inside. Who knows how it got there."

"Hey, Leo," Caitlin said, growing impatient. "Are you just going to stare at the envelope all night?"

Leo smiled. "Sorry. My head's still throbbing a bit, and I guess I'm a little confused—and surprised. Would you mind turning on the light on the nightstand for me?"

"Sure," Phil said, leaning over and switching it on.

"Thanks." Leo removed the letter from the envelope and gently unfolded its two pages. As he read, his eyes grew wide and a soft whistle escaped his lips.

Caitlin leaned forward. "Well, what does it say?"

"Don't be so insistent," Phil chided. "He doesn't have to tell us if he doesn't want to."

"No," Leo said quietly, "I'd like to share it with you. This letter is amazing. It's a miracle you guys found it, and you deserve to hear what it says."

Phil and Caitlin settled themselves in chairs at the foot of the bed and listened intently as Leo read the letter aloud.

My dear Leo,

By the time you read this, I will have departed this life, having left my mark, such as it is, upon the world. By way of thanks for all your assistance, and as a token of my **esteem** for you, I give you this little book by Poe. It doesn't look like much, I know, but it's quite rare—one of my most cherished pieces.

Now, on to more pressing matters—and the real reason for this letter.

As you know, I have led an **unconventional** life, perhaps (if I may flatter myself as I face eternity) even a **notable** life. Throughout my **diverse** career, three things have **motivated** and sustained me: an **insatiable** appetite for knowledge and experience; a **disdain** for **complacency**; and, perhaps most important, a **vivacious** sense of humor.

In you, Leo, I detect similar qualities. You are **modest, articulate**, and mature for your age, with an admirable sense of humor. (We've had many a good laugh, haven't we?) You are also a **perceptive** fellow, brimming with potential and a **keen** intelligence that, in the best sense, begs to be put to the test. And that is precisely what I intend to do.

Now, please don't think I'm teasing you, for the challenge I have devised will demand all your **insight** and powers of **deduction**. Allow me to explain what it **entails**.

Among the many valuable items in my collection is something no one knows about, something unique, my most prized possession. Without doubt it would be the crown jewel of any library or museum, but I already have given generously to such institutions. Instead I have decided it should go to someone worthy and eager to prove his **mettle**.

If you're clever enough to uncover the map and follow the **arduous** trail to the treasure, you will be richly rewarded, for the prize is also a **heretical** truth (that's a clue!) whose unveiling, I am sure, will astound not only you but also the world.

Many would consider it **perverse** to keep such a **prodigious** thing secret, but whenever that **scruple** troubled me I thought of a line from Poe. "There are some secrets," he once wrote, "which do not permit themselves to be told." Indeed, over time I came to feel a **profound** moral satisfaction in knowing I was the **judicious** guardian of something that might tempt **corrupt** people to do great evil if they knew of it.

As a man of wisdom and **restraint**, I have been **steadfast** in keeping this secret, but the time has come to pass it on, for I cannot presume to take something of such significance with me into the grave. That would make my death—and in **retrospect,** my life—only a **hindrance** to the advancement of knowledge and the quest for truth.

I am old. My day is nearly done. I no longer yearn for **self-aggrandizement**. I want only to set my house in order and go peacefully to the great theater of the beyond. I **bequeath** my secret to you because you have proved yourself both an able young scholar and a trustworthy friend. I know you will use this gift wisely and well.

I have great faith in you, Leo. I know you will **prevail**. Good luck and Godspeed.

With affection, E. A. P.

As he read the final lines, Leo's voice cracked with emotion. When he finished, they all sat in stunned silence. Finally Caitlin spoke.

"That really was amazing, Leo. Do you have any idea what this treasure might be?"

Leo pondered the question for a moment. "It's hard to say. Prospero had all kinds of incredible stuff: autographed books by Steinbeck, Faulkner, and Hemingway; first editions of Twain, Melville, and Hawthorne; beautiful old originals by Locke, Voltaire, and Rousseau from the Enlightenment; musical scores by Mendelssohn, Brahms, Mozart, and Bach; letters and poems by Goethe and Dante; a couple of Gutenberg Bibles; a bunch of **medieval** and Anglo-Saxon **illuminated** manuscripts—you name it, he had it. And all of these things, of course, are tremendously valuable but hardly secret."

"What about Shakespeare?" Phil asked. "Did Prospero have anything by him?"

Leo smiled. "No one has anything by him, Phil."

"Get out of here! He's the most famous writer ever."

"Famous, yes, but still largely unknown."

"You're being **cryptic**," Caitlin said. "What do you mean?"

"Simply that no one has seen anything actually *written* by Shakespeare. His work was printed and **disseminated** both during his lifetime and after his death, but there are no **extant** manuscripts. Nothing in his handwriting has ever turned up—nothing, at least, that could be **verified**."

"Not even a letter?" Caitlin asked.

Leo shook his head. "Not the merest scrap of paper."

The three students were quiet for a moment.

"Well, whatever it is," Caitlin said finally, "I'm sure it'll be the scoop of the century. I want to be right there with my notebook and pen when you find this great literary treasure."

"I'm glad to hear that, Caitlin," Leo said. "I think I'm going to need all the help I can get on this." He looked at Phil. "How about you, my man? You want in?"

"Sure. I don't know how much help I'll be, but I'll do whatever I can."

"Then it's settled. We're a team."

"So what's our next move?" Caitlin asked.

Leo shrugged. "Beats me. Got any good ideas?"

"Would you mind if I took a look at the letter?" Phil asked.

"Be my guest."

While Leo and Caitlin brainstormed, Phil **scrutinized** the letter. Prospero's handwriting was **distinctive**—so small as to be almost **minute**, yet entirely **legible**. The delicate lines of words were perfectly straight and evenly spaced down the length of the two unruled pages, which were of light and somewhat **translucent** stock. Phil thought it remarkable that a ninety-three-year-old man could write with such a steady and **scrupulous** hand. Then something else occurred to him.

"Leo," he said, looking up, "you remember the other night in the dining hall when you were telling us about Prospero?"

"Of course."

"You said he was a good calligrapher, didn't you?"

"Yes, very good."

"And he was crazy about puzzles and riddles, right?"

"Right. He would spend hours solving the most **esoteric** crosswords and acrostics I've ever seen."

"And didn't he also **decipher** codes during World War II?"

"He never actually told me that, but that's what I've heard. Why do you ask?"

"I'm not sure yet," Phil said, "but I think I'm getting an idea. This letter was supposed to be included with the book by Edgar Allan Poe that Prospero gave you, right?"

Leo nodded.

"Did you ever notice that Edgar Allan Poe and Edward Anthony Prospero have the same initials, E. A. P.?"

"My God, I never thought of that," Leo said. "What an interesting coincidence. Do you think it's significant?"

Before Phil could answer, Caitlin interrupted. "What's the meaning of this **interrogation**, Phil? I'm dying to know what you're getting at."

Phil stood up. "If what I'm thinking is right, you'll see in a second." He handed Caitlin one of the two pages of the letter. Then he walked to the head of Leo's bed, removed the shade from the lamp on the nightstand, and proceeded to hold the other page directly over the hot, exposed bulb.

Caitlin jumped up. "Are you crazy? You'll burn it!"

"Don't worry," Phil said as he began moving the paper in a slow circle to distribute the heat evenly. "Even if this doesn't work, the letter should be fine."

"What are you up to?" Leo asked, craning his neck in an effort to see.

"Just hang on and I'll explain in a minute."

Caitlin peered over Phil's shoulder as he continued to move the paper **methodically** over the bulb. To her amazement, within a few seconds, **cryptic**, **obscure** markings began to appear between the lines of handwriting on the page. "Holy cow! What's happening?"

"Son of a gun, I was right!" Phil cried.

"Hey, keep it down or the night nurse'll hear you," Leo commanded in a stern whisper. "What's going on?"

"Get a load of this," Phil said, turning to show Leo and Caitlin the paper. While they marveled at it, Phil heated the second page of the letter over the bulb, and soon more writing appeared. He placed the two pages side by side on the bed so they could examine what had been revealed.

This is what they saw:

1. HLTLA LORWE TASSD NEAGA TLLAD
   NMEEH ODWNA ENMEM PLYER RYEALS.
   NMIAI FISHT TESRO NDINA ANSAM EARPPL.

2. 0001104 2925207 1270226 1877106
   2910221 0966123 1528331-S 0966123
   1253312 2181134 0836228.

3. O I know two O may a man undo.

4. O8I3 093W O35534 5Y3 E9D7J3H5 8W
   Q5 YQHE 59 7W3 59 T99E 07409W3.

"Wow, this is incredible!" Caitlin exclaimed. "Prospero hid the map to his treasure right in his own letter."

"Excellent job, Phil," Leo said. "You're a **paragon** of **ingenuity**. Prospero would be proud."

Caitlin looked at Phil. "That was really **astute**. How in the world did you figure it out?"

Phil was about to explain when he remembered Caitlin's **callous** and **patronizing** remark during *Romeo and Juliet*. Here was a perfect opportunity to return the **condescension** in kind. "It was pretty simple, actually," he said with a sly smile. "I guess you just have to learn to read between the lines."

Caitlin groaned and slumped into a chair. "Touché. All right, are we even now?"

Phil grinned. "The slate is clean."

"Now that you two have settled whatever **petty** rivalry you had going," Leo said, "Phil, would you please tell us how you **deduced** that the map was hidden in the letter?"

"I guess I just put two and two together and got lucky," Phil said. "When you mentioned the letter was supposed to accompany the book by Poe and when it dawned on me that Poe's and Prospero's initials were the same, something clicked. I remembered that Poe's story 'The Gold Bug' is all about a coded map, written in invisible ink, that leads to a fantastic treasure. That made me wonder if the story might have been Prospero's inspiration here."

Phil pointed to the letter. "Look at the lines of the original. See how even they are, with the same amount of space between them? The whole thing's so neat and **meticulous**, it practically looks typed. Why would someone leave spaces like that in a handwritten letter? I figured it might be to make room to write a message in between, in invisible ink."

"I thought invisible ink was something kids played with," Caitlin said. "I had no idea it really worked." She paused. "How *does* it work, anyway?"

"There are lots of ways to make invisible ink," Phil explained, "with sugar water, honey water, various juices, even straight white vinegar. When the ink dries, it disappears. Usually all you need to do to reveal the message is expose the paper to heat. In 'The Gold Bug' they held the parchment before a fire, but as you can see, the heat from a lightbulb will also do the job."

"How do you know all this stuff?" asked Caitlin.

Phil chuckled. "I used to mess around with invisible ink when I was a kid, and I've learned a few things about codes and ciphers from reading a lot of mysteries and spy novels."

"Well, guys, we've made it over the first hurdle," Leo said. "But now it looks as if we've got four more to go. I'd love to stay up and try to **decipher** these messages, but it's late, my head's pounding, and I'm exhausted. I think we should pack it in and get a fresh start on it in the morning."

Phil looked at his watch. "Yeah, you're right. It's already after one. C'mon, Caitlin, let's let Leo get some rest. He's had a rough night. I'll walk you back to your dorm."

"Wait a minute, everybody," Caitlin said. "Aren't we forgetting something?"

"What's that?" Leo asked.

"The letter. What are we going to do with it?"

"Why can't Leo just keep it here?" Phil asked.

"We need to put it in a safe place."

"I see what you mean, Caitlin," Leo said. "Now that we know that the letter is also the map, it's even more **imperative** that we guard it carefully. Unfortunately, I'm still a **vulnerable** target. Whoever clobbered me could come after me again anytime. There's really no place to hide the letter here at CHS. Why don't you guys hold onto it until I get out?"

"I'll keep it," Phil offered. "It'll be safe with me."

"I'm not so sure about that," Caitlin said. "The letter was in your library book. Whoever put it in there could easily discover that you checked the book out and track you down."

"Excellent point," Leo said. "Can you hide it safely?"

"Oh, absolutely," Caitlin said. "Women are very **subtle** creatures. We have lots of good hiding places."

Caitlin had just climbed into bed and gotten comfortable when the telephone rang. Lucy groaned and rolled over, but Juliet leapt out of bed like a sprinter off the starting blocks.

"I knew it. I just knew it," she cried as she scampered

into the living room. "It's my parents. They're worried because I didn't call tonight."

After a moment, Juliet appeared in the doorway to the bedroom. "Caitlin, it's for you. It's Phil. He says it's important."

Caitlin rushed to the phone. "Hello?"

"Caitlin, are you all right?"

"Yes, of course," she said, suddenly **apprehensive** at the **solicitous** tone of Phil's voice. "I was just going to bed. What's wrong?"

"I've got some more bad news."

Caitlin sat down on the couch, gripping the receiver hard. "Are you okay?"

"Yeah, I'm fine. But we've got major trouble."

"What do you mean?"

"I think you were right about the library book. My room was searched tonight. Somebody came up the fire escape and through the open window. When Jimmy and Chris got back here around midnight they found the place ripped apart."

Caitlin could feel her heart pounding in her ears.

"It's the letter, Caitlin. Somebody's definitely looking for that letter."

Chapter 18

Round Up
the Usual Suspects

Tuesday

"Did you get that?" asked Bill Berkowitz, reaching for the thermos of coffee on his desk and pouring himself a cup.

Caitlin took a moment to **scrutinize** her notes before replying. The previous night's excitement had taken its toll. She had overslept and just missed the morning staff meeting. Now they were going over her assignment alone.

She yawned, covering her mouth. "I think so. You want me to track down Professor Bibb and see what he has to say about the assaults on Harold Hargrave and Leo. My last class ends at two-thirty today, so I can do that this afternoon."

"Good," Bill said. "And don't forget to ask if he thinks there's any connection between the assaults and the contents of Prospero's rare book collection."

"Okay, but what about Professor Martext?"

"Steve Rosenblum's handling him."

Caitlin nodded. "There's also Teddy Prospero. Isn't he the most likely suspect? Shouldn't his interview be a **priority**?"

"Don't worry about Teddy. I've got him covered. I'm running an article by Tony Scolari tomorrow on the lawsuit Teddy's been threatening to file against the college and the executors of the collection. You just talk to Bibb. I'll handle the rest." Bill took Caitlin's cup, refilled it from the thermos, and handed it back to her.

"Thanks," she said, taking a sip of the hot brew. "And what about Hargrave? As chief curator, he's probably best acquainted with the collection. Maybe he knows something about whatever it is this person wants."

"Maybe he does," Bill said, "but as a victim, he's off our list of suspects. Besides, you talked to him already, and he didn't mention anything specific that might have **instigated** the attacks. As I recall, he felt the **motive** was personal."

"True. However, you've left out one executor."

"Carmen Torres?"

"Yeah. Why's that?"

"Why do you think?"

Caitlin sipped her coffee. "Well, I don't know her that well, but I don't think she's the type. She seems so **upright** and **virtuous**. Besides, she and Leo are close."

"It wouldn't be the first time **avarice**—the desire to accumulate a little cash—came between friends." Bill stood up and began pacing behind his desk. "Think about it, Caitlin," he went on, playing the **devil's advocate**. "If you could get a pile of money, let's say a million dollars, by committing some small offense, some **peccadillo,** would you do it?"

"What do you mean?"

"Suppose you could get the money free and clear by just hitting a friend over the head, no serious injuries, just knock him out, and he never has to know you hit him. Would you do it?"

"I don't think so."

"Honest?"

"How could you be sure you wouldn't injure the person?"

Bill sensed her **vulnerability** and applied more pressure. "Caitlin, think of what you could do with all that dough! You could buy a yacht and sail around the world, or live in a mansion, or collect nice cars, or give it all to charity, or start a newspaper. You could be as **exotic** or as **conventional** as you liked. Whatever your fantasy was, you could fulfill it. One brief, **ultimately innocuous** action resulting in a lifetime of **serenity**—you can't say the idea doesn't have a certain **allure**."

"Of course I'm **intrigued** by it, but—"

"But what?"

"It's just too **repugnant**. I mean, maybe if I was really desperate, then for a million dollars I'd let someone hit me, but I don't think I could bring myself to hit somebody else. On the other hand, if the guy knew he was going to be hit, and we were planning on splitting the money afterward, then, yeah, it's possible I'd consider doing it."

"You mean, under certain circumstances you'd do it?"

"I suppose so, but what are you getting at?"

Bill sat down again and put his feet up on his desk. "Caitlin," he said, teasing her, "do you consider yourself an **ethical** person?"

"Of course I do."

"And if you could commit a crime—**hypothetically** at least—don't you think there are certain circumstances under which even Carmen Torres, despite all her **integrity**, could commit a crime?"

"Okay, okay," Caitlin **acquiesced**. "I suppose so."

"Right, especially since she hasn't gotten **tenure** yet. When an associate professor signs a contract at Holyfield, do you know how long it's for?"

"Five years?"

"Three, and it's renewable only twice. That means the longest she could teach here without receiving **tenure** would be nine years."

Caitlin recalled that when she'd met Carmen in the dining hall the professor had said this was her ninth year at the college. "That would mean this is her last year."

"Precisely."

Caitlin leaned forward. "So what are you **implying**?"

"I'm **implying** that whatever it is she's after, if she can get her hands on it first, it could be a scholarly **coup**—the basis for an article, which in turn could be the basis for a book, which in turn could be the basis for a comfortable little **niche** at Holyfield for the rest of her life."

"But wouldn't academic advancement be **motive** enough for any junior faculty member in the humanities?"

"Sure, anyone who can wield a blunt instrument and administer chloroform is a candidate. But we're trying to narrow our list of suspects, so we have to look at those closest to the crime. And Carmen, as a friend of Prospero's and an executor of his collection, probably has some idea of its contents."

Bill continued to **augment** the evidence against Torres, **elucidating** a set of ordinary circumstances that might turn an **amiable** professor into a **callous** felon. Yet no matter how logical and **rational** his **deductions** seemed, Caitlin remained **incredulous**. Every time she tried to imagine Carmen hitting Leo on the head or sneaking up behind Hargrave, her mind rebelled.

"Look, Bill," she said finally, "isn't this a little **far-fetched**? I mean, if we wanted to we could **fabricate motives** and make anyone look guilty."

"You really think it's **implausible**?"

"Yes, I do."

Bill stood up. "Then I'm definitely not going to let you interview her."

"I'm glad," Caitlin said with a laugh. "I wouldn't want to be in that awkward position. Any more news about Leo?" she asked, standing up and gathering her notes.

Bill nodded. "He called this morning, said he was sore but should be out of CHS this afternoon."

"That's great!"

"Yeah, he's pretty **resilient**," Bill said, walking Caitlin to the door.

Caitlin trotted up the stairs, then stopped at the top and turned. "Hey, Bill?"

"Hey, what?" he replied, sticking his head out the door.

"I'm sorry I was late this morning."

"Forget about it and get to class!"

Caitlin smiled and hurried off across Longman Green. Looking up, she saw that the sky had grown bleak and menacing. The morning air was chilly and moist. So much for Indian summer, she thought, shivering. It's going to pour.

Shortly before noon, the sky opened up. Lightning crackled and thunder roared. Slanting sheets of rain pounded rooftops and pelted the street. Caught in the **deluge**, Phil began to run, leaping over the puddles that had quickly accumulated on the sidewalk. By the time he reached CHS, he had abandoned all hope of remaining dry.

The sliding glass doors parted and Phil dashed into the shelter of the lobby. He paused to take a quick inventory of the damage. His sneakers, socks, and blue jeans were soaked. Water had dripped from his bare head to his neck, then under his jacket and down his back. About the only thing that wasn't drenched was his backpack. Thank goodness for waterproof nylon, he thought.

He took the elevator up to the third floor and signed the visitors' book at the nurses' station. Then he dripped and squished down the **immaculately** buffed hallway to Leo's room.

The door was open. Phil looked in and saw Leo lying in bed, on top of the covers, reading a magazine. Apparently he had already **perused** the day's editions of the *Herald* and *The Plains*, for both newspapers lay crumpled on a chair beside the bed. He wore a maroon terry-cloth bathrobe over a white T-shirt and jeans, and there was a fresh, somewhat less **conspicuous** bandage on his head.

"Hey, Leo. How ya doing?"

Leo looked up. "Phil, good to see you, my man," he said in a **sonorous** bass voice. "Hey, did you get caught in the storm? You look like a sewer rat."

"Yeah, it's a monsoon out there. I'm soaked to the gills."

"Well, come on in and dry off. Grab a towel from the bathroom."

"Thanks." Phil set his backpack on the floor, doffed his jacket, and draped it on a chair. He found a towel and began rubbing his hair. "So, what's new?" he asked Leo.

"What's new is that the doctor checked me out this morning and the **diagnosis** was merciful. She pronounced me full of **vitality** and said my **bondage** in this sanitary wasteland would end at four o'clock."

"I'm glad to hear that," Phil said, sitting down on the end of the bed, "because something else happened last night. My room was searched."

Leo scowled. "Is Caitlin . . . is the letter . . ."

"Don't worry. They're both okay." Phil **recounted** the details of the break-in. "I think they were looking for the book your letter was in. Nothing was stolen, so what else could it be?"

Leo pounded the bed with his fist. "I knew someone was onto us. This **confirms** it. You haven't told anybody about the letter, have you?"

"No, of course not."

"Not even your roommates?"

"They don't suspect any **malicious** intent. They just think the whole thing was some kind of **eccentric** freshman **initiation ritual**."

"And the campus police?"

"They were gone by the time I got back to the room."

"Good," Leo said with a sigh of relief. "But there's no time to lose. We'd better get to work solving those clues."

Phil got up from the bed. "That was my first thought, too, which is why I took the liberty of getting you some **per-tinent** reading material." He unzipped his backpack, removed several books, and set them down on the bed. "I had a break this morning between calculus and history, so I dug these out of the stacks for you."

"Good thinking," Leo said. As he examined the books, his face lit up with delight. "*A History of Codes and Ciphers, Elementary Principles of Cryptanalysis, Cryptography: A Manual for Students*—excellent! You are one **resourceful** dude, Phil. Thanks for taking the **initiative**."

Phil shrugged. "Don't mention it." He put on his jacket and zipped up his backpack. "I thought maybe we could get together with Caitlin later on and start figuring things out."

"Absolutely. I'll check out these books and see what I can come up with. You want to meet for dinner at the commons?"

"Sure, what time?"

"How about six o'clock?"

"Okay. See you then," Phil said and started to leave.

"Yo, wait up a second," Leo called out.

Phil stuck his head back inside the doorway. "What?"

"A word to the wise from your freshman counselor. Get an umbrella, will ya? Otherwise you'll be spending the rest of the semester right here in CHS with the flu."

Phil grinned. "Sure, Mom. Anything you say."

Chapter 19

Professor Bibb's
Eminent Domain

Professor Bibb took Caitlin's drenched raincoat and dripping umbrella and smiled **cordially**. "Perhaps you should remove your footwear as well."

Caitlin looked down at her battered sneakers. A small puddle was beginning to form around them on the gleaming parquet floor.

"Sorry about that, Professor," she said, prying them off by stepping on their heels.

"No need to worry. Just taking precautions," he said, opening the front hall closet and hanging up her coat. "You may put them on the tray next to the door."

Caitlin placed her shoes next to an old pair of galoshes. They were **reminiscent** of the ones her mom had made her wear over her shoes whenever it rained in grade school. She had thought the black rubber boots made her feet look like tree stumps, and she remembered the day in the sixth grade when she had **vehemently** refused to put them on and her mother had **relented**.

"Right this way, Ms. Ciccone."

Caitlin followed Bibb to an archway at the end of the hall. She could hear the soothing strains of classical music coming from the room beyond.

"May I get you anything? Juice or tea?" Bibb asked, ushering her into the living room.

"Tea would be great, thank you."

"Ah, good. Well, then, I'll be right with you. In the meantime, please make yourself at home."

As Bibb disappeared back down the hallway, Caitlin looked around in wonder at the **lavish** furnishings. The **capacious** room was crammed with antique furniture and objets d'art. **Luxuriant** plants sprouted in the corners, and at the far end a white-lacquered baby grand piano stood to one side of a tiled fireplace with a mahogany mantel. On the walls **traditional** landscapes and still lifes hung next to **contemporary abstract** expressionist paintings, in no **discernible** order. The sheer **plenitude** of **acquisitions**, and their **diversity**, convinced Caitlin that Bibb was an **eclectic connoisseur** with expensive tastes.

She wandered through this thicket of things and passed under another arch that led into what appeared to be Bibb's library. On one side of the room, tall glass cases displayed old leather-bound volumes. On the other, open shelves rising to the ceiling housed books that probably were used on a more regular basis—well-thumbed scholarly **tomes**, sets of classics, and **abstruse treatises** in French, Italian, German, and Latin.

In the middle of the room an **intricately** carved wooden stand supported an enormous book that looked like an **archaic unabridged** dictionary. Its cover was studded with dark gems and embossed with **exotic** lettering. She opened the book and was surprised by the brightly **illuminated** pages. They seemed to shine with an inner light.

"Ms. Ciccone!"

She looked up to see Bibb set a serving tray down on a table and rush toward her. Startled, she let go of the book and stepped back. The cover dropped shut with a thump.

"Ms. Ciccone, are your hands clean?" he blustered, carefully examining the first few pages to check for marks.

Caitlin was amazed at how the possibility of a smudge could **dismantle** the **composure** of this **renowned** scholar.

"I'm sorry."

"It's all right," Bibb said with a frown. "There doesn't appear to be any damage. I shouldn't have left the book sitting out in the open where someone could **tamper** with it."

Bibb unlocked one of the glass bookcases, then picked up the volume and lovingly put it in its place. He turned, wiped his forehead with his handkerchief, smoothed his hair, and glanced at Caitlin.

"All's well that ends well," he said with a **convivial** laugh, regaining his **equanimity**. He pointed to the serving tray. "Would you mind setting that on the table by the picture window in the living room? I'll be just another moment."

Caitlin ferried the tea set to its appointed spot without a **mishap**, then sat down in an armchair and looked out the window.

The **panoramic** view from the penthouse apartment was impressive. The rain had **abated** and the **oppressive** gray storm clouds, which had **dominated** the city's skyline and the **arable** Iowa farmland stretching beyond, finally were beginning to lift. The whole city seemed to be at her feet. Nine blocks down College Street she could see the distinct group of buildings that made up the central Holyfield campus.

"Here we are," Bibb said, returning with a plate of cookies. "I see you've discovered another one of my apartment's prime **assets**."

"This view is great," Caitlin said. "It must make you feel like a king looking out over his **domain**."

Bibb chuckled. "Some say I do live like a king. Unfortunately, the days of **monarchy** are long gone and my **regal** ambitions must be otherwise **gratified**."

The professor lowered his sizable **girth** into a high-backed armchair opposite her. With pronounced effort, he leaned forward and began to serve. "I found this tea in a little shop in London last summer. It's delightful. One sugar or two?"

"None, thank you."

"Cream?"

"No, thanks."

"How **abstemious** of you, my dear!" Bibb exclaimed. "But I should have known. Your article on the Shakespeare radio **colloquium** was so evenhanded."

"Thank you," Caitlin replied.

"Perhaps too evenhanded."

"What do you mean?"

"I must say, there was a **veritable plethora** of **outlandish speculation** being bandied about. Not all theories deserve equal space, you know."

"That may be," Caitlin said, trying to steer clear of any **ideological** booby traps, "but as a reporter my job is to relate what's said and report the facts. I'm not an editor."

"Ah, yes. Of course," Bibb sighed. "Tell me, Ms. Ciccone, what facts are you looking for today?"

"We're investigating the attacks on Professor Hargrave and Leo Kabnis."

"Leo Kabnis, the honors student?" Concern clouded Bibb's usually **jovial** expression.

"Yes," Caitlin said, monitoring his reaction beneath a casual mask. "It happened last night. Someone clubbed him on the head in his room."

"That's dreadful, simply dreadful!"

"The doctors think he's going to be okay."

"I hope so," Bibb said. "I'd read about poor Hargrave—in your newspaper, in fact. But now Leo Kabnis too? That's absolutely **appalling**."

"There's reason to believe that the incidents are somehow connected to the Prospero collection."

"Yes?"

"I was hoping you could answer a few questions."

"Gladly," he said, holding out a plate of cookies. "Please, help yourself."

"Thanks. That book I was just looking at, that's a rare book, right?"

"Very. It's an eighteenth-century copy of a famous Sufi text, *Secrets of Illuministic Wisdom*, by Ibn Sabin."

"Sufi—what's that?"

"The Sufis are a **sect** of Islam. They claim to teach the **arcane doctrine** behind all religions. Recent scholarship indicates that the **ascetic** St. Francis of Assisi may have practiced Sufism, and of course you remember King Arthur's famous Knights of the Round Table?"

"Yes?"

"They and other chivalrous organizations—and even the fraternities on our very own campus—may be **derivative**, whether they know it or not, of a **sect** of Sufis called the Khidr Order. In fact, the Black Prince's Order of the Garter was quite likely a mistranslation of that."

Caitlin took a sip of her tea. "So the Khidr Order was a kind of **prototype**."

"Yes, although its many **emulators** have always managed to misunderstand the **radical** mysticism at the heart of its practices."

"How did you get your hands on this book? Was it expensive?"

"Luck," Bibb said with a **subtle** wink. "Years ago, when I was a junior faculty member in Alabama, I went to an estate auction on the outskirts of Tuscaloosa. The recently deceased had at one time inherited an odd miscellany from a forebear who had dabbled in theosophy, alchemy, phrenology, and other nonsense. No one knew what the books were, let alone what they were worth. I picked up the whole lot for $150."

"What would a collector pay for the Sufi book now?"

"It's insured for two hundred thousand dollars."

"Two hundred thousand? Why don't you sell it?"

Bibb frowned. "I'm a collector, not a **speculator**. A book like that is priceless to me."

"Aren't you afraid someone will steal it?"

"Ms. Ciccone, the world of rare book collectors, especially those who buy and sell items of this caliber, is **relatively** circumscribed and, shall we say, incestuous. It would be **foolhardy** for one of them to **purloin** it. Besides, I'm a leading expert in this field. I'm a contributing editor of the *Journal of the International Antiquarian Society*. I receive all the newsletters and catalogues and attend most of the auctions. If anyone attempted to resell it, at least in a lawful manner, I'd be sure to find out about it."

"What if, like you, the thief didn't want to sell the book but just wanted it for its **intrinsic** value and beauty?"

Professor Bibb's shaggy eyebrows twitched and then relaxed. He looked down his bulbous nose at Caitlin and chuckled.

"So I'm a suspect? I'm honored, Ms. Ciccone. Yes," he added with a **devious** glint in his eye, "if I were you, I'd put me right at the top of your list. My qualifications are **impeccable**: I'm a **bibliophile**. I'm one of the executors. My lifestyle appears to be **opulent**. I was friends with Edward Anthony Prospero."

"So do you think," Caitlin cut in, "there could be a valuable document that might have **motivated** the attacks?"

"Do you think," Bibb asked in response, "I'd be chatting over tea with you if I thought there was some **exceptional** treasure for the taking at Tillinghast Library?"

Before Caitlin could answer the question, the professor stood and shuffled over to an escritoire in the corner of the living room. He opened a drawer, removed a manila envelope, and returned to his seat. "Here's a **preliminary** list of the contents of the Prospero collection," he said. "**Peruse** it at your leisure. I doubt you'll find any surprises."

Caitlin set down her cup and took the envelope. "Who **compiled** this list?"

"I did," Bibb said with a **complacent** smile.

Chapter 20

Words, Words, Srdow

After finishing dinner at seven o'clock, Caitlin, Phil, and Leo went up to Leo's room to try to **decipher** the first clue in Prospero's letter. By nine-thirty, after much **speculation** and **virtually** no progress, the two freshmen were ready to abandon the whole business.

Languid and **sluggish** after a long day of difficult classes, Phil sprawled **apathetically** on the couch, an arm draped over his eyes. He thought about his essay for Professor Torres's English 112. It was Tuesday night, the paper was due Friday, and he still had neither a **rudimentary** understanding of Dickinson's poem nor the slightest notion of how he could manage to write something **articulate** and **coherent** about it. Fatigue had wrapped him in a soft **shroud** of **stupefaction.**

Caitlin, on the other hand, resolved to get something worthwhile accomplished. She stretched out on the carpet, stuck a cushion under her head, and began reading a chapter in one of her textbooks.

Leo continued to sit quietly in his armchair by the window, **perusing** the books on cryptography that Phil had brought him and scribbling notes on a yellow legal pad.

After several minutes of silence, Phil lifted his arm and looked at Caitlin.

"What are you reading?" he asked.

She glanced up at him and smiled. "Words, words, words."

Phil looked puzzled.

"It's from *Hamlet*," she explained.

"You're reading *Hamlet*?"

"No, the quotation's from *Hamlet*."

"No, it's not from *Hamlet*," Leo mumbled from his chair in the corner. "It's from something else."

"It most certainly is from *Hamlet*," Caitlin said.

"What is?" asked Phil.

"What I just said."

"What did you just say?"

"'Words, words, words,'" Caitlin said.

Phil frowned. "What about 'words, words, words'?"

"It's a quotation from *Hamlet*!"

"No, I think it's from another play by Shakespeare," Leo said, his attention still fixed on his notes.

"Which play?" Phil asked.

"I don't know yet," Leo said.

"It is too from *Hamlet*," Caitlin said. "Polonius thinks Hamlet may be insane, so he tries to have a **rational** conversation with him to find out. But when he sees Hamlet with a book and asks what he's reading, Hamlet, who's being sullen and **intractable**, just says, 'Words, words, words.'"

"That's right," Leo said, scribbling another note on his pad. "You must know the play well, Caitlin."

"Well enough," Caitlin said, **exasperated.**

"So you're reading *Hamlet* for an English class?" Phil asked.

Caitlin rolled her eyes. "No, I was quoting from it."

"Yes, I know you were," Leo said.

"That's what I'm trying to tell you!" Caitlin shouted.

"Let me get this straight," Phil said. "You're not actually reading *Hamlet*. You're reading something else?"

Caitlin groaned. "Right."

"I see," Phil said.

"But when I quoted from *Hamlet*, Leo said the line was from something else by Shakespeare."

"I didn't say that," Leo said.

"Oh yes you did!" Caitlin insisted. "You said 'words, words, words' was from some other play by Shakespeare!"

"I think you did, Leo," Phil said.

"No I didn't," Leo **asserted**.

"Yes you did!" cried Caitlin.

Leo slapped his pencil down on his notepad and looked up. "Look, I know that line's from *Hamlet*, but I wasn't talking about *Hamlet*. I was referring to this **complex** doggone cipher I'm trying to figure out!"

"Oh," said Caitlin.

"Which seems to be a quotation from another Shakespearean play," Leo said.

"I see," said Phil.

"Sorry," Caitlin said. "I guess I wasn't following your train of thought."

Leo grunted and turned his attention back to his notes.

There was an awkward pause.

Finally Phil said, "So, what *are* you reading, Caitlin?"

Caitlin **grimaced**. "Something for my psychology class. It's called *Principles of Human Communication*."

"I did it!" Leo cried half an hour later. He set down his notepad and pencil, closed his book, and released a deep sigh. "I finally **deciphered** the first clue."

Phil, who had **succumbed** to the **soporific** effect of a soft couch, was deep in the grip of a catnap.

Caitlin snapped her book shut. "You're kidding! That's great!" She got to her feet and shook Phil. "Phil, wake up! Leo's figured out the clue."

Phil sat up slowly and looked at them through bleary eyes. "Sorry guys. I'm feeling a bit **scatterbrained**. It was kind of a rough day."

Caitlin sat down on the couch next to Phil. "C'mon, Leo. Don't keep us in suspense. What did you find out?"

"Well, for one thing, that Prospero sure was a master of **obfuscation**. The clue turned out to be a transposition cipher. It's two quotations from Shakespeare."

"Shakespeare again?" Phil said, **stifling** a yawn.

"What's a transposition cipher?" Caitlin asked.

"Two of the most common methods for writing secret messages are the substitution cipher and the transposition cipher," Leo explained. "In the substitution cipher, one letter—or number or symbol—stands for another. For example, *x* might stand for *e,* 8 for *a,* the plus sign for *o.* It's **arbitrary**—whatever the person writing the code decides. In a transposition cipher, the letters of the message are arranged into groups of the same number of letters, then the letters in each group are jumbled according to a formula—first letter last, last letter second, fourth letter third, whatever. Of course, there are a great many possible jumbling formulas, which makes it difficult to decode."

"How'd you manage to figure it out?" asked Phil. He was feeling more awake now, and his curiosity was piqued.

"Here, I'll show you," Leo said, picking up his yellow notepad and motioning for Phil and Caitlin to join him. When they had positioned themselves on either side of his armchair, Leo pointed to three rows of gibberish:

HLTLA LORWE TASSD NEAGA TLLAD
NMEEH ODWNA ENMEM PLYER RYEALS.
NMIAI FISHT TESRO NDINA ANSAM EARPPL.

"That was the original clue from Prospero's letter," he said. "As you can see, there are periods at the ends of the second and third lines, which would indicate that there are two sentences. Each sentence is arranged in groups of five letters, with the last group consisting of six letters."

"Got it," said Phil.

"Go on," said Caitlin.

"Once I determined this was a transposition cipher, I started testing different formulas for decoding the five-letter groups. That was the hard part. By trial and error and process of elimination I finally figured out it was a 5-3-4-2-1 arrangement, with the two final six-letter groups 5-3-4-2-1-6."

"And so?" said Caitlin.

"And so this is what I got for the first sentence," Leo said. He flipped back several pages of notes and pointed to two neatly penciled lines:

> ALL THE WORLD'S A STAGE AND ALL
> THE MEN AND WOMEN MERELY PLAYERS.

"Isn't that from Shakespeare's *As You Like It*?" Caitlin asked.

"It is indeed," Leo said. "And so is the second sentence." He flipped another page and pointed again.

> I AM IN THIS FOREST AND IN MAN'S APPAREL.

"That's **ingenious**!" Phil said.

"It sure is," Caitlin said, "but I still don't understand how you did it. Can you explain it again?"

"Sure," Leo said. "Maybe if I work backward it'll be easier to understand." He turned to a fresh page in his notepad and began to write. "If you take the first sentence of the decoded message—'All the world's a stage, and all the men and women merely players'—and break it up into five-letter groups, this is what it would look like:"

> ALLTH EWORL DSAST AGEAN DALLT
> HEMEN ANDWO MENME RELYP LAYERS.

"Now," he went on, continuing to write, "following the 5-3-4-2-1 formula, if you put the fifth letter in each group first, the third letter second, the fourth letter third, the second letter fourth, and the first letter fifth, this is what you get:"

HLTLA LORWE TASSD NEAGA TLLAD
NMEEH ODWNA ENMEM PLYER RYEALS.

"Now I follow you," Caitlin said.

Leo scribbled quickly again. "So, if you break up the second sentence—'I am in this forest, and in man's apparel'—into five-letter groups, it reads like this:"

IAMIN THISF OREST ANDIN MANSA PPAREL.

"And when you switch the letters around according to the formula, this is the code:"

NMIAI FISHT TESRO NDINA ANSAM EARPPL.

"Leo, you're a genius!" Caitlin exclaimed.

Leo flashed a smile. "Just a minor one."

"But a member of that most **sagacious** and **perspicacious** league nonetheless," said Phil.

Caitlin poked Phil in the ribs. "Whoa, listen to those ten-dollar SAT words. You're even a poet, and you don't know it."

Phil chuckled. "I seem to rhyme all the time." He turned to Leo. "So, what now, chief?"

Leo looked up. "What do you mean?"

"Now that you've **deciphered** the clue," Phil said, "what are we supposed to do with it?"

"Yeah, Leo," Caitlin said, "what do those quotations mean?"

Leo frowned and began pacing the floor. "That's a good question."

"Here's an idea," Caitlin said brightly. "Since the quotations are from Shakespeare, maybe their meaning has something to do with Shakespeare."

"And maybe with this Elizabethan Festival," Phil suggested.

"But Prospero's dead," Caitlin **countered**. "He couldn't have known about the festival."

"He might have been involved in planning it, or known it was in the works."

"That seems **tangential**. I think the clue is some kind of riddle."

Leo stopped pacing and flung himself into his armchair. "I agree it's probably a riddle, but what does it **imply**?"

"That it has something to do with Shakespeare," said Phil.

"And Shakespeare was a playwright," said Caitlin.

"Meaning he wrote for the stage," said Leo.

"So maybe it's something to do with the theater?" Phil asked hopefully.

"Yes," Leo said. "The first sentence would seem to suggest that: 'All the world's a stage, and all the men and women merely players.'"

"What are 'players'?" Phil asked.

"Actors—people in the play," Leo said.

"Okay, so you've got a stage, and you've got actors—that's the theater, right?"

"Right, but which theater? The theater of the world? The theater of human relations? The theater of the **absurd**?"

"I think you're being too intellectual and **abstract**," Caitlin said. "It's a riddle, right? So it probably refers to the theater right here on campus—the Stink."

Leo nodded. "I think you've got something there."

"Yeah, Caitlin. That was very **perceptive**," Phil said. "But what about the second quotation?"

Leo picked up his notepad and read aloud: "'I am in this forest, and in man's apparel.'"

"That doesn't seem **pertinent** to the theater," Phil said.

"No, it doesn't," Caitlin said. "What would the Stink have in common with a forest and men's apparel? That sounds more like a garment factory in the woods or something."

"Maybe it's a **metaphor**," Leo suggested.

"That makes sense," Caitlin said. "Riddles are often **metaphorical**."

"So maybe the forest stands for something else?" Phil suggested.

"Right," Leo said.

"Like what, a lumber yard full of mannequins dressed in men's suits?" Caitlin said.

Phil grinned. "Talk about **tangential**!"

Leo gently scratched his head just below his bandage. "No, I don't think Caitlin's too far off the mark."

"Well, what's your **analysis**, chief?" Phil asked.

Leo tapped the eraser end of his pencil against his notepad several times. "If the stage and the actors indicate a theater, and if, as Caitlin so **insightfully inferred**, the theater in question is our very own Stink, then where in the Stink might there be a 'forest' full of men's apparel?"

"In the costume room!" cried Caitlin.

"Precisely," Leo said.

"Took the words right out of my mouth," Phil mumbled.

Leo checked his watch: 10:45. His head was still throbbing despite the aspirin he'd taken earlier. "Are you sure you guys'll be all right without me?" he asked.

"Yes, of course," Caitlin said. "We'll do everything just as you said—sneak into the theater when the play's over at eleven, hide until midnight when everything's closed up, then get down to the basement and find the costume room."

"Be sure to check all the Shakespearean costumes, especially the ones for men," Leo said. "'I am in this forest, and in *man's* apparel,' remember?"

"Right," Caitlin said. "Now you just get some rest and get rid of that headache, okay? We need you well if we're going to solve all these clues and find this treasure."

"Thanks," Leo said, patting her on the shoulder. He turned to Phil. "Did you get a flashlight?"

Phil nodded. "Chris lent me one. It's right here." He patted the side of his jacket.

"Good luck, guys," Leo said as the two freshman started out the door. "As they say in the theater, break a leg."

Caitlin turned and looked at Leo. "I know you're worried, but don't be. We won't disappoint you."

"I know you won't," Leo said, hoping she was right.

Chapter 21

Clothes Make the Man

"Caitlin?"

"Uh-huh?"

"Did you hear something?"

Caitlin and Phil stood absolutely still in the dark hallway in the basement of the Stink. In the silence, Caitlin could almost hear her heart beat as Phil's flashlight swept the shadowy space. Every object the moving beam of light touched—stray props, sections of painted scenery, a broom, a mannequin, a rickety table on its side—loomed out of the dark with **uncanny** liveliness.

"No, I didn't," Caitlin replied. She half expected the beam to reveal some **amorphous, chimerical** monster—the Phantom of the Stink—lying in wait for them. Not wanting to **succumb** to her fears, she added, "You must be imagining things."

"No, I'm not. Listen." Phil cocked his head and concentrated.

What might have been a **suppressed** sigh or cough or a padded step or an **indistinct** rustling seemed to come from directly behind them. Or was it above them? Caitlin couldn't be sure. In fact, she wasn't even sure she'd heard anything at all.

"I think it came from over there," Phil said. He took a few steps forward and aimed the beam at a gray door halfway down the hall on the right. "Let's try that one," he suggested.

Caitlin turned the knob. Although it seemed unlocked, the door didn't budge. She turned the knob again and, leaning against the gray metal, gave it a good shove. Again her efforts were **ineffectual**; the heavy door remained fixed.

Phil joined her at the door. The metal surface felt warm against their hands. They looked at each other for a moment, and then, when Caitlin nodded, they threw their shoulders against the door. This time it gave.

Phil waved the flashlight around the small, cramped room. A large furnace **dominated** the left side. Thick **insulated** pipes and electrical conduits ran along the ceiling. To the right of the door a fuse box and a row of switches hung on the wall.

Phil shook his head. "The boiler room. I guess I got worked up over nothing. You were right. I must've been hallucinating."

"It's easy to do that in the dark," Caitlin said. "Maybe this will help." She flipped on several of the switches by the door. A bare bulb hanging from a cord filled the cinderblock cubicle with harsh light. Out in the hall, a row of fluorescent lamps stuttered to life. Caitlin and Phil turned and saw the **spectral** props and flats that had seemed so **evocative** and **forbidding** in the semidarkness dissolve into the **mundane** and **literal** objects that they were.

Phil turned off the flashlight and put it in the inside pocket of his varsity jacket. Caitlin, wasting no time, began checking the doors on the left side of the hall.

Phil followed her lead and began checking the ones on the right. He peeked into a small rehearsal space, a storage room, and a janitor's closet with a sink.

"Hey, Phil. Over here." Caitlin's voice was muffled and distant.

Phil looked down the hall. At the far end a door was ajar. He could see that inside the room was lit.

He walked to the doorway. The **commodious** room was a wonderland of costumes and accessories. Along the right wall were two working tables, a sewing machine, three chairs, a mannequin, an ironing board, and a small curtained area for dressing. Racks and racks of outfits, separated by narrow aisles, ran across the room. More garments were heaped on shelves along the walls. Here and there boxes, bags, or piles of clothing for which no better place could be found had been deposited. The room was packed to the brim, **surfeited** with a smorgasbord of garb.

"Caitlin, where are you?"

Above the sea of shirts and coats and dresses, a hand waved to him. "Over here."

Phil charted a course down the left side of the room and found Caitlin standing behind a mound of petticoats. She was engaged in a **methodical** search—removing articles of clothing from their hangers, carefully examining them, then hanging them back up. Phil looked at the long aisle and multiplied that by the number of rows he guessed the room contained.

"We're never going to find it," he mumbled.

"We're certainly not going to find it if you keep thinking like that," Caitlin replied. "Let's just work together on one aisle at a time. Why don't you start on the other side of this one and work toward the front. I'll work toward the back."

"It's a plan," Phil said without enthusiasm.

"And remember," Caitlin added, "if you come across any Shakespearean costumes—especially ones for men—let me know."

"How will I know it's a Shakespearean costume?"

"Oh, come on. That's simple. Doublets, long gowns with trains, **regal** robes—that kind of **archaic** stuff."

Phil felt she was **belittling** his intelligence. "What do you think I am, a **philistine**?" he asked in a **sarcastic** tone. "I hate to remind you, but that's not the kind of stuff they were wearing in *Romeo and Juliet* the other night. They were wearing **contemporary** clothing."

"All right, fine," Caitlin said, throwing up her hands with impatience. "We'll check the modern clothing too. Why **differentiate**? We'll check everything, if you want. Just pay close attention to anything that looks Elizabethan, okay?" She turned her back to him and continued to **scrutinize** the items on the rack.

Phil shrugged and walked around to the other side of the aisle. "So what exactly are we looking for in these costumes?"

"Something written, probably. Maybe a symbol. Maybe a book. I don't know."

"How can you find something if you don't know what you're looking for?" he protested.

"We'll know it when we find it," was her **enigmatic** reply.

"That makes no sense at all," he insisted.

"Yes, it does. If you knew what you were looking for, you wouldn't have to look for it."

"Isn't it possible that if you don't know what it is, you won't know it when you find it?"

"Yes, I guess so. We may not find it. But if we look, at least we'll have a chance of finding it. If we don't, we won't."

Phil couldn't **refute** this last argument, so he laid aside his doubts and joined the search.

For a solid hour they worked their way through the racks in silence. The sheer **abundance** of outfits was overwhelming. In addition, there seemed to be no **discernible** scheme according to which the items had been stored. The aisles did not progress according to historical and geographical origins, moving from one era and country to the next, nor was the collection arranged by function. The whole thing seemed **haphazard** and **arbitrary**.

Caitlin sighed. She looked at the **plethora** of costumes running down the aisle and shook her head. Maybe Phil was right, she thought. This is **futile**, like looking for a needle in a haystack. She removed a pair of commedia dell'arte pantaloons from the rack, gave them a **perfunctory** search, then hung them back up in disgust.

She yawned. "Phil?"

"Yeah?" came his **lethargic** response from the next aisle.

"How's it going over there?"

"All right, but I'm a little beat."

"Me too," she **conceded**. She felt too **enervated** and **listless** to continue the search, so she slumped down on the floor and leaned against a box of shoes. "Well, what are we going to do?" she asked.

There was no response. She noticed the room had grown silent. "Phil? Are you there?"

Phil popped out of a thicket of costumes a few feet from where Caitlin reclined. He was wearing a flowing purple robe **embellished** with gold crescent moons and brandishing a black staff with a small star affixed to its end.

"Cute!" she said **sarcastically**.

"Thanks," he said. "I thought you needed a little cheering up. You sounded so discouraged."

"Where did you find that wild costume?"

"Over in the corner. The tag says 'TPST.'"

"TPST?" Caitlin jumped to her feet.

Before he knew what was happening, she was all over him, delving into pockets and running her hands up and down his sides.

"Hey, that tickles! Stop it!"

"Hold still," she commanded, **dispensing** with **decorum** in the heat of excitement. "Don't you see, Phil? 'TPST' stands for *The Tempest*—by Shakespeare! The **protagonist** is an old magician named Prospero."

"Prospero?"

"Yeah, as in Edward Anthony. I think you're wearing the very thing we've been looking for!"

"I am?"

"Yes. Turn around," she ordered.

Bewildered, Phil did as he was told.

He could feel her fingers checking the hood and slipping inside the collar. Then she started down the back seam. Her fingers paused about halfway.

"There's something in the lining. Bend over."

Phil obeyed and Caitlin flipped back the tail of the robe. He felt a tug and then heard a rip.

"Eureka!" Caitlin shouted. "Look at this!"

Phil stood and turned. In her thumb and forefinger Caitlin held a yellowed piece of parchment.

Phil tossed the robe on a nearby mound of clothing. "What is it? Let me see."

Caitlin gently unfolded the brittle paper. There were several incomplete lines of writing in **florid** penmanship, much of it smudged and **illegible**. Two edges of the parchment were clean and two were ragged. It seemed to be a fragment torn from a larger document.

"You're brilliant!" Phil cried. He threw his arms around Caitlin and hugged her.

"You're the one who found the robe," she told him. "If I ever go looking for gold, remind me to bring you—"

Suddenly a door banged shut.

"What's that?" Caitlin whispered, grabbing Phil's arm.

"I don't know," he whispered back as all the lights in the room went out.

Through the darkness they could hear slow, heavy, **inexorable** footsteps approaching.

Caitlin quickly slipped the parchment into her shirt pocket. Phil removed the flashlight from his jacket, switched it on, and aimed it at the sound.

Out of the shadows, an **obscure**, towering figure lumbered toward them. It was a man, dressed in black, his face covered by a hideous Harlequin half-mask.

A blade glinted in his hand.

"Caitlin, quick. Take the flashlight and stand back," Phil whispered. "This guy's got a knife. When he goes for me, run for the door, okay?"

Caitlin took the flashlight, but before she could do much else the menacing **assailant** was upon them.

Phil assumed a martial arts posture.

The huge man crouched, then lunged at Phil's chest with the knife.

Phil stepped back **adroitly** and the thrust fell short. He feinted with his left hand, throwing his **antagonist** off guard, then slammed his right fist in the man's belly. As his opponent bent forward in pain, Phil spun around and delivered a roundhouse kick to the side of his head.

Caitlin saw the man drop the knife and fall **headlong** toward her. He hit the floor with a thud and groaned.

"Come on, Phil! Let's get out of here!"

They jumped over the body and fled from the room, knocking over clothes and boxes.

XXI XII MDXCIX

From the shallow drawer on top of his new two-volume boxed set of *The Oxford English Dictionary,* affectionately known as the *OED,* Leo removed a heavy, black-handled magnifying glass. He turned to Phil and Caitlin, who were sitting on the couch. "I didn't know we had a karate expert on our floor," he said.

"Tae kwon do, actually," Phil corrected him. "And I'm no expert. My dad was in special forces in Vietnam. He taught me a few moves, just in case."

"Good thing he did," Leo said, slapping the weighty lens against his palm. "That guy in the costume room meant business."

"No question about that," Caitlin muttered, the image of the **grotesque** mask and **lethal** knife still fresh in her memory.

"I wonder if he was acting independently or working for someone else," Leo **mused.** "Or maybe there are several people out there trying to follow us to the treasure."

"Are you **implying** there's a **conspiracy**?" Caitlin asked.

"I have no idea. All I'm suggesting is that when a guy pulls a knife on you, it's **prudent** to consider every possible **motive** for his behavior."

Phil leaned forward and looked at his freshman counselor. "Do you think we should go to the police?"

Leo pondered the proposal for a moment. "Normally I
wouldn't hesitate to report something this serious, but this is
an **exceptional** situation."

He sat down in an armchair opposite the two freshmen.
"In the first place, you guys weren't supposed to be inside
the theater any more than the guy who attacked you was. So
you'd have to **prevaricate** about what you were doing down
there. Also, if the police got involved, *The Plains* would report the incident. That would put Bill in an awkward position because then he'd have to run something in the *Herald*,
and publicity just isn't something we want right now."

Leo paused and gently probed the slim bandage on his
head. "Going to the police and the newspapers might help
bring the culprit to justice. But submitting to grueling **inter-
rogations** and having our names splashed all over the front
page clearly would **impede** our search for the treasure. It
might also make whoever's on our trail even more desperate
and **ruthless**. So for now I think we need to be **circumspect**
and guard our secret **diligently**, even if it means taking some
unusual risks." He released a deep sigh. "I feel bad about
what happened to you guys. I shouldn't have let you go
alone."

"Don't worry about it, chief," Phil said. "It turned out
okay. We didn't get hurt and, miraculously enough, we
found what we were looking for."

"We'll see." Leo picked up the piece of parchment from
the coffee table and held it up to the light. The script was **inscrutable**. He set the fragment back down and examined it
with the magnifying glass. Caitlin and Phil watched the expression on his face **oscillate** between curiosity and perplex-
ity. Then suddenly he looked uneasy, as if he were in the
grip of some **quandary**.

"What does it say?" Caitlin asked.

Leo stood up. "I'm not sure, but I have an idea."

As Leo crossed the room to his bookcase, Phil picked up the magnifying glass and he and Caitlin leaned forward to have a closer look at the **paltry** scrap of paper. Through the lens the enlarged handwriting appeared more consistent and neat, but still alien and **incomprehensible**.

"I can't make out a word of this," Phil said.

Caitlin nodded. "It's as if someone's trying to tease us. Do you think this is another one of Prospero's practical jokes?"

"I bet it is," Phil **surmised**. "I bet it's another one of his codes, where every letter in our alphabet **correlates** with a letter in some other alphabet."

Leo pulled a thick **tome** from one of his shelves. "It's not a code and there's no other alphabet. This is in our alphabet, only a much earlier version." He set the **ponderous** book on the coffee table next to the piece of parchment.

"What's that?" Caitlin asked him.

"A history of typography. I'm hoping we'll find a type-face or script that roughly corresponds to the handwriting in the fragment. That will help us **transcribe** the message into something we can read. If we're lucky, that something will turn out to be in English."

Caitlin began flipping through the thick, creamy pages. "Where do we start?"

"Let's try the late Middle Ages," Leo said. "I once saw a facsimile of the Kelmscott Chaucer that looked similar to the writing on this parchment—and that was equally **arcane**." He reached under the coffee table and retrieved a notepad and pen. "Phil, want to play scribe?"

"Sure, chief."

"P-l-a-y-e-r," Leo spelled, studying the document with the magnifying glass and comparing what he saw to the sample on the page. "Did you get that?"

"Sure did." Phil laid the **transcription** on the table and they **scrutinized** their hour's worth of work.

> xxi xii mdxcix
>
> lind,
>
> y at playing with one
> I am no clownish custard,
> tion. When I say 'Not one
> ivocate. Again, know well
> hat authority rules longest
> elf **manifest**. The player

Caitlin pointed to the left and bottom edges of the parchment. "Too bad it's torn. As it stands, it's gibberish."

"Not entirely," Leo said. "The content may be **opaque** but the form is **lucid**. Look at the upper right-hand corner."

Caitlin looked at the **amalgam** of x's and i's and drew a blank. "Another code?"

"I don't think so."

"How about an algebra problem? Or a diagram for a football play?" Phil joked.

"They're Roman numerals, like the ones on the cornerstones of buildings," Leo said. "It's a date."

Phil leaned over the piece of parchment and studied the Roman numerals. "Let's see. Twenty-one, twelve, fifteen hundred and ninety-nine." He looked up, a puzzled expression on his face. "How can this be a date? There's no twenty-first month."

"Maybe the writer was British," Caitlin said. "Don't the British put the day first, then the month, then the year?"

Leo smiled. "Very **astute**, Caitlin."

"Which would make it the twenty-first of December, 1599," Phil said. "Wow, this thing's almost four hundred years old!"

Caitlin looked at Leo. "Do you think this is a fragment of a letter?"

"Probably," Leo replied, rubbing his chin. "But we won't know for sure until we solve Prospero's other clues, which I suspect will lead us to the rest of the document."

Phil let out a loud, **protracted** yawn. "I don't know about you guys, but I'm definitely not looking forward to waking up tomorrow morning."

"What do you mean 'tomorrow'?" Caitlin said. "It's already today." She pointed to the digital clock on the table beside the telephone. "It's practically four in the morning."

"No wonder I feel so **listless** and **apathetic**," Phil said as he snuggled into a corner of the couch.

Caitlin yawned. "Me too. My brain's getting **sluggish**."

"To tell the truth," Leo said, "I'm feeling pretty **phlegmatic** and **incoherent** myself. Why don't we get together again after we get some rest—"

"Amen," Caitlin murmured.

"—and then go see Carmen Torres."

At the mention of his English professor's name, Phil opened his drooping eyelids. "Why do we need to see her, Leo?"

"She's a good friend and mentor who also happens to know a lot about the Renaissance. I think she could help us place the writing on this piece of parchment you found tonight. Besides, I was planning to ask her if she'd keep Prospero's letter for us. Now I'm hoping she'll keep both documents."

"Why do you want her to have them?" Caitlin asked.

"She once told me she has a safe in her house. Phil's room and my room have already been ransacked. Yours could be next. Carmen has office hours from one to three tomorrow—I mean today. I think we should all go see her then. Any objections?"

Caitlin shook her head.

"It's okay by me," Phil said, "as long as nobody mentions the paper I'm supposed to write for her by Friday. I haven't the slightest idea yet what I'm going to say."

"I hear you," Leo said, giving Phil a knowing wink. "I'll help you with it Thursday if you want, and you can type it up on my computer when you're done."

Phil smiled. "Thanks, chief. I owe you one."

"Don't worry about it." Leo stood up. "Caitlin, you won't take it as an insult if Phil and I offer to walk you back to LaSalle, will you?"

"Of course not," Caitlin said, getting up. "As my dad always says, 'The better part of **valor** is **discretion**.' I'm independent but not **foolhardy**."

Phil stretched out into the space Caitlin had vacated on the couch. "What do you mean, 'Phil and I'? I'm happy right here."

"You're going to have to get up eventually," Caitlin said. "Besides, after what happened tonight there's no way I'm going to walk across campus at this hour without Mr. Phil Kwon Do."

Phil laughed. "All right, I'm coming," he said, dragging himself to his feet.

Ay, Here's the Rub

Wednesday

Torres took off her thin-rimmed glasses and leaned back in her chair. "This really is most extraordinary!"

"Then you'll help us?" Leo asked.

The professor stood and walked over to the window. The warm midafternoon sun fell across her **contemplative** face. "He could have been a prince during the Italian Renaissance," she **mused**, momentarily **oblivious** to Leo's question.

"Who could have?" Caitlin asked.

"Prospero. Edward Anthony Prospero." Torres turned from the window. "Leo, do you recall that painting of Cosimo de' Medici by Giuseppe Abbruzzese?"

"The one in which he's **portrayed** with his arm resting on the picture frame, only the frame isn't really a frame but an illusion painted on the canvas?"

"Yes. It was a common technique meant to **convey** the presence of a person's influence even in his or her absence."

"I don't get the connection," Phil said.

"In sending Leo on this quest," Carmen explained, "it's as if Prospero wanted to **exert** control and guide Leo's destiny, even from the grave. His will was powerful indeed."

She returned to her desk and sat down. "In answer to your question, Leo, yes, I will keep these documents in my safe at home and assist you in any way I can. As your professor and friend, that's the least I can do. Besides," she said with a **conspiratorial** grin, "how could I resist the chance to help solve such an **engrossing** mystery?"

"Thanks, Carmen," Leo said. "I knew we could count on you."

"Don't mention it." Torres put on her glasses and picked up Prospero's letter-map. "Tell me, does anyone beyond this room know about this?"

"Just Bill Berkowitz," Caitlin said.

"But someone else definitely knows we have it," Phil added.

Torres frowned. "Who?"

"We're not sure," Leo said, "but whoever it is wants it in a serious way." He described the encounter with the knife-wielding thug in the costume room.

"Generally speaking, people don't resort to force based on **speculation**," Torres said. "It would seem that this person must know something we don't about the nature and value of this treasure. But there's one thing I don't understand."

"What's that?" Leo asked.

"You received Prospero's letter at last Sunday's meeting. Since then you've **divulged** its contents to only four people: Bill, Caitlin, Phil, and me. How could anyone else have found out enough about it to **harass** Hargrave and the three of you?"

"Carmen, that's not the letter I got at the executors' meeting. Something—**intuition**, I guess—told me the one I got there was **apocryphal**. Certain things about it didn't look right. We found the real letter by pure coincidence. It was inside a Shakespeare primer that Phil took out of the library Monday morning."

Torres took off her glasses and leaned across her desk. "Are you **implying** someone made a switch before the meeting?"

"Yes. I think someone saw Prospero's letter, made a **forgery** to give to me, then hid the original in that Shakespeare book temporarily, intending to retrieve it later. By sheer luck it got back into the appropriate hands."

"Did you share that suspicion with anyone?"

"I went to Professor Hargrave's office that afternoon to tell him I thought the letter was **spurious**. Reggie was there too. He said he was certain Prospero didn't write it."

"That's interesting. And Hargrave was attacked that night, wasn't he?"

Leo nodded. "The question is, by whom?"

"I'll bet it was Teddy," Phil said. "Bill said Prospero left him nothing in his will. Maybe Teddy saw Prospero's letter to Leo and thinks this treasure is his rightful inheritance."

"So it could be the **vindictive** grandson," Torres said, "or it could very well be Prospero's trusted valet."

Caitlin giggled. "You mean the butler did it? That's so **hackneyed**."

"The notion may seem **trite**," Torres said, "but consider the facts. Reggie probably knew Prospero better than anyone. Moreover, he was the one who handed out the gifts at the executors' meeting last Sunday, so he had access to the original letter and could have made a switch. Also, he appears to have been the last person with Hargrave before he was attacked. Reggie's a big, **imposing** man. He could have gone after Hargrave and Leo, figuring one of them was lying and had the real letter. Physically, he also fits the description of the man in the Harlequin mask who attacked you in the theater."

Leo sighed. "If it were Teddy, it wouldn't surprise me. I know he and Tooth and Nail are in financial trouble. Plus he hates my guts. But Reggie? I just can't believe he's **culpable**. He's got money—Prospero left him a small fortune in his will. He'd never betray the old man like that. Or attack me. Reggie is the **epitome** of **rectitude** and loyalty. I consider him a friend."

"Money tests friendship," Torres said, "and it's not un-usual for people who have plenty of it to want even more."

"Maybe it was someone else close to Prospero, someone who got wind of this treasure and knew of his plan," Caitlin said. She looked at Leo. "You worked with Prospero. Any ideas?"

"The most logical suspects would be the executors—ex-cluding ourselves, of course," Leo added, smiling at Torres.

"And Hargrave too," Caitlin said.

"Why him?" asked Phil.

"He can't be a criminal and a victim **simultaneously**."

"Maybe he staged the assault and knocked himself out to throw the authorities off the scent."

Caitlin laughed. "Phil, you've been reading too many de-tective novels."

"So that leaves Bibb and Martext," Torres said, "who **revered** Prospero but also had considerable **reverence** for his **prosperity**—enough, perhaps, to become envious and **cov-etous** of it." She leaned back in her chair and put her hands behind her head. "Which means we now have four **plausible** suspects. It could be the **depraved** grandson, the **renegade** valet, the **avaricious** theater director, or the **acquisitive** Re-naissance Studies professor. I suppose it could even be some combination of the above—or even all of the above."

"Geez, it sounds like that board game Clue," Phil said.

Everyone laughed.

"Well, if we can't **deduce** who the culprit is, perhaps we can **dupe** him into revealing himself," Phil suggested.

"What do you mean?" asked Caitlin.

"Set a trap and draw him out. We could pretend to find the treasure. Then maybe he'd show up."

"Yeah," Caitlin said, growing excited. "Maybe we could ask Bill to run a bogus article in the *Herald*—"

"That just happens to mention where the treasure's being kept," Phil said, **galvanized** by Caitlin's enthusiasm.

"He'd be drawn to it like a bee to honey," Caitlin said.

"Then whammo!" Phil jumped up and **mimed** the act of taking a photograph. "We catch him red-handed."

"Wait a minute. Time out," Torres said, waving her arms like a referee. "Who do you think you are, the Mod Squad?"

Caitlin and Phil exchanged a baffled look.

"Mod squad? What's a mod squad?" Leo asked.

Torres chuckled. "'The Mod Squad' was a TV show years ago about a trio of young investigators like you guys—only they were undercover cops and you're not. Look. Your mission is not to **apprehend** and **incarcerate** criminals. It's to solve Prospero's clues and find the treasure, taking as few risks as possible." The professor slipped on her glasses and carefully picked up the piece of parchment on her desk. "Let's take a look at matters closer at hand, shall we?"

While Caitlin and Phil joined Torres in examining the fragment, Leo explained how they'd **transcribed** it. When he had finished, Torres said, "If this document is genuine, the date would **coincide** nicely with the two quotations from *As You Like It* that led you to the costume room."

"How's that?" Phil asked.

"The play was entered in the old English copyright records in August 1600. This fragment is dated late in 1599. Perhaps this is no **fortuitous** correspondence."

Caitlin looked at the torn scrap of parchment in the professor's hand. "Are you **implying** Shakespeare wrote that?"

Torres gave her a solemn nod. "There's not much to go on at this point, but I must confess, when I saw what Prospero wrote in his letter to Leo—that the treasure would 'astound not only you but also the world'—I immediately assumed it had something to do with Shakespeare, either some new biographical material or perhaps an actual manuscript. After all, Prospero was a **prominent** Shakespearean scholar."

"The coincidence of the clues and the date may simply be **attributable** to the old man's mania for quoting Shakespeare," Leo said. "It would have been normal for him to quote Shakespeare regardless of the nature of the prize. He practically thought in Shakespeare."

"True," Torres **conceded**. "Either way, I suppose, this fragment is quite a find." She removed a magnifying glass from her desk drawer and compared the writing on the fragile document with Leo's **transcription**. After a minute she said, "Leo, everything looks great, except for one **minuscule discrepancy**. The *u* in 'custard' looks more like an *o* to me."

"I wasn't sure about that," Leo replied. "But 'clownish costard' didn't make any sense to me."

"Is 'clownish custard' any less **cryptic**?"

"Not really, but at least 'custard' is a real word."

"So is 'costard,' if you change the *c* to upper case. 'Costard' is the name of a clown in *Love's Labour's Lost*."

"Isn't that one of Shakespeare's earliest plays?" Caitlin asked.

"Yes, it was probably completed about 1593. Shakespeare apparently revised it after that, for when it was first printed in 1598 the phrase 'newly corrected and **augmented**' appeared on the title page."

"But isn't that still too early for the date on this fragment?" Leo asked.

"Not if Shakespeare was working on a sequel. There is **credible** evidence showing that there was also a later play called *Love's Labour's Won*. In 1598 the English critic Francis Meres, in his *Palladis Tamia*, listed both *Love's Labour's Lost* and *Love's Labour's Won* as written by Shakespeare. So did a bookseller's catalogue from 1603 that was discovered in the 1950s. Until that catalogue turned up, most scholars thought *Love's Labour's Won* was simply another title for the play we know as *The Taming of the Shrew*, but now many believe it was a separate play that was mysteriously lost. Of course no copy has ever been found, so we know practically nothing else about it."

"That's fascinating," Caitlin said. "If in fact there was a sequel, maybe the same characters were carried over into it, and perhaps the writing on this piece of parchment is part of a letter that refers to this missing play."

"And if that's the case," Phil said, taking the **hypothesis** to its logical conclusion, "then maybe the treasure Prospero's letter refers to is that play itself."

A moment of silence fell over the room. Torres stood up and went to the window. "If Phil's right," she said finally, "then there's no telling how much money it would be worth."

"Or what someone would be willing to do to get it," Leo added.

Chapter 24

Use Your Dictionary

It was a little after midnight when Caitlin and Phil climbed the stairs to the fifth floor of Ericson Hall.

"You think Leo's still awake?" Caitlin asked as they reached the landing.

"Look," Phil reasoned, holding a piece of paper up as evidence. "His note specifically says, 'Come by my room after you're done with whatever you're doing tonight.' We went to the library. After that we saw Fellini's *La Strada*, which was excellent. And after that we went to Salerno's—"

"Which was also excellent."

"Now we're here," he continued. "If he's asleep, which I doubt, and we wake him up, we can say we were simply doing what he asked us to do."

They knocked on 5-A and Leo opened the door with **alacrity**, as if he had been standing there waiting for them to arrive.

"Well, hello!" he said, smiling broadly. "Come on in."

They stepped inside and Leo quickly closed the door. "You guys have good timing. Come over here and help me out."

He strode to the couch, where what appeared to be an old **unabridged** dictionary lay spread out on the cushions. The two freshmen followed and stood by his side.

"What can we do for you, chief?" asked Phil.

"Read me the numbers from the second clue." Leo pointed to the armchair. "They're over there, on my legal pad."

Phil headed toward the armchair, and Leo looked at Caitlin. "When I locate each word in this dictionary, write it down for me, okay?"

Caitlin nodded. She dug pen and paper out of her purse and sat down on the couch.

"Okay, Phil. Let's go," Leo said, bending over the old dictionary. "Read me the first set—slowly, okay?"

"Right, chief." Phil looked down at Leo's notepad, cleared his throat, and carefully **articulated** each number in the first set: "*0-0-0-1-1-0-4.*"

"*0-0-0-1-1-0-4,*" Leo repeated as he began thumbing through the front part of the big book. After a moment he stood up straight. "*A,*" he announced.

Caitlin looked back, puzzled. "'*A*'?"

"Yes, the letter *A*—it's the first word in the clue."

"Okay, whatever you say," Caitlin said, writing it down.

Leo signaled Phil for the next set of numbers.

"*2-9-2-5-2-0-7.*"

Leo flipped to the back pages of the dictionary. "*Wild,* Caitlin," he said after a moment.

"Yes," she agreed, "this *is* pretty wild."

"No, I meant *wild* is the second word."

"Oh, sorry," Caitlin said and wrote it down.

Phil read the next group: "*1-2-7-0-2-2-6.*"

Leo flipped to the middle of the dictionary and slowly ran his finger down a page, stopping near the bottom. "*Indulgent*!" he cried. "Now we're getting someplace. You got that, Caitlin? *Indulgent*?"

"Yeah." She wrote it down, then looked up at Leo. "I hate to say it, but I'm confused. What exactly are we doing here?"

"You're **facilitating** the process, Caitlin. Just hang on and I'll explain in a second. Phil, give me the next set."

A few minutes later Caitlin jotted down the final word of the decoded message. She looked at what she had written and shook her head. "This is weird. Leo, are you sure it's right?"

"Of course. It's a dictionary code. The numbers refer to specific words in this dictionary."

Caitlin rolled her eyes. "I think we gathered that much."

"All right, let me explain," Leo said, holding up his hands. "When I saw some examples of dictionary codes in one of the cryptography books, I noticed they looked similar to Professor Prospero's second clue. The thing about dictionary codes, though, is that both the code-writer and the code-reader have to know which dictionary the code refers to. In this case, Prospero knew and I didn't, so right away we had a major problem."

Phil laughed. "No kidding. There must be hundreds of dictionaries out there."

"That's right," Leo said, pointing an index finger at him, "but only one of them is the 1934 *Webster's New International*, Second Edition—the dictionary Prospero gave me last April on my twentieth birthday." He laughed and sat down on the couch. "I can't believe I was so **obtuse** and wasted all that time looking through the *OED*. In **retrospect**, it seems so obvious that he would use the dictionary he gave me as the code-breaker."

Caitlin patted Leo's shoulder. "Even an **indefatigable** mind like yours has to take a break once in a while."

"Anyway," Leo went on, "once you know which dictionary you're working with, cracking the code is simple. This baby here," he said, patting the dictionary beside him, "has more than three thousand pages, and each page has three columns. Now, you probably noticed that each group of numbers in the clue has seven digits. I figured the first four

digits would indicate the page number; the fifth would indicate the column—left, middle, or right; and the sixth and
seventh would indicate the headword, or boldfaced entry,
counted down from the top of the column."

"That's pretty **ingenious**," Phil said.

"I'm not sure I followed all of that," Caitlin said. "Can
you give me an example?"

"Be glad to." Leo set the big dictionary on his lap. "Pick a
word, any word," he told Caitlin. She pointed to a headword
at **random**.

"Okay," Leo said, "you chose *instinct.* It's on page 1287.
It's in the right-hand column—the third column. And," he
paused and counted down the column, "it's the twenty-third
word from the top. So, if you put all those numbers together,
the seven-digit code for the word *instinct* would be *1287323*:
page 1287, column three, twenty-third word down. Does
that help **clarify** it for you?"

Caitlin nodded. "Phil," she said, getting up from the
couch, "may I see the whole clue again?"

"Sure."

Phil handed her the notepad and Caitlin looked at the
numbers.

0001104 2925207 1270226 1877106
2910221 0966123 1528331-S 0966123
1253312 2181134 0836228.

"What about this group that ends with *S*?" she asked.

"That was for the verb *to meet,*" Leo explained. "Prospero
simply added the *S* to indicate the present tense form, *meets,*
which doesn't have a separate headword."

"Okay. So let me get this straight," Caitlin said, turning
to face Leo. "The first number group stands for page one, column one, fourth word down, right?"

"Right," Leo answered.

"Which was *A.*"

"Yes."

"And the second word, *wild*, was on page 2925, in column two, seventh word down."

"Exactly. You see how **lucid** and simple it is?"

"Sure," said Caitlin, "once you know the system."

It was almost two in the morning. Leo paced the floor in silence. Phil and Caitlin **languished** on the couch, staring dully at the piece of paper on which she had written the decoded message:

A wild, **indulgent** place
where flesh meets flesh in rude embrace.

Phil yawned. "I still have no idea what this means. All I can say is it sounds a little kinky." He poked his finger at the page. "Look at these words: *Wild*, **indulgent**, *flesh*, *embrace*. Do those suggest some **conventional**, everyday activity to you?"

Caitlin folded her arms. "Maybe."

"Like what?"

"A wedding reception."

Phil laughed. "Get out of here. That's the most **ludicrous** thing I've ever heard."

"What's so **ludicrous** about it? All the wedding receptions I've seen are wild and **indulgent**, and everybody's hugging and kissing and embracing."

"Yeah, but what about the word *rude* before *embrace*? There are no 'rude embraces' at wedding receptions."

Caitlin pondered the question for a moment. "There's the part when the groom takes off the bride's garter."

"That's not rude," Phil said. "A little lewd, maybe, but definitely not rude."

Caitlin retreated to the corner of the couch and hugged a cushion. "All right, then. Since you don't like that idea, how about a rock concert? Those can be pretty **hedonistic**, with everybody engaging in **wanton** behavior and 'rude embraces,' screaming and yelling and dancing and slamming into each other."

"Now that's more **plausible**," Phil said. He looked at Leo, who was still pacing and brooding. Then he turned to Caitlin. "You know what I think?"

"What?" Caitlin said.

Phil hesitated. "You won't laugh, will you?"

"I might. I can't make any promises."

"I think it may refer to someplace in a red-light district, a striptease joint or a massage parlor or something."

"Oh, get off it, Phil! I'll admit my suggestion wasn't exactly **scintillating**, but yours is **fatuous**."

"No, I'm serious. Think about it. *Wild, **indulgent**, flesh, embrace*—doesn't that suggest the kind of kinky stuff you'd find in a red-light district?"

Caitlin made a **skeptical** face. "I think you're just being **prurient**. Besides, Prospero would never hide the treasure—or a part of it—in a **sordid** place like that."

"Who knows. The guy was pretty **eccentric**." Phil looked at Leo, who continued to pace **incessantly**. "Hey, Leo. Does the city of Holyfield have a red-light district?"

Leo, apparently **oblivious** to their conversation, didn't answer.

Caitlin tossed the cushion at Phil. "I can't believe it! You're really serious, aren't you? Well," she scoffed, "if you're so sure it's something kinky, how about a sultan's harem? That meets all your **criteria**. No, wait. How about a mud wrestling arena? That's even better. Or maybe a—"

"Football stadium!" Leo blurted. He clapped his hands and spun around, laughing. "It's the football stadium!"

Giddy with **insight**, Leo sat down in the armchair and leaned toward the two freshmen. "When the college built a new stadium back in the '70s, Prospero helped bankroll the project. And in spite of his objections, they named it after him. It's called Prospero Stadium, guys."

"Then this clue must be **metaphorical**, like the first one," Caitlin said. "Football's a violent sport, full of blocking and tackling. That's what Prospero must mean by 'where flesh meets flesh in rude embrace.'"

"And the stadium is the 'wild, **indulgent** place,'" Phil said, completing the thought, "where all the fans go nuts and do crazy, **impetuous** things to cheer on their team."

"Precisely," Leo said.

Caitlin gave Phil a mildly **contemptuous** look. "This makes a lot more sense than a stupid red-light district."

"It was just a **hypothesis**," Phil mumbled. "You have to start somewhere."

"Listen," said Leo. "Holyfield's playing its first game of the season Saturday at one o'clock. I think you guys should go up there then and look around."

"You're not coming with us?" Caitlin asked.

Leo shook his head. "Unfortunately, I can't. I've got an executors' meeting at noon at the faculty club, then an appointment at two with Dr. Benson at CHS to have my stitches taken out."

"Maybe we should go sometime tomorrow, when you can come with us," Phil said. "There's bound to be a big crowd during the game, which will **hamper** the search. Wouldn't it be better if we went when there were fewer people around?"

"Under normal circumstances, yes," Leo said, "but there's another consideration. Whoever's on our trail is not exactly the **urbane**, cultivated type who's going to ask you politely to hand over the merchandise. If he follows you to the stadium, it'll be harder for him to try anything with lots of people around."

Phil nodded, remembering the knife.

"That's a good point," Caitlin said, yawning. "Which reminds me. It's really late and there aren't a lot of people around. Would you guys mind walking me back to LaSalle again?"

Chapter 25

Up a Tree

Saturday

It was a perfect day for a game. Above the media booth Old Glory flapped in a cloudless blue sky, and the stadium, which consisted of two levels of bleachers on both sides and one end of the field, was packed. According to the announcer, 5,237 people had turned out to see Holyfield and Stratford College battle it out for the region's bragging rights.

Caitlin and Phil stood in the aisle between the two levels of bleachers, overlooking the fifty-yard-line. For more than an hour they had been conducting a **desultory** and **fruitless** search of the stadium, wondering where in all this space and confusion they might find a tiny scrap of four-hundred-year-old paper.

"Pennants, get your Holyfield pennants here," shouted a young vendor walking toward them with his **abundant** bag of wares.

"*Hot* dogs, s*oda*!" chanted another, carrying an **unwieldy** tray from the opposite direction.

They found some empty seats and sat down. Phil looked at the scoreboard, which stood behind the end zone at the open end of the stadium. The teams were tied at fourteen with two minutes to go in the third quarter. Down on the field, a Holyfield linebacker emerged from a **writhing** pile of bodies with the ball. The Grangers' quarterback had just fumbled and the Crusaders had recovered deep in their opponents' territory.

"Hey, 22. Try using your hands!" **taunted** a pennant-waving yahoo two rows below where Caitlin and Phil sat.

"Kill! Kill! Kill!" whooped a **vociferous** band of weekend warriors wearing matching sunglasses, baseball caps, sweatsuits, and **jovial** grins.

Phil frowned. "Caitlin, are you sure there wasn't some kind of number attached to the clue?"

"No, why?" Caitlin replied. She had removed a small set of binoculars from her jacket pocket and was scanning the sea of **raucous** fans on the other side of the field.

"If I wanted someone to find something in a stadium, you can be sure I'd provide some coordinates."

"Like what?"

"Row, seat number, yard line, something like that. As it is, I don't see how we're going to find it. This place is huge. There are several thousand people here. It could be anywhere."

"Don't worry," Caitlin said, still peering through the binoculars. "We'll find it. We just have to keep looking."

Caitlin's gaze settled on an older man. A **dilapidated** hat was perched on his head and a maroon and gold button that said "Holyfield 1950" **embellished** the lapel of his **weathered** overcoat. She watched the old alumnus jump up and **vehemently** shake his fist in the air, a look of **exultation** on his jowled face. No wonder they call them fans, she thought. The word is probably short for **fanatic**.

A loud whistle blew, signaling the end of the third quarter. As the players headed to the sidelines for a pep talk and the referees repositioned the football, Caitlin proposed that they check the perimeter of the stadium.

"You walk around one way, I'll go the other, and we'll meet on the other side by the statue," she said.

"What statue?" Phil asked.

"It's outside the main gate. We passed it when we arrived."

"Oh, yeah. Now I remember," he said as they made their
way out of the stadium.

They split up and Caitlin ambled along the broad sidewalk. Phil's complaint was **valid**, she thought. The stadium
was indeed massive, with a **myriad** of potential hiding places.
How could they possibly **scrutinize** every one? she wondered.
The more she thought about how **problematic** their task was,
the more she felt her enthusiasm for the search **wane**.

Nevertheless, she continued to scan the **periphery** of the
stadium, stopping frequently to make at least a **cursory** inspection of each **obscure** nook or cranny that looked as
though it might contain the **minute** piece of paper she
hoped to find.

In the **commodious** parking lot to her left, she saw several **impromptu** parties taking place. Pennants fluttered from
aerials and music blared from car speakers. Tailgates were
down and barbecues were smoking. **Copious** amounts of
food and drink were being served and consumed.

A **collective** roar rose from inside the stadium and a
tinny voice came over the P.A. "Touchdown, Holyfield. Extra
point, good. Holyfield leads Stratford 21-14." In response, a
dissonant chorus of horns swelled from the parking lot—a
cacophony of cars, Caitlin thought. The jarring, **discordant**
sound reminded her of the **notoriously sluggish** traffic back
in New York, where the horn often was employed more than
the accelerator.

Glancing over her shoulder, Caitlin noticed a big man
wearing an olive drab army jacket and sunglasses strolling
along the stadium fence about twenty-five yards behind her.
Something about him seemed vaguely familiar—and vaguely
ominous. What was it?

She casually walked over to a souvenir stand and took in

the **gaudy array** of T-shirts, hats, cards, posters, mugs, stat-uettes, memorabilia, and **tawdry** trinkets, gimcracks, and gewgaws.

An older woman leaned over the counter and smiled at her. "Can I help you, miss?"

"I'm trying to decide."

"Take your time, dear."

"Thanks," Caitlin said, wondering if the strange man was still nearby. She took a **surreptitious** look around and saw that he had stopped and turned his back to her. He seemed to be staring at something on the other side of the chain-link fence.

She turned to the woman behind the counter, bought a pencil that had a football for an eraser and said "Holyfield Crusaders" on the side, and resumed walking.

After a short distance she glanced back. The man still appeared to be looking through the fence at something, only he had resumed walking too, and, if anything, had lessened the gap between them. She quickened her pace until she arrived at the main gate.

As she approached the statue, she tensed. Phil was nowhere in sight. Suddenly she was angry. Here I am being followed by some creep and Mr. Phil Kwon Do is late, she thought.

She walked to the other side of the statue and peered **furtively** around it. The man was loitering by the gate, reading a newspaper as people strolled in and out of the stadium.

She looked up at the patinated bronze statue. The larger-than-life figure was rendered in flowing academic robes, with the mortarboard on top of the head tilted at a rakish angle. While the bushy eyebrows arched as if in surprise, a **subtle** smile curled up at one corner of the otherwise stern mouth, creating an expression that wavered somewhere between **levity** and **gravity**. One powerfully wrought hand rested on a large stone book; the other reached out in a **magnanimous** gesture, as if welcoming all those approaching the stadium. On a metal plate affixed to the **pedestal** the name Edward Anthony Prospero was carved in block letters. Below it the date 1900 was followed by a dash.

It figures, Caitlin thought. Why fill in the year of his death when he's still having fun pulling the strings of the living? As she **ruminated** on the **eccentricity** of the man who had gotten her into this mess, she checked the gate out of the corner of her eye. The **forbidding** stranger was still there. "Great," she muttered to herself. "I wish Phil would hurry up!"

"Hey, Caitlin!"

Phil's voice startled her. She looked around but couldn't see him.

"Up here!"

She turned and saw a monumental tree with long, **sinuous** branches and a thick, gnarled trunk. She ran over to it. Inside the chained-off area around the base, a plaque was set into the ground:

> The house of George Wilcox,
> who in 1875 donated the land
> on which the central campus
> of Holyfield College was built,
> once stood beside
> this **venerable** tulip tree.

With a hand shading her eyes, Caitlin looked up into the **diffuse** sunlight and dense foliage and spotted Phil clinging to one of the upper branches, his body partly **obscured** by the trunk.

"Phil," she called out, "I don't think this is a good time to be climbing trees. Somebody's following me and I need you—"

"Here, catch!"

A small object plummeted down at her. She tried to catch it, but the splintered shafts of sunlight breaking through the canopy of leaves were so bright that she **inadvertently** blinked. The object bounced off her arm, fell to the ground, and broke.

Caitlin bent over. Resting amid a pile of clay **shards** was a sealed plastic bag with a piece of parchment inside.

"Phil, you found it!"

"Yeah, I was standing here waiting for you," he said as he shinnied down the trunk of the tree, "and I just flashed on it."

Caitlin carefully picked up the plastic bag and put it in her purse. She glanced over her shoulder. The big man had tucked his newspaper under his arm and was strolling toward them.

"I was looking at that statue of Prospero," Phil went on, "and I thought of that Edgar Allan Poe story, 'The Gold Bug'—"

"Phil, I think your explanation will have to wait."

He stepped over the chain surrounding the huge tree. "Why?"

"Never mind." She grabbed his hand and led him into a crowd of people moving between the stadium and the parking lot.

"What's going on?" he asked.

"Somebody's following us. I'll explain later. Let's just get out of here!"

They crossed the parking lot with **celerity**. When they reached College Street, Caitlin spied a gray station wagon with a white bonnet on the roof waiting at the curb. She waved her arm, then broke into a run, pulling Phil with her.

They jumped in and slammed the door. Caitlin quickly locked it. Through the rear window she could see the man leaning **nonchalantly** against the parking lot fence, staring at the cab.

"You in trouble, Caitlin?" asked the driver.

Caitlin flipped around and saw the driver tip back the brim of her Minnesota Twins baseball cap and eye her **quizzically** in the rearview mirror.

"Annie! You don't know how glad I am to see you!"

Leo snapped back the tops of three sodas, put them on the table, and sat down next to Caitlin on the couch. Phil leaned forward in the armchair and continued his story.

"So I saw the statue and thought, maybe Prospero's playing a big joke on us. Maybe there's no treasure and everything we've done has been **futile**. But as I turned away, upset by that thought, I saw this enormous old tree—and it just hit me. I looked back at the statue and saw that Prospero's arm was pointing right at the tree. It couldn't have been more obvious!"

"It's not obvious to me," Leo confessed. "How did you make this **spontaneous** connection?"

"It was Edgar Allan Poe's 'The Gold Bug' again."

"Really? How so?"

"In the story they locate the treasure by dropping this scarab—the gold bug of the title—through the eye socket of a skull that's nailed to the branch of a gigantic tulip tree. When I saw the plaque identifying this as a tulip tree, I started climbing. And sure enough, about halfway up I saw a small clay skull tied to a branch with the piece of parchment sealed in a plastic bag and tucked neatly inside the eye socket."

"Boy," Caitlin said, "first the invisible ink and now this crazy skull. You're sure getting some good mileage out of that story."

Phil grinned. "What can I say? Poe's one of my favorite writers. I learned a lot of SAT words reading him."

"Actually, the **symmetry** between Poe's plot and Prospero's scheme isn't perfect," Leo said. "In the story, didn't they drop the scarab through the eye socket and then find the treasure by digging in the spot where it hit the ground?"

Phil nodded. "Right, but in this case burying it in a place with so much **pedestrian** traffic would have been **irrational**. It might've been **inadvertently** uncovered by someone else or damaged by the digging—not to mention the fact that conducting an excavation in public is bound to attract attention. Up in the tree, the fragment was safely hidden but still accessible."

"Also, if we'd had to dig it up," Caitlin said, "we wouldn't have been able to **evade** that guy who was following us."

"I especially like how the clay skull protected the document from the elements while it provided a neat **correlation** to a detail of the tale," Leo said. "You know," he added, looking at Caitlin, "I wonder if that guy was the same creep who came after you in the costume room."

Before she could answer, there was a knock on the door. Leo opened it and Professor Torres entered holding a slender leather valise. She was a little out of breath.

"How did you get here so fast?" Caitlin asked.

"When I called for a cab, I took Leo's advice and asked for your friend Annie. I must say, she's quite a speed demon!"

Caitlin and Phil laughed. Leo seated Torres in the unoccupied armchair, served her a soda, and returned to his place on the couch. "Did you bring the first fragment?" he asked.

In answer to his question, Torres calmly reached into her valise, removed the piece of parchment, and set it on the coffee table. Caitlin placed the one they had just found beside it, and the three students watched as Carmen delicately adjusted the two pieces until their ragged edges fit together almost seamlessly.

"Ready?" she asked, looking up.

With Carmen's guidance, the **transcription** went quickly, and their **initial** assumptions were **confirmed**: The two fragments turned out to form the top half of a letter. This is what it said:

xxi xii mdxcix

Dear Hippolyta and Rosalind,

Take care, lest you play at playing with one better versed in play. I am no clownish Costard, prating for your delectation. When I say 'Not one sou more!' I do not **equivocate**. Again, know well this soundest sense: that authority rules longest that need not make itself **manifest**. The player

Phil took a sip of soda and frowned. "What's a 'sou'?" he asked, pronouncing the word *sow*.

"Not *s-o-w*," Leo said, spelling it out. "*S-o-u*. *Sow* rhymes with *cow*. A *sou*, which rhymes with *you*, is a denomination of money—an old French coin. Apparently Hippolyta and Rosalind have demanded payment for some sort of service rendered, and the writer is refusing to **comply**."

"What kind of service could it be?" Caitlin wondered aloud.

"I think that sounds too **legitimate**," Phil said. "Look at the last complete sentence. Doesn't it seem **furtive**, as if the writer's urging them to be **evasive** and keep quiet?"

"There certainly is a lot of **ambiguous** wordplay in the text," Leo said. "And you do get the feeling that there's some kind of **covert** operation afoot."

"What about blackmail?" Caitlin suggested. "Maybe that's why it's addressed to two Shakespearean characters. I played Hippolyta in high school once. She's the Queen of the Amazons in *A Midsummer Night's Dream*. And Rosalind is from *As You Like It*, isn't she? Those might be aliases."

Leo stroked his chin. "Interesting point. The two quotations from the first clue were from *As You Like It*."

"There are a lot of references to plays and playing and players here," Phil said.

"No kidding," Caitlin said. "And who is 'better versed in play' than Shakespeare himself?"

"Indeed," Torres said quietly.

The three students looked at the professor, who had hitherto remained silent and **pensive**. Her chin rested on top of her hands as she studied the document.

Leo leaned forward. "But if these fragments are in fact from Shakespeare, why would he write a **clandestine** letter to two women? I thought that in his **benighted** day women were denied access to the stage and had little or nothing to do with money."

"Quite true," said Torres. "But that would make it an **exceptionally** valuable letter, wouldn't it?"

Chapter 26

One **Conjecture** Is Better Than None

Sunday

Leo sat at the kitchen table in Carmen Torres's **modest**, two-bedroom cottage on Cedar Street, four blocks from campus, drinking coffee and eating a fresh croissant smeared with butter and strawberry jam. It was nine o'clock on a **halcyon** fall morning. Already the sun was out in full force and the bright blue sky was **unblemished** by clouds. There wasn't the slightest hint of the monstrous rainstorm that, according to an article Leo had read in *The Plains*, was supposed to arrive by nightfall.

The kitchen window was open and the gauzy white curtains swayed in the warm breeze. Torres's cat, an **amiable** tabby named Raza, sat on the windowsill basking in a shaft of sunlight. Torres studied the pattern the light made on the black-and-white checkered floor of her kitchen. Then she looked at Prospero's third clue, which she had copied on a notepad:

O I know two O may a man undo.

"I can see why you wanted help figuring out this anagram," she said, getting up from the table and giving Raza a loving pat. "It reminds me of those scrambled word puzzles in the newspaper, only those are **rudimentary.** This is much more **complex.**"

Torres refilled their cups and set the coffeepot back on the warmer on the counter. Then she sat down at the table again, took a sip of the dark brew, and reflected. "Solving this anagram may be especially tough because it's also a lipogram."

"What's a lipogram?" Leo asked, adding a dollop of milk to his coffee.

"Any piece of writing composed without using a certain letter or letters. Did you notice that Prospero's line has lots of *a*'s and *o*'s but no *e*'s?"

"Yes, I was wondering about that." Leo poured two spoonfuls of sugar into his cup, stirred, and took a sip. "Does that mean we have to decipher both an anagram and a lipogram?"

"Oh, no," Torres said. "A lipogram isn't a puzzle in and of itself; it's just a **novelty**, a text with something self-consciously omitted. All I'm saying is that, in this case, the fact that Prospero's anagram has no *e*'s will make whatever message lies hidden in it that much more difficult to unravel."

Leo swallowed the last bite of his croissant and wiped his mouth. "I bet it's hard to write much more than a sentence without using an *e*."

"You're telling me," Torres said. "But some people love to test their mental **mettle**. A Frenchman named Georges Perec once wrote a whole novel without ever using an *e*. And there was an **obscure** Greek poet named Tryphiodorus who wrote a version of the *Odyssey* that had no *a*'s in the first book, no *b*'s in the second book, and so on."

Leo was amazed. "Why would anyone do something like that?"

"Oh, partly to be intellectually **ostentatious** and partly to be **esoteric**, I suppose." Torres sipped her coffee, then selected a croissant from the basket on the table, set it on her plate, broke it carefully in half, and began applying butter to its fluffy center. "Wordplay is such a pleasant pastime, and a **perennial** one too; people have been riddling and punning probably since the beginning of language. The ancient Greeks and Romans loved palindromes—sentences that read the same backward as they do forward, like 'Live not on evil'—and the eighth-century English poet Cynewulf artfully concealed acrostics of his name in several of his most **pious** works."

Leo helped himself to a second croissant. "What about Shakespeare? He was one of the all-time greats when it came to wordplay, right?"

"Indeed. Shakespeare was such an **inveterate** punster that he sprinkled some three thousand puns into his plays. I pity the poor **pedant** who counted them all. Obviously Professor Prospero loved wordplay too or he wouldn't have made you go to all this trouble decoding these tricky ciphers."

Leo looked at the clue on his notepad and frowned. "I think I'm beginning to wish he hadn't."

Torres smiled. "But aren't you curious about this literary **largess** he promised you'll find at the end of the rainbow?"

"Of course," Leo said. He took a long sip of coffee and sighed. "I'm just worried about how we're going to weather the storm that precedes the rainbow."

"Must there be a storm to reveal a rainbow?"

Leo pondered the question. "Carmen, you know that since we started looking for this treasure, it's been nothing but close calls and"—he gestured toward his head—"not-so-close calls." He paused and swallowed the rest of his coffee.

Torres got up and fetched the pot, poured Leo another cup, and topped off her own. Then she sat down again and looked at him. "What are you trying to tell me?" she asked gently.

Leo glanced at Raza. She had stretched out **languidly** on

the windowsill, her eyes half-closed, her paws dangling over the edge. She seemed so **serene** and content.

"I guess I'm saying that I think the storm's **inevitable**, that it's building fast, and that whatever force is driving it is trying to make sure we never get to see that rainbow."

A few minutes later, Torres slipped on a pair of stylish reading glasses and picked up her ballpoint pen. "Okay. We've got eleven vowels, counting *y*, and only ten consonants: three *n*'s, two *m*'s, two *w*'s, a *d*, a *t*, and a *k*. An odd assortment, to say the least, but let's see what we can do with it."

"What do you make of this capital *I*?" Leo asked.

Torres looked at Prospero's clue again:

O I know two O may a man undo.

"I'm not sure," she said. "But the fact that there's only one *i* leads me to believe that it's going to be used the same way it is in the anagram—as a nominative pronoun. Somehow I doubt it'll be part of a longer word."

Leo nodded. "That's what I'm thinking too. Shall we proceed with that working **hypothesis**?"

"Sure, why not. When you're dealing with a conundrum, one **conjecture** is better than none, right?"

They set to work. After fifteen minutes of **assiduous** effort, Leo looked at what he had written and shook his head. "Well, I've got a sentence, but unfortunately it's missing an *a* and an *o*, and it doesn't make any sense." He read the line aloud:

O no I won't wonk a mud yam.

Torres laughed. "That gets an A for **inventiveness** and a B for grammatical **coherence**, but I'm afraid it fails dismally as a **plausible** solution."

"Back to the drawing board," Leo said.

A few minutes later Torres looked up from her notepad. "Here's one that's just as **frivolous**," she said, and read her line aloud:

OK, I am not a woody man now.

Leo chuckled. "I won't presume to grade the professor on her **scintillating** work. Let's just say it needs **refinement**."

"It could use another *u* somewhere too. That was the one letter I couldn't work in."

"I like the 'woody,' though. That's **innovative**. Do you think there might be an **allusion** to a forest buried in here somewhere?"

"It's a reasonable **surmise**," Torres said. "Let's see where it leads us."

They tried to incorporate the word *woody* into a solution but met with **dubious** success. The best line Leo could come up with, "I am now a woody nook nut," was again two letters short of the twenty-one in Prospero's clue. Torres's best offering, which still lacked a *u*, was equally **preposterous**: "I woo a woody ant man monk."

"I'm not so sure this 'woody' thing's going to work out," Leo said.

"Neither am I," Torres said. She leaned back in her chair and sighed. Raza interpreted the movement as an invitation to leap from the windowsill onto her lap. Torres stroked the cat's head, then set the tabby on the floor. "Well, I guess we'll just have to start again from square one."

For nearly an hour they worked in intense silence.

Finally Leo leaned across the table. "Carmen," he said quietly, "I think I've got something good."

"I think I do too," she answered without looking up. "Hold on a minute."

He waited patiently while she finished writing. When

she was done, she sat back in her chair and took a deep breath, releasing it slowly.

"Take a look at this," Leo said, pushing his notepad across the table and turning it around so she could read what he had written.

Torres leaned forward and looked at the sentence:

Do you know I am not a woman?

"It uses all twenty-one letters, and it makes sense," Leo said.

She glanced up at him, an **inscrutable** smile on her face.

"What do you think?" he asked. "Am I onto something?"

She started to nod her head, but the gesture was interrupted by an **involuntary** chuckle, which erupted into **vigorous** laughter.

This was not the reaction Leo had expected after an hour of hard work, with solid results. "What's so funny?" he asked **tentatively** when she began to calm down.

Torres had laughed so hard that her eyes were filled with tears. "Oh, Leo, I'm sorry, but I just can't believe it. This is truly amazing."

"What is?"

"What we both came up with. I guess, as they say, great minds think alike." She picked up her notepad and handed it to him. "Look at the last line on the page."

Leo looked and his jaw dropped.

Do you not know I am a woman?

"My God, Carmen. That's incredible!" he cried, slapping the table. "We came up with the same words but our solutions are **antithetical**."

"Or, to be a bit more precise, antonymous," Torres said.

"The sentences are opposite in meaning: Yours indicates the speaker is a man and mine indicates the speaker is a woman."

"And all we did was put the word *not* in a different place." Leo scratched his head, trying to **fathom** the coincidence.

"It's interesting that you made the speaker a man and I made her a woman," Torres said. "Do you think we just unconsciously displayed our respective gender **biases**?"

"That's a good question for your seminar on the politics of sexuality in Renaissance literature."

Torres laughed. "Yes, there's **fertile** ground here for intellectual inquiry, I'm sure."

Leo looked at the professor hopefully. "Carmen, do you think one of our sentences is the right solution?"

"Yes, I do."

"Which one?"

"Let me check something and I'll tell you in a minute."

Torres stood up and walked out of the kitchen, her slippers slapping briskly against her heels. A short while later she returned with a book in her hand.

Leo saw the title of the volume and felt his pulse quicken. "It's a quotation from Shakespeare's *As You Like It*?"

Torres nodded as she sat down and flipped through the pages. "Here it is, in act 3, scene 2. It's one of Rosalind's lines." She handed the open book to Leo with her finger pointing to a spot about halfway down the page.

Leo took the book and read the lines:

> Do you not know I am a woman?
> When I think, I must speak.

"So you had it right," he said, feeling **simultaneously** disappointed and **elated**.

"But so did you, except for the placement of one small word," Carmen consoled him.

"A small word, but of great significance." Leo read Rosalind's lines again and thought for a moment. "So, if I remember this scene correctly from looking at it the other night, Celia is trying to explain to Rosalind that she's just seen Orlando—"

"Who is Rosalind's amorous interest, as they say," Torres interjected.

"But Rosalind gets excited and keeps interrupting her. Finally Celia grows impatient and tells Rosalind to shut up. That's when Rosalind says, 'Do you not know I am a woman? When I think, I must speak.'"

"Yes, and frankly, those lines have always **irked** me. I've always thought their **implication** was **discriminatory** and sexist, that Shakespeare was **belittling** women as shallow thinkers and **impetuous** talkers." She paused. "But I suppose you could look at it another way. Since Rosalind is disguised as a man at the time, perhaps Shakespeare was being **ironic, subtly** scoffing at that **offensive stereotype** by having Rosalind **denigrate** or **disparage** women as though she were a typical male chauvinist. It's hard to tell."

"That's interesting," Leo said. "You know, when I checked Prospero's Shakespeare concordance for the quotation about being in a forest, dressed in man's apparel, and found out it was from *As You Like It*, for some reason it never occurred to me that it referred to how Rosalind hides in the Forest of Arden and disguises herself as a man."

"Yes, that's one of the many **satirical** moments in the play when Shakespeare pokes fun at the ideal of romantic love," Torres said.

An **amorphous** notion began taking on **coherence** in Leo's brain. "Carmen, remind me. Isn't Rosalind dressed up as a character from Greek mythology?"

Torres nodded. "She assumes the **guise** of Ganymede, the Trojan boy Zeus took to Olympus to be the cupbearer to the gods."

"Then that must be it!" Leo exclaimed.

"Ganymede?"

"Yes!"

"I don't get it. How does Ganymede fit into this?"

Leo jumped up and began pacing the kitchen floor. "Prospero once donated a painting of Ganymede to the Holyfield Art Gallery. Every time I go there I see it—with that plaque beside it, thanking Prospero—because it's hanging right in the lobby."

In his excitement Leo almost stepped on Raza, who had reentered the kitchen for a drink from her bowl. Torres rescued her cat and set her out of harm's way.

"I know the painting you're talking about," she said. "Are you **implying** that the clue has something to do with it?"

"Yes, and I'd bet my B.A. that the next fragment of the old letter is hidden somewhere on it or near it." He looked around the room. "May I use your phone?"

"Of course. It's on the wall over there by the door." Torres watched him walk to the phone and pick up the receiver. "What do you have up your sleeve, Leo?"

He checked his watch. "The gallery opens at noon on Sundays, right?"

"Yes."

"It's 11:25 now. I'm going to call Caitlin and Phil and tell them to meet us there in twenty minutes."

Chapter 27

Operation Ganymede

Outside the entrance to the Holyfield Art Gallery a small crowd had gathered, waiting for the doors to open. Caitlin, Phil, Leo, and Carmen Torres sat together on the steps, quietly plotting how to proceed with what Phil had already **facetiously** dubbed "Operation Ganymede."

"You said it was hanging in the lobby?" Caitlin asked.

"That's right," Leo said. "As you go in it's on the right, just past the information desk. You can't miss it. It's big."

"I don't know how we're going to search a painting that's in the middle of the lobby," Caitlin said. "Everybody and his mother will be walking by." She waved a hand at the entrance. "Look at all those people waiting to get in."

"She's right, Leo," Torres said. "Sundays are busy here, and I imagine especially so today because of this popular exhibit on Elizabethan artists for the festival. On top of that **impediment** there'll be gallery workers just a few feet away at the information desk. They'll have a great view of us."

"And don't forget the security guards," Phil said. "I'm sure they won't appreciate it if we start monkeying around with the merchandise."

"No kidding," said Caitlin. "There might even be some kind of alarm system too."

"I think we're okay there," Torres said. "They do have an

alarm system but the gallery director once told me that they activate it only when the building's closed." She looked at Leo. "I trust you're not planning to do anything **unethical**."

Leo chuckled. "I'm certainly not going to try to steal the painting or **dismantle** it, if that's what you're **implying**. But I think we'll have to figure out a way to look behind the frame, because it seems to me that's the only place on a painting you can hide anything. So I guess we'll need to move it a little, which clearly is a problem since we'll be so **conspicuous**."

"What if we try this later, maybe around closing time?" Caitlin suggested. "There might be fewer people then."

"Perhaps," Torres said, "but that's when the guards and gallery workers are intent on getting everyone out and clos-ing up the building, so they're likely to be even more **vigilant**."

"Then there's only one other way to go," Leo said. He paused, and everyone looked at him expectantly. "We'll have to create a **diversion**."

"What kind of **diversion**?" Phil asked.

"A big one. Something that will **wreak** enough havoc to get everyone's attention and hold it for a couple of minutes while we check out the painting."

"That sounds more like a disturbance than a **diversion**," Torres said.

Caitlin looked at Leo. "Do you have something in mind?"

"As a matter of fact, yes. It's pretty outrageous, but it just might work."

Forty minutes later, Leo and Phil returned from Ericson Hall accompanied by a beefy student with long dark hair slicked back and tied in a ponytail. Although it was warm, he wore an oversized army-surplus trenchcoat with the collar turned up.

The threesome trotted up the art gallery steps and approached Caitlin and Torres.

"We were beginning to wonder if you boys had given up and gone for lunch," Torres said.

"Sorry we took so long. Max was in the shower when we got there," Leo explained. "We had to wait till he got dressed."

Torres extended her hand to the newcomer. "Hi, I'm Carmen Torres. I teach in the English Department."

"Max Meyerhoff, sophomore, biology major," the student said in clipped, nasal tones. He shook Torres's hand.

Torres introduced Caitlin, then gave a **circumspect** look around the gallery steps. "Max," she said in a low voice, "I presume you have . . . the '**diversion**'?"

"Right here where it's cozy," Max said, patting a bulge under his lapel. "And by the way, his name's Irwin."

A few minutes later, after settling the last few details of their plan, the five members of Operation Ganymede entered the Holyfield Art Gallery.

Once inside the **commodious** lobby, the group split up.

Max headed for the marble staircase at the far end and climbed the steps to the landing. He turned and leaned **nonchalantly** over the balustrade.

Torres approached the circular information desk in the middle of the lobby, where a man and a woman **dispensed** brochures and catalogues and answered visitors' questions. She picked up a catalogue and began thumbing through the pages.

Phil strolled toward an archway on the left under a banner announcing the gallery's current exhibit, "Shakespeare's Colleagues: Artists and Artisans of Elizabethan England." Next to the archway a stout, **impassive** security guard stood with her feet apart and her hands behind her back. Phil lingered in the vicinity of the guard, **feigning** interest in a **dour** portrait of Queen Elizabeth I that hung on the wall nearby.

While the others took their positions, Leo led Caitlin to the right side of the lobby and paused in front of an **imposing** rectangular oil painting, about eight feet long, in an **ornate** gilded frame. He indicated the bronze plaque on the wall, and Caitlin stepped forward to read it:

"Ganymede Serving the Olympians"
Giacomo Bruzzi (1684–1749)

Gift of Edward Anthony Prospero,
Distinguished Alumnus and
Harcourt Professor of English Emeritus,
Holyfield College
Donated in 1987

Caitlin moved back and surveyed the painting. The scene **depicted** a group of ancient Greek gods and goddesses, dressed in elegant white togas or tunics, enjoying a **sumptuous** feast while reclining on pillows and divans.

In the center and foreground of the picture stood a **lithe**-limbed boy of perhaps thirteen, wearing only a loincloth and leather sandals. He held a pewter pitcher from which he poured an amber liquid into the goblet of an attractive older woman. A strikingly muscular old man with a curly white beard and an **imperious** expression reclined beside the woman, raising his cup to be served next. Caitlin **surmised** that the boy was Ganymede, the old man Zeus, god of the heavens, and the woman Hera, queen of the heavens and goddess of women.

She leaned toward Leo. "The drink Ganymede is serving—is that where the **cliché** 'nectar of the gods' comes from?"

"Yes. The gods drank nectar and ate ambrosia to ensure their **immortality**."

"I could use a cup of that stuff right now."

"Too bad they lost the recipe. Hey, hold on a second, will you?" Leo approached the painting and began making a **cursory** examination of the frame.

Caitlin glanced over her shoulder. There were at least fifty people milling around the lobby. She saw Max occupying his **vantage point** on the landing and Carmen Torres at the information desk, still browsing through the catalogue. She located Phil across the wide room and saw that he was looking at her. When their eyes met, he smiled and gave her a **surreptitious** thumbs-up sign, which she returned.

"I don't see anything on the outside of the frame," Leo said, appearing at her side. "Are you ready to move?"

Caitlin nodded.

Leo touched his index finger to his nose—the signal to begin the "**diversion**." Caitlin saw Max touch his nose in response, then sit down on the landing with his feet on one of the steps. She watched him slip a hand under the flap of his trenchcoat. A moment later, from the bottom of the coat, a pointy head emerged, followed by a long, scaly, **sinuous** body that slithered wildly down the stairs and onto the lobby floor.

"Look out!" she heard Phil yell right on cue. "There's a snake in here!"

Operation Ganymede was underway.

At the sound of Phil's voice, Carmen Torres dropped the catalogue and leapt up onto the information desk like a cat. "Snake!" she shouted, hopping up and down and pointing at the floor. "Snake! Snake!"

Caitlin marveled at how persuasively Torres played the **stereotyped** role of a hysterical woman.

The professor's shrill cries **galvanized** the crowd. People pushed and shoved and screamed as they attempted to locate the threat and get out of its path. An **erratic** wave of people rushing for the double doors collided with the flow of visi-

tors entering through them, causing a human logjam. Phil
did everything he could, short of knocking people over, to
exacerbate the panic.

Leo waited until he saw the stout security guard **jostling**
toward the source of the commotion, then turned to Caitlin.
"Come on. Let's go!"

He grasped the frame of the painting and lifted it several
inches away from the wall. "Check back there. Quick! And be
careful not to tear the parchment."

Caitlin stuck her head behind the painting and peered
up and down. Nothing in plain sight. She pulled her head
out and reached in with her hand, exploring the back of the
canvas and then running her fingers along the inside of the
frame. She checked as much area as she could reach, finally
stretching on tiptoes to touch the top corner. Nothing.

She glanced at Leo and shook her head.

"Try the other side—and hurry!"

As Caitlin scurried around Leo, she saw the security
guard waving her billy club in the air.

"Calm down, everyone," the guard commanded. "Everything's under control."

But everything was far from under control. Bodies continued to surge in every direction, and the lobby reverberated
with shouts and screams as the shiny blue serpent slithered
one way and then the other across the slick marble floor.

"It's huge!"

"It's coming this way!"

"It's going to bite me!"

Caitlin ducked her head behind the painting. Again,
nothing. With one hand she searched every inch of the canvas and frame that she could reach. Still nothing. She could
feel drops of sweat beading on her forehead. She wanted to
scream with frustration. Where was the stupid piece of
parchment?

Maybe Leo was wrong, she thought as she leaned behind

the painting and searched the frame again. Maybe he'd mis-interpreted Prospero's clue. Maybe they'd caused this insane disturbance for nothing, and the whole thing was just a hor-rible **fiasco**.

She heard Leo's deep voice **admonishing** her. "C'mon, Caitlin. What's taking you so long? Time's running out."

On the other side of the room the security guard, with the crowd behind her, now had the big snake cornered.

"Stand back, everyone," she warned. "This fella may be poisonous. Just keep back. I've already radioed for help."

"Kill it!" screeched a woman perched on the information desk next to Torres.

"Crush its **noxious** head!" a man bellowed.

Torres's stentorian voice rose above the others. "No, don't touch it! That's cruelty to reptiles!"

Phil, who had jockeyed to the front of the crowd, ad-vanced toward the guard. "Hold on a minute, ma'am," he said calmly. "That snake's not going to hurt anybody."

The guard scowled. "What do you think you're doing, young man? I told you to keep back. Do you want to get poi-soned?"

"No, he's right!" Max Meyerhoff said as he broke through the **throng**. "This **wayward** creature is my pet."

The crowd fell silent as Max brushed past Phil and the guard, lifted the snake from the floor, and slung it over his shoulders.

"Irwin, you bad boy," he said, shaking his finger at the snake's head. "What are you doing here? Don't you know these awful people were going to kill you?"

Leo glanced over his shoulder and saw Max holding the snake. "Only a few more seconds, Caitlin. Hurry up!"

Max turned to face the astonished crowd. "I don't know why you all got so worked up," he said, flashing a crooked smile. "Irwin's just a common blue racer snake, *Coluber con-strictor flaviventris*. You can find them all over the Midwest, from Ohio to Texas. They can get pretty big—as long as six feet—but they're totally harmless."

Leo could hear the crowd beginning to **disperse**. "Time's up, Caitlin. Let's get out of here before somebody sees us."

Caitlin sighed and brushed away the damp hair that clung to her face. Then, with her head tilted back, she saw it—the yellowed and ragged edge of a piece of parchment. It was wedged inside a deep crack in the upper corner, between the stretcher and the back of the frame. How could she have missed it?

She reached up and carefully **extracted** the fragment with her fingernails. "Leo, wait. Here it is!"

Chapter 28

The Method in the Madness

The afternoon had grown still and dark. Raza the cat sat on the windowsill staring out at the fat raindrops that had just begun to fall, splattering on roofs and sidewalks. Across the street a blue sedan pulled up to the curb and lingered, idling under the branches of a sycamore tree. Raza looked across the study and meowed.

"Raza, honey, I'm sorry but I've already fed you," Carmen Torres said without looking up from her work. She was sitting at her computer, typing in a final **transcription** of the writing on the three fragile pieces of parchment that Leo, who was sitting beside her, had assembled on the surface of a clipboard in his lap. He was spelling out the words for her, letter by letter. Caitlin and Phil stood behind them, eagerly watching the message materialize on the screen. They were nearly done.

"'Does in play and player too'? It sounds like a double homicide," Phil remarked.

Torres looked over her shoulder at Phil. "Or it might be a reference to that **disconcerting** moment when an actor forgets his lines or falls out of character. The dramatic 'mask' comes off, the spell over the audience breaks, and so the play's 'done in.'"

"—*e-r*, break, *t-h-a-n*," Leo dictated.

"Carmen, that last line looks bungled," Caitlin said.

Torres turned around and looked at the screen. She had just typed "R3HD3 95Y34 5YQH." "Oh lord," she said.

"What happened?" Leo asked, taking a look for himself.

"Wait a second. Let me delete this and then we can go over it again."

Torres hit a key and Leo watched the line of gibberish disappear from the screen with a blip. His eyes widened as an idea took hold of him.

"Okay," Torres said. "Where were we?"

"Carmen, is there some way you can retrieve what you just deleted?" Leo's tone was urgent.

"I'm afraid not. Why?"

"Just a hunch. Mind if I use the keyboard?"

"Go right ahead. But what's this all about?"

"I'm not sure yet," Leo said as they switched seats, "but I think I may have figured out Prospero's last cipher." He glanced at the fragment they'd been working on and began to type, slowly pecking the keys with his index fingers. The characters "R3HD3 95Y34 5YQH" appeared on the screen.

"There," he said. "Isn't that what you had before?"

Torres was amazed. "How did you recall all that from a glimpse?"

"I didn't. I reconstructed it."

"But it looks like the mess Raza makes when she walks across the keyboard. How could you possibly reconstruct it when there's no pattern?"

"Typographical errors are usually **random**, but this thing's **uniformly** off. When you turned to talk to Phil, your hands must have moved one row up and to the left."

"So are you saying that the key to the fourth cipher is some kind of keyboard shift?" Torres asked.

Leo nodded.

"As usual, Leo, I'm impressed." Torres got up and crossed the room to the bookcase.

"Won't the fourth clue tell us exactly where the treasure is?" Caitlin asked Leo.

"That's what I'm hoping."

Torres removed several volumes from the middle shelf of her bookcase, reached through the clearing into a small wall safe, and pulled out Prospero's letter. "I believe we'll be needing this," she said, unfolding it and waving it in the air.

"Okay, let's get the cipher on the screen first," Leo said.

"And then it's on to the treasure," Phil added, rubbing his hands together in expectation.

Torres sat down and handed Leo the document. He set it on the table and typed in the code for the final clue. It looked like this:

> O8I3 093W O35534 5Y3 E9D7J3H5 8W
> Q5 YQHE 59 7W3 59 T99E 07409W3.

"Well, it's definitely a shift down," Phil said. "Look at all the numbers. The numbers are on the top row of the keypad."

"Let's try down and to the left then," Torres suggested.

Leo hunted and pecked. Caitlin watched the *o* become a *k* and the *8* turn into a *u*. The key below and to the left of *i* was *j*. "*K-u-j*? That's weird," she said. "How about down and to the right?"

This time the results were **comprehensible**. Phil and Caitlin almost danced with anticipation as the message began to unfold on the screen.

> Like Poe's letter . . .

Phil pointed at the screen. "That must be 'The **Purloined** Letter'!"

> . . . the document is at hand to use to good purpose.

"I think I know the very passage," Torres said, rising from her chair again and striding across the room to the bookcase. "I've taught that story to freshmen for years." She pulled out an old dog-eared **anthology** and flipped through it. When she found the appropriate page, she read the passage aloud:

> The more I reflected . . . upon the fact that
> the document must always have been *at
> hand,* if he intended to use it to good pur-
> pose . . . the more satisfied I became that, to
> conceal this letter, the Minister had resorted
> to the **comprehensive** and **sagacious expedi-
> ent** of not attempting to conceal it at all.

Torres looked up and saw anticlimax written across the faces of the three students.

"Well, if this 'document' isn't concealed, then where is it?" Caitlin asked.

Phil shrugged. "Out in the open, I guess."

"No kidding, Einstein," Caitlin said. "But where out in the open? Up in another stupid tree somewhere?"

Leo leaned back in his chair. "I suppose the least **covert** and most natural place for a document is a library," he said without much **conviction**. "We could check the **archives**."

Torres shook her head. "If it's already been catalogued and shelved somewhere in Tillinghast, it might be **obscure**, but it wouldn't be a secret."

Leo stared **glumly** at the screen. The message displayed there seemed **paradoxically** both **lucid** and **opaque**, its meaning maddeningly **tangible** yet **evanescent**.

Torres patted Leo on the shoulder. "You didn't expect this to be a piece of cake, did you?"

"No, but you'd think that at least once Prospero could be a little less **ambiguous** and a little more **candid**. Why must he always **revel** in these riddles and **circumlocutions**? I get the feeling that if he were alive right now he'd be having himself a big laugh."

"C'mon, chief. We're really close. I can feel it," Phil said, trying to **revitalize** his counselor's spirits.

"If it's 'at hand,' then it must be fairly accessible and **conspicuous**," Caitlin reasoned. "What about these fragments? They're right here."

"That's right," Phil **concurred**. "Maybe Prospero isn't teasing us at all. Maybe he's just trying to tell us to take a closer look."

Reluctantly, Leo turned his attention to the last fragment and typed in what little was left to **transcribe**.

xxi xii mdxcix

Dear Hippolyta and Rosalind,

> Take care, lest you play at playing with one
> better versed in play. I am no clownish Costard,
> prating for your delectation. When I say 'Not one
> sou more!' I do not **equivocate**. Again, know well
> this soundest sense: that authority rules longest
> that need not make itself **manifest**. The player
> who removes the mask before play's done, does
> in play and player too. Why **hamper** your own
> good office? Why must you always haggle with
> me tooth and nail? Know well it is well within my
> office to enforce our law, and I know well how to
> fence other than with words.

Yours, D. Constable

"There's that word 'play' again," Phil observed, studying the computer screen. "And look at 'mask.' We were right: Hippolyta and Rosalind must be actors."

"We don't have to take it **literally**," Caitlin said. "Whoever D. Constable is could be using the word 'mask' **metaphorically**. Perhaps the author's urging them not to **divulge** their identities."

"And the term 'authority' in the earlier sentence puts their role as actors into question," Torres said. "After all, who 'rules' in the realm of the Elizabethan theater?"

Leo scratched his head. "If Shakespeare's case was representative, the 'author' had 'authority' over the **troupe**. Perhaps these two are playwrights, and they're demanding payment for a script."

"But if they had so much power, why wouldn't they be more frank about it?" Phil asked. "Why the **pseudonyms** and masks?"

"Good question," said Torres. "Any thoughts, Caitlin?"

"Maybe these people with authority weren't supposed to have it, and therefore the authority of this D. Constable depends on their not letting on they're the ones with the real authority."

"Who wasn't supposed to have authority?" Phil asked, not following Caitlin's **convoluted analysis**.

"Hippolyta and Rosalind."

"Why?"

"Well, to begin with, what if they were women?"

"I thought they were."

"We can't take their sex for granted," Leo said. "They may have adopted **pseudonyms** as a **deception**."

"What about this D. Constable?" Phil asked **dubiously**. "Do you think that's a man?"

"In the play he is," Torres said.

"Which play?" Caitlin asked.

"*Love's Labours Lost*. The *D* stands for *Dull*, specifically Anthony Dull, a minor character who happens to be a constable. As I pointed out before, Costard, the clown, is also a character in the play."

"Correct me if I'm wrong," Leo said, "but are we beginning to entertain the notion that this D. Constable is none other than Shakespeare himself?"

Torres nodded. "I must admit, the **allusions** to the theater, the choice of aliases, and the date of the letter all make that a distinct possibility."

"If that's the case," Phil said, "then isn't Shakespeare being **ironic** when he calls himself 'dull'? That's not the usual adjective you'd think of to describe the Bard of Avon."

"True," Torres said, "but let's consider the situation in historical and psychological **context**. It's no secret that many great creative artists have difficulty dealing with the pressures of success. Harried by their own and others' expectations, they often become unproductive and **ineffectual**. Perhaps this was the case with Shakespeare. Remember, his output was **prodigious**.

"By 1599, when this letter was written, he'd composed twenty plays in half as many years and was establishing himself at The Globe. This deep involvement in the theater, the need to produce more work, and the responsibility he felt toward his actors all might've begun to take their toll. Thus it wouldn't surprise me if Shakespeare wrote this letter at a point when he had begun to feel a bit worn around the edges—in other words, 'dull.'"

"And so," said Caitlin, picking up the professor's train of thought and taking it one step further, "this letter could demonstrate the **validity** of the theory you proposed last Sunday at the radio panel. You said that Shakespeare may have hired a woman to write for him. This might prove that Shakespeare hired *two* **anonymous** women to write a play for him, possibly even the sequel to *Love's Labours Lost*."

Torres smiled. "Exactly. Nor do we have to assume that Shakespeare played the employer's—or constable's—role only once. Look at the phrase 'your own good office.' That seems to **imply** a relationship that had already proved **fruitful**."

"The 'always' in the next sentence would **substantiate** that reading," Leo said.

"However," Torres said, "fascinating as this theory may be, it's still **inconclusive** because it's only **conjecture**. There's nothing **explicit** in the letter that links it to Shakespeare. We still need **incontrovertible** proof."

"Which brings us right back to where we started," Leo said **ruefully**, "sitting here with the answer to the puzzle right under our noses and not knowing where to look." He sighed. "Maybe what I need to do is put myself in Prospero's place, just try to get inside his head for a minute and think, if I were an old practical joker, I'd probably hide my literary treasure in—"

"Tooth and Nail!" Caitlin shouted. She was staring at the **transcription** of the letter on the monitor.

"Huh?" Leo said.

"Look at this sentence," she cried, pressing her finger to the screen. "It says, 'Why must you always haggle with me tooth and nail?'"

"What about it?" Phil asked.

"Tooth and Nail. The secret society. It's where the treasure's hidden!"

"Of course. That must be it!" Leo said, slapping his forehead. "Way to go, Caitlin."

Torres chuckled. "It figures. Prospero founded the place."

"So it was right under our noses after all," Phil said. He looked at Caitlin and Leo. "Well, what are we waiting for?"

"Hold on just one minute," Torres said. "You're not thinking what I think you're thinking, are you?"

"We're not thinking anything, Carmen," Caitlin said, flashing the professor her most **ingenuous** smile.

Torres, unconvinced, gave the three students a **dubious** frown. "Look here," she **remonstrated**. "Don't do anything **impetuous** or **unethical**. I have to go to *The Taming of the Shrew* tonight at the Stink. We can discuss this **problematic** situation tomorrow, okay? Just be **prudent** and sleep on it."

The three students nodded. "Sure, Carmen," they replied in unison.

Once outside the professor's house, Caitlin could hardly contain herself. "How are we going to get in?" she asked her companions as they began walking down Cedar Street toward campus.

Phil zipped his jacket up against the light rain. "Good question," he said. "Got any ideas, chief?"

"Maybe Bill can help us. I think he once interviewed a **disgruntled** Tooth and Nail member who'd gotten sick of Teddy's shenanigans and quit the fraternity."

"Great," Caitlin said, taking hold of Leo's arm. "Then let's go see what our **intrepid** *Herald* editor has to say."

"Wouldn't you know," Bill Berkowitz said to the ceiling. "Just as I was getting into it." He put a marker in *The Impossible H. L. Mencken: A Selection of His Best Newspaper Stories* and set the volume on the coffee table on top of Bliss and Patterson's *Writing News for Broadcast*. Then he dragged himself out of his chair and trudged across the living room.

The digital clock next to the phone said 11:58. He picked up the receiver and answered in a tone that was not particularly **cordial**.

"It's me," said the voice on the other end of the line.

Bill's face relaxed into its usual **benign** expression. It was Tony Scolari, his assistant editor for campus affairs and right-hand man at the *Herald*.

"Hey, Tony. What's up?"

"Something big, and I thought I'd better call in case you wanted to make any last-minute changes for tomorrow's edition."

"Well?"

"Somebody broke into Professor Torres's house up on

Cedar. Apparently a neighbor found Torres's cat howling on her front stoop in the storm, and it's a house cat, so when the neighbor went over and rang the professor's doorbell—"

"Forget about the neighbor. Was there any **vandalism**? Anything stolen?"

"The town police are checking the place out. All I know so far is that they found some Sasquatch-sized footprints, broken glass, and a wall safe that'd been forced open."

"Tony, you're an ace. Where are you now?"

"Down at campus security."

"Can you meet me at the professor's house in ten?"

"I'm on my way," Tony said and hung up the phone.

Bill threw on a raincoat and grabbed an umbrella. As he flew down the stairs, his brain raced, wondering about the documents Leo said he'd given to Carmen Torres and worried about what might be happening to his friends right now inside of Tooth and Nail.

Chapter 29

Descent into the Maelstrom

It was pouring. The granite tombstones in the old cemetery behind Holyfield Chapel were tilted at odd angles, as though huddling for warmth against the storm.

Just inside the spiked iron fence, Leo knelt in the mud, trying to remove the hinges from the heavy wooden door that Bill's **clandestine** contact had said would lead to a **subterranean** passage into Tooth and Nail. On one side, Caitlin, in foul-weather gear, aimed a flashlight, while on the other Phil, in a jacket that was far from **impermeable**, held a bag of tools he'd borrowed from the radio station.

Leo gave the screwdriver a good twist. It slipped. "It's no use. The heads of the screws are caked with paint and I can't get any purchase."

For a few moments the three students looked at the seemingly **impregnable** door, trying to think of what to do next. Then Caitlin, shivering, broke the silence.

"Are you sure this is the way Bill's friend said to get in?" she asked Leo.

"I don't see any other doors around here, do you?"

"Why don't we try knocking out the pins," Phil suggested.

"Good idea," Leo said. "Got a hammer?"

Phil pulled one from the bag and handed it to Leo. As he

wedged the head of the screwdriver under the lip of the pin and then tapped the butt of the screwdriver with the hammer, the **tumultuous** storm seemed to redouble its efforts. The **tempestuous** clouds rumbled and the **malevolent** wind howled through the graveyard, lashing the old elms and oaks and whipping the wet clothes of the students.

Caitlin jumped up and down to stay warm. "We sure picked a great night," she said **ironically**.

Tap, tap, tap. The first pin popped out.

Phil leaned against the heavy door to keep it steady.

Tap, tap, tap. Out came the second pin.

Phil and Leo shimmied the door to free the **protruding** deadbolt. Then, grunting with the effort, they slid the door sideways and leaned it against the wall. As Phil gathered the pins and tools and put them in the bag, Caitlin aimed the beam of the flashlight into the opening.

The dark maw was **forbidding**, but whatever **indecision** they might have felt at the prospect of crossing the threshold was **obliterated** when a bolt of lightning and **concomitant** thunderclap exploded in the sky. The storm was right on top of them. Before they knew what they were doing, the three students scrambled down the stairs into the gloom.

"Well, we're in a tunnel," Leo said. "That's a good sign."

"If anybody's **claustrophobic**, it's too late to apologize," Caitlin joked.

"I'm just not wild about cramped spaces," Phil quipped back.

As they made their way along the narrow tunnel, Caitlin kept the flashlight focused a few feet ahead. The brick walls and low brick ceiling were damp and stained, and the dirt floor was slick with a thin layer of mud. Here and there the **serpentine** roots of trees had burst through the surface of the earth in their search for **sustenance.**

"Now I know how Jonah felt," Leo said.

"Who's Jonah?" Phil asked.

"A character in a biblical **allegory**," Leo explained. "While fleeing from God, Jonah was thrown overboard, swallowed by a whale—otherwise known as Leviathan—and after a **protracted sojourn** in the belly of the beast, spewed forth."

"So the whale barfed him up?" Phil said.

"In no uncertain terms."

"I'm not so sure the analogy holds," Caitlin said. "What happened to him was **involuntary**. But we're down here of our own **accord**. And we're not running away from anything. We're on our way toward something."

"I certainly hope so," Leo said.

A moment later Caitlin's flashlight revealed a concrete platform and the foot of a spiral stairway. Slowly and silently they ascended the winding steps. At the top was a small landing that ended abruptly at a wall.

Caitlin shone the beam over the smooth surface. There was no door—only a door-sized rectangle recessed into the brick wall. There were no knobs, handles, or levers in sight.

Caitlin turned to Leo. "What now?"

Leo studied the surface of the wall. "It doesn't look too promising," he **conceded**.

"It figures," Phil muttered. "First 'The Gold Bug' and now 'The Cask of Amontillado.' I think I'm living in a tale by Edgar Allan Poe."

"Why's that?" Caitlin asked.

Phil's face was grim. "In the story, a character named Fortunato is fettered to a wall in a crypt and then sealed in, brick by brick."

"Sealed in? You mean he was buried alive in there?"

"That's right. It's a revenge story."

"Hey, keep it down," Leo whispered.

Phil and Caitlin watched as Leo, his head half-turned in concentration, began to rap the wall gently. The recessed area produced a more **resonant** sound than did the area around it. After half a minute, Leo stood up and stroked his chin. "It must be a trick door. Phil, will you give me a hand?"

"Sure, chief."

Phil and Leo tried to slide the panel open, but it was too heavy and smooth. It wouldn't budge.

Phil reached into his bag and produced a small crowbar. "Maybe this will help."

Leo wedged the tapered tip into the crack between the panel and the brick wall and pulled hard. A chunk of brick broke off and fell to the landing, but that was all. The effort was **futile**. They were at an **impasse**. Phil scowled and gave the **intractable** wall a swift kick.

"Kicking won't help," Caitlin said. "What we need to do is think."

"More like pray," Phil sighed.

Leo began to pace the small landing. "There's got to be some way to get inside, probably a secret switch or something."

"This is a secret society, so maybe there's some kind of chant or password," Caitlin suggested half-seriously. "Anybody know any **incantations**?"

Leo shrugged. "Abracadabra? Shallakazam?"

"How about 'Open Sesame'?" Phil suggested.

Caitlin laughed and leaned against the wall. Her hand pressed against a brick, which moved under her weight. There was a grinding sound as the recessed panel slid to the left, disappearing into the surrounding wall.

"Well, how about that," she said. "Phil, I didn't know you dabbled in necromancy."

Phil grinned. "There's a lot you don't know about me."

"A subject for some other enchanted evening," Leo said, ushering them quickly through the opening.

The beam of Caitlin's flashlight searched the interior. **Indistinct, amorphous** objects danced in the light. Phil felt along the wall until he found a switch.

The three students could not believe their eyes. Speechless, they wandered around the room, marveling at all the **relics** of hunting, heraldry, and war from bygone eras. On one wall, stuffed hawks and falcons hovered over the menacing heads of wild boars and elk, their glass eyes bulging fiercely. On a second wall, and in several display cases around the room, were all manner of **archaic** implements of mayhem and carnage: pikes, battle-axes, crossbows, broadswords, sabers, muskets, and pistols. There were spiked maces for breaking armor, stout shillelaghs for cracking skulls, and dirks for swiftly cutting a throat or skewering a belly. On the other two walls hung less grisly fare: a row of shields bearing colorful coats of arms and splendid tapestries **depicting valorous** knights and **vanquished** dragons.

"Wow, look at this," Caitlin said.

"What is it?" Phil asked, joining her.

On a small, ornamental table lay a very large, very old book, its faded cover studded with dark gems and embossed with peculiar, **esoteric** lettering. Phil carefully lifted the cover and frontispiece to reveal the title page, on which "Secrets of Illuministic Wisdom, by Ibn Sabin" was written in beautiful calligraphic script.

Caitlin's jaw dropped. "This is the same book I saw in Professor Bibb's apartment."

"Really?"

"Yes, he said it was a spiritual text based on the **doctrine** of the Sufis."

"Who the heck are they?"

"An **obscure** Islamic **sect** that had something to do with St. Francis of Assisi, the Knights of the Round Table, the Order of the Garter, and all kinds of crazy stuff. And get this—he told me he had the book insured for two hundred thousand dollars."

"What's it doing here?"

"Maybe Tooth and Nail is involved in stealing rare books, or maybe Bibb and Teddy Prospero are partners in a plot to raid the Prospero collection. I don't know. All I know is I've got a strong hunch that something **insidious** is going on around here."

Phil nodded. "I think I know what you mean. This place is like a **bizarre** museum—for maniacs and murderers."

"And other **nefarious** characters," Caitlin added dryly as Phil picked up a blunderbuss and sighted down the barrel.

"Don't shoot," Leo called from a doorway on the other side of the room. "There doesn't seem to be anybody around. C'mon, we've got some searching to do."

As Leo and Phil headed down the hall, Caitlin opened the door across the way and found the switch. A row of sconces came on, casting a rosy glow over a paneled room. She looked around.

A billiards table occupied the center. A dartboard hung on the far wall. A card table stood in the corner. She headed for the cabinets that lined the wall on the left and began going through them.

The first contained several athletic trophies, none with a date later than 1983. The second held a rack of pool balls, a stack of magazines, cards, and other odds and ends. The third was entirely empty.

Just an **exalted** clubhouse for boys, she thought.

"Hey, Caitlin!"

Phil stood in the doorway, nearly jumping out of his shoes with excitement. "Come on. Leo found the library!"

They hurried down the hall. When they got to the library, Leo was already busy. All four walls of the spacious room were lined with bookshelves, and he had started in a corner near the fireplace, **methodically** looking through each book on each shelf.

"Check this out!" he said, waving a faded volume. "*Fifteen Seconds to Play*, a Chip Hilton sports story."

"Not exactly the most **edifying** fare," Caitlin said as she walked to the middle of the room and staked out a section of shelf to search.

Leo laughed. "That's an **understatement**. I read these things when I was ten."

Phil stood in front of the large fireplace, put down the tool bag, and surveyed the room. Another big job, just like the costume room, he thought. He noticed that there were two doors, one at each end of the room. "Maybe we should lock these doors, just in case," he suggested.

"Good idea," Leo responded, flipping through several paperbacks.

Phil turned the night latches on both doors, then walked back to the fireplace and removed the screen. There was a small pile of embers still burning under white ash. When he crouched down and blew on them, they reddened. He took several logs from the woodbox beside the hearth and placed them on the andirons. He fanned the embers with a book and the bone-dry wood caught almost immediately. When the logs began to blaze, he stood and looked around the room.

"Any suggestions on where to begin?" he asked Leo.

"Anywhere you want. There doesn't seem to be any order. Just start somewhere and be **meticulous**."

"Okay," Phil said, opting for a spot near the fireplace.

Leo's right, he thought, as he began searching. At one time the library might have been ruled by a system, Dewey Decimal or otherwise, but it had long since **deteriorated** to the point where any concept of organization was impossible to **discern**. The collection was also a peculiar study in contrasts, from the **profound** and sober to the **superficial** and **fatuous**.

Phil noticed that this literary disarray was not the only sign that the library had become the victim of neglect. An oriental carpet that covered most of the floor was faded and **threadbare**. One of the two sleek art deco ceiling lamps hung askew. Cracks in the green leather club chairs stationed about the room had been clumsily mended with duct tape. And over everything lay a thin film of dust.

"It looks like this place has seen better days," Phil said, pulling down a well-thumbed potboiler from the shelf.

"Prospero founded Tooth and Nail as a literary club," Leo said. "I guess they've let the original vision slide."

Phil held up a **dilapidated** volume and shook his head. "Forget about the treasure. We'll be lucky if we find a book that's worth more than five bucks. Take a look at the mold on this one."

"Stop yapping about standards, you guys," Caitlin said. "I've got a whole stack of quality material over here." She was sitting on the floor, surrounded by piles of books.

Leo and Phil hurried to her side.

Crouching down, Leo examined several of the titles. *"Pericles, Coriolanus, Timon of Athens, The Winter's Tale.* Why didn't you tell us?"

"I haven't found anything **noteworthy** yet," Caitlin replied. She pulled several more old books from the bottom shelf. As she did so, a worn leather-bound **tome** fell over on its side with a resounding thump.

"Check out that big fat one," Phil said, pointing to it. "It looks really old."

Caitlin reached over and wiped the dust off the cover. Then she laughed. *"All's Well That Ends Well.* How **auspicious**!" She grunted as she attempted to lift the cumbersome book.

Leo leaned forward to assist her. "Be careful. It looks as if the spine's broken."

"Don't worry. I've got it," Caitlin said, but the weight was too much and the book slipped from her grasp. The cover flipped open and a sheaf of brittle, yellowed papers slid onto the floor.

"Oh my God!" Phil exclaimed.

Caitlin scrambled to pick up the loose papers.

"Wait!" Leo commanded. "That manuscript could be four hundred years old. Let me handle it."

Leo got on his knees and gently gathered the papers together. When he was done, he transported the bundle to a table next to a chair. Phil and Caitlin were right behind him, eagerly looking over his shoulder.

"What does it say?" Caitlin asked.

Leo took a deep breath, released it slowly, and read the words on the first page of the manuscript. "Love's Labours Won, a romantic comedy by Rowena Hester," he recited slowly. Then, **exultant**, he thrust his fists into the air. "This is it! This is Shakespeare's missing play! I can't believe it!"

"You mean Rowena and Hester's play," Caitlin said. "It looks as though the two authors have combined their first names into one full name."

"Who are Rowena and Hester?" Phil asked her.

"The letter, Phil. It was addressed to the Shakespearean characters Rosalind and Hippolyta, remember?"

"So?"

"So *Rosalind* and *Rowena* both start with *R* and *Hippolyta* and *Hester* both start with *H*. Get it?"

Phil eyes widened. "Rowena and Hester are their real names! So the letter *was* from Shakespeare, and it *was* addressed to two women who were writing for him."

"Precisely, Einstein," Caitlin said. She tapped Leo's shoulder. "Aren't you going to look through the manuscript?"

"Yeah. Let's see what's inside," Phil urged.

Tentatively, Leo turned a few pages. Here and there in the margins and between the lines of neatly printed text were notes scribbled in the same crabbed and **cryptic** handwriting in which the letter fragments had been written.

"These must be Shakespeare's comments to the authors," Leo said. "The handwriting **corroborates** Carmen's theory.

Too bad she couldn't be here with us. Her help was **crucial**."

Caitlin **reverently** ran her fingers along the edge of one of the pages, taking care not to touch any of the handwriting. "I don't mean to sound **mercenary**," she said, "but do you have any idea what this might be worth?"

Leo shrugged. "I can't even begin to guess. Several million, maybe? And with the letter, a whole lot more."

Phil patted him on the back. "Now that you've finally got it, chief, what do you plan on doing with it?"

The sound of rattling keys interrupted the conversation.

The three students looked at the door. There was a click as the bolt drew back and the latch turned.

Chapter 30

Double, Double, Toil and Trouble

While the others stared, Caitlin picked up the precious manuscript. She tried to hide it behind her back, but it was too **unwieldy**. She didn't want to appear **furtive**, so she held the sheaf of papers in front of her as **nonchalantly** as she could.

"I see I have some unexpected guests this evening," Teddy Prospero said, closing the door behind him. There was a **smirk** on his face and a revolver in his hand.

"Somehow I knew you'd show up," Leo said.

"Have you forgotten? I live here. This is my home." Teddy delivered the lines with a **contemptuous** sneer, then waved the gun toward the corner of the room. "Get over there, all three of you. Now!"

The group retreated and huddled together in the shadow of the dusty bookshelves.

"What do you want from us?" Leo asked.

"For starters, how about an explanation of why you're trespassing. Tooth and Nail is private property, and in case you haven't noticed, you guys are here without an invitation. I could have the cops arrest you for breaking and entering—not to mention stealing," he added, eyeing Caitlin. "What's that you've got there?"

Caitlin clutched the manuscript close to her chest. "What we came for tonight has nothing to do with you."

"Correction," Teddy said. "It has everything to do with me. Would you want somebody to break into your home?"

Caitlin shook her head.

"Then why don't you tell me exactly what you did come for?" Teddy pressed, advancing toward Caitlin. "C'mon. Let's see what you've got there."

Leo stepped in front of Caitlin and glared at Teddy. His face tensed but his voice remained **placid**. "You knew about the letter, didn't you?"

Teddy looked perplexed. "What letter?"

"The letter from Professor Prospero—from your grandfather."

"I don't know anything about any letter. In fact, I haven't the faintest idea what you're talking about."

"Don't be **obtuse**. You know exactly what I'm talking about. You're **culpable**. Don't deny it. You chloroformed Hargrave. You knocked me out and searched Phil's room. And then you hired some creep to attack Phil and Caitlin in the theater and **harass** them at the football stadium."

Teddy's response to these allegations was a **derisive** laugh. "Everybody says you've got such a wonderful mind, Leo, but I think you're losing it. Unlike you people, I don't need to **violate** the law to get what I want—which in this case is only what I'm entitled to from my grandfather's estate. As soon as my suit against the college is resolved, I'll be set."

He sat down in a club chair in the middle of the room and looked at Leo. "I never laid a finger on Harry, and I didn't attack you either, Leo. But frankly I'm glad somebody did. You deserved to get your **complacent**—"

Leo lunged at Teddy.

"Chill out, man!" Phil said, grabbing Leo's jacket with both hands before his counselor could do anything **foolhardy**. "The guy's a jerk," he added under his breath, "but he's a jerk with a gun."

While Phil **restrained** Leo, Caitlin turned on Teddy. "You wanted to get back at your grandfather for cutting you out of his will. And you wanted to get even with Leo at the same time. So when you found out about Prospero's letter, you figured you'd just let us solve all the clues and then snatch the treasure away from—"

"Caitlin!" Leo shouted.

A grin spread across Teddy's face. "How **intriguing**," he said, raising the gun and pointing it at Caitlin. "Tell me. What's this about a treasure?"

Chagrined, Caitlin looked at Leo, hoping he would supply a suitable answer. But before anyone could speak, the door opened.

Harold Hargrave stood on the threshold, one hand on the doorknob. His open trenchcoat was dripping wet. "Yes, Ms. Ciccone, please tell us all about the treasure," he said.

Teddy stood up. "Harry, how nice of you to join us. Are you part of this treasure-hunting party too?"

Hargrave stepped into the room. "Yes, I suppose you could say that."

Teddy aimed the gun at the librarian. "Then that's too bad, because I'll have to ask you to step over there and join your friends."

A **devious** smile tugged at the corners of Hargrave's rigid mouth. "I don't think so, Teddy," he said in a **dispassionate** tone.

"Don't be difficult now. Just get in the corner and I'll be happy to continue this little chat."

"Do you know what a **quagmire** is?" Hargrave asked.

Teddy snorted. "Do I look like a walking dictionary?"

"Your **inane** brand of **levity** is not amusing," Hargrave said, his voice filled with **disdain**. "It's unfortunate that you don't know what a **quagmire** is, because I think you're about to step into one."

Teddy's finger tightened on the trigger. "Harry, just shut up and get over in the corner. Now!"

Phil tensed, preparing to take advantage of any opportunity this **diversion** might afford him, when a **minuscule** movement at the other end of the room caught his attention. The latch on the door was turning. Then the door opened silently. Phil glanced at Leo and Caitlin and knew from the astonished expressions on their faces that they saw the man too.

He was large—enormous, in fact.

Even without the mirror sunglasses, Caitlin knew instantly who he was. He wore the same bulky army fatigue jacket, and in his hand he held a long, shiny switchblade. He glided silently across the carpet while Hargrave and Teddy continued their **altercation**.

"I don't think you understand," Hargrave was saying. "You are the dunce who'll be sitting in the corner presently, not I."

Teddy started to laugh, but only half a laugh came out. The rest of the sound got stuck in his throat when the big man threw a **brawny** arm around his neck.

"You try anything and I'll cut out your kidneys," he hissed, pressing the knife against Teddy's side.

"Drop the gun," Hargrave commanded.

Teddy obeyed. The revolver landed on the floor with a thud. Hargrave bent down and picked it up. He looked over at Leo, Caitlin, and Phil, who stood frozen in the corner.

"Don't do anything **rash** or **impulsive**," Hargrave told them. He looked at Teddy. "Are you comfortable?" he asked.

Teddy's eyes bulged and his face was **pallid**. His shoes dangled an inch off the ground.

"Let him go, Melvin," Hargrave ordered. "I think I'd like him present for the final act of our little play."

Melvin released his grip and Teddy slumped to the floor, gasping for breath.

"Now, Ms. Ciccone, would you step forward, please?"

Caitlin hesitated.

"Don't be afraid. You won't get hurt if you cooperate."

Reluctantly, Caitlin took a step forward.

"A little further, please. To the chair."

Caitlin obeyed.

"Good. Now, put that manuscript you're holding down on the table next to the chair."

Caitlin looked back at Leo, who shrugged sadly.

"There's nothing we can do about it," he said.

She set the manuscript on the table.

Hargrave picked it up greedily. "Melvin, keep an eye on our friends," he said, sitting down in the club chair to examine his prize.

Melvin bent over, yanked Teddy to his feet, and gave him a shove. Teddy stumbled to the corner and stood beside Leo. **Disgruntled**, he hung his head.

Leo looked at him and whispered, "If you didn't know about the letter or the treasure, then what were you after?"

"What's mine," was Teddy's **succinct** and **dour** response.

"So you didn't knock me out and search Phil's room?"

"No."

"And you didn't chloroform Hargrave?"

Teddy shook his head.

"Then if you didn't, who did?" Leo asked, half to himself.

"This **surpasses** all my expectations!" Hargrave exclaimed. As the librarian gloated over the manuscript, Melvin turned to Caitlin and grinned, revealing a **lurid** gold incisor.

"*Ciccone.* That's a nice name," he said.

When she didn't respond, Melvin leaned over and grabbed a handful of her hair.

Caitlin screamed.

"Knock it off!" Phil yelled, taking a step forward. Melvin ignored him.

"Get your hands off me!" Caitlin howled. She kicked her **assailant** hard in the shin.

Melvin didn't flinch. Instead he jerked her head back and bent over her. "I oughtta cut your throat," he said, his **fetid**, **malodorous** breath enveloping her.

The blade flashed. Caitlin felt the sharp tip against the soft flesh beneath her chin. Enraged, Phil rushed the big man.

Melvin shoved Caitlin aside and spun around with a backhand swipe of his knife. Phil sprang back as the **keen** steel opened a gash in the sleeve of his jacket.

"Come on, chump," Melvin growled, beckoning with the blade.

A deafening blast shook the room. Chunks of plaster fell from the ceiling. The smell of cordite hung in the air.

Harold Hargrave stood in front of his chair, pointing the revolver at the two **combatants**. "Step back, McKnight."

Phil took Caitlin's hand and they rejoined Leo and Teddy.

The chief curator turned to Melvin. "Behave yourself or I swear I'll use this gun on you too."

"Sorry. I just wanted to teach him a lesson."

"I fail to see how stabbing Mr. McKnight can serve a **didactic** purpose."

"I wasn't gonna kill him. I just wanted to make him bleed."

"I'm sorry, Melvin, but there's no time for **wanton barbarity**. As the Preacher says, 'To every thing there is a season, and a time to every purpose under the heaven: a time to be born, and a time to die; a time to plant, and a time to pluck up that which is planted'; and most important, 'a time to get, and a time to lose.'"

"Ecclesiastes," Leo observed. "I see you've been **perusing** that King James Bible Prospero gave you, Professor."

Hargrave smiled **indulgently** at Leo's remark. "Yes, and it appears that this is my time to get and your time to lose. One might say it's your day of **reckoning**."

"I'm not so sure about that," Leo said. "I know a few lines from Ecclesiastes too: 'I saw under the sun the place of judgment, that wickedness was there; and the place of right-eousness, that **iniquity** was there.'"

A dry, crackling laugh erupted from the chief curator's mouth. "Very **adroit banter**, Leo. Unfortunately, **rhetoric** won't alter the outcome of this literary treasure hunt." From a pocket inside his trenchcoat Hargrave removed an enve-lope and held it up before the group. "It's too bad, really, that you worked so hard only to fail dismally. I have all your papers right here: Prospero's letter, with your notes on his ci-phers; the three fragments of the Shakespeare letter; and now the priceless manuscript itself. And what do all of you have? Nothing."

Caitlin gasped. "That envelope was in Carmen's safe! How did you get it?"

"Melvin's more **dexterous** than he appears, Ms. Ciccone. I must thank you for keeping all the **pertinent** papers in one place. It was quite helpful in **deducing** where you were headed tonight."

"But how did you find out about Prospero's letter, any-way?" Phil asked.

The librarian looked at him **imperiously**. "Does my **per-spicacity** surprise you?"

"No, but I think you owe us an explanation," Leo said.

Hargrave grinned. "It would be a pleasure to explain how I outfoxed you." He sat down again in the club chair, crossed his legs, and rested the revolver in his lap. "Make yourself comfortable for a minute," he told Melvin, "while I **endeavor** to **enlighten** these poor simpletons."

Melvin seated himself in a chair nearer the group, his eyes trained on Phil and his switchblade at the ready.

Hargrave set the envelope down on the manuscript, which lay on the table beside his chair. "When Reggie deliv-ered Prospero's gifts to the executors the day before our first meeting, I took the precaution of examining each one before locking them in the closet of the Bohring Conference Room. You see, I never trusted the old man. He was an **incorrigible** practical joker, and I had already been grievously **deceived** by him once. Naturally, I wasn't about to let him have a **posthumous** laugh at my expense, so I opened the letters.

"When I saw that Prospero intended to **bequeath** a special prize to Leo, I couldn't help but wonder about its nature and monetary value. Given Prospero's **renown** for **munificence**, I knew the gift would be very generous indeed. I thought, 'Why should a mere undergraduate receive this treasure? Wouldn't justice be better served if it were given to someone more **meritorious**, someone who had sweated and toiled in the world of books and devoted his life to knowledge?'"

"And you decided that someone should be you," Phil said, making Hargrave's **implication explicit.**

"I didn't decide. I knew. This **invaluable** document deserves my guardianship as much as I deserve its rewards. Would you prefer that it belong to some **insignificant pedant** or, worse, fall into the **frivolous** and **capricious** hands of the **vulgar, unenlightened** masses? I can imagine no greater tragedy or injustice."

"So you believe you're acting in the interests of justice?" Caitlin asked **incredulously.**

"I was in the right place at the right time. I saw an opportunity I had earned and I seized it. That, Ms. Ciccone, is justice."

Caitlin rolled her eyes, disgusted by Hargrave's **arrogance.** "How **virtuous!**" she said **ironically.**

Leo looked Hargrave in the eye. "So, you kept Prospero's letter, forged a replacement, and put it in my book. Then, when I came to your office to tell you I suspected something was wrong, you **implicated** Teddy and tried to blame the **deception** on him."

"Can you think of a more suitable scapegoat?" Hargrave asked with a **supercilious** smile. "After all, he was threatening to sue the college. In fact, he tried to get me to enter into **collusion** with him. He wanted me to use my influence as principal executor to persuade the committee to settle his suit by liquidating a million dollars' worth of items in Prospero's collection. He promised me a kickback and said he planned to keep half the money for himself."

"That's a lie," Teddy protested. "You wanted me to drop the suit because you were afraid I'd win and you'd lose your precious collection." He sniggered and looked at Leo. "He tried to bribe me by offering me books. Can you believe that?"

"A valiant effort, Teddy," Hargrave said, "but you're hardly the master of **duplicity** your grandfather was. The truth is that you and your pathetic secret society are in financial straits because of your obsessive gambling and **intemperate speculation** in the stock market."

Caitlin cut in. "We found Prospero's letter in a book on Shakespeare that Phil took out of the library. It's by Margaret Hargrave. Is she your wife?"

"Was. She died a year and a half ago. She was a **prominent** Shakespearean scholar. It's a pity she isn't here to share the thrill of my discovery tonight."

"You mean your theft. It was our discovery," Leo said bitterly.

Hargrave's thin lips stretched into a grin. "The rest of the world will never know that."

"How did Prospero's letter get into your wife's book?" Caitlin asked.

"I hid it there temporarily, just before I was assaulted in my office. When I got back from CHS the next morning, the book and the letter were gone. So I hired Melvin to search Leo's room. Unfortunately Leo returned unexpectedly and Melvin had to take **drastic** measures. When I realized that whoever attacked me either wasn't looking for the letter or didn't find it, I figured a staff person must have reshelved the book without my authorization, which turned out to be the case."

"The question is," Caitlin said, "if Teddy didn't attack you, and obviously Leo didn't, then who did?"

The chief curator pressed the tips of five spidery fingers against his forehead. "I don't know. Maybe one of them is lying. It doesn't matter now."

Leo wasn't so sure about that. Something told him there was still a wild card left to be played in this game.

"So you traced the book to me through the library's records and had Melvin search my room," Phil said.

Hargrave nodded. "After I knew who my **adversaries** were, it was easy, with Melvin's assistance, to keep up with you. Although I didn't have the map, I knew it was only a matter of time before you'd lead me to the treasure."

"What do you plan to do now?" Caitlin asked, afraid that she already knew the answer.

The librarian leaned back in his chair, his eyes **suffused** with the glow of triumph. "I'm an orderly person. I don't like to leave any messes." He turned to his **accomplice** and nodded.

"If you think you're going to get away with this, Professor Hargrave, you're wrong," Caitlin said. "You can't silence the truth. Besides, people know where we are. I'm sure they'll be here any minute."

"Maybe so, Ms. Ciccone," Hargrave said, getting to his feet. "But by the time your rescuers arrive, if they do arrive, you can rest assured that all your 'truth' will have gone up in smoke." He reached into the pocket of his trenchcoat and produced a quart-sized glass bottle. "Gasoline," he said. He unscrewed the cap and took a whiff. "High octane."

Melvin removed several pairs of handcuffs from his jacket and rattled them cheerfully as he approached the group. While he handcuffed Caitlin to Teddy and Teddy to a metal ring on the mantel of the fireplace, Hargrave worked his way around the perimeter of the room, pouring a thin stream of the **combustible** amber liquid onto the carpet.

"I think we're ready," he said as he splashed the last few drops at the four students' feet.

Suddenly the door to the library opened and a **sonorous** voice boomed from the hallway.

"Cease and desist, you **despicable scoundrel**!"

Chapter 31

Fire Burn
and Cauldron Bubble

An ancient, **wizened** man shuffled into the room, supporting his stooped and shriveled frame with a stout oaken staff. A long oilskin cloak hung from his hunched shoulders. His face was **sallow** and deeply wrinkled; his cheeks were sunken and his crown was entirely bald. But for his eyes, which twinkled roguishly, he was a picture of death.

"Professor?" Leo cried.

"Prospero?" gasped Hargrave.

"Oh my God, it's a ghost!" Teddy screamed.

"No more an apparition than you are," said Reginald Burton-Jones, stepping into the room behind Prospero.

"I can't believe you're alive," Leo said.

"What the devil are you *doing* alive?" Hargrave demanded.

"Don't you remember *The Tempest*, Harold? I've come to play the good magician to your **scurrilous, usurping** Antonio."

Melvin abandoned Teddy and lumbered to Hargrave's side. "You want me to handle these clowns?" he asked, cocking a thumb at Prospero and Burton-Jones.

Prospero looked at the **bestial** henchman. "Ah, I see we have already cast our Caliban," he quipped.

"Just a moment," the librarian told Melvin. "This is an

interesting development in the plot. Let's see where it leads."

"I don't get it," Teddy said, aghast at the sight of his grandfather returned from the grave. "How did you manage to fake your death?"

Prospero shook his head **ruefully**. "Obviously you still haven't read *Romeo and Juliet*."

Teddy scowled **defiantly** and looked away.

"Did you drink something, like Juliet, that made you appear dead?" Caitlin asked.

The old man nodded. "Yes. As you remember, Friar Laurence gives Juliet an elixir that will put her in a state of suspended **animation**. 'In this borrowed likeness of shrunk death,' he instructs her, 'thou shalt continue two-and-forty hours, and then awake as from a pleasant sleep.'"

"Where did you get this elixir?" Phil asked.

"On one of my archaeological expeditions I came to know a group of Yaqui Indians in Sonora, Mexico. They had maintained their **primordial** ways, living an **austere** existence entirely isolated from society. Among them was an old **soothsayer** and **savant** who knew the many secrets of roots and cacti and herbs. During one of their sacred ceremonies he gave me an **acrid** potion to drink. I didn't know what it was, but not wanting to offend him, I took it.

"When I awakened, I felt strangely **rejuvenated**. I was told that I had died and that my soul had **sojourned** in the house of the spirits and returned two days later, reborn. I was so impressed by this **potent** bit of wizardry that I persuaded the shaman to give me the recipe. To **feign** my death, I simply **procured** the necessary ingredients and repeated the procedure. Reggie handled all the bureaucratic details, of course—the death certificate, cemetery plot, and so forth."

"An enchanting tale," Hargrave said, his voice reeking with **sarcasm**. "It's too bad you had to come back to life."

"Too bad for your **avaricious** schemes, perhaps," Prospero said, shaking his staff at the librarian. "I'd hoped for a **tranquil** and **obscure** retirement, but when Reggie **apprised** me of Leo's visit to your office, I suspected you had uncovered my coded letter to Leo and were attempting to **subvert** my plans. I was **compelled** to **intervene**. I instructed Reggie to try to recover the original, which resulted in your being chloroformed."

"See, I told you I had nothing to do with that," Teddy said.

Prospero gave his grandson a **contemptuous** look. "That may be true, Teddy, but it hardly **exonerates** you from the host of **improprieties** you've committed, all of which have **debased** the Prospero name." He turned toward Caitlin and Phil. "At any rate, it was **fortuitous**, and in this case most fortunate, that my letter wound up in the hands of Leo's **resourceful** friends, Mr. McKnight and Ms. Ciccone."

"If you don't mind my asking, sir," Phil said, "in your condition how did you . . . how could you know . . . "

Caitlin interrupted. "Let me **clarify** Phil's question. After we got your letter to Leo, how were you able to follow what we were doing and know we'd be in Tooth and Nail tonight?"

"Ariel," Prospero said, extending a gnarled hand in the direction of Burton-Jones. "Like Shakespeare's Prospero, I had a **covert** and **discreet** assistant. Reggie was my eyes and ears and, in not a few cases, my hands and feet."

Burton-Jones chuckled. "It was my pleasure, considering the **magnanimity** you showed me in your will."

"My will, of course, was not to die but to disappear," Prospero said. "After all," he added in a **droll** tone, a wry smile spreading across his wrinkled face, "death is a rather **irrevocable** event that tends to lend an air of finality to things. It's curious, but people are more likely to take you seriously when you're dead than when you're alive. All in all, I felt there were **singular** advantages to appearing to have made my exit while remaining onstage, as it were."

Hargrave sighed and sat down in a club chair. "Since you're so **loquacious**, Professor, why don't you turn your gift of gab to a subject that I'm curious about. This remarkable manuscript—how did you ever manage to obtain it?"

"I'd be glad to tell you that story," Prospero said, "but I'm afraid I must rest my decrepit old bones. May I sit down?"

Hargrave **acquiesced** and Burton-Jones helped the old man get seated.

"In June of 1973," Prospero began, his **resonant** voice filling the room and showing none of the **ravages** of time that had **debilitated** his once sturdy and **vigorous** physique, "I was invited to attend an academic conference in the north of England and deliver a paper entitled 'The Ontology of Place: Landscapes in English Literature.' As you know, these conferences are not wholly devoted to **studious endeavors**.

"One night I found myself at the gaming table. There were four of us playing: a cold-eyed fellow named Benjamin Bulben from Trinity College, Dublin, who was a specialist on William Butler Yeats; some **ostentatious** fop from the Continent who claimed he was Baron-Something-or-Other—the exact title escapes me now; and a roly-poly young Welshman who fancied himself a poet. He was an **impetuous** player and drank heavily at the table. He had pluck, I'll grant him that. During one hand he tried to bluff me by betting a huge amount of money on nothing but a pair of fives."

"I don't have time for **senile digressions**," Hargrave interrupted. "Get to the point, and try to be **concise**."

Professor Prospero gave the chief curator an obliging smile. "This fellow, who had recently come into a sizable estate, ended up owing me quite a sum. When I mentioned that I collected books, he said that his inheritance had included a fine library, and he proposed that I take my pick of it in lieu of cash. As one who has found many treasures in unexpected places, I agreed to the arrangement without reservation.

"At first, however, I was sorely disappointed. The young man's collection, not unlike the one you see here in this room, had more than its share of undistinguished volumes and worthless junk. But something told me not to give up. Finally, in a dusty corner of the attic, underneath a pile of old records of **negligible** value, I found the extraordinary manuscript now resting on that table."

"What about Shakespeare's letter to Rowena and Hester?" Leo asked, gesturing toward the envelope lying on top of the manuscript. "How did you come across that?"

The lines on Prospero's face deepened as he smiled. "To my utter astonishment and delight, the three fragments were tucked right inside the manuscript of the play. It was, as they say, a **veritable** gold mine."

"Precisely what I was thinking," Hargrave said. "Why on earth did you keep these manuscripts so long? You could have sold them for a fortune or used the discovery to further your career."

"This may be hard for you to understand, Harold, but I had no desire for money or fame. When the materials came into my hands, I was about to retire. My wealth was already great, and as a scholar I had long since established my **niche** in academia. The last thing I wanted was to be in the midst of the **tumult** such a **revelation** would **inevitably** ignite around the world.

"And so, although I had always intended to share my discovery, I found myself constantly putting off the difficult decision of how and when to do it. My **procrastination** was **exacerbated** by my growing fear of the evil that would **ensue** should these texts fall into the **corrupt** hands of those who would **exploit** them for personal gain. I felt **compelled** to protect these wondrous documents, even if that meant withholding them from **conscientious** scholars with the most **upright** and lofty intentions."

The old professor sighed deeply and shifted in his seat. "Months turned into years and the years into two decades. Then one day, after coming through a bad bout of pneumonia, I realized something had to be done, for my days were surely numbered. It **irked** me to think that I would die and the letter and manuscript might be lost again on account of my indecision; after all, they had already **languished** in **obscurity** for nearly four hundred years. Finally, I devised a plan.

"I wanted to leave a **legacy** of **benevolence**, not just money and material things. In Leo Kabnis I saw all the qualities the teacher in me admired and, though he was not my flesh and blood, everything I had hoped for but been denied as a father and grandfather. So I created an **ambitious** puzzle worthy of his talents and arranged things so I could observe his progress and enjoy his success from the wings—before permanently departing the theater, so to speak."

Prospero paused and looked up at Hargrave, then at the gleaming gun in the librarian's hand. "The only flaw in my plan was making you principal executor. I'm bitterly disappointed in you, Harold. I thought you had **integrity**—or at least a conscience."

Hargrave glared at the old professor. "You **arrogant, hypocritical egotist**," he said, spitting out the words. "You think your role in this is entirely **altruistic**, yet you fail to **perceive** how all along you've tried to control events and **dominate** others' lives to suit your **whims**. You spent your whole life **masquerading** as a great **philanthropist** when you were actually building a shrine to your own magnificence. Your muchvaunted generosity was nothing but a **charade**. You thought giving money to found a library in your name and making me its curator would **eradicate** the ill will between us. Well, I'm no dog, professor; you can't just toss me a bone. I'm not so easily **assuaged**."

Hargrave dug a handkerchief out of his pocket, wiped the beads of sweat off his brow, and continued his **tirade**. "You were always so **officious**, weren't you, always butting in, always trying to get a laugh at someone's expense. Have you forgotten how one of your **ill-conceived** pranks nearly **sabotaged** my career? I was the **laughingstock** of the whole college, for God's sake! Did you expect me to forget that?"

"I certainly didn't expect you to cherish a grudge for twenty-five years and allow it to **undermine** your sanity and **corrupt** your soul."

"That's enough, you **dotard**!" Hargrave shouted. "I don't have to put up with the ravings of a **senile** fool."

From his position with the others in the corner by the fireplace, Leo watched the librarian approach Prospero and raise the gun until the muzzle was only inches from the old man's forehead. Prospero sat perfectly still and calm, a **stoic** expression on his face.

"I'm sick of your **smug** soliloquies," Hargrave said through clenched teeth. "I'm sick of you and everything about you."

"Back off, Harold," Burton-Jones said, stepping from behind Prospero's chair. "Don't be a fool."

Hargrave turned and shoved the gun in the valet's belly. "You're the fool, you **toady**."

Leo saw Hargrave's finger tense on the trigger and his heart slammed against his ribs. He dashed across the room. In one swift motion he grabbed Hargrave's wrist, forced the gun up and away, and jammed the chief curator's head back with the palm of his other hand.

Hargrave groaned and staggered backward. Leo pinned him against the wall. The librarian sank his teeth into Leo's thumb. Leo howled and smashed his forehead into Hargrave's nose.

"Jolly good show!" cried Burton-Jones. "They're at it tooth and nail."

"Reggie, look out!" Caitlin shouted as Melvin charged.

The **stalwart** Englishman dodged the knife and landed a lightning right cross to the big man's jaw. Melvin absorbed the blow like a bag of sand. Grinning, he raised the knife to strike again.

Phil took two long steps and sailed through the air. He landed with one knee in the middle of Melvin's back, driving the big man to the floor. Melvin grunted, then heaved Phil from his back like a water buffalo shaking off a pesky tsetse fly. Phil rolled aside and swiftly regained his feet as Melvin struggled to get up from the floor.

"Make Caliban a knight," Prospero said, handing his oaken staff to Burton-Jones.

"With pleasure." Burton-Jones, no stranger to the **pugilistic** arts, hefted the sturdy wood and smacked it across Melvin's shoulders.

"Take that, you **reprobate**," Prospero cried.

From the corner, Teddy echoed the old man's **sentiment** in considerably less **genteel** terms.

Melvin, roaring in pain and fury, rose to his feet. Phil wound up and let fly with everything he had. The uppercut caught the big man square in the face. As he reeled and slammed against the wall, his back hit a switch and the lights went off.

In the half-light from the blazing fire, the fight raged on. **Distorted** shadows **grappled** and **writhed** in a **grotesque** dance. Tables and chairs overturned. Books tumbled from shelves. A shot rang out. Someone screamed.

The fire shifted suddenly and a burning log rolled off the andirons onto the hearth. Red-hot embers crackled and sprayed onto the carpet. There was a horrifying whoosh as the trail of gasoline ignited.

The **ardent** flames quickly stormed the walls, scaling the shelves and feeding on the dusty volumes. **Acrid** smoke choked the room.

The door flew open.

Bill Berkowitz, Carmen Torres, and three Holyfield police officers, their guns drawn, burst into the room.

"Oh my God, the manuscript!" Caitlin cried. "And Shakespeare's letter!"

Beside a broken table, a pile of papers curled and blackened into ashes. *Love's Labours Won*, the object of so much love and so much labor, had been lost.

Epilogue

At eight o'clock Monday morning, a crowd formed as students lingered on their way to breakfast and classes to gawk at the result of the previous night's **conflagration**. Although the stone exterior of the building appeared **relatively unscathed**, the damage to the interior of Tooth and Nail had been extensive. Through the blackened doorway workers carried out charred furniture and sodden, partially consumed beams. A **vigilant** security guard and a cordon of yellow ribbon marking the **periphery** of the premises kept the **inquisitive** at a safe remove.

Two hours later, Harold Hargrave, his nose broken, and Melvin Rudnik, his hulking body battered, were arraigned separately at the Holyfield Municipal Courthouse on State Street downtown. Both men were remanded into custody to be held without bail pending trial on numerous charges, including breaking and entering, burglary, assault with a deadly weapon, arson, and **conspiracy** to commit murder. The district attorney assured *The Plains* that both were open-and-shut cases and predicted that Melvin, a repeat offender, would get fifteen to twenty, while Hargrave, for his **transgressions**, could look forward to at least ten **contemplative** years behind bars to catch up on his reading.

Late that afternoon, Lucy Kwon and Juliet Jacques sat in Java Jones discussing a special edition of the *Herald* that covered the fire at Tooth and Nail, the charges against Hargrave and Melvin, and the **complex** events leading up to their arrest. Their interest in the story was especially **keen**, as the article carried the byline of Caitlin Ciccone.

That night, after gamely trying to read a few chapters of Immanuel Kant's *Critique of Pure Reason*, Phil gave up and joined Jimmy Thomas, Chris Bednarski, and Max Meyerhoff for a round of pool in the Student Center. He was so **enervated** and fatigued, however, that he nearly fell asleep on the table trying to line up a bank shot.

On Tuesday morning, Teddy Prospero appeared before the Campus Rules Committee, which voted **unanimously** to expel him for "**malicious** and **incorrigible** behavior," "**wanton** disregard of the rules and regulations governing campus life," and "**egregious** failure to meet the minimum standards of academic performance required of all students enrolled at Holyfield College."

On Tuesday afternoon Leo and Caitlin were interviewed by *Newsweek, Time*, and *USA Today*.

That night, a limousine driven by Annie Howe quietly left the confines of a sprawling estate on the outskirts of town. Two hours later it arrived at a small airfield outside Des Moines, where a private jet was waiting to fly to an undisclosed destination in Mexico. On board that flight were two passengers: Reginald Burton-Jones and Edward Anthony Prospero.

Meanwhile, "Lend Me Your Ears," the evening call-in show hosted by Randy "The Maniac" Malone, featured Leo, Caitlin, and Phil answering questions about their adventure. The first caller was Ben Schofield from CHS, who offered Caitlin "**covert** congratulations from an **anonymous** source." After that, the telephone lines were jammed for two solid hours.

The following afternoon, Professor Torres returned the essays on Emily Dickinson to her students in English 112. Phil was **jubilant** when he saw "Well thought out!" written on his title page below a grade of A minus.

On Thursday morning, the college's board of directors voted in special session to promote Carmen Torres from associate to full professor and grant her **tenure**—"in recognition," they said, "of her **laudable** contributions to literary scholarship and her **meritorious** commitment to the advancement of pedagogy at Holyfield College."

The next night, Caitlin finally sat still long enough for Phil to sketch her face, as she'd promised to let him do the night they'd met at *Romeo and Juliet*. She was so pleased with the results that she treated him to a Megaworks Special at Salerno's and, in a gesture of supreme **benevolence**, let him have the last slice.

On Saturday morning Leo went to CHS to have the stitches removed from his thumb. Dr. Abigail Benson **drolly apprised** him that he would live to type again.

That evening, two hundred-odd **notable** guests—faculty, alumni, visiting dignitaries, **philanthropists**, and a handful of selected undergraduates—gathered in the Rococo Room in Guild Hall for a **sumptuous** reception celebrating the opening of the new Prospero Memorial Library. The soft strains of lute and lyre wafted through the **capacious** chamber, accompanying the **genteel** conversation.

In the heart of the crowd, Caitlin, Phil, and Leo stood chatting **amiably** with Professors Bibb, Martext, and Torres.

"One thing still confuses me," Caitlin said as she watched Bibb devour a heap of **lavish** hors d'oeuvres. "Remember your rare book on the Sufis?"

Bibb gave his busy mouth a **fastidious** wipe with the corner of a linen napkin. "It's not something I'm **apt** to forget. Why?"

"What was it doing in Tooth and Nail?"

Bibb took a gulp of mineral water and swallowed **audibly**. "Teddy was telling the truth for once, Ms. Ciccone. That wasn't my book. Mine is real. Theirs is a **facsimile**."

"But it looked exactly like yours."

"A **superficially alluring** volume, of course, but it can't be worth more than a hundred dollars."

Caitlin took a **tentative** bite out of a chunk of cheddar cheese and washed it down with diet cola. "Then Tooth and Nail was a Sufi organization?"

"Not by any stretch of the imagination. The Sufis are **ascetic** and **spartan** in their ways. However, I believe some of Tooth and Nail's modus operandi are **derivative**."

"How do you mean?" Leo asked.

"Their costumes and **initiation rituals**, their **occult** chants and runes, their allegedly magical formulas, that sort of thing. One might say that they took a more **literal** approach to the Sufi text, whereas my interest has always been in its historical, **mystical**, and **aesthetic** value."

"Nor have you overlooked its economic value," Martext joked.

Professor Bibb let out a **robust** laugh. "Well, I'd be a fool if I did. But since you bring it up, Bart, you certainly have never been one to close the door when opportunity knocked."

Martext took a sip of white wine. "Not quite never, Theo."

"Is that so? To what do you refer?"

"As you know, the Theater Studies Department is always on the qui vive for stray funds. The college subsidizes only half of our production costs. The rest we must raise through ticket sales and donations. Well, I don't need to tell you that over the past twenty years the chief benefactor to the theater program was Edward Anthony Prospero. He supplied the money to **renovate** the Stink, and when we wanted to bring opera to Holyfield he—"

"Yes, of course, Bart. We've heard this all before. Prospero's **beneficence** is **proverbial**."

"Quite. So a couple of weeks ago I made a visit to Tooth and Nail to see if a **magnanimous** interest in theater was something that could be passed down genetically."

"What did you find out?" Torres asked.

"Teddy offered to contribute a generous amount to the program, but demanded that in return I use my vote as an executor to approve a settlement of his lawsuit. At first I told him I'd consider his offer because I thought I might be able to reason with him. It soon became clear, however, that any **capitulation** would have **catastrophic** consequences. So I told him **categorically** that I'd rather rot in hell than agree to his sleazy deal."

The director paused and looked at Professor Bibb, who was grinning at him. "I am a man of the theater," he said, glaring at his plump colleague, "but I do have principles, you know."

"Indeed," said Bibb, popping a bite-sized quiche into his mouth.

At the far end of the hall, Dean Arthur Calvin Herbert tapped his crystal glass with a fork, calling everyone to attention, and the conversation **dwindled**. As the administrator began to address the crowd, Phil looked across the wide hall.

Above a **voluminous** fireplace, a **grandiose** portrait of Professor Prospero had been displayed for the occasion. The painting **depicted** the old man at a somewhat younger stage of life. He was dressed in an Elizabethan doublet and ruff; in one hand he held a quill pen, in the other a yellowed manuscript. Two rosy-cheeked cherubs fluttered around his head and seemed to be whispering something amusing in his ear. In the background, **arable** farmland extended to the horizon.

"And so it is with great pleasure," Dean Herbert intoned, "that I introduce to you the guiding spirit of this great institution, President Harriet O'Donnell."

As the applause died down, Phil yawned and decided it was time to stretch his legs.

"I would like to thank everyone who has made this historic moment possible," O'Donnell began.

Phil burrowed through the dense crowd and found an empty alcove where a set of French doors stood open to the expanse of West Quad. He walked onto the moonlit terrace and breathed deeply. The evening air was chilly but crisp and **rejuvenating** after the stuffy atmosphere inside. He was loosening his tie when he felt a warm hand touch his shoulder. It was Caitlin.

"It's hot in there," she said.

The moon bathed them in **pallid** light. For a while they stood together in silence, gazing up at the sky. Then they looked in each other's eyes.

Caitlin took Phil's hand and smiled. "Well?"

Phil felt his heart begin to pound. "Well what?"

"What do you mean, 'what'?" She squeezed his hand. "Don't be such a **reluctant** Romeo. Kiss me."

He pulled her close and they kissed, briefly but tenderly.

"'O trespass sweetly urged,'" Caitlin whispered, quoting *Romeo and Juliet.* "'Give me my sin again.'"

Phil grinned. "With pleasure."

They kissed again, deeply.

"It's about time," Caitlin sighed and rested her cheek against his chest. Phil held her tightly.

When they walked back through the alcove into the crowded hall, Caitlin laughed and pointed to the portrait of Prospero.

"Phil, do you see what I see?"

"Yes," he said, and burst out laughing too.

There was no question about it. The old codger was nictitating.

Exercises

Below are some exercises designed to help prepare you for the SAT. They serve two **beneficial** purposes: First, they give you some practice with the three question types in the verbal sections of the test—analogies, sentence completions, and reading comprehension (or critical reading) questions. Second, they give you a chance to reinforce your understanding of the SAT words you've just learned by seeing some of them in yet another **context**—the kind of **context** in which you'll see them on the SAT.

In format, these exercises are exactly like the questions on the real test. In content, they're a little different. Most of them, particularly the analogies and the sentence completions, contain a lot more tough words than the average SAT question. So don't be discouraged if you find them challenging. We wanted to provide you with as much reinforcement as possible. Also, not all SAT questions test vocabulary as **overtly** and **explicitly** as these do. Some primarily test your verbal reasoning skills. These questions do that too, but since the express purpose of this book is to help you build and strengthen your vocabulary, they test word knowledge as much as logic.

After you've worked through the exercises for each question type, be sure to read the explanations that follow. You'll find some **shrewd** strategies in them as well as the "best" answers—which, by the way, are the answers you're instructed to find on the SAT. As far as the test is concerned, *best* means "the only answers you're going to get credit for," but by using *best* rather than *correct*, the test makers are acknowledging that there is often more than one "good" answer to a question—especially a verbal question. So don't be too hasty about picking your answers; read all the choices for each question before you decide which one is "best."

Analogies

Let's start with an example:

> **TRIVIAL**:DEEP::
> (A) **inane**:foolish
> (B) intellectual:**profound**
> (C) **petty**:small
> (D) lighthearted:**grave**
> (E) **voracious**:hungry

As you can see, an SAT analogy consists of six pairs of related words, one question pair and five answer pairs. Your task is to pick out the answer pair that expresses a relationship most similar to the relationship expressed in the question pair.

The best way to approach an analogy question is to start by forming a sentence that captures the relationship between the two words in the question pair. We call that sentence a *bridge*. For this example, your bridge might be "*Trivial* is the opposite of *deep*" or "Something *trivial* is not *deep*." Once you've built your bridge, then use it to test out each of the answer choices:

—— is the opposite of ——.

Inane is the opposite of *foolish*.
> Wrong. *Inane* and *foolish* have almost the same meaning.

Intellectual is the opposite of *profound*.
> Wrong. These words are neither antonyms nor synonyms.

Petty is the opposite of *small*.
> Wrong. *Petty* and *small* are nearly synonymous.

Lighthearted is the opposite of *grave*.
> Bingo. One meaning of *grave* is "serious," and *serious* is the opposite of *lighthearted*.

Voracious is the opposite of *hungry*.
Wrong. To be *voracious* is to be very *hungry*.

So the best answer is choice D.

Three words of caution: First, don't expect the first bridge you construct to work for every analogy. Sometimes your bridge will connect more than one answer pair. In that case it's too broad, or general, and you'll have to make it narrower. Other times your bridge won't connect any of the answer pairs. In that case it's too narrow, or specific, and you'll have to make it broader.

Second, don't be **seduced** by answer pairs that are related in meaning to one or both of the words in the question pair. In our example, for instance, choices A, B, and C are **superficially** attractive because *inane* and *petty* have almost the same meaning as *trivial*, and *profound* is a synonym for *deep*. However, as we've already seen, the words in these answer pairs are not related in the same way as the words in the question pair. Remember that you're looking for similar relationships, not similar meanings.

Finally, don't think that you have to follow the order of the words in the question pair when you're building your bridge. If it's more convenient to reverse them, then do so. Just remember to reverse the words in the answer pairs too when you test them out.

There are many common analogy types. The following questions illustrate some of those types.

1. **METICULOUS**:SLOPPY::
   (A)   obsessive:**indifferent**
   (B)   **insatiable**:hungry
   (C)   **gregarious:abject**
   (D)   **evanescent**:fleeting
   (E)   forgetful:**reminiscent**

2. BIRD:FLOCK::
   (A) **combatant**:contest
   (B) **shard**:pottery
   (C) word:**concordance**
   (D) actor:**troupe**
   (E) chapter:book

3. **CATASTROPHIC**:UNFORTUNATE::
   (A) **tempestuous**:unhealthy
   (B) helpful:**adverse**
   (C) **abhorrent**:distasteful
   (D) **apocryphal**:unknown
   (E) **acute**:dull

4. **PECCADILLO**:SIN::
   (A) **heresy**:religion
   (B) fault:defect
   (C) **tome**:book
   (D) **iniquity**:wickedness
   (E) **turret**:tower

5. PLEASURE:**HEDONIST**::
   (A) **solitude**:recluse
   (B) flattery:**sycophant**
   (C) future:**soothsayer**
   (D) good:**beneficiary**
   (E) drama:**protagonist**

6. YIELD:**ADAMANT**::
   (A) talk:**terse**
   (B) **procrastinate**:lazy
   (C) perform:**hidebound**
   (D) combust:**spontaneous**
   (E) **prevaricate**:sincere

7. SHRINE:DEVOTION::
   (A) church:**seclusion**
   (B) **edifice**:construction
   (C) prison:**incarceration**
   (D) monastery:**repression**
   (E) court:**incantation**

8. **CASTIGATE**:PRAISE::
   (A) **captivate**:charm
   (B) protest:**acquiesce**
   (C) **divulge**:disclose
   (D) **corrupt:glorify**
   (E) **coerce**:encourage

9. **DELUGE**:RAIN::
   (A) sleet:hail
   (B) **conflagration**:fire
   (C) **tirade**:language
   (D) **ordeal:fiasco**
   (E) **tumult**:earthquake

10. HEAR:**CACOPHONY**::
    (A) transmute:**alchemy**
    (B) view:eyesore
    (C) smell:**clamor**
    (D) balance:**symmetry**
    (E) **decipher**:code

11. MEDDLE:**OFFICIOUS**::
    (A) **intervene**:presidential
    (B) doubt:**incredulous**
    (C) **irk:pompous**
    (D) interfere:**authoritative**
    (E) **verify:legitimate**

12. **FOOLHARDY**:BOLD::
    - (A) **erudite**:learned
    - (B) **intractable:obstinate**
    - (C) **imprudent**:cautious
    - (D) **haughty**:proud
    - (E) **intrepid**:courageous

13. DOCUMENTS:**ARCHIVE**::
    - (A) **theses**:library
    - (B) **relics:mausoleum**
    - (C) **anecdotes**:encyclopedia
    - (D) statues:**niche**
    - (E) **artifacts**:museum

14. **NOXIOUS**:HARM::
    - (A) **tedious**:boredom
    - (B) **toxic**:waste
    - (C) **voracious**:hunger
    - (D) **lethal**:injury
    - (E) **ominous**:misfortune

15. **FACILITATE**:EASIER::
    - (A) **infer**:clearer
    - (B) **fathom**:deeper
    - (C) **elucidate**:brighter
    - (D) **augment**:greater
    - (E) **validate**:truer

16. ENERGY:**ENERVATED**::
    - (A) **vigor:invigorating**
    - (B) innocence:**ingenuous**
    - (C) **bias**:intolerant
    - (D) interest:**apathetic**
    - (E) fame:**infamous**

17. **FACADE**:APPEARANCE::
    - (A) **pseudonym**:name
    - (B) costume:**guise**
    - (C) **masquerade**:party
    - (D) **facsimile**:copy
    - (E) **euphemism**:phrase

18. **AVARICIOUS**:WEALTH::
    - (A) **winsome**:charm
    - (B) **chimerical**:fantasy
    - (C) **vindictive**:revenge
    - (D) **impoverished**:money
    - (E) **furtive:conspiracy**

19. FIND:**UBIQUITOUS**::
    - (A) touch:**tangential**
    - (B) understand:**subtle**
    - (C) avoid:**inexorable**
    - (D) **pervade:universal**
    - (E) **apprehend:salient**

20. **DUPE:HOAX**::
    - (A) **charlatan:deception**
    - (B) **pugilist**:fight
    - (C) **laughingstock:ridicule**
    - (D) **malcontent**:rebellion
    - (E) **scoundrel:stratagem**

Explanatory Answers

1. A "X is or means the opposite of Y" is a common analogy type: *meticulous* is the opposite of *sloppy*; *obsessive* is the opposite of *indifferent*. Another way to express this is "Someone or something that is X is seldom or never Y."

2. D This question is one of the many variations on the "whole:part" or "part:whole" analogy. In this case, the whole is a group and the part is one member of the group: a *flock* is a group of *birds*, and a **troupe** is a group of *actors*.

3. C The bridge for this common analogy type is "X is extremely Y": something that is **catastrophic** is extremely *unfortunate*, and something that is **abhorrent** is extremely *distasteful*.

4. E This question illustrates the "X is a Z type of Y" analogy: a **peccadillo** is a small *sin*, and a **turret** is a small *tower*.

5. A This analogy type links a group or class of people with something that they are by definition associated with: a **hedonist** is someone who by definition seeks *pleasure* just as a **recluse** is someone who by definition seeks **solitude**. Notice that this bridge is broad (or general) enough to capture the relationship between an answer pair as well as the question pair, but it's narrow (or specific) enough to eliminate other attractive answer pairs. For example, although a **soothsayer** (choice C) is by definition closely associated with the *future*, he or she doesn't seek it but instead tries to predict it. Similarly, a **beneficiary** (choice D) receives rather than seeks *good*.

6. E This analogy type also links a class of people (all those who can be characterized as **adamant**) with something (the action of *yielding*) that they are by definition associated with. In this case, however, the association is negative rather than positive: someone who is **adamant** does not *yield* just as someone who is *sincere* does not **prevaricate**, or lie.

7. C This question links a place with its primary purpose. Since the purpose can be expressed in different ways, there are several variations on the bridge for this analogy type. A simple "X is a place primarily for Y" works here: a *shrine* is a place primarily for *devotion*; a *prison* is a place primarily for **incarceration**.

8. B This is another "X is or means the opposite of Y" analogy: **castigate** is the opposite of *praise*; *protest* is the opposite of **acquiesce**.

9. B This is another "X is a Z type of Y" analogy: a **deluge** is a great (as in heavy, intense) *rain*; a **conflagration** is a great (as in violent and destructive) fire.

10. B This analogy is similar to the ones in questions 5 and 7. The only difference is that it involves a thing (in the grammatical sense) rather than a person or a place. To construct your bridge, recall the meaning of **cacophony**: a **cacophony** is something that, by definition, is unpleasant to *hear*; similarly, an *eyesore* is something that is unpleasant to *view*.

11. B This is the positive version of the analogy type illustrated by question 6: someone who is **officious** by definition is inclined to *meddle*, or interfere; likewise, someone who is **incredulous** by definition is inclined to *doubt*, or disbelieve.

12. D This is a variation on the "X is extremely Y" analogy type: to be **foolhardy** is to be overly *bold*; to be **haughty** is to be overly *proud*. Choices A and E, though very tempting, are both wrong for the same reason. They fit the "X is extremely Y" pattern, but they don't fit the "X is *overly* Y" variation on this pattern. In other words, whereas **foolhardy**, like **haughty**, has a negative connotation, **erudite** and **intrepid** both have positive connotations.

13. E This analogy is similar to the one in question 7: an **archive** is a place for storing and preserving *documents*; a *museum* is a place for storing and preserving **artifacts**.

14. A This is one of the variations on the "cause:effect" or "effect:cause" analogy: by definition, something that is *noxious* causes *harm* and something that is **tedious** causes *boredom*. Choices D and E are both tempting, but each is wrong for a different reason. In D the effect is **understated**: by definition, something that is **lethal** causes *death*, not just *injury*. In E the relationship is not strictly causal: by definition, something that is **ominous** foreshadows but doesn't necessarily bring about *misfortune*.

15. D This is another variation of the "cause:effect" analogy: by definition, to **facilitate** something is to make it *easier* and to **augment** something is to make it *greater*.

16. D This analogy, like the sixth one, involves a definition by negation: to be **enervated** means to be "without *energy*"; to be **apathetic** means to be "without *interest*."

17. A This analogy is similar to the tenth one. To construct your bridge, think back to the definition of **facade**: a **facade** is a false *appearance* just as a **pseudonym** is a false *name*.

18. C By definition, a person who is **avaricious** is **motivated** by a desire for *wealth* just as a person who is **vindictive** is **motivated** by a desire for *revenge*.

19. E By definition, something that is **ubiquitous** is everywhere; therefore, it is easy to *find*. Analogously, something that is **salient** is by definition **conspicuous**; therefore, it is easy to **apprehend** (in the sense of **perceive**).

20. C This analogy is similar to the fifth one: a **dupe** is the butt (or victim) of a **hoax** (or trick) just as a **laughingstock** is the butt (or target) of **ridicule**.

Sentence Completions

A sentence completion is simply a fill-in-the-blank question. You're given a sentence with one or two words missing, and you're asked to pick out the word or words that fit best in that **context**. There are no special tricks to answering sentence completions. All you have to do is pay attention to the key words in each sentence.

Key words come in two common varieties. One variety consists of words like *but, after, therefore, for example,* and so on. These are function words that clue you in to the structure of a sentence and tell you how the ideas are related. The second variety consists of content words—nouns, verbs, adjectives—that tell you what the tone and style, as well as the ideas, of the sentence are.

When you're approaching a sentence completion question, try to come up with your own answer before looking at the choices given. Study the sentence carefully, paying close attention to the key words, and decide which word or words you would use to complete the sentence. Then look for the answer that best matches yours. This strategy will prevent you from reading a sentence too hastily, overlooking a small but important word, and choosing a **superficially** attractive—but wrong—answer.

The following questions illustrate some of the ways that SAT sentence completions test your verbal reasoning skills as well as your vocabulary.

1. Despite the fact that the Shaker communities are all but
   ----, they leave behind a ---- **legacy** of architecture and
   furniture design.
   (A) dormant..**modest**
   (B) self-sufficient..**prodigious**
   (C) extinct..**vital**
   (D) **obsolete**..transitory
   (E) isolated..**robust**

2. Such ---- explanations fail to address the real depth of the question; the universe was not made in jest, but in ----, **unfathomable** earnest.
    (A) **superficial**..transparent
    (B) **perfunctory**..jocular
    (C) penetrating..**somber**
    (D) facile..solemn
    (E) **trite**..**inane**

3. Stephen Crane's first novel, *Maggie: A Girl of the Streets,* which ---- in grimly ---- detail the world of New York's slums, has been credited with introducing realism into American fiction.
    (A) **portrays**..fantastic
    (B) **embellishes**..**lurid**
    (C) reveals..**ornate**
    (D) **glorifies**..**sordid**
    (E) **depicts**..accurate

4. Each new step in science ---- twenty seemingly ---- facts as merely the various **manifestations** of a single principle.
    (A) unifies..**harmonious**
    (B) **reconciles**..**discordant**
    (C) **integrates**..identical
    (D) **undermines**..erroneous
    (E) **illuminates**..consistent

5. One can prevent a child from becoming left-handed by **restraining** that arm; however, most experts agree that this kind of ---- measure is ----, since right-handedness carries no **discernible** advantages.
    (A) **drastic**..**ineffectual**
    (B) **coercive**..pointless
    (C) **sophisticated**..costly
    (D) **discriminatory**..**innocuous**
    (E) **repressive**..**invaluable**

6. Such ---- in a matter that concerns themselves, their
   eternity, their all, ---- me more than it moves me to
   compassion; to be unable to respond even to one's own
   life is **appalling.**
   (A) **fanaticism**..repulses
   (B) **egotism**..angers
   (C) **apathy..intrigues**
   (D) **complacency**..amuses
   (E) **indifference..exasperates**

7. The majority of the inhabitants are ---- vegetarians;
   that is, they eat meat only when they can afford it,
   which, because of the **ludicrously** high prices, is
   almost never.
   (A) **reluctant**
   (B) **adamant**
   (C) **clandestine**
   (D) **resourceful**
   (E) **staunch**

8. Since the tin ears of reporters were tuned to capture only
   the mediocre remarks of mediocre men, one had to look
   for the most ---- and ---- formulation for each press
   release in order to have any chance at all of making it
   into print.
   (A) lofty..**grandiloquent**
   (B) **eloquent**..**lucid**
   (C) **lackluster..pedestrian**
   (D) **droll**..humorless
   (E) dull..**abstruse**

9. Geologists believe that two hundred million years ago
   there was a single, ---- supercontinent, Pangaea, which
   subsequent plate movements have split and ---- into the
   continents we know today.

(A) original..**obliterated**

(B) **primordial**..coalesced

(C) **subterranean**..sunk

(D) **monolithic**..shifted

(E) **immutable..differentiated**

10. This **indulgence** in modern entertainment ---- some of the explorers, who, in their great **zeal** for adventure, had eagerly expected a more ---- life in this remote part of the world.

(A) disappointed..**spartan**

(B) pleased..**stoic**

(C) **disoriented..mundane**

(D) frustrated..**affluent**

(E) **gratified..exotic**

11. Because the nation grew ---- through the continual conquest of new lands, richly endowed with **exploitable** natural resources, we came to equate democracy with free-wheeling individualism, **unrestrained** mobility, and ---- growth.

(A) powerful..**sluggish**

(B) **impoverished..incessant**

(C) **egalitarian**..controlled

(D) **prosperous**..perpetual

(E) **frugal..prodigious**

12. The quality, not the quantity, of the spiritual cures is ----; as in the case of Lourdes, a healing shrine can maintain its reputation on a **modest** percentage of successes, provided a few of them are ----.

(A) **decisive**..medical

(B) **dubious..incontrovertible**

(C) critical..**insignificant**

(D) **relevant..salutary**

(E) **crucial**..spectacular

13. It is an illusion to think that there is anything ---- about
the organism we call Earth; surely, this is the most ----
membrane imaginable in the universe.
   (A) unique..**fertile**
   (B) **exotic..vulnerable**
   (C) fragile..**impermeable**
   (D) **hostile..commonplace**
   (E) **impregnable..resilient**

14. The film's production is ---- by shooting delays, a
ballooning budget, and personal ----: the two on-screen
lovers are said to **abhor** each other.
   (A) jeopardized..**accord**
   (B) **impeded..cupidity**
   (C) **galvanized..idiosyncrasies**
   (D) **motivated..animosity**
   (E) plagued..**discord**

15. The Third Punic War was no ---- struggle; after charging
Carthage with breach of treaty and declaring war, Rome
wasted no time in blockading and razing the city.
   (A) **decisive**
   (B) **protracted**
   (C) **rash**
   (D) **covert**
   (E) **conventional**

16. The world around us seems to contain a bewildering ----
of materials; yet, properly seen, the light from ---- bodies
reveals they are all made from a few common building
blocks.
   (A) **array..corpulent**
   (B) **dearth..scintillating**
   (C) **diversity..**luminous
   (D) **uniformity..translucent**
   (E) **plethora..opaque**

17. The sense of diminishing food is an **apt** symbol for the
    less ---- sense that spiritual ---- is also diminishing as
    their once rich culture becomes watered down.
    (A) concrete..**inertia**
    (B) **intuitive..conviction**
    (C) **tangible..sustenance**
    (D) **subtle..vitality**
    (E) **metaphysical**..nourishment

18. Brought before the Inquisition, a tribunal **renowned** for
    quashing dissent, Galileo was made to ---- all of his ----
    writings supporting the Copernican theory.
    (A) **divulge..antithetical**
    (B) **promulgate..subversive**
    (C) **disown..orthodox**
    (D) renounce..**heretical**
    (E) **clarify..arcane**

19. Bruno, a major artist of the Renaissance, **imparted** ----
    sense of ---- to the human figure, which had for so long
    been **trivialized** by **flamboyan**t ornamentation.
    (A) a revolutionary..**austerity**
    (B) a **hackneyed..embellishment**
    (C) a **radical..insignificance**
    (D) an **unprecedented..symmetry**
    (E) a **spurious..grandeur**

20. The ---- of our environment and the hidden, **amorphous**
    menace that is always afloat in our air oblige us to close
    ourselves in, like those plants that ---- by storing up
    liquid within their spiny exteriors.
    (A) **animosity..succumb**
    (B) **hostility**..survive
    (C) **largess..languish**
    (D) **benevolence..flourish**
    (E) **magnitude..prevail**

Explanatory Answers

1. C The key word *Despite* signals a contrast between the two parts of the sentence, so the two words should be opposites or near opposites. Only in choice C is this true.

2. D The first half of the sentence tells you that certain (unspecified) explanations "fail to address the real depth of the question," so for the first blank an adjective that means "not deep" (or something similar) would be a good choice. The second half of the sentence contains the key word *but*, which denotes a contrast, so for the second blank an adjective that means "not in jest" would be a good choice. Choices A, B, D, and E all fit well in the first blank, but only choices C and D fit well in the second blank. Choice D, therefore, is the best answer. (Although *facile* is not in the glossary, it has a close relative there: **facilitate**. As you can **infer** from the question, one definition of *facile* is "**superficial**." You'll find others in the dictionary.)

3. E The key here is the word *realism*. You would not expect a realistic novel to **embellish** or **glorify** its subject, so choices B and D are out. Likewise, you would not expect to find either *fantastic* or **ornate** details in a realistic novel, so choices A and C are out as well. That leaves only choice E.

4. B The key word *new* indicates a before-and-after structure: before, there were twenty facts; now, there is a single principle. Choices A and C offer the best possibilities for the first blank, since *unifies* and **integrates** both denote a change from many to one. However, if the facts were **harmonious** or *identical* to begin with, they would not need to be *unified* or **integrated**. So choices A and C are out after all. Of the remaining three choices, **reconciles** in B is the next best candidate for the first blank, and since it pairs well with **discordant** in the second blank, it is the best answer.

5. B The key word *however* indicates that the second half of the sentence will oppose the successful practice of **restraining** the left arm to force right-handedness. For the first blank, even a supporter would be unlikely to call the practice *sophisticated*, so choice C is out. For the second blank, only *pointless* in choice B is consistent with the idea that "right-handedness carries no **discernible** advantages."

6. E For the first blank, you need a noun that means "unable to respond." For the second blank, you need a verb that is opposed in meaning to "moves me to **compassion**." Choices C, D, and E satisfy the first need. Choices A, B, and E satisfy the second need. Choice E, then, which satisfies both needs, is best.

7. A The key phrase *that is* indicates that the second half of the sentence explains or elaborates on the meaning of the first half. Since the inhabitants eat meat whenever they can afford it, they must be *reluctant* vegetarians. If they were *adamant* (choice B) or *staunch* (choice E) about their vegetarianism, they would never eat meat, and if they were *clandestine* (choice C) about it, no one (including the author of the sentence) would be likely to know about it. Though the inhabitants might very well be *resourceful* (choice D), there is no suggestion in the sentence that they are.

8. C The key word *since* indicates that this sentence has a cause-and-effect structure: because what gets into print is "mediocre," press releases must be "mediocre." The *and* between the two blanks suggests that the missing words will be closely related or at least compatible in meaning. Choices A, B, D, and E are out because *lofty*, **grandiloquent**, *eloquent*, *lucid*, *droll*, and *abstruse* are all, in their own ways, **antithetical** in meaning to *mediocre*, and *droll*, moreover, means the opposite of *humorless*. Choice C fits the bill.

9. D The main idea of this sentence is that a single large land mass split into a number of smaller ones. The action of splitting precludes ***immutable***, meaning "unchangeable," and *coalesced*, meaning "merged" or "united," so choices E and B are out. And if the single large land mass either had been ***obliterated*** or had started out ***subterranean*** and then *sunk* further below the earth's surface (assuming that to be possible), we wouldn't know the pieces today, so choices A and C are out, too. That leaves D.

10. A For the second blank, you need a word that is opposed in meaning to *modern*, and since comfort and convenience are usually associated with modernity (as the word ***indulgence*** suggests), ***spartan*** and ***stoic*** (choices A and B) are the best candidates. For the first blank, you need a verb that expresses how people "eagerly" expecting one thing would be likely to feel when confronted with another. That's *disappointed* (choice A) rather than *pleased* (choice B).

11. D For the first blank, a nation that continually conquered lands "richly endowed with ***exploitable*** natural resources" almost surely would not grow ***impoverished*** or *frugal*, and there's no reason to believe it would grow ***egalitarian*** either, so choices B, E, and C (respectively) are out. For the second blank, "***sluggish*** growth" is not consistent with the notions of "continual conquest," "free-wheeling individualism," and "***unrestrained*** mobility," so choice A is out, too. That leaves D, which fills both blanks nicely.

12. E The key word *as* indicates that the second half of the sentence is presenting an example of the rule stated in the first half, which is that a healing shrine maintains its reputation on the quality rather than the quantity of its spiritual cures. So the missing words must reinforce each other. *Crucial* and *spectacular* in choice E do that best.

13. C The content and balanced structure of this sentence both suggest a direct opposition between the two main ideas, so the missing words must be antonymous. *Fragile* and *impermeable* in choice C are near opposites; the words in the other choices are not.

14. E The colon indicates that the second half of this sentence—which says that two on-screen lovers *abhor*, or hate, each other—is intended to explain the phrase "personal ----." Starting with the second blank, then, you can narrow your choices to D and E because *animosity* and *discord* suggest conflict, while *accord*, *cupidity*, and *idiosyncrasies* do not. Moving to the first blank, you can easily see that choice E is better than D because bad things (delays, ballooning budgets, conflict) have bad effects—they *plague* rather than *motivate*.

15. B Again, you can **infer** from the structure of this sentence that the second half is intended to explain or elaborate on the point made in the first half. Since the second half says that Rome "wasted no time" in "razing" (or leveling) Carthage, the war clearly was no *protracted* (or drawn out) struggle.

16. C The key word *yet* signals a contrast between the two halves of this sentence. If, as the second half says, everything in the world is actually made from just a few common building blocks, then it must appear to contain a bewildering *array* (choice A), *diversity* (choice C), or *plethora* (choice E) of materials. For the second blank, the *luminous* bodies in C can **emit** light, but the *corpulent* and *opaque* ones in A and E cannot. So C is best.

17. C The structure here compares something in the physical world (a diminishing food supply) with something in the spiritual world. Spiritual things are more, not less, *intuitive*, *subtle*, and *metaphysical* than material things, so choices B, D, and E are out. As for the second blank, the word *sustenance* best fits the analogy between real food and spiritual food.

18. D The implicit structure of this sentence is one of rule and example. The beginning of the sentence says that the Inquisition quashed dissent in general, so you can expect the rest of the sentence to say that it quashed Galileo's dissent in particular. Choice D does that.

19. A The phrase "which had for so long been" suggests that Bruno started something new, so the best choices for the first blank are *revolutionary* (choice A), *radical* (choice C), and *unprecedented* (choice D). For the second blank, you need a word that is opposed in meaning to the phrase "**trivialized** by **flamboyant** ornamentation." The best choice for that is *austerity* in choice A.

20. B The verb *oblige* indicates that the structure of the first part of this sentence is causal: conditions X and Y cause us to do Z. The action of closing in is a defensive one, and one defends oneself against something negative, like an "**amorphous** menace." *Largess* and *benevolence* are positive, and *magnitude* is neutral, so choices C, D, and E are out. As for the second blank, plants obviously store up liquid to *survive* (choice B), not to *succumb* (choice A).

Reading Comprehension

All SAT reading comprehension questions test vocabulary implicitly. Some, like most of the questions below, also test it **explicitly** by asking you what a word means in the **context** of a particular passage. Since many words—even words you think you know well—have more than one meaning, the key to answering questions of this type is to go back and study the **context** before choosing an answer. In fact, this is a good strategy for reading comprehension questions in general because, according to the directions, the best answer to each one must be either stated or **implied** in the passage.

We've based our reading comprehension questions on the novel portion of this book. On the real SAT I, the passages will be shorter (400 to 850 words) and will cover a variety of (mostly nonfiction) topics. The questions, however, will be similar to these.

1. In the phrase "maneuvered through the press like an **erratic** driver" (page 8), the word "press" refers to
   (A) a **throng**
   (B) an apparatus or machine for printing
   (C) the media
   (D) vehicles
   (E) journalists

2. On page 13 of the novel, the word "**ambitious**" most nearly means
   (A) desirous of personal advancement
   (B) elaborate or extensive
   (C) **pretentious** and showy
   (D) **erudite**
   (E) extremely costly

3. The word "marked" in the phrase "marked contrast" on page 25 means
   (A) labeled
   (B) identified
   (C) rated
   (D) singled out
   (E) decided

4. When the authors say that Caitlin Ciccone "eschewed" the chocolate cake served at Steinbach Commons her first night at Holyfield College (page 30), they mean that she
   (A) ate the cake **voraciously**
   (B) chewed the cake **diligently** before swallowing
   (C) found the cake as **repugnant** as the main dish
   (D) decided to be **abstemious** and forgo the cake
   (E) took only a few **tentative** bites of the cake

5. When Caitlin says to Phil, "Nice shirt" (page 41), Phil considers the remark to be
   (A) sincere
   (B) **facetious**
   (C) **derisive**
   (D) **ambiguous**
   (E) **implausible**

6. The word "**precipitated**" is used on page 53 to mean
   (A) brought about
   (B) condensed
   (C) separated
   (D) **impeded**
   (E) hurled downward

7. On page 73 the phrase "**ostentatious allusions**" refers to
   (A) big words used in a **pedantic** manner
   (B) **egregious** errors in grammar and **syntax**
   (C) **pretentious** references to Shakespeare's plays
   (D) deliberately **deceptive** words and phrases
   (E) glaringly false **perceptions**

8. According to page 94, Prospero's "preference for American spellings and **idioms**" can best be described as
   (A) **dispassionate**
   (B) **ardent**

    (C) **eccentric**

    (D) **unorthodox**

    (E) conservative

9. The phrase "**vulgar** pastime" on page 105 refers to

    (A) a drama written in the **vernacular**

    (B) a **commonplace** activity

    (C) a play performed for the public

    (D) a **diversion** engaged in by the common people

    (E) an indecent or obscene form of entertainment

10. Which of the following best captures the meaning of the word "**inscrutable**" as it is used on page 125?

    (A) mysterious

    (B) **esoteric**

    (C) puzzling

    (D) **erudite**

    (E) **illegible**

11. When Carmen Torres says, "No novels, please—and no haikus either" (page 140), she is urging her students in English 112 to make their essays

    (A) both **diffuse** and **succinct**

    (B) **concise** but adequately developed

    (C) neither **prosaic** nor poetic

    (D) **verbose** but not **abstruse**

    (E) **coherent** and **rhetorical**

12. When Leo Kabnis says that Shakespeare's work was "**disseminated**" both before and after the Bard died (page 157), he means that it was

    (A) performed

    (B) **revered**

    (C) **compiled**

    (D) **promulgated**

    (E) applauded

13. It can be **inferred** from page 164 that the phrase "playing the **devil's advocate**" most nearly means
    (A) teasing a colleague
    (B) **refuting** an accepted argument
    (C) championing a popular cause for the sake of argument
    (D) arguing both for and against some proposition
    (E) defending a weak or questionable position

14. On page 171, the phrase **"eclectic connoisseur"** most nearly means someone who
    (A) has informed but **diverse** tastes
    (B) collects art
    (C) prefers **lavish** furnishings
    (D) appreciates beautiful things
    (E) enjoys a variety of fine food and expensive wines

15. When Leo calls Prospero "a master of **obfuscation**" (page 179), he means that Prospero
    (A) was a **prominent** Shakespearean scholar
    (B) had a **predilection** for solving puzzles
    (C) was a gifted cryptanalyst
    (D) knew how to baffle others
    (E) was an **ingenious** practical joker

16. On page 202, when Carmen Torres says, "Perhaps this is no **fortuitous** correspondence," she means that
    (A) the proximity of the two dates may not be accidental
    (B) there is a good chance the letter dated 1599 is genuine
    (C) it is unfortunate that the two events are not more closely related
    (D) it would be a remarkable coincidence if the letter and the play were both written by Shakespeare
    (E) the two dates may be closely related only by chance

17. On page 215, the phrase **"levity** and **gravity"** most nearly means
    - (A) life and death
    - (B) **absurdity** and **futility**
    - (C) **frivolity** and sobriety
    - (D) **ridicule** and **animosity**
    - (E) gaiety and **adversity**

18. On page 249, the phrase "can't get any purchase" most nearly means
    - (A) can't make an **acquisition**
    - (B) can't get a fast hold
    - (C) don't have enough light
    - (D) don't have the right tool
    - (E) don't see any way around this **impediment**

19. Prospero's remark that "death is a rather **irrevocable** event that tends to lend an air of finality to things" (page 272) can best be described as
    - (A) a sober **precept**
    - (B) an **astute** observation
    - (C) a **prophetic conjecture**
    - (D) an **unsettling paradox**
    - (E) a humorous **understatement**

20. It can be **inferred** from the novel that on page 283 the word "nictitating" most nearly means
    - (A) twitching **involuntarily**
    - (B) frowning **ominously**
    - (C) winking **conspiratorially**
    - (D) **grimacing irascibly**
    - (E) grinning **obsequiously**

Explanatory Answers

1. **A** This is a typical SAT-style reading comprehension question. It gives you five meanings of a familiar word and asks you which of those meanings is intended in a particular **context**. In this case, there are at least three clues to the correct answer: the phrase itself on page 8 ("maneuvered through the press like an **erratic** driver"), the reference to "mass of people" on page 6, and the reference to "human traffic" on page 9—all of which suggest that *press* here means "**throng**" or "crowd."

2. B This question illustrates the importance of going back to a passage and seeing how a word is used in **context**. Choice A, the primary definition of *ambitious*, is not the correct (or "best") answer here. In the phrase "**ambitious** two-week program of lectures and symposia," *ambitious* means "demanding great effort or enterprise"—in other words, "elaborate or extensive" (choice B).

3. E In other **contexts**, *marked* could mean "labeled" (choice A), "identified" (choice B), "rated" (choice C), or "singled out" (choice D), but in the phrase "marked contrast," it means "noticeable, obvious, **conspicuous**." *Decided* also has this meaning when it is used as an adjective rather than a verb. So does another familiar word, *pronounced*, which is used in this sense on page 172.

4. D *Eschewed* is an "extra-credit" word, so you won't find it in the glossary. However, if you reread the reason Caitlin gives for *eschewing* the cake—"One had to give up certain other temptations to accommodate a passion for pizza" (page 30)—you can figure out that *eschew* means "forgo, do without, pass up, abstain from, avoid, **shun**."

5. D This may not look like a vocabulary question, but if you don't know the meanings of the five words in the answer choices, that's exactly what it is. Look back at what Phil thinks after Caitlin makes the remark: "He wondered if she was serious or just making fun of him" (page 41). A remark that can be interpreted in two or more ways is ***ambiguous***.

6. A "Brought about" (choice A), "condensed" (choice B), "separated" (choice C), and "hurled downward" (choice E) are all meanings of ***precipitated***. To find out which is intended in this **context**, substitute each one into the sentence in which ***precipitated*** is used on page 53: "He also knew that their deaths would be **precipitated** by Romeo's killing Tybalt, Juliet's cousin, in revenge for Tybalt's killing Mercutio, Romeo's friend." The only choice that makes sense is *brought about*.

7. C *Ostentatious* means "showy," and *allusions* are indirect references. In this case, the **ostentatious allusions** are to two of Shakespeare's plays: *Othello* and *King Lear*.

8. B On page 94, Leo describes Prospero as "a **zealous** defender" of the American language and says that he was "**adamant**, perhaps even **fanatical**, in his preference for American spellings and **idioms**." Of the five choices, therefore, the best answer is ***ardent***, which means "very enthusiastic, passionate, **fervent**, **zealous**."

9. D The phrase "**vulgar** pastime" is used by Professor Bibb, who says that Shakespeare "was probably a front for a member of the **aristocracy**, a class that **shunned** association with the theater, which was considered a **vulgar** pastime" (page 105). You can **infer** from this statement that a **vulgar** pastime is some form of entertainment for people who are not in the **aristocracy** (the upper or ruling class). In other words, it's "a **diversion** engaged in by the common people" (choice D).

10. E "Mysterious" (choice A) and "puzzling" (choice C)

are both among the meanings of *inscrutable*, but in the **context** on page 125, where it is used to describe penmanship, *inscrutable* most nearly means "**illegible**" (choice E).

11. B   Choice C is an attractive answer since a novel is **prosaic** in the sense that it's written in prose, and a haiku is a poem—specifically, a three-line poem consisting of only seventeen syllables. However, Torres makes the remark immediately after she **specifies** how long the students' essays should be, and she would naturally expect the students to write in prose rather than verse. Therefore, she must mean that she wants the essays to be neither too long nor too short—in other words, "**concise** but adequately developed" (choice B).

12. D   Reread the sentence in which the word is used on page 157: "[Shakespeare's] work was printed and **disseminated** both during his lifetime and after his death, but there are no **extant** manuscripts." Since works are usually printed in order to be circulated or distributed, you can guess from the **context** that the correct answer is *promulgated*, which means "published."

13. E   If you don't remember what "playing the **devil's advocate**" means, look back at the **context** in which the phrase is used on page 165. Bill is trying to make a case for including Carmen Torres on the list of suspects who might have attacked Leo, but neither he nor Caitlin is really convinced that she could have done it. That's what "playing the **devil's advocate**" means: "defending a weak or questionable position for the sake of argument" (or sometimes out of sheer **perversity**).

14. A   All of the answers describe Bibb accurately, but only choice A, "has informed but **diverse** tastes," precisely captures the meaning of the phrase "**eclectic connoisseur**."

15. D It is right after he has finally **deciphered** the first clue that Leo calls Prospero "a master of **obfuscation**." The phrase is a tribute to Prospero's ability to baffle others—that is, to confound or confuse them by making something unclear or difficult to understand. That's what *obfuscation* means.

16. A As the usage note in the glossary reminds you, *fortuitous* is not synonymous with *fortunate*. A *fortuitous* correspondence is one that merely happens by chance; it may be good (fortunate), bad (unfortunate), or **indifferent**. So when Carmen Torres says on page 202, "Perhaps this is no **fortuitous** correspondence," she means it's probably no accident that the letter fragment is dated not long before *As You Like It* was entered in the copyright records. That's choice A. *Proximity*, by the way, is an "extra-credit" word meaning "nearness" or "closeness."

17. C The phrase appears in a description of the statue of Prospero that stands outside the stadium: "While the bushy eyebrows arched as if in surprise, a **subtle** smile curled up at one corner of the otherwise stern mouth, creating an expression that wavered somewhere between **levity** and **gravity**" (page 215). You can tell from this **context** that *levity* and *gravity* are opposites. The only pair of opposites with meanings similar to those of *levity* and *gravity* is *frivolity* and *sobriety* in choice C.

18. B It's Leo who uses the phrase on page 249. After trying unsuccessfully to remove some screws with a screwdriver, he says, "It's no use. The heads of the screws are caked with paint and I can't get any purchase." In this **context**, *purchase* clearly means "fast (or firm) hold on the screw heads."

19. E Look back at page 272. Prospero utters the remark

"in a **droll** tone" with a smile on his face, so he obviously intends it to be humorous. Since he is talking about death, his use of *rather* before **irrevocable** and *tends to lend* instead of *lends* both indicate that the remark is an **understatement**. Therefore Choice E is the best answer.

20. C The process of elimination works very well for this question. Prospero would be acting out of character if he were *grinning* **obsequiously** (choice E) at anyone, and if he were *twitching* **involuntarily** (choice A), *frowning* **ominously** (choice B), or **grimacing irascibly** (choice D), Caitlin and Phil would not be laughing. Therefore, *nictitating* (an "extra-extra-credit" word) most nearly means "winking **conspiratorially**."

Glossary

Key to Abbreviations

adj.	adjective
adv.	adverb
cf.	compare
esp.	especially
n.	noun
pert.	pertaining
pl.	plural
sing.	singular
spec.	specifically
usu.	usually
v.	verb

Note: This glossary includes only selected definitions—those that apply to the ways in which the SAT words are used in this book. For additional definitions, as well as for guidance on pronunciation, consult your dictionary. The numbers in brackets refer to the pages in this book on which you'll find the words used.

A

abate, *v.* to reduce or become less in value, amount, or intensity: The storm *abated*. [172]

abhor, *v.* to regard with hatred or disgust, loathe, detest. **abhorrent**, *adj.* [46, 287, 291, 298, 303]

abject, *adj.* miserable, wretched. **abjectly**, *adv.* [132, 286]

abridge, *v.* to make shorter, reduce, compress. [98]

abstemious, *adj.* eating and drinking sparingly or in **moderation**, temperate. [173, 306]

abstract, *adj.* 1. not thought of as an object or real thing or in connection with any specific example: *Honesty* and *love* are *abstract* words. 2. not dealing with or representing anything concrete or particular: *abstract* ideas; *abstract* art. [xi, 171, 182]

abstruse, *adj.* very hard to understand, deep, complicated. [101, 132, 171, 296, 301, 307]

absurd, *adj.* unreasonable, nonsensical, foolish, stupid, ridiculous (SAT synonyms: **farcical, ludicrous, preposterous**). **absurdity**, *n.* [20, 59, 104, 309]

absurd, *n.* the state or condition of **ultimate** meaninglessness in human life and in the universe: the theater of the *absurd*. [182]

abundance, *n.* a large amount, great supply, more than enough (SAT synonyms: **plenitude, plethora, profusion**). [2, 188]

abundant, *adj.* in great supply, plentiful (SAT synonym: **copious**). [212]

accomplice, *n.* someone who knowingly aids another in committing a crime. [268]

accord, *n.* agreement, harmony, concord. **—of one's own accord:** by a person's own choice or will, without outside influence, voluntarily. [251, 298, 303]

accordance, *n.* agreement, harmony: in *accordance* with your wishes. [68]

accost, *v.* to approach and speak to, often in an aggressive manner: A stranger *accosted* her on the street. [39]

acquiesce, *v.* to give in or agree without protest or complaint but also without interest or excitement. [153, 165, 273, 288, 292]

acquisition, *n.* 1. something acquired or owned. 2. the act of acquiring or owning things. [171, 309]

acquisitive, *adj.* eager to acquire or own things. [201]

acrid, *adj.* harsh, burning, or biting to the taste or smell: the *acrid* smell of cigarette smoke. [271, 277]

acute, *adj.* sharp, intense (SAT synonym: **keen**). **acutely,** *adv.* [101, 287]

adage, *n.* an old saying, a maxim or proverb. [79]

adamant, *adj.* stubborn, unyielding, inflexible (SAT synonyms: **hidebound, intractable, obdurate, obstinate**). [94, 287, 291, 296, 301, 311]

adept, *adj.* very skillful, expert (SAT synonyms: **adroit, deft, dexterous, proficient**). [viii, 98]

adjacent, *adj.* close, lying near but not necessarily in contact with. [7, 16, 35]

adjunct, *n.* something separate and less important that is added to a main thing: The wallpaper section is an *adjunct* to the paint store. [68]

admonish, *v.* to warn, caution, scold, or criticize gently, esp. against doing something wrong or bad: The teacher *admonished* the class (cf. **castigate, censure, upbraid**). **admonishment,** *n.* [134, 237]

admonition, *n.* a mild criticism or **reprimand**, a gentle warning: an *admonition* to tell the truth. [xiii, 146]

adorn, *v.* to decorate or make beautiful. [11, 24]

adroit, *adj.* skillful or clever at doing a difficult thing (SAT synonyms: **adept, deft, dexterous, proficient**). **adroitly,** *adv.* [viii, 191, 265]

adversary, *n.* a person one fights against, enemy, opponent. [150, 268]

adverse, *adj.* unfavorable, damaging to one's interests: *adverse* criticism. [73, 287]

adversity, *n.* hardship, misfortune, great trouble or difficulty. [107, 309]

advocate, *n.* a person who speaks or writes in support of another person or of a cause or issue; defender, champion (cf. **devil's advocate**). [101]

aesthetic, *adj.* of or pert. to beauty, showing appreciation of or sensitivity to beauty in art or nature, tasteful, artistic. [131, 281]

affable, *adj.* easy to talk to, pleasant, kindly, courteous, gracious (SAT synonyms: **cordial, jovial,** and see **amiable**). [18, 65]

affinity, *n.* a natural attraction, close relationship, or intense liking. [106]

affluent, *adj.* wealthy (SAT synonym: **prosperous**). [44, 70, 104, 297]

affront, *n.* an intentional offense or insult. [103]

alacrity, *n.* eager willingness and promptness, speed, quickness: She performed the task with *alacrity*. [141, 205]

alchemical, *adj.* pert. to an early form of chemistry primarily concerned with changing common metals into gold and **concocting** a potion that would ensure eternal youth; hence, possessing a seemingly magical power to change something or someone's form or appearance. **alchemy,** *n.* [103, 288]

alienate, *v.* to make unfriendly or hostile, lose the support of. [42]

alleged, *adj.* declared or assumed to be true but not proven; supposed: an *alleged* burglar. **allegedly,** *adv.* [36, 101, 102]

allegory, *n.* a story or play with a symbolic meaning usu. intended to teach a moral or lesson. [251]

allot, *v.* to distribute or assign a share or portion: to *allot* sufficient space for everyone. [97]

allude, *v.* to refer to indirectly, mention casually: She *alluded* to a scandal. [101, 105]

allure, *n.* the power of fascination or attraction, charm. [165]

alluring, *adj.* highly attractive, tempting, charming (SAT synonym: **tantalizing**). [40, 281]

allusion, *n.* a slight mention or an indirect reference. [73, 226, 245, 306, 311]

aloof, *adj.* distant or removed in manner or action, cool, reserved: She tried to remain *aloof* from the argument. [23, 65, 99]

altercation, *n.* an angry, loud dispute. [262]

altruistic, *adj.* unselfishly concerned with or interested in the welfare of others. [82, 275]

amalgam, *n.* a mixture or combination. [195]

ambiguous, *adj.* having more than one possible meaning or interpretation, unclear, indefinite, uncertain, vague. **ambiguity,** *n.* [34, 66, 101, 142, 220, 242, 306, 311]

ambitious, *adj.* 1. eager to succeed or achieve something, such as wealth or power. 2. requiring great ability or effort, challenging: an *ambitious* goal. [13, 275, 305, 310]

ambivalent, *adj.* simultaneously having opposite or conflicting feelings, such as love and hate, toward a person or thing. [78, 138]

amenable, *adj.* willing to yield or cooperate, responsive to advice or authority, agreeable: He was *amenable* to the group's decision. [135]

amiable, *adj.* friendly, good-natured, agreeable (SAT synonyms: **affable, cordial, jovial**). **amiably,** *adv.* [39, 74, 122, 166, 222, 280]
—*Amiable* and *affable* both mean friendly and likable. *Amiable* suggests someone with a pleasant personality; *affable* suggests someone easy to approach and talk to.

amorphous, *adj.* lacking definite form or shape. [16, 185, 229, 252, 299, 304]

analysis, *n.* a close examination; spec., the process of separating a whole into its parts to study or interpret them (SAT synonym: **dissection**). **analyze,** *v.* [ix, xiii, 30, 67, 97, 103, 105, 113, 137, 183, 244]

anecdote, *n.* a short, entertaining, often humorous story. [67, 141, 289]

animated, *adj.* lively, spirited (SAT synonym: **vivacious**). [56, 59]

animation, *n.* the state of being alive and capable of motion, having life, or
appearing to have life (SAT synonym: **vitality**). [271]

animosity, *n.* hatred, bitterness, extreme dislike (SAT synonyms: **antagonism,
enmity, hostility**). [39, 298, 299, 303, 309]

annotated, *adj.* accompanied by explanatory or critical notes: an *annotated*
edition of *Hamlet*. [45]

anonymous, *adj.* by or from a person who is not named or is not identified.
anonymity, *n.* [102, 125, 245, 279]

antagonism, *n.* active opposition, ill will, or hatred (SAT synonyms: **animosity, enmity, hostility**). [144]

antagonistic, *adj.* opposed, unfriendly (SAT synonyms: **belligerent, hostile**).
antagonist, *n.* [41, 191]

antediluvian, *adj.* before the biblical flood (the **deluge** in the time of Noah, as
described in Genesis: 6–8). [7]

anthology, *n.* a collection of selected writings. [242]

antiquated, *adj.* old-fashioned, outmoded, out-of-date (SAT synonyms: see
obsolete). [130]

antithetical, *adj.* directly opposite, contradictory: *antithetical* opinions. [227,
299, 301]

apathetic, *adj.* lacking interest or concern, unresponsive (SAT synonyms: **perfunctory** and see **phlegmatic**). **apathetically,** *adv.* **apathy,** *n.* (SAT synonym: **indifference**). [176, 196, 289, 293, 296]

apocryphal, *adj.* probably not true, genuine, or authentic; spec., of questionable authorship. [95, 199, 287]

appalling, *adj.* causing dismay or amazement, frightful. [73, 173, 296]

appraise, *v.* to officially decide the worth or price of, evaluate, estimate, judge
(SAT synonym: **assess**). [45, 71]

apprehend, *v.* 1. to become aware of through the senses; to understand, grasp
mentally (SAT synonyms: **discern, perceive**). 2. to arrest (a suspected criminal). [202, 290, 293]

apprehension, *n.* 1. fear or worry of what may happen, dread. 2. the ability to
understand, a mental grasp. [22, 118]

apprehensive, *adj.* fearful, anxious about something in the future. [162]

apprise, *v.* to inform, notify. [72, 77, 271, 280]

apt, *adj.* 1. having a natural tendency, likely: *apt* to agree. 2. to the point,
suitable: an *apt* proposal. **aptly,** *adv.* [1, 280, 299]

arable, *adj.* suitable for plowing, planting, and growing crops; fit for cultiva-
tion (cf. **fertile, prolific**). [172, 282]

arbitrary, *adj.* based only on one's own will or feelings, not based on reason
or law: an *arbitrary* order. **arbitrarily,** *adv.* [28, 179, 188]

arcane, *adj.* understood or known only by a few, mysterious (SAT synonym:
esoteric). [174, 194, 299]

archaic, *adj.* of an earlier period, of a time long past, old-fashioned, no longer
in ordinary use: Words such as *methinks* and *forsooth* are *archaic* (SAT synonyms: see **obsolete**). [11, 52, 84, 171, 187, 253]

archive, *n*. (usu. *pl*.) 1. records, documents, or papers of a government, organization, or institution. 2. a place in which such records are kept. [132, 242, 289, 292]

ardent, *adj*. 1. burning, fiery, glowing, shining (SAT synonyms: **fervid, torrid**). 2. filled with enthusiasm and eagerness: an *ardent* supporter (SAT synonyms: **avid, fervent, zealous**). [277, 306, 311]

arduous, *adj*. very hard, difficult, strenuous, laborious. [14, 22, 118, 155]

aristocracy, *n*. 1. the ruling class, nobility. 2. any privileged group thought to be superior. [104, 105, 311]

array, *n*. a large and impressive display or number: an *array* of royal gems; an *array* of knights in full armor. [84, 109, 215, 298, 303]

arrogant, *adj*. acting superior or self-important, aggressively proud, making false claims to greatness (SAT synonyms: **haughty, imperious, pretentious, supercilious**). **arrogance**, *n*. [43, 57, 266, 275]

articulate, *adj*. 1. able to express oneself clearly, easily, and effectively. 2. expressed in such a manner. [25, 82, 114, 140, 155, 176]

articulate, *v*. to utter clearly and distinctly. [206]

artifact, *n*. an object produced by human work or art, esp. something of historical or archaeological interest. [45, 78, 289, 292]

artisan, *n*. a worker trained or skilled in some trade, craftsperson. [10, 79]

ascertain, *v*. to find out, make certain of. [xi, 71, 118, 129]

ascetic, *adj*. holding back from pleasures or comforts, self-denying (SAT synonyms: **austere, spartan**). [174, 281]

aspiration, *n*. a strong desire (as to attain a goal), ambition: to have *aspirations* for high office. [61]

aspiring, *adj*. having great ambition for something, possessing a desire to attain a goal: an *aspiring* athlete. [58, 105]

assailant, *n*. an attacker. [121, 150, 152, 191, 263]

assent, *n*. agreement, acceptance, consent. [80]

assert, *v*. to state confidently or declare firmly. **assertion**, *n*. [x, 9, 73, 108, 178]

assess, *v*. to determine the value, importance, or extent of; to evaluate, estimate, weigh (SAT synonym: **appraise**). **assessment**, *n*. **assessor**, *n*. [xii, 20, 77, 118, 134, 145]

asset, *n*. a valuable thing, quality, or resource. [13, 172]

assiduous, *adj*. showing careful, constant attention (SAT synonyms: **diligent, industrious**). **assiduously**, *adv*. [xvi, 2, 225]

assuage, *v*. 1. to make less severe or intense, mitigate, pacify: The passage of time will *assuage* his disappointment. 2. to satisfy: to *assuage* one's thirst. [117, 275]

astute, *adj*. very smart, intelligent, clever, cunning (SAT synonyms: **discerning, insightful, keen, perceptive, perspicacious, sagacious, shrewd**). [xi, 121, 139, 159, 195, 309]

attest, *v*. to state that something is true, correct, or genuine, give evidence of, **confirm**. [111]

attire, *n*. clothes, dress, apparel, esp. if fancy or elaborate. [66]

attribute, *v.* to put forward as the source, origin, or author of; assign, ascribe. **attributable,** *adj.* [98, 106, 111, 202]

attribute, *n.* quality, characteristic, trait. [102]

audacious, *adj.* daring, bold, adventurous. **audaciously,** *adv.* [110]

audible, *adj.* able to be heard. **audibly,** *adv.* [70, 281]

augment, *v.* to increase, make or become greater (in size or amount). **augmented,** *adj.* [29, 70, 166, 203, 289, 293]

auspicious, *adj.* showing signs of future success, indicating a happy or fortunate outcome, favorable. [110, 256]

austere, *adj.* 1. stern or severe in appearance, grim (SAT synonyms: **grave, somber, staid**). 2. severely simple, without luxury (SAT synonyms: **ascetic, spartan**). **austerity,** *n.* [10, 122, 271, 299, 304]

authenticate, *v.* to establish the truth of or show to be genuine (SAT synonyms: **confirm, corroborate, substantiate, validate, verify**). **authentication,** *n.* [45, 69]

authenticity, *n.* the condition or quality of being genuine or true. [101]

authoritative, *adj.* commanding, giving orders, showing authority. [19, 288]

autonomy, *n.* independence, self-reliance, self-government. **autonomous,** *adj.* [6, 99]

avaricious, *adj.* greedy for wealth or possessions, miserly. **avarice,** *n.* (SAT synonym: **cupidity**). [93, 164, 201, 271, 290, 293]

avid, *adj.* enthusiastic, having a **keen** interest in or intense desire for something (SAT synonyms: **ardent, fervent, zealous**). [24]

B

banter, *n.* good-humored, playful teasing or joking conversation. [147, 265]

barbarity, *n.* cruelty, brutality, savagery. [264]

beguiling, *adj.* charming, amusing, delightful (SAT synonyms: **captivating, engaging, winsome**). [40]

belittle, *v.* to make something or someone seem small or unimportant (SAT synonyms: **denigrate, disparage**). [187, 229]

belligerent, *adj.* ready and eager to fight, quarrel, or make war (SAT synonyms: **antagonistic, hostile**). [53]

beneficence, *n.* the doing of good; generosity or kindness. [282]

beneficial, *adj.* contributing to health and well-being. [85, 284]

beneficiary, *n.* a person who receives a benefit, spec. an inheritance, **bequest,** or **legacy**. [64, 287, 291]

benevolence, *n.* an inclination to do good; kindliness. [275, 280, 299, 304]

benighted, *adj.* in a state of mental or moral ignorance (SAT synonym: **unenlightened**). [221]

benign, *adj.* kind, good-natured, arising from or indicative of goodness or happiness, not **malevolent** or **malicious**. [11, 66, 139, 247]

bequeath, *v.* to pass on or hand down, to leave by means of a will. [156, 266]

bequest, *n.* money or property given or left to someone by means of a will (SAT synonym: **legacy**). [13]

bestial, *adj.* having the qualities of a beast, cruel, brutish. [270]

bias (*pl.* **biases**), *n.* preference, inclination, prejudice, often one that is unfair or unjust. [60, 129, 137, 228, 289]

—*Bias* and *prejudice* both refer to feelings that make a fair judgment impossible. *Bias* may refer either to a reasonable preference or opinion or to one that is unfair and unjust: a *bias* in favor of one's children; a *bias* against foreigners. *Prejudice* always refers to an unfair or unjust judgment made without concern for the facts: a *prejudice* against all new ideas. Unreasonable or harmful *biases* are forms of *prejudice*.

biased, *adj.* showing a strong preference or inclination, having one's opinion already formed, prejudiced in someone's favor (SAT synonym: **discriminatory**). [25, 82, 114]

bibliophile, *n.* a lover of books, a book collector. [28, 69, 175]

bizarre, *adj.* extremely unusual in style or manner (SAT synonym: **outlandish**). [10, 254]

blithe, *adj.* carefree, showing no concern, thoughtless. **blithely,** *adv.* [151]

boisterous, *adj.* noisy and wild, lacking **restraint** (SAT synonyms: **raucous, vociferous**). [39]

bolster, *v.* to support, prop, buoy up, or strengthen: They piled sandbags to *bolster* the levee. [100]

bombastic, *adj.* using or pert. to speech or writing that sounds grand or impressive but has little meaning or substance (SAT synonym: **grandiloquent**). [67]

bondage, *n.* slavery, servitude, subjection, serfdom. [168]

boor, *n.* a crude, insensitive person. [43]

bourgeoisie, *n.* the middle class, the class between the working class and the very wealthy class. [135]

brawny, *adj.* strong and muscular (SAT synonym: **stalwart**). [8, 262]

breadth, *n.* width, the measure of something from side to side. [8, 105]

burgeoning, *adj.* growing or developing quickly (SAT synonym: **flourishing**). [83, 140]

C

cacophony, *n.* a harsh or unpleasant blending of sounds. [214, 288, 292]

callous, *adj.* unfeeling, insensitive, hardhearted. [73, 160, 166]

candid, *adj.* open and direct, frank, straightforward. [242]

cantankerous, *adj.* quick to dispute or quarrel, argumentative (SAT synonym: **irascible**). **cantankerously,** *adv.* [134]

capacious, *adj.* able to contain a large quantity, roomy, large: The school's *capacious* auditorium could seat the entire student body (SAT synonym: **commodious**). [29, 171, 280]

capitulate, *v.* to yield, surrender, esp. under specifically negotiated terms. **capitulation,** *n.* [73, 282]

capricious, *adj.* unpredictable, changing suddenly for no apparent reason, inconstant (SAT synonyms: **fickle, impulsive, wayward**). [65]

captivate, *v.* attract, fascinate, charm, capture the attention of. **captivating,** *adj.* (SAT synonyms: **beguiling, engaging, winsome**). [25, 288]

castigate, *v.* to criticize harshly or severely, berate (SAT synonym: **upbraid;** cf. **admonish, censure**). [101, 288, 292]

catastrophic, *adj.* involving or pert. to a great disaster, terrible misfortune, or total failure. [9, 282, 287, 291]

categorical, *adj.* absolute, without any question or condition: The company issued a *categorical* denial of all the charges that had been made. **categorically,** *adv.* [73, 282]

celerity, *n.* speed, quickness: The soldiers followed their commander's orders with *celerity.* [217]

censor, *v.* to ban, prevent from becoming known or circulated (SAT synonym: **suppress**). [103]

censure, *v.* to officially condemn as wrong, criticize harshly (cf. **admonish, castigate, upbraid**). [46]

chagrined, *adj.* embarrassed or annoyed as a result of failure, humiliation, or disappointment. [261]

chaos, *n.* 1. utter confusion or great disorder. 2. an unformed state or condition. [27, 99]

chaotic, *adj.* completely disordered and confused. [84]

charade, *n.* an elaborate and obvious show or illusion. [104, 275]

charlatan, *n.* a fake, phony, quack, or fraud, esp. one who pretends to have great knowledge or skill. [115, 290]

chasten, *v.* to discipline or punish in order to correct or improve (cf. **chastise**). **chastened,** *adj.* [79]

chastise, *v.* to criticize or scold harshly (cf. **chasten**). [54, 101]

chimerical, *adj.* imaginary, unrealistic, wildly **improbable.** [185, 290]

chronicler, *n.* a person who records events in order of time. [102]

circumlocution, *n.* a roundabout or wordy way of expressing an idea. **circumlocutory,** *adj.* [97, 243]

circumspect, *adj.* cautious, careful, considering all conditions before acting (SAT synonyms: **discreet, prudent, vigilant, wary**). [193, 233]

circumvent, *v.* to go around, avoid, bypass, get around by clever maneuvering. [103]

cite, *v.* to refer to or quote. **citation,** *n.* [100, 106, 137]

clamor, *n.* a loud and continuous noise, strong and noisy protest or outcry, hubbub, uproar (SAT synonym: **din**). [54, 288]

clandestine, *adj.* done in secret, kept hidden, esp. to conceal something that is illegal or immoral (SAT synonyms: **covert, devious, furtive, surreptitious**). [221, 249, 296, 301]

clarify, *v.* to make clear or easier to understand (SAT synonyms: **elucidate, enlighten, illuminate**). [xi, 35, 208, 272, 299]

claustrophobic, *adj.* afraid of being in a small or enclosed space. [250]

cliché, *n.* an overused expression that has become stale and has almost lost its meaning: "As good as gold" is a *cliché.* [234]

coerce, *v.* to force or **compel** by threats, intimidation, or violence. **coercive,** *adj.* [125, 288, 295]

coherence, *n.* order, consistency, logical relationship of parts. [225, 229]

coherent, *adj.* expressed or constructed in an orderly, consistent, logical manner. [140, 176, 307]

coincide, *v.* 1. to occur at the same time or be in the same position in space at the same time. 2. to agree exactly. [96, 202]

coincidental, *adj.* happening or existing at the same time merely by chance or accident. [106]

collaboration, *n.* a working with another or others, as on a literary or scientific project. [69, 98, 99, 100, 109, 114]

collaborative, *adj.* done by working together, cooperative, pert. to or produced by **collaboration.** [98, 100]

collective, *adj.* pert. to or done by a number of persons acting as a group. **collective,** *n.* [70, 98, 100, 113, 214]

colloquium, *n.* a meeting for discussion, esp. an academic seminar to exchange views on a particular subject. [173]

collusion, *n.* a secret agreement or cooperation between persons for an illegal or wrongful purpose. [72, 267]

colossal, *adj.* very great in size, gigantic, enormous. [15, 117]

combatant, *n.* a person engaged in a fight or contest. [264, 287]

combustible, *adj.* capable of catching fire and burning. [269]

commendable, *adj.* praiseworthy, admirable: Promoting literacy is a *commendable* endeavor (SAT synonyms: **laudable, meritorious**). [vii, viii, 10]

commodious, *adj.* having plenty of room, spacious (SAT synonym: **capacious**). [134, 187, 214, 233]

commonplace, *adj.* ordinary, dull, unremarkable (SAT synonyms: **lackluster, mundane, pedestrian, prosaic**). [114, 129, 298, 307]

communal, *adj.* of or relating to a community; public: All freshmen must eat in the *communal* dining room. [19, 99]

compassion, *n.* sympathy for the suffering of others combined with a desire to help. [135, 296, 301]

compel, *v.* to force, drive. [76, 272, 274]

compelling, *adj.* forceful, powerful, moving, convincing. [111]

compensate, *v.* 1. to make up for, offset, counterbalance. 2. to pay (money) for, recompense, reimburse. **compensation,** *n.* [2, 101]

competence, *n.* sufficient skill, ability, or fitness; the state or condition of being qualified or capable. **competent,** *adj.* [9, 118, 133, 146]

compile, *v.* to gather from different sources and put together in an orderly form, assemble, compose. [ix, 7, 28, 45, 175, 307]

complacent, *adj.* uncritically pleased with oneself or one's circumstances, esp. in a narrow-minded or annoying way; self-satisfied (SAT synonym: **smug**). **complacency,** *n.* [155, 175, 260, 296]

complex, *adj.* having two or more interrelated parts, complicated or involved, not simple (cf. **convoluted**). [9, 48, 68, 142, 144, 178, 279]

compliant, *adj.* willing to give in or go along, obedient, submissive. [135]

comply, *v.* to act in agreement; to submit to another's request, wish, rule, or command. [220]

composure, *n.* calmness, control over one's emotions. [172]

comprehensible, *adj.* understandable, capable of being understood: The professor's lecture helped make the text *comprehensible.* [142, 241]

comprehensive, *adj.* including much, large in scope, inclusive, extensive, wide-ranging. [45, 99, 105, 242]

concede, *v.* to acknowledge as being true, reasonable, or proper. [189, 203, 251]

concise, *adj.* short and to the point, brief and clear (SAT synonyms: **succinct, terse**). [xii, 273, 307, 312]

conclusive, *adj.* serving to settle a question or put an end to doubt, final, definitive (cf. **crucial, decisive**). [111, 114]

concoct, *v.* to make up, invent, cook up. [30]

concomitant, *adj.* existing with something else, accompanying. [250]

concordance, *n.* an alphabetical index of the important words in a written work (or the works of an author) indicating the passages in which they occur: She consulted a *concordance* to the works of Shakespeare. [42, 45, 287]

concur, *v.* to agree. [103, 139, 243]

condescension, *n.* a proud, snobbish attitude toward anyone considered inferior. [56, 66, 160]

confidant, *n.* a person to whom one entrusts personal matters or secrets. [78]

confirm, *v.* to establish as true or certain, make firm or binding, strengthen, support (SAT synonyms: **authenticate, corroborate, substantiate, validate, verify**). [168, 219]

conflagration, *n.* a great, destructive fire. [278, 288, 292]

congregate, *v.* to come together in a crowd, assemble. [3]

conjecture, *n.* an opinion or conclusion based on insufficient evidence, a guess (SAT synonyms: **speculation, surmise**). [222, 225, 246, 309]

connoisseur, *n.* an expert, esp. a person with special training in a field or an informed taste for something. [70, 92, 171, 308, 312]

conscientious, *adj.* 1. guided by conscience (SAT synonyms: **ethical, upright, virtuous**). 2. showing thought and care: *conscientious* work (SAT synonyms: **fastidious, meticulous, painstaking, scrupulous**). **conscientiously,** *adv.* [ix, 274]

consequence, *n.* a logical or natural result, outcome, or effect. [9, 50, 73, 152]

conspicuous, *adj.* 1. easy to see, obvious (SAT synonyms: **prominent, salient**). 2. striking, outstanding. [28, 67, 81, 167, 232, 243, 293, 310]

conspiracy, *n.* a secret plot to commit an evil or illegal act. [136, 192, 278, 290]

conspiratorial, *adj.* pert. to or characteristic of a **conspiracy** or of the persons involved in it. **conspiratorially,** *adv.* [199, 309, 314]

constraint, *n.* a restriction or limitation. [100]

contemplative, *adj.* thoughtful, devoted to meditation (SAT synonym: **reflective**). [3, 198, 278]

contemporary, *adj.* current, modern, of the present time. [52, 53, 59, 171, 188]

contemporary, *n.* a person living at the same time as another. [98, 100, 103, 105, 111]

contempt, *n.* the feeling that someone or something is low, undesirable, or disgusting; a display of this feeling (SAT synonym: **disdain**). [101]

contemptuous, *adj.* full of **contempt**, thinking of or treating as inferior or worthless (SAT synonyms: **disdainful, supercilious**). [211, 159, 272]

contention, *n.* a claim that someone supports and argues for: It is the *contention* of many environmentalists that life on earth is in danger. [142]

context, *n.* the part of something written or spoken that comes before or after a word or passage and affects or casts light upon its meaning; surrounding material, setting. [xi, xii, xvi, 11, 245, 284, 294, 304, 305, 310, 311, 312, 313]

continuity, *n.* an unbroken flow or succession, connectedness. [137]

contradiction, *n.* opposition or lack of agreement, logical inconsistency. [100]

conventional, *adj.* established by widely accepted custom or practice, according to generally accepted standards or rules (SAT synonyms: **orthodox, traditional**). [10, 44, 98, 129, 165, 209, 298]

convey, *v.* **literally,** to carry, transport, or transmit; figuratively, to make known, express, or communicate. [25, 198]

conviction, *n.* a strong belief or opinion. [242, 299]

convivial, *adj.* 1. festive. 2. fond of good company, esp. when eating and drinking, sociable (SAT synonym: **gregarious**). [61, 172]

convoluted, *adj.* **literally,** coiled or twisted; hence, extremely complicated or **complex.** [68, 97, 109, 244]

copious, *adj.* large in quantity, great in number, yielding or containing much (SAT synonym: **abundant**). [109, 214]

cordial, *adj.* warm, friendly, hearty (SAT synonyms: **affable, amiable, jovial**). **cordially,** *adv.* [27, 133, 170, 247]

corpulent, *adj.* fat, fleshy, stout, obese (cf. **portly, rotund**). [67, 108, 298, 303]

correlate, *v.* to correspond, be mutually related: Grades *correlate* with class participation. [194]

correlation, *n.* a link, relationship, correspondence. [219]

corroborate, *v.* to support with more evidence, make more certain or believable, provide further proof (SAT synonyms: **authenticate, confirm, substantiate, validate, verify**). [71, 98, 257]

corrupt, *v.* to make dishonest, evil, wicked, or impure (SAT synonyms: **debase, undermine**). **corrupt,** *adj.* (SAT synonyms: **depraved, unethical**). [36, 156, 274, 276, 288]

corruption, *n.* immoral or dishonest behavior. [73, 85]

counter, *v.* to offer in response, meet or return, oppose. [20, 108, 143, 182]

coup, *n.* a brilliant move or action, clever maneuver. [166]

covert, *adj.* secret, concealed, hidden, sheltered; not done in an open, visible manner; not **overt** (SAT synonyms: **clandestine, devious, furtive, surreptitious**). [220, 242, 272, 279, 298]

coveted, *adj.* possessing so much value as to inspire greed or envy. [79]

covetous, *adj.* having a strong desire for something that belongs to someone else. [43, 201]

credence, *n.* belief or confidence in the truth of something: The darkening sky gave *credence* to the storm predictions. [65]

credible, *adj.* believable, trustworthy, reliable: The plaintiff's testimony was not *credible*. **credibility,** *n.* [104, 107, 115, 203]

criterion (*pl.* **criteria**), *n.* a standard, rule, or test on which a judgment or decision is based. [210]

critique, *n.* a critical review or commentary, as of an artistic work. [82, 279]

crucial, *adj.* of great importance, essential to resolving an issue or crisis (cf. **conclusive, decisive**). [122, 153, 258, 297, 302]

cryptic, *adj.* mysterious, baffling, having a hidden meaning (SAT synonyms: **enigmatic, inscrutable**). **cryptically,** *adv.* [105, 115, 157, 159, 203, 257]

culpable, *adj.* deserving blame, guilty. [200, 260]

cupidity, *n.* greed (SAT synonym: **avarice**). [73, 298, 303]

cursory, *adj.* done quickly with little attention to detail (SAT synonyms: **perfunctory, superficial**). [214, 235]

cynical, *adj.* expressing disbelief in or distrust of others out of a sense that everyone's motives and actions are selfish. [32, 147]

D

dearth, *n.* scarcity, scant supply, lack. [103, 298]

debase, *v.* to make lower in value, quality, character, or dignity (SAT synonyms: **corrupt, undermine**). [272]

debilitate, *v.* to make weak, enfeeble. [273]

decadent, *adj.* in a state of decline (as in art, literature, morals, etc.), self-indulgent or self-gratifying. [77]

deceive, *v.* to lie, trick, mislead (SAT synonym: **dupe**). [79, 266]

deception, *n.* 1. the act of **deceiving** or tricking (SAT synonym: **duplicity**). 2. something that **deceives**, a trick (SAT synonym: **hoax**). **deceptive,** *adj.* [244, 266, 290, 306]

decipher, *v.* 1. to change from code into ordinary language, decode. 2. to make out (something **illegible** or difficult to understand). [45, 123, 158, 161, 176, 181, 288, 313]

decisive, *adj.* 1. determining an outcome, ending doubt, settling an issue or question (cf. **conclusive, crucial**). 2. showing firmness and determination. **decisively,** *adv.* [132, 151, 153, 297, 298]

decorum, *n.* formal, proper, or suitable behavior, dress, speech, etc.; conduct suitable to a situation. [189]

deduce, *v.* to reach a conclusion by reasoning (SAT synonym: **infer**). [201, 265]

deduction, *n.* the act of **deducing** or a conclusion reached by reasoning or **inferring.** [155, 166]

defiant, *adj.* refusing to obey or submit, boldly opposing power or authority. **defiantly,** *adv.* [271]

deflate, *v.* to reduce the confidence or lessen the importance of. [123]

deft, *adj.* skillful in a quick, smooth way (SAT synonyms: **adept, adroit, dexterous, proficient**). **deftly,** *adv.* [viii, 91]

deluge, *n.* a great flood or downpour. [167, 288, 292]

demeanor, *n.* behavior, bearing, manner, deportment. [144]

denigrate, *v.* to defame, damage the reputation of (SAT synonyms: **belittle, disparage**). [229]

depict, *v.* to represent in a picture, drawing, sculpture, etc. (SAT synonym: **portray**). [15, 128, 234, 253, 282, 295]

deplorable, *adj.* 1. very bad or unfortunate, regrettable. 2. deserving strong disapproval or condemnation. [36, 119]

depraved, *adj.* wicked, immoral, evil (SAT synonyms: **corrupt, unethical, wanton**). [201]

derision, *n.* scornful or sneering laughter, taunting, mockery (SAT synonym: **ridicule**). **derisive,** *adj.* (SAT synonym: **sarcastic**). [41, 260, 306]

derivative, *adj.* traced or received from a source, descended or originating from. [174, 281]

despicable, *adj.* deserving of dislike and scorn, vile, low. [269]

desultory, *adj.* moving or passing from one thing to another, not proceeding in an orderly or organized way, aimless, disconnected (SAT synonyms: see **random**). [131, 212]

deteriorate, *v.* to grow worse, fall into disrepair, become lower in quality or value. [255]

deviant, *adj.* not normal, standard, or acceptable; abnormal. [32]

devil's advocate, *n.* a person who upholds an unpopular cause or defends a questionable position for the sake of argument or out of sheer **perversity** (cf. **advocate**). [164, 308, 312]

devious, *adj.* not honest and straightforward, sly, shifty, tricky (SAT synonyms: **clandestine, covert, furtive, surreptitious**). [175, 261]

dexterous, *adj.* skillful and **competent** with the hands or body (SAT synonyms: **adept, adroit, deft, proficient**). [viii, 265]

diagnosis, *n.* a careful examination of the facts or nature of something or a decision based on such an examination, esp. one by a physician. [18, 168]

dialect, *n.* a form of language spoken in a particular region or by a certain class that differs somewhat in vocabulary, **idioms**, and pronunciations from the standard language. [53]

diction, *n.* manner of expression, choice and arrangement of words. [110]

didactic, *adj.* designed to instruct or guide behavior: A *didactic* story includes a moral. [264]

differentiate, *v.* to distinguish, make a distinction, see the difference between, become distinct. [188, 297]

diffuse, *v.* to spread out widely, scatter (SAT synonym: **disperse**). **diffused**, *adj.* [71, 128]

diffuse, *adj.* 1. spread out, not concentrated or localized. 2. wordy (SAT synonym: **verbose**). [216, 307]

digress, *v.* to depart from the main subject in writing or speaking, stray, ramble. [109]

digression, *n.* something written or spoken that has little or no relation to the main subject. [118, 131, 273]

dilapidated, *adj.* falling to pieces, broken-down, in disrepair. [9, 213, 256]

dilemma, *n.* a situation in which one must choose between equally unpleasant or unfavorable options (SAT synonym: **quandary**). [73, 125]

diligence, *n.* steady and careful attention, esp. to work or duties. [2, 118]

diligent, *adj.* 1. hard-working (SAT synonyms: **assiduous, industrious**). 2. characterized by or done with steady and careful effort (SAT synonyms: **painstaking, studious**). **diligently**, *adv.* [ix, 107, 116, 129, 138, 193, 306]

din, *n.* a continuous, loud, annoying noise; uproar: They could hear the *din* of traffic through the open window (SAT synonym: **clamor**). [29]

dire, *adj.* causing great fear or distress, disastrous, terrible: a *dire* situation. [73]

directive, *n.* an order or instruction, esp. as issued by a high authority. [137]

disaffected, *adj.* discontented, rebellious. [147]

discern, *v.* to detect with the eyes or other senses, recognize mentally: We could barely *discern* his features in the dim light (SAT synonyms: **apprehend, perceive**). **discernible**, *adj.* [xi, 171, 188, 255, 295, 301]

discerning, *adj.* having or showing sharp perception and judgment, rapidly noticing small differences or fine distinctions (SAT synonyms: **astute, insightful, keen, perceptive, perspicacious, sagacious, shrewd**). [18]

disclose, *v.* uncover, expose to view, reveal (SAT synonym: **divulge**). [124]

disconcerting, *adj.* upsetting, frustrating, or embarrassing. [123, 140, 239]

discord, *n.* conflict, lack of harmony or agreement. [298, 303]

discordant, *adj.* disagreeing, conflicting, clashing, not in harmony (SAT synonyms: **dissonant, strident**). [11, 214, 295, 300]

discourse, *n.* formal and orderly speech or writing on a subject. [97]

discourse, *v.* to talk, carry on a conversation. [55]

discreet, *adj.* cautious in one's speech or actions, tactful (SAT synonyms: **circumspect, prudent**). [272]

discrepancy, *n.* a lack of agreement or an inconsistency. [203]

discretion, *n.* the exercise of caution or good judgment. [197]

discriminatory, *adj.* unfair, prejudiced (SAT synonym: **biased**). [229, 295]

disdain, *n.* scorn, a feeling or show of dislike or disregard for something or someone considered inferior (SAT synonym: **contempt**). **disdainful**, *adj.* (SAT synonyms: **contemptuous, supercilious**). [155, 261]

disgruntled, *adj.* dissatisfied, resentful, discontented. [247, 263]

dismantle, *v.* to pull down or take apart, disassemble: The movers had to *dismantle* the bookcase to get it through the door. [172, 232]

disorient, *v.* to disturb someone's sense of time, place, or identity. [134, 297]

disown, *v.* to refuse to recognize or claim as one's own, reject. [43, 299]

disparage, *v.* to speak of, treat, or regard as inferior or unimportant (SAT synonyms: **belittle, denigrate**). [114, 229]

dispassionate, *adj.* not affected by passion, emotion, or prejudice (SAT synonyms: **impartial, indifferent, objective, stoic,** and see **phlegmatic**). [261, 306]

dispel, *v.* to cause to disappear; drive away, scatter. [153]

dispense, *v.* 1. to deal out in portions, distribute, administer. 2. to get rid of, do away with, do without. [67, 189]

disperse, *v.* to move or scatter in different directions (SAT synonym: **diffuse**). [149, 238]

disposition, *n.* arrangement, makeup, composition. [68]

dissection, *n.* a cutting into parts in order to study or a part-by-part examination (SAT synonym: **analysis**). [104]

disseminate, *v.* to scatter widely, spread abroad. [157, 307, 312]

dissertation, *n.* a lengthy, formal piece of writing, spec. a **thesis** prepared for a doctoral degree. [101]

dissonant, *adj.* harsh and disagreeable in sound, jarring to the ear (SAT synonyms: **discordant, strident**). [214]

dissuade, *v.* to persuade not to do something. [125]

distinctive, *adj.* serving to set apart as different or characterize as special. [81, 92, 157]

distort, *v.* 1. to twist out of shape. 2. to change so as to create a false impression: The editorial *distorted* the facts (SAT synonym: **pervert**). [115, 277]

divergent, *adj.* branching off, departing from a set course or opinion, deviating. [99]

diverse, *adj.* varied, not alike, different (SAT synonym: see **eclectic**). [25, 66, 155, 308, 312]

diversion, *n.* 1. something that distracts the attention. 2. pastime, recreation, sport. [232, 233, 235, 262, 307, 311]

diversity, *n.* variety, difference, dissimilarity. [10, 82, 98, 171, 298, 303]

divulge, *v.* to make known, reveal (usu. something private or secret) (SAT synonym: **disclose**). [152, 199, 244, 288, 299]

doctorate, *n.* the highest degree awarded by a university. [45]

doctrine, *n.* a theory or set of principles actively taught and promoted by those who believe it. [174, 253]

documentation, *n.* the provision of documents or published information as proof or evidence; the documents or information provided: We cannot publish this information without adequate *documentation*. [104]

dogged, *adj.* refusing to give up despite difficulties: *dogged* determination (SAT synonym: **persistent**). **doggedly**, *adv.* [21]

dogmatic, *adj.* stating opinions in an overbearing manner, opinionated, dictatorial. [103]

domain, *n.* an area over which control is exercised, sphere of activity, field of interest or knowledge. [170, 172]

dominate, *v.* 1. to occupy a commanding position, rise high above, tower over, overlook from a height. 2. to rule, control, or influence by superior power. **dominant**, *adj.* [10, 22, 64, 84, 172, 186, 275]

dotard, *n.* a feeble old person (cf. **senile**). [276]

dour, *adj.* gloomy, severe, stern (SAT synonyms: see **morose**). [233, 263]

drastic, *adj.* extreme, severe, harsh, having a strong effect (SAT synonym: **radical**). [29, 267, 295]

droll, *adj.* amusingly strange, humorously odd. **drolly**, *adv.* [58, 272, 280, 296, 301, 314]

dubious, *adj.* 1. arousing doubt, questionable, vague, uncertain, undecided. 2. feeling or full of doubt (SAT synonyms: **incredulous, skeptical**). **dubiously**, *adv.* [43, 105, 114, 146, 154, 226, 244, 246, 297]

dupe, *v.* to fool, trick, cheat (SAT synonym: **deceive**). [46, 201]

dupe, *n.* someone easily fooled, tricked, or cheated. [290, 293]

duplicity, *n.* dishonesty, double-dealing, acting contrary to one's real feelings and beliefs in order to fool or cheat (SAT synonym: **deception**). [267]

dwindle, *v.* to decrease steadily, shrink, diminish. [6, 146, 282]

E

ebullient, *adj.* overflowing with high spirits, enthusiasm, or excitement. [82]

eccentric, *adj.* deviating from what is considered normal or accepted, out of the ordinary, peculiar, odd (SAT synonym: **idiosyncratic**). **eccentricity**, *n.* (SAT synonym: **idiosyncrasy**). [10, 32, 46, 142, 168, 210, 216, 307]

eclectic, *adj.* selecting, or consisting of selections, from a variety of sources, esp. the best of those sources; varied. [44, 171, 308, 312]
—*Diverse, miscellaneous,* and *eclectic* all suggest variety. A *diverse* collection contains strikingly different elements; *diverse* stresses difference. A *miscellaneous* collection is a mixture or jumble of things, often unrelated and often put together with little attention to quality or arrangement. An *eclectic* collection contains the best material selected with care from a wide variety of sources.

eclipse, *v.* to darken, diminish the brightness or importance of, overshadow, **surpass**, outshine (SAT synonym: **obscure**). [11, 129]

ecstatic, *adj.* overcome by intense emotion, esp. delight or bliss. [26]

edification, *n.* moral, spiritual, or intellectual improvement or instruction (SAT synonym: **enlightenment**). [xiv, 68]

edifice, *n.* a building, esp. a large or elaborate one. [7, 22, 81, 122, 288]

edifying, *adj.* morally, spiritually, or intellectually instructive (SAT synonyms: **enlightening, illuminating**). [12, 254]

efficacy, *n.* effectiveness, the ability to produce a desired result: It was too soon to measure the *efficacy* of the new irrigation system. [104]

egalitarian, *adj.* promoting equal treatment for people, esp. as to social, political, and economic rights. [10, 297, 302]

egotist, *n.* a boastful, conceited, self-centered person. **egotism**, *n.* [275, 296]

egregious, *adj.* very bad or **offensive** in an obvious way, flagrant. [279, 306]

elated, *adj.* full of joy or happiness, blissful. [228]

elicit, *v.* to bring out, draw forth. [24, 122]

elite, *adj.* belonging to or characteristic of a class of people considered the best, brightest, most powerful, etc. [107]

elitism, *n.* a preference for rule or leadership by the **elite** class. **elitist,** *adj.* [36]

eloquent, *adj.* expressed in a strong, clear, graceful, and persuasive way; moving, forceful. **eloquence,** *n.* [1, 59, 138, 296, 301]

elucidate, *v.* to make clear, explain (SAT synonyms: **clarify, enlighten, illuminate;** cf. **lucid**). [67, 110, 166, 289]

elude, *v.* to escape, avoid (SAT synonym: **evade**). [85]

elusive, *adj.* 1. hard to get hold of or capture. 2. hard to define, describe, understand, or remember. [106, 129]

emaciated, *adj.* excessively thin, wasted away. [143]

embed, *v.* to fix firmly in a surrounding mass. [105]

embellish, *v.* to make beautiful by adding decoration. **embellishment,** *n.* [28, 122, 189, 213, 295, 299, 300]

eminence, *n.* great distinction, superiority, or importance. **eminent,** *adj.* (SAT synonyms: see **prominent**). [11, 170]

emit, *v.* to give or send out, utter, issue, discharge. [48, 303]

empathy, *n.* an identification with and ability to share another person's feelings or situation. [135]

emphatic, *adj.* expressed or done with emphasis, forceful. **emphatically,** *adv.* [34, 74]

emulate, *v.* to try to do as well as or better than, esp. by imitating; compete with, rival. **emulator,** *n.* [84, 174]

enamored, *adj.* filled with love or desire, charmed. [114]

endeavor, *v.* to make a serious effort, strive: I shall *endeavor* to improve my attitude. [265]

endeavor, *n.* a serious attempt or effort. [27, 72, 97, 129, 273]

endorse, *v.* to support, give one's approval to. [114]

enervated, *adj.* weakened, drained of strength or energy. [xii, 143, 189, 279, 289, 293]

engaging, *adj.* appealing, charming, interesting: an *engaging* smile (SAT synonyms: **beguiling, captivating, winsome**). [133]

engross, *v.* to absorb the complete attention or interest of, fascinate. **engrossing,** *adj.* [132, 141, 199]

enhance, *v.* to intensify, heighten, set off. [xi, 31]

enigma, *n.* a riddle, mystery, puzzle; a person, situation, statement, or text that causes confusion, doubt, or bewilderment. [22, 39, 96]

enigmatic, *adj.* puzzling, mysterious, hard to understand or explain (SAT synonyms: **cryptic, inscrutable**). **enigmatically,** *adv.* [21, 103, 135, 139, 188]

enlighten, *v.* to make the truth or nature of something clear; to free from ignorance or prejudice, educate (SAT synonyms: **clarify, elucidate, illuminate**). **enlightening,** *adj.* (SAT synonyms: **edifying, illuminating**). [42, 70, 109, 265]

enlightenment, *n.* knowledge, understanding, instruction, education (SAT synonym: **edification**). [xiv, 11]

enmity, *n.* a deep-seated mutual hatred or mistrust (SAT synonyms: **animosity, antagonism, hostility**). [42]

ensconced, *adj.* settled securely or snugly. [45]

ensue, *v.* to follow as a consequence or result, occur next. [274]

entail, *v.* to require as a necessary consequence, necessitate: To execute the plan successfully will *entail* precise teamwork. [63, 143, 155]

entity, *n.* something that exists and can be recognized as a particular and distinct unit. [100]

enumerate, *v.* to list one after the other, count off, name individually (SAT synonym: **specify**). [131]

epic, *adj.* pert. to or having the qualities of a long poem, novel, or play, usu. written in a dignified or elevated style, celebrating heroes and heroic deeds. [64, 77]

epitome, *n.* an embodiment of an idea or quality. [200]

equanimity, *n.* the quality or state of being calm, composed, and even-tempered. [42, 172]

equivocate, *v.* to intentionally mislead or confuse by using language that can be understood in two or more ways. [220, 243]

eradicate, *v.* to get rid of as if tearing up by the roots, uproot, destroy, remove, wipe out (cf. **radical**). [116, 275]

erratic, *adj.* 1. not regular or consistent (as in quality or progress): *erratic* work. 2. odd or peculiar: *erratic* behavior. [8, 19, 235, 305, 310]

erudite, *adj.* having or exhibiting deep and extensive learning. [107, 289, 292, 305, 307]

erudition, *n.* deep and extensive learning. [105]

esoteric, *adj.* intended for or understood only by a select group (SAT synonym: **arcane**). [67, 131, 158, 223, 253, 307]

espionage, *n.* the practice of using spies to obtain secret information. [45]

esteem, *n.* high regard, respect. **esteemed,** *adj.* (SAT synonym: **prestigious**). [75, 97, 154]

estimable, *adj.* deserving **esteem**: an *estimable* **endeavor**. [69]

ethical, *adj.* 1. of or dealing with **ethics** and morality. 2. in **accordance** with principles of right or good conduct (SAT synonyms: **conscientious, upright, virtuous**). [125, 165]

ethics, *n.* 1. the study of the general nature of morals and moral choices. 2. the standards or rules governing proper conduct. [58, 152]

euphemism, *n.* a more pleasant word or phrase used in place of another felt to be unpleasant: "The bathroom" is a *euphemism* for "the toilet." [20, 290]

evade, *v.* to escape or avoid through trickery or cleverness: to *evade* responsibility (SAT synonym: **elude**). [100, 132, 219]

evanescent, *adj.* vanishing, short-lived, fleeting: the *evanescent* autumn. [xv, 242, 286]

evasive, *adj.* meaning to **evade,** not **forthright**; indirect, intentionally vague or misleading: an *evasive* maneuver. [21, 146, 220]

evocative, *adj.* having the power to call forth certain ideas or memories: an *evocative* poetic image. [186]

evolution, *n.* the gradual process of the development of something: the *evolution* of an idea into a work of art. [66]

exacerbate, *v.* to increase the severity of, aggravate: Her attitude *exacerbated* the tension. [236, 274]

exalted, *adj.* elevated in position, character, rank, etc. or made to seem so (SAT synonym: **glorified**). [254]

exasperate, *v.* to irritate extremely, to try the patience of. [117, 152, 177, 296]

exceptional, *adj.* extraordinary, outstanding. **exceptionally,** *adv.* [34, 70, 175, 193, 221]

exclusive, *adj.* admitting only certain people as friends or members: an *exclusive* sorority. [36]

exegesis, *n.* detailed explanation or **analysis**, esp. of a text. [140]

exemplary, *adj.* worthy to serve as a model. [37]

exert, *v.* to put forth or bring to bear: to *exert* pressure. [xi, 24, 198]

exonerate, *v.* to declare blameless, find innocent: They were *exonerated* of any responsibility in the affair. [272]

exorbitant, *adj.* far beyond what is usual or proper; excessive: *exorbitant* rents; *exorbitant* expectations (SAT synonym: **extravagant**). [2, 73]

exotic, *adj.* 1. unfamiliar, strikingly different. 2. from faraway places of the world, alien. [57, 109, 165, 171, 297, 298]

expanse, *n.* a wide and open space: an unlimited *expanse* of prairie. [23]

expedient, *n.* a means to an end. [242]

expertise, *n.* specialized skill or knowledge. [69]

explicit, *adj.* clearly defined, definite, precise: He made his expectations *explicit.* **explicitly,** *adv.* [xi, 246, 266, 284, 304]

exploit, *n.* a daring deed, heroic feat: the *exploits* of King Arthur and his knights. [39]

exploit, *v.* 1. to use productively or to greatest advantage: to *exploit* an idea. 2. to use in a selfish way: to *exploit* others' labor. **exploitable,** *adj.* [9, 39, 65, 102, 139, 274, 297, 302]

expound, *v.* to explain by giving detail: to *expound* a point of view. [41, 93]

exquisite, *adj.* of extreme beauty and excellence. [61]

extant, *adj.* still existing: the few *extant* works of the Etruscans. [79, 157, 312]

extract, *v.* to remove with effort, to obtain despite resistance. [238]

extracurricular, *adj.* not part of the regular course of study of a school or college. [12]

extravagant, *adj.* excessive, immoderate, extremely wasteful (SAT synonyms: **exorbitant, lavish**). [46]

exultant, *adj.* filled with great joy, expressing triumph (SAT synonym: **jubilant**). [213, 257]

exultation, *n.* great rejoicing and jubilation, the state of being **exultant.** [213]

F

fabricate, *v.* to make up, invent, devise: to *fabricate* a story. **fabrication,** *n.* [74, 101, 166]

facade, *n.* an artificial or **deceptive** appearance. [104, 290, 293]

facetious, *adj.* meant to be funny or playfully disrespectful. **facetiously,** *adv.* [59, 142, 231, 306]

facilitate, *v.* to make easier. [99, 207, 289, 293, 300]

facsimile, *n.* an exact copy: a *facsimile* of a painting. [281, 290]

faculty, *n.* a power or capability of the mind or body, either natural or acquired. [107]

fanatic, *n.* a person **motivated** by extreme, unreasoning enthusiasm. **fanaticism,** *n.* [213, 296]

fanatical, *adj.* excessively enthusiastic or devoted (SAT synonym: **zealous**). [65, 94, 311]

farcical, *adj.* laughable, comical, ridiculous (SAT synonyms: **absurd, ludicrous, preposterous**). [73]

far-fetched, *adj.* not likely to be true or to happen: a *far-fetched* story; a *far-fetched* plan. [166]

fastidious, *adj.* 1. overly particular, hard to please. 2. excessively sensitive in matters of taste. 3. extremely careful about details (SAT synonyms: **conscientious, meticulous, painstaking, scrupulous**). [25, 92, 280]

fathom, *v.* to figure out or get to the bottom of (cf. **unfathomable**). [131, 228, 289]

fatuous, *adj.* silly or stupid in a **complacent** way (SAT synonym: **inane**). [210, 255]

feign, *v.* to fake, make believe, pretend: to *feign* illness. [107, 145, 233, 271]

feisty, *adj.* full of spirit or nerve. [33]

felicitous, *adj.* well suited or appropriate: a *felicitous* expression (SAT synonym: **apt**). [65]

fertile, *adj.* productive; able to produce offspring, seeds, fruit, etc. in great quantities: *fertile* land (SAT synonym: **prolific**; cf. **arable**). [7, 228, 298]

fervent, *adj.* full of intense feeling or spirit: a *fervent* plea (SAT synonyms: **ardent, avid, zealous**). [104, 138, 140, 311]

fervid, *adj.* glowing with feeling, fiery: a *fervid* desire (SAT synonyms: **ardent, torrid**). [65]

fetid, *adj.* having an **offensive** smell (as of decay), stinking. [264]

fiasco, *n.* a total and ignominious failure. [237, 288]

fickle, *adj.* not loyal or constant (as in affections), given to casual change (SAT synonym: **capricious**). [135]

fidelity, *n.* faithfulness to a person, cause, or duty; loyalty. [32]

fitful, *adj.* irregular, intermittent: *fitful* sleep. [127]

flamboyant, *adj.* 1. flashy, showy, striking (SAT synonym: **ostentatious**). 2. colorful or showy in style. [53, 139, 299, 304]

florid, *adj.* overly decorated, flowery: a *florid* writing style (SAT synonym: **ornate**). [26, 52, 190]

flourish, *v.* to grow with **vigor,** thrive, succeed. **flourishing,** *adj.* (SAT synonym: **burgeoning**). [44, 299]

flourish, *n.* a loud, lively sounding of trumpets. [51]

foolhardy, *adj.* bold in a foolish, reckless manner (SAT synonyms: **imprudent, rash**). [175, 197, 260, 289, 292]

forbidding, *adj.* grim, sinister, menacing. [186, 216, 250]

forge, *v.* to make or imitate in order to **deceive;** to counterfeit: to *forge* a check. [46]

forgery, *n.* an imitation (as of a signature or document) intended to be passed off as the real thing; a counterfeit. [154, 200]

formidable, *adj.* 1. inspiring fear, dread, or amazement. 2. awesome, intimidating. [11, 44, 95]

forthright, *adj.* going straight to the point without hesitation, frank, direct: a *forthright* answer. [33]

fortuitous, *adj.* occurring by chance, accidental (SAT synonyms: see **random**). [202, 272, 308, 313]
Usage note: Be careful not to confuse *fortuitous* with *fortunate,* meaning "lucky." A *fortuitous* discovery is accidental, unexpected, and may or may not be *fortunate.*

frivolous, *adj.* 1. unimportant, not worth serious attention (SAT synonyms: **insignificant, paltry, petty, trivial**). 2. lacking seriousness, irresponsible, silly. **frivolity,** *n.* [74, 135, 226, 266, 309]

frugal, *adj.* careful in spending, using one's money or resources carefully and sparingly, thrifty, economical (SAT synonym: **prudent**). [5, 49, 147, 297, 302]

fruitful, *adj.* yielding good or rich results, productive: a *fruitful* meeting. [245]

fruitless, *adj.* producing nothing, useless, not successful. [212]

furtive, *adj.* sly, stealthy, shifty, underhanded (SAT synonyms: **clandestine, covert, devious, surreptitious**). **furtively,** *adv.* [54, 67, 215, 220, 259, 290]

futile, *adj.* of no use, ineffective, pointless. **futility,** *n.* [29, 67, 189, 218, 252, 309]

G

galvanize, *v.* to rouse to action, excite (SAT synonym: **stimulate**). [201, 235, 298]

garish, *adj.* excessively showy, flashy (SAT synonyms: **gaudy, tawdry**). [72]

garrulous, *adj.* overly talkative, esp. about unimportant things (SAT synonym: **loquacious**). [3, 29]

gaudy, *adj.* excessively showy in a tasteless way (SAT synonyms: **garish, tawdry**). [215]

genteel, *adj.* elegant, courteous, refined (SAT synonyms: **sophisticated, suave, urbane**). [277, 280]

germane, *adj.* pert. to what is under consideration or being discussed (SAT synonyms: **pertinent, relevant**). [72]

giddy, *adj.* dizzy, lightheaded. [210]

girth, *n.* a measure around something, esp. a person's waist; circumference; size. [172]

glorify, *v.* 1. to honor or praise highly. 2. to make something seem much better than it actually is. **glorified,** *adj.* (SAT synonym: **exalted**). [36, 288, 295, 300]

glum, *adj.* gloomy, moody, dejected (SAT synonyms: see **morose**). **glumly,** *adv.* [54, 242]

grandeur, *n.* magnificence, splendor. [23, 299]

grandiloquent, *adj.* speaking in a lofty, **pompous,** or overblown manner (SAT synonym: **bombastic**). [2, 296, 301]

grandiose, *adj.* 1. impressive, magnificent (SAT synonym: **imposing**). 2. affectedly grand (SAT synonym: **ostentatious, pretentious**). [7, 36, 121, 282]

grapple, *v.* to engage in a struggle at close quarters, wrestle, vie. [29, 277]

gratify, *v.* to please, satisfy, delight. **gratified,** *adj.* [10, 35, 59, 144, 172, 297]

grave, *adj.* 1. serious, dignified, formal, grim: a *grave* person; a *grave* occasion (SAT synonyms: **austere, somber, staid**). 2. extremely important, momentous: a *grave* decision. [35, 72, 128, 285]

gravity, *n.* seriousness, importance, weight. [215, 309, 313]

gregarious, *adj.* liking the companionship of others, sociable (SAT synonym: **convivial**). [46, 286]

grimace, *v.* to twist the face in an expression of pain, disapproval, frustration, or **contempt.** [26, 114, 178, 309, 314]

grotesque, *adj.* odd, misshapen, or horrible in appearance. [192, 277]

guise, *n.* external appearance, esp. if false. [103, 229, 290]

H

hackneyed, *adj.* made **commonplace** or dull by overuse: a *hackneyed* plot (SAT synonym: **trite**). [200, 299]

halcyon, *adj.* calm, peaceful, unruffled (SAT synonyms: **placid, serene, tranquil**). [222]

hamper, *v.* to restrict the movements of, hinder, interfere with (SAT synonym: **impede**). [139, 211, 243]

haphazard, *adj.* characterized by lack of order or direction, accidental, not planned (SAT synonyms: see **random**). [28, 90, 188]

harass, *v.* to annoy or irritate, trouble, worry, pester, badger, torment. [94, 199, 260]

harmonious, *adj.* 1. orderly and pleasing in sound or arrangement. 2. in **accord** or agreement. [11, 151, 295, 300]

haughty, *adj.* self-satisfied and scornful of others, excessively proud (SAT synonyms: **arrogant, imperious, supercilious**). [56, 93, 100, 289, 292]

headlong, *adv.* **literally,** headfirst; figuratively, recklessly. [191]

hedonist, *n.* a person who follows a way of life devoted to the pursuit of pleasure and the avoidance of pain. **hedonistic,** *adj.* [77, 209, 287, 291]

heresy, *n.* a belief that differs from an **orthodox** religious doctrine or from an established belief or standard. **heretical,** *adj.* [90, 155, 287, 299]

heterogeneous, *adj.* consisting of dissimilar parts, elements, or members: American society is *heterogeneous*. [10]

hidebound, *adj.* inflexible, close-minded, conservative, stubbornly stuck in one's ways (SAT synonyms: **adamant, intractable, obdurate, obstinate**). [32, 287]

hierarchy, *n.* a rigid ranking of persons or things with each rank subject to or dependent upon those above it: a corporate *hierarchy*. [109]

hindrance, *n.* someone or something that delays or blocks progress; an obstruction (SAT synonym: **impediment**). [102]

histrionic, *adj.* 1. pert. to actors or acting. 2. overly dramatic or emotional, affected, insincere (SAT synonym: **melodramatic**). [26, 99]

hoax, *n.* an act meant to trick or fool, fraud, fakery (SAT synonym: **deception**). [111, 290, 293]

hostile, *adj.* exhibiting opposition, open distrust, dislike, ill will, or hatred: a *hostile* attitude (SAT synonyms: **antagonistic, belligerent**). **hostility,** *n.* (SAT synonyms: **animosity, antagonism, enmity**). [41, 144, 298, 299]

hypocritical, *adj.* appearing to possess a virtue one lacks, insincere, fraudulent, two-faced. [275]

hypothesis (*pl.* **hypotheses**), *n.* an assumption made for the sake of argument or further study. [90, 113, 137, 140, 145, 204, 211, 225]

hypothetical, *adj.* based on a **hypothesis** (cf. **theoretical**). **hypothetically,** *adv.* [165]

I

iconoclastic, *adj.* attacking or opposing accepted, established beliefs or customs. [77]

ideological, *adj.* relating to or based on ideas, esp. the ideas characteristic of a particular culture or group. [173]

idiom, *n.* 1. an expression whose meaning cannot be understood by putting together the usual meanings of each separate word: "To put your nose to the grindstone" is an *idiom* meaning "to stick to a job and work hard." 2. the way of speaking typical of a certain group of people: the *idiom* of the South; political *idiom* (cf. **jargon**). [94, 306, 311]

idiosyncrasy, *n.* a characteristic or quality peculiar to a particular person; a quirk (SAT synonym: **eccentricity**). **idiosyncratic,** *adj.* (SAT synonym: **eccentric**). [65, 110, 298, 303]

ill-conceived, *adj.* badly planned. [74, 275]

illegible, *adj.* difficult or impossible to read, printed or written unclearly. [190, 307, 312]

illicit, *adj.* unlawful, illegal. [36]

illuminate, *v.* 1. to light up, brighten. 2. to make clear, provide understanding, enable to understand (SAT synonyms: **clarify, elucidate, enlighten**). 3. to decorate (a manuscript, page, letter) in gold or silver or colors. **illuminated,** *adj.* **illuminating,** *adj.* (SAT synonyms: **edifying, enlightening**). [46, 52, 91, 111, 156, 171, 295]

illustrious, *adj.* very well known, celebrated (SAT synonyms: see **prominent**). [42, 142]

immaculate, *adj.* spotlessly clean. **immaculately,** *adv.* [27, 167]

imminent, *adj.* about to happen: an *imminent* crisis (SAT synonym: **impending**). [80]

immortality, *n.* unending life or fame. [234]

immune, *adj.* not susceptible to (as a disease), unaffected by. [74, 103]

immutable, *adj.* not changeable; fixed: the *immutable* laws of nature. [98, 109, 297, 302]

impart, *v.* to give or grant a share or portion of. [149, 299]

impartial, *adj.* fair, just, not **biased**, not prejudiced (SAT synonyms: **dispassionate, indifferent, objective**). **impartiality,** *n.* [24, 97, 115, 137]

impasse, *n.* a predicament from which there is no escape, a deadlock. [252]

impassive, *adj.* unaffected by emotion, giving no sign of feeling (SAT synonyms: **stoic** and see **phlegmatic**). [233]

impeccable, *adj.* without fault, flaw, or blemish. **impeccably,** *adv.* [39, 175]

impede, *v.* to hinder, interfere with, obstruct (SAT synonym: **hamper**). [117, 193, 298, 306]

impediment, *n.* an obstacle, something that interferes with progress (SAT synonym: **hindrance**). [95, 153, 231, 309]

impending, *adj.* about to happen: an *impending* storm (SAT synonym: **imminent**). [95]

imperative, *adj.* absolutely necessary, urgent. [120, 126, 161]

imperious, *adj.* proud, overbearing, dictatorial (SAT synonyms: **arrogant, haughty, supercilious**). **imperiously,** *adv.* [234, 265]

impermeable, *adj.* not permitting passage (as of a liquid) through or into: an *impermeable* membrane. [249, 298, 303]

impervious, *adj.* unreceptive to, unaffected by: *impervious* to all pleas (SAT synonym: **immune**). [103]

impetuous, *adj.* acting suddenly and forcefully, with much emotion and little thought; hasty, overeager, impatient. [211, 229, 246, 273]
    —*Impetuous, rash,* and *impulsive* all refer to hasty or sudden actions or to people who act first and think later. *Impetuous* suggests great energy, eagerness, or impatience. *Rash* suggests reckless haste and foolish daring. *Impulsive* suggests an ungovernable inner force that drives one to act without thinking.

implausible, *adj.* difficult to believe, not **plausible**. [32, 114, 166, 306]

implicate, *v.* to connect (someone) to a plot, crime, etc. [266]

implication, *n.* a hint, suggestion, something **implied** (cf. **insinuation**). [107, 229, 266]

imply, *v.* to say indirectly, suggest without directly stating: His manner *implied* that he didn't believe us (see **infer**). **implied,** *adj.* **implying,** *adj.* [xi, 115, 142, 165, 166, 182, 192, 199, 202, 230, 232, 245, 305]

imposing, *adj.* impressive in appearance, manner, or size (SAT synonym: **grandiose**). [7, 64, 122, 200, 234]

impoverished, *adj.* without money or resources. [44, 297, 290, 302]

impregnable, *adj.* not able to be entered, penetrated, conquered, or overcome. [249, 298]

impressionable, *adj.* easily affected or influenced, sensitive. [104]

improbable, *adj.* unlikely to be true or to occur. [108, 111]

impromptu, *adj.* not planned or prepared, produced on the spur of the moment, offhand (SAT synonym: **spontaneous**). [98, 214]

impropriety, *n.* an improper act or an unacceptable use of language. [272]

imprudent, *adj.* unwise, lacking good judgment, not **prudent** (SAT synonyms: **foolhardy, rash**). [73, 289]

impudent, *adj.* rude, disrespectful (SAT synonym: **insolent**). [57]

impulsive, *adj.* acting or occurring suddenly without plan or forethought, **mo**tivated by impulse (SAT synonyms: **capricious, spontaneous,** and see **impetuous**). [4, 262]

inadvertent, *adj.* not intentional. **inadvertently,** *adv.* [217, 219]

inane, *adj.* without point or meaning, silly, foolish: an *inane* comment (SAT synonym: **fatuous**). [20, 57, 261, 285, 286, 295]

inaudible, *adj.* not capable of being heard, not **audible**. [142]

incantation, *n.* a formula of words used to produce a magical result. [252, 288]

incarcerate, *v.* to put in prison, imprison. **incarceration,** *n.* [202, 288, 292]

incessant, *adj.* unceasing, continuing without interruption: *incessant* noise. **incessantly,** *adv.* [117, 210, 297]

incoherent, *adj.* not expressed in a clear, orderly manner; hard to make sense of, disjointed, disorganized, not **coherent**. [138, 142, 196]

incompetent, *adj.* without ability or skill, not **competent**. [116]

incomprehensible, *adj.* impossible to understand, not **comprehensible** (SAT synonym: **unfathomable**). [194]

inconceivable, *adj.* not possible to imagine, unbelievable, unthinkable. [105]

inconclusive, *adj.* not definite or final, leaving room for doubt, without conclusion or result, not **conclusive**. [246]

inconspicuous, *adj.* not easily noticeable, not obvious, not **conspicuous**. [132]

incontrovertible, *adj.* indisputable, unquestionable, not possible to argue with. [246, 297]

incorrigible, *adj.* incapable of being corrected, improved, or reformed. [45, 74, 266, 279]

incredulous, *adj.* unable or unwilling to believe, doubting (SAT synonyms: **dubious, skeptical**). **incredulously,** *adv.* [118, 166, 266, 288, 292]

indecision, *n.* inability to choose or decide. [250]

indefatigable, *adj.* never lacking energy, tireless. [207]

indeterminate, *adj.* indefinite, unclear, not fixed or settled. [130]

indifferent, *adj.* 1. uncaring, having no particular interest in, detached (SAT synonyms: **perfunctory** and see **phlegmatic**). 2. not for or against, having no preference (SAT synonyms: **dispassionate, impartial, objective**). **indifference,** *n.* (SAT synonym: **apathy**). [25, 28, 39, 286, 290, 296, 313]

indignation, *n.* anger aroused by something unjust or unfair (SAT synonym: **resentment**). [59]

indistinct, *adj.* unclear, hard to recognize, blurred, dim, faint. [185, 252]

indulge, *v.* allow to act without **restraint**, give in to or satisfy (an appetite, **whim,** desire, etc.). **indulgence,** *n.* [97, 297, 302]

indulgent, *adj.* 1. not holding back or exercising **restraint**, giving in to. 2. putting up with, tolerating. **indulgently,** *adv.* [206, 209, 210, 211, 264]

industrious, *adj.* hardworking, persevering (SAT synonyms: **assiduous, diligent**). **industriously,** *adv.* [8, 131]

ineffectual, *adj.* not producing the desired effect. [186, 245, 295]

inert, *adj.* not having the power to move or respond. **inertia,** *n.* [144, 299]

inevitable, *adj.* certain to happen, impossible to prevent, unavoidable. **inevitably,** *adv.* [1, 34, 225, 274]

inexorable, *adj.* relentless, not able to be stopped, changed, or moved by persuasion. [190, 290]

infamous, *adj.* having a very bad reputation (SAT synonym: **notorious**). [59, 78, 289]

infer, *v.* to reason or conclude from evidence, figure out a meaning (SAT synonym: **deduce**). [115, 134, 183, 289, 300, 303, 308, 309, 311]
Usage note: Be careful not to confuse the verbs *imply* and *infer.* To *imply* is to hint or suggest rather than to state something outright: Her statement *implies* support for his position. To *infer* is to come to a conclusion based on something said or written: He *inferred* from her statement that she supported his position. One may *infer* (come to a conclusion, derive a meaning) from something *implied* (hinted at, suggested).

ingenious, *adj.* clever, creative, imaginative: an *ingenious* plan. **ingeniously,** *adv.* [45, 103, 180, 208, 308]

ingenuity, *n.* cleverness, skill, imagination (SAT synonym: **inventiveness**). [159]

ingenuous, *adj.* showing innocence or trust; childlike, sincere (SAT synonym: **naive**). [246, 289]

inherent, *adj.* essential, existing within someone or something as a natural, permanent element (SAT synonyms: **innate, intrinsic**). [65]

inhibition, *n.* an inner **restraint** that stops a person from acting or thinking freely. [97]

inimitable, *adj.* not able to be copied or imitated, matchless. [67]

iniquity, *n.* great injustice, wickedness, sin. [265, 287]

initial, *adj.* of or coming at the beginning, earliest, first. [219]

initiate, *v.* 1. to set going, start, begin. 2. to admit as a member of a club or society, usu. through a special or secret ceremony. **initiation,** *n.* [25, 97, 168, 281]

initiative, *n.* the act of or the responsibility for taking the first step in doing something. [116, 169]

innate, *adj.* inborn, possessed at birth, natural as opposed to acquired (SAT synonyms: **inherent, intrinsic**). [107]

innocuous, *adj.* harmless, causing no injury or ill will: an *innocuous* remark. [46, 165, 295]

innovative, *adj.* 1. fresh, marked by a change in the usual way of doing things (SAT synonym: **novel**; cf. **unprecedented**). 2. introducing or tending to introduce new ideas or ways of doing things. [vii, viii, 110, 114, 226]

innumerable, *adj.* too many to be numbered, countless (SAT synonym: **myriad**). [10]

inquisitive, *adj.* inclined to ask questions, extremely curious: He was amused by the very *inquisitive* child. [24, 121, 278]

insatiable, *adj.* always unsatisfied, never getting enough (SAT synonym: **voracious**). [155, 286]

inscrutable, *adj.* mysterious, difficult to interpret or understand (SAT synonyms: **cryptic, enigmatic**). [66, 125, 193, 227, 307, 312]

insidious, *adj.* evil or treacherous in a sly, underhanded manner; working or spreading ill or harm in a hidden, dangerous way. [73, 104, 254]

insight, *n.* the power to sense or understand the inner nature of someone or something. **insightful,** *adj.* (SAT synonyms: **astute, discerning, keen, perceptive, perspicacious, sagacious, shrewd**). **insightfully,** *adv.* [85, 114, 138, 155, 183, 210]

insignificant, *adj.* not important, meaningless, small in size or value: The error was *insignificant* (SAT synonyms: **frivolous, negligible, paltry, petty, trivial**). **insignificance,** *n.* [103, 266, 297, 299]

insinuation, *n.* a sly hint, indirect or **covert** suggestion, esp. of something unpleasant or disagreeable (cf. **implication**). [123]

insipid, *adj.* 1. without flavor or taste, bland: an *insipid* meal. 2. not interesting, dull: an *insipid* person. [x, 29]

insolent, *adj.* insulting, intentionally rude or disrespectful: an *insolent* response (SAT synonym: **impudent**). [95]

instigate, *v.* to cause to happen by stirring up, incite. [5, 164]

insulated, *adj.* set apart, isolated, protected, detached. [151, 186]

intact, *adj.* entire, with no part removed or damaged. [107]

integral, *adj.* essential, necessary for completion. [64]

integrate, *v.* to form into a unified whole, incorporate into a larger whole, unite. [99, 295, 300]

integrity, *n.* moral or artistic honesty, strength of character. [57, 107, 165, 275]

intemperate, *adj.* excessive, unruly, lacking in **moderation**. [267]

interrogation, *n.* an examination by questioning. [99, 158, 193]

intervene, *v.* to come between, interfere, esp. to change a situation. [44, 272, 288]

intolerance, *n.* unwillingness to accept or respect others' beliefs or practices. [103]

intractable, *adj.* difficult to control, lead, or **manipulate** (SAT synonyms: **adamant, hidebound, obdurate, obstinate**). [153, 177, 252, 289]

intrepid, *adj.* extremely brave, daring, unafraid. [247, 289, 292]

intricacy, *n.* something detailed, complicated, **complex**, entangled, or involved: the *intricacies* of a computer. [124]

intricate, *adj.* elaborately detailed, complicated, or **complex**. **intricately**, *adv.* [171]

intrigue, *v.* to arouse the interest, desire, or curiosity of; fascinate. [33, 106, 165, 261, 296]

intrinsic, *adj.* belonging to the essential nature of a thing (SAT synonyms: **inherent, innate**). [175]

intuition, *n.* the faculty of knowing instinctively, without conscious reasoning; the knowledge so acquired. **intuitive**, *adj.* [94, 135, 199, 299, 303]

invaluable, *adj.* valuable beyond what can be reasonably estimated, priceless. [266, 295]

inventiveness, *n.* originality, creativity (SAT synonym: **ingenuity**). [225]

inveterate, *adj.* fixed in a habit or custom: an *inveterate* liar. [224]

invigorating, *adj.* giving strength and energy to (SAT synonym: **rejuvenating**). [145, 289]

involuntary, *adj.* done by reflex rather than by choice, beyond control of mind or will (SAT synonym: **spontaneous**). **involuntarily**, *adv.* [227, 251, 309, 314]

irascible, *adj.* easily provoked, very irritable (SAT synonym: **cantankerous**). **irascibly**, *adv.* [117, 309, 314]

irk, *v.* to bother, annoy, vex. [229, 275, 288]

irony, *n.* a manner of expression that implies the opposite of what the words **literally** mean, as when one says "Thanks for sharing" after hearing something unpleasant (see **sarcasm**). **ironic**, *adj.* (SAT synonym: **satirical**). **ironically**, *adv.* [33, 66, 90, 229, 245, 250, 266]

irrational, *adj.* not according to reason, senseless, not **rational**. [143, 144, 219]

irrevocable, *adj.* not possible to bring back, undo, or alter: an *irrevocable* decision. [272, 309, 314]

J

jargon, *n.* the technical language used by members of a particular profession or class: psychological *jargon* (cf. **idiom**). [30, 125]

jostle, *v.* to crowd or brush against, push, elbow, shove. [236]

jovial, *adj.* jolly, good-natured (SAT synonyms: **affable, amiable, cordial**). [173, 213]

jubilant, *adj.* filled with or showing joy (SAT synonym: **exultant**). [280]

judicious, *adj.* characterized by good judgment, sensible, wise. [156]

K

keen, *adj.* 1. sharp. 2. intellectually sharp, penetrating, piercing: a *keen* observation; a *keen* critic (SAT synonyms: **astute, discerning, insightful, perceptive, perspicacious, sagacious, shrewd**). 3. intense (SAT synonym: **acute**). **keenly**, *adv.* [116, 155, 264, 279]

kindle, *v.* to ignite or light; hence, to stir up or excite. [10, 138]

L

laceration, *n.* a jagged tear or wound. [149]

lackluster, *adj.* without brilliance or sheen, **literally** or figuratively dull or colorless (SAT synonyms: **commonplace, mundane, pedestrian, prosaic**). [66, 296]

languid, *adj.* having no energy or interest, slow, weak (SAT synonyms: see **phlegmatic**). **languidly,** *adv.* [176, 224]

languish, *v.* to lose strength or health, become weak, droop from longing or desire, pine, suffer: to *languish* in bed with a broken heart. [28, 209, 275, 299]

largess (or **largesse**), *n.* 1. a generous or **lavish** gift. 2. generous or **lavish** giving, generosity (SAT synonym: **munificence**). [75, 224, 299, 304]

latent, *adj.* present but not visible or active: *latent* musical ability. [30]

laudable, *adj.* worthy of praise or approval (SAT synonyms: **commendable, meritorious**). [280]

laughingstock, *n.* a person or thing that is the object of laughter, the butt of a joke or **ridicule**. [275, 290, 293]

lavish, *adj.* characterized by excess, more than enough, rich or fancy: a *lavish* meal (SAT synonyms: **extravagant, luxuriant, opulent, sumptuous**). [46, 171, 280, 308]

legacy, *n.* money or property that has been left to someone by a will; an inheritance, anything handed down from the past (SAT synonym: **bequest**). [73, 275, 294]

legible, *adj.* able to be read or **deciphered** easily: The document must be signed with a *legible* signature. [157]

legitimate, *adj.* lawful, legal. [220, 288]

lethal, *adj.* deadly, fatal. [125, 192, 289, 293]

lethargic, *adj.* having little or no energy, drowsy, dull (SAT synonyms: see **phlegmatic**). [189]

levity, *n.* joking or gaiety, esp. at inappropriate moments: There was an unacceptable amount of *levity* in the classroom. [215, 261, 309, 313]

listless, *adj.* lacking spirit, energy, or interest (SAT synonyms: see **phlegmatic**). [135, 189, 196]

literal, *adj.* 1. real, actual, without exaggeration or decoration. 2. exact, word-for-word, closely following the original. 3. adhering to the original, primary, or ordinary meaning of a word, not figurative or **metaphorical**. **literally,** *adv.* [85, 186, 244, 281]

lithe, *adj.* flexible in a graceful way, limber, supple. [234]

loquacious, *adj.* talkative, esp. excessively (SAT synonym: **garrulous**). [24, 272]

lucid, *adj.* capable of being readily understood, clear, plain: a *lucid* response. [107, 142, 195, 209, 242, 296, 301]

ludicrous, *adj.* provoking laughter, scorn, or **ridicule**: a *ludicrous* situation (SAT synonyms: **absurd, farcical, preposterous**). **ludicrously,** *adv.* [20, 66, 108, 209, 296]

lurid, *adj.* causing horror or fear, terrible, shocking, sensational: *lurid* head-lines. [263, 295]

luscious, *adj.* having a pleasing taste and smell. [146]

luxuriant, *adj.* 1. showing thick and **abundant** growth, lush: *lush* vegetation. 2. very rich, fancy, or elaborate, as in decorations or furnishings (SAT synonyms: **lavish, opulent, sumptuous**). [121, 171]

lyric, *adj.* expressing strong personal feelings. **lyrical,** *adj.* [77, 106]

M

magnanimous, *adj.* 1. generous in overlooking insults or injuries. 2. noble, high-minded, unselfish. **magnanimity,** *n.* [77, 139, 215, 272, 282]

magnitude, *n.* size, extent, dimensions: a crowd of great *magnitude.* [70, 299, 304]

malcontent, *n.* a dissatisfied, discontented, rebellious person. [93, 290]

malevolent, *adj.* wishing or doing evil to others, showing ill will (SAT synonym: **malicious**). [250]

malicious, *adj.* desiring to hurt or injure someone, full of ill will, evil, nasty, spiteful (SAT synonym: **malevolent**). [43, 50, 72, 139, 144, 168, 279]

malodorous, *adj.* having a disagreeable odor, foul-smelling. [264]

manic, *adj.* having or showing an exaggerated enthusiasm, interest, desire, or level of activity. [17]

manifest, *v.* to show plainly, reveal, demonstrate, make evident or obvious. **manifestation,** *n.* [27, 105, 295]

manifest, *adj.* clear, apparent, obvious, easily seen or understood. [195, 220, 243]

manipulate, *v.* to control, handle, or influence cleverly or dishonestly, often to one's own advantage. [58]

masonry, *n.* stonework, brickwork, or a structure made of stone or brick. [7]

masquerade, *n.* a social gathering at which masks and elegant costumes are worn by the guests. [5, 290]

masquerade, *v.* to wear a disguise, pose, assume a false identity. [275]

mausoleum, *n.* a large tomb or a building that houses many tombs. [36, 289]

meager, *adj.* of inadequate quality or quantity, inferior. [53]

meandering, *adj.* winding, turning, rambling, wandering aimlessly. [139]

mediate, *v.* to bring about a settlement between disputing parties, act as a peacemaker or go-between. [109]

medieval, *adj.* pert. to or characteristic of the Middle Ages, the period in European history between the fall of the Roman Empire and the Renaissance, lasting from 476 to about 1450. [156]

melancholy, *adj.* causing, suggesting, or feeling sadness, gloom, dejection, depression (SAT synonyms: see **morose**). [151]

melodramatic, *adj.* exaggerated in emotion or sentiment, overly dramatic (SAT synonym: **histrionic**). **melodramatically,** *adv.* [59, 147]

mercenary, *adj.* greedy, **motivated** solely by the desire for money or material gain. [258]

meritorious, *adj.* deserving of praise, admiration, or reward; worthy (SAT synonyms: **commendable, laudable**). [vii, viii, 280]

mesmerize, *v.* to fascinate, capture and hold the attention of, bind as if in a spell. **mesmerizing,** *adj.* [44, 142]

metamorphosis, *n.* 1. a change from one form, shape, substance, or structure into another. 2. a complete transformation, as in a person's character or appearance. [108, 147]

metaphor, *n.* a figure of speech that suggests a likeness between two otherwise unlike things, an **implied** comparison: "The road was a *ribbon* of black" and "Love is a *rose*" are *metaphors*. [183]

metaphorical, *adj.* expressing one thing in terms of another, figurative, not **literal. metaphorically,** *adv.* [183, 211, 244]

metaphysical, *adj.* of or pert. to metaphysics, the branch of philosophy that explores the nature of being and reality; hence, highly **abstract** or difficult to understand. [142, 299, 304]

methodical, *adj.* carried out in an orderly or systematic way: a *methodical* search. **methodically,** *adv.* [159, 187, 254]

meticulous, *adj.* extremely (often excessively) careful about details (SAT synonyms: **conscientious, fastidious, painstaking, scrupulous**). **meticulously,** *adv.* [19, 27, 121, 255, 286, 290]

mettle, *n.* spirit, courage, strength of character: a person of *mettle*. [155, 223]

mime, *v.* to act out something silently with body movements and facial expressions. [202]

minuscule, *adj.* very small, tiny (SAT synonym: **minute**). [61, 203, 262]

minute, *adj.* extremely small, tiny (SAT synonym: **minuscule**). [157, 214]

misanthrope, *n.* a person who regards all others with hate or distrust. [92]

misapprehension, *n.* misunderstanding. [118]

mishap, *n.* an unlucky or unfortunate accident. [172]

mock, *adj.* pretended; not real but made to look so: *mock* remorse. [141]

moderation, *n.* the condition or quality of avoiding extremes and staying within reasonable limits. [19]

modest, *adj.* 1. not vain or boastful, humble. 2. limited in number, size, scope, etc. 3. simple, not elaborate or **pretentious.** [46, 155, 222, 294, 297]

monarch, *n.* 1. a hereditary sovereign (as a king), the sole ruler of a state. 2. a person with supreme power in some **domain.** [93, 104]

monarchy, *n.* government by, or a country ruled by, a **monarch.** [30, 172]

monolithic, *adj.* made of or resembling a single large block of stone; hence, solid, rigid, massive, and **uniform** in appearance or character. [7, 297]

morose, *adj.* gloomy and irritable. [54]

—*Morose, dour, glum,* and *melancholy* all are used to describe a gloomy, downcast, unhappy mood or attitude. *Morose* and *dour* suggest a feeling of irritation, bitterness, or ill will masked by gloomy silence or reserve. *Glum* and *melancholy* suggest a sad or depressed state of mind, often as a result of disappointment.

mortified, *adj.* humiliated, having one's self-respect or pride injured. [59]

motivate, *v.* to provide with a reason or cause to behave in a certain way, provide with a **motive**, move to action, impel. **motivated**, *adj.* [xiv, 144, 155, 175, 293, 298, 303]

motivation, *n.* a reason or cause to act, impulse, incentive (SAT synonym: **motive**). [145]

motive, *n.* something (an emotion, desire, need, etc.) that makes a person behave in a certain way (SAT synonym: **motivation**). [135, 164, 166, 192]

mundane, *adj.* common, everyday, ordinary: a *mundane* occupation (SAT synonyms: **commonplace, lackluster, pedestrian, prosaic**). [186, 297]

munificence, *n.* great generosity (SAT synonym: **largess**). [266]

muse, *v.* 1. to consider, be absorbed in one's thoughts, contemplate, think or say in a **reflective** manner (SAT synonym: **ruminate**). 2. to ask oneself, wonder. [8, 127, 192, 198]

muse, *n.* a source of inspiration. [111]

myriad, *adj.* consisting of a vast, indefinite number; countless (SAT synonym: **innumerable**). [61]

myriad, *n.* an indefinitely large number. [214]

mystical, *adj.* having a quality or meaning that is spiritual or beyond human understanding. [281]

N

naive, *adj.* showing a lack of worldly wisdom or **sophistication**; hence, simple, childlike, and innocent (SAT synonym: **ingenuous**) or foolish, impractical, and inexperienced. [104]

nefarious, *adj.* extremely wicked, villainous, evil. [254]

negligible, *adj.* too small or unimportant to be worth considering (SAT synonyms: **insignificant, paltry, petty, trivial**). [274]

niche, *n.* 1. a place or situation especially suited to a person or thing. 2. a recess in a wall, as for holding a small statue or other art object. [166, 289]

nonchalant, *adj.* cool and unconcerned. **nonchalantly**, *adv.* [95, 217, 233, 259]

nondescript, *adj.* lacking distinguishing features or characteristics, not easily described or classified. [81]

notable, *adj.* worthy of note, distinguished, important, outstanding (SAT synonyms: see **prominent**). **notably**, *adv.* [70, 155, 280]

noteworthy, *adj.* deserving attention, worthy of notice. [12, 86, 256]

notorious, *adj.* widely known, esp. unfavorably (SAT synonym: **infamous**). **notoriously**, *adv.* [67, 214]

novel, *adj.* fresh, new, unusual (SAT synonym: **innovative**; cf. **unprecedented**). [vii, viii, ix, xvi, 6, 32, 110]

novelty, *n.* something that is fresh, different, unusual, or the first of its kind. [104, 223]

noxious, *adj.* harmful to a person's health or morals, not **wholesome**: *noxious* influences; *noxious* smoke (SAT synonym: **pernicious**). [84, 237, 289, 293]

nurture, *v.* to care for, help to grow and develop, provide with physical or intellectual nourishment. [10, 108]

O

obdurate, *adj.* not easily moved by pity or persuasion, stubborn, inflexible (SAT synonyms: **adamant, hidebound, intractable, obstinate**). [66]

obfuscation, *n.* the often intentional act of confusing or making something unclear or difficult to understand. [179, 308, 313]

objective, *adj.* 1. not influenced by personal feelings or opinions, not **biased**: A judge must always remain *objective* when hearing a case (SAT synonyms: **dispassionate, impartial, indifferent**). 2. having to do with what is real, as opposed to what exists only in the mind (cf. **subjective**). **objectivity,** *n.* [82, 97, 103, 137]

oblique, *adj.* expressed in an indirect manner, not straightforward: an *oblique* reference. **obliquely,** *adv.* [100]

obliterate, *v.* to destroy completely, wipe out, remove any trace of: The storm *obliterated* the village. [250, 297, 302]

oblivious, *adj.* showing no awareness of, not minding: *oblivious* to the commotion. [198, 210]

obscure, *v.* to hide or conceal; to make vague, confusing, dim, or **indistinct**: The clouds *obscured* the view (SAT synonym: **eclipse**). [216]

obscure, *adj.* 1. unclear, difficult to understand: an *obscure* message. 2. indistinct, hard to make out: an *obscure* sound. 3. hard to find, hidden: an *obscure* trail in the woods. 4. not well-known: an *obscure* sonnet by Shakespeare. 5. dark, dim. **obscurely,** *adv.* **obscurity,** *n.* [xi, 22, 51, 67, 79, 96, 98, 101, 103, 105, 119, 129, 159, 190, 214, 223, 242, 253, 271, 275]

obsequious, *adj.* too eager to please, flatter, or obey; fawning (SAT synonyms: **servile, sycophantic**). **obsequiously,** *adv.* [50, 309, 314]

obsolete, *adj.* no longer in use, out-of-date, outmoded. [36, 294]
  —*Antiquated, archaic,* and *obsolete* all refer to that which is old and out of general use. *Antiquated* means no longer in style, out of fashion: *antiquated* ideas. *Archaic* suggests another era, a time long past: an *archaic* custom. *Obsolete* describes that which has been discarded or has fallen into disuse: *obsolete* technology; an *obsolete* word.

obstinate, *adj.* stubborn, unyielding, inflexible, esp. in the face of argument, attack, or criticism (SAT synonyms: **adamant, hidebound, intractable, obdurate**). **obstinately,** *adv.* [65, 108, 115, 289]

obtuse, *adj.* slow in understanding or feeling, dull, stupid: She couldn't tell if he did not understand her or was being deliberately *obtuse*. [207, 260]

occult, *adj.* beyond human comprehension, mysterious, magical. [281]

offensive, *adj.* objectionable, insulting, disagreeable, disgusting (SAT synonym: **repugnant**). [57, 229]

officious, *adj.* overly eager or presumptuous in offering unsolicited assistance or advice, meddlesome. [69, 275, 288, 292]

ominous, *adj.* threatening or foreboding, sinister, full of or indicating potential evil or harm. **ominously,** *adv.* [64, 214, 289, 293, 309, 314]

onerous, *adj.* hard to bear, burdensome, heavy, troublesome (SAT synonym: **oppressive**). [103]

opaque, *adj.* 1. not allowing the passage of light, not transparent. 2. difficult to understand, unclear. [195, 242, 298, 303]

oppressive, *adj.* harsh, difficult, hard to bear, burdensome: *oppressive* living conditions (SAT synonym: **onerous**). [172]

opulent, *adj.* very rich, costly, expensive, indicative of great wealth: an *opulent* estate (SAT synonyms: **lavish, luxuriant, sumptuous**). [175]

oracle, *n.* a priest through whom the gods were thought to respond to questions put to them by the ancient Greeks and Romans; hence, any person thought to possess great wisdom or authority. [142]

orator, *n.* a person who gives a speech, esp. a long, formal one (called an *oration*). [142]

oratory, *n.* the art of speaking effectively in public. [91]

ordeal, *n.* an experience that is very difficult or painful. [108, 142, 125, 288]

ornate, *adj.* highly and often excessively decorated; fancy, showy (SAT synonym: **florid**). [23, 84, 92, 130, 234, 295, 300]

orthodox, *adj.* in **accordance** with long-established and commonly accepted beliefs or practices, esp. those of a religion; proper, generally accepted, customary: an *orthodox* approach to science (SAT synonyms: **conventional, traditional**). [103, 299]

oscillate, *v.* to move back and forth in a regular way, like a pendulum. [193]

ostentatious, *adj.* showy or flashy in an attempt to impress, making a **conspicuous** display to attract attention (SAT synonym: **flamboyant, grandiose, pretentious**). [31, 36, 73, 223, 273, 306, 311]

outlandish, *adj.* strange, unfamiliar, strikingly different or odd: *outlandish* clothing; *outlandish* notions (SAT synonym: **bizarre**). [102, 173]

overt, *adj.* done or shown openly, observable, not hidden or concealed, not **covert. overtly**, *adv.* [143, 284]

overwrought, *adj.* under considerable emotional strain; extremely nervous, excited, or tense. [18]

P

painstaking, *adj.* careful, showing great effort (SAT synonyms: **conscientious, diligent, fastidious, meticulous, scrupulous**). **painstakingly**, *adv.* [20, 104]

pallid, *adj.* pale, wan; lacking color, strength, or **vitality**: *pallid* skin; a *pallid* performance. [134, 144, 262, 283]

paltry, *adj.* so small as to be worthless or unimportant; trifling (SAT synonyms: **frivolous, insignificant, negligible, petty, trivial**). [73, 194]

panoramic, *adj.* wide and **comprehensive**, usu. describing a view in every direction: the breathtaking *panoramic* view of the valley below. [172]

paradox, *n.* 1. a statement that appears to contradict itself and thus seems to be false or **absurd** but may actually be true, such as the often-quoted *paradox* of modern architecture: "Less is more." 2. a person, thing, situation, etc. with an apparently contradictory or inconsistent nature. **paradoxical**, *adj.* **paradoxically**, *adv.* [46, 65, 110, 242, 309]

paragon, *n.* a model of excellence or perfection: a *paragon* of virtue. [159]

paraphrase, *v.* to express, using different words, the meaning of something spoken or written; restate, reword. [142]

patronizing, *adj.* tending to treat others as inferior, acting with an air of **condescension** (SAT synonyms: **haughty, imperious, supercilious**). [160]

paucity, *n.* lack, scarcity, insufficiency of amount or number: a *paucity* of volunteers. [111]

peccadillo, *n.* a minor sin, fault, or error. [164, 287, 291]

pedant, *n.* 1. a person who makes a showy display of knowledge to impress others. 2. a person who pays excessive attention to rules or details in learning or scholarship. **pedantic,** *adj.* [224, 266, 306]

pedestal, *n.* the base supporting a column, statue, lamp, or the like. [216]

pedestrian, *adj.* dull, ordinary, uninteresting: *pedestrian* prose (SAT synonyms: **commonplace, lackluster, mundane, prosaic**). [118, 219, 296]

penchant, *n.* a strong liking or inclination: a *penchant* for flashy sports cars. [44]

pensive, *adj.* deeply thoughtful, often in a sad or dreamy way. **pensively,** *adv.* [11, 62, 129, 151, 221]

penury, *n.* extreme poverty, indigence, want, destitution. [108]

perceive, *v.* to become aware of through the senses, esp. the sight; to observe, take notice of; to grasp mentally, understand (SAT synonyms: **apprehend, discern**). [275, 293]

perception, *n.* 1. the act or process of becoming aware of something through any of the senses: a **keen** *perception* of sound. 2. knowledge, **insight**, comprehension. [85, 101, 132, 306]

perceptive, *adj.* capable of quickly understanding: a *perceptive* student (SAT synonyms: **astute, discerning, insightful, keen, perspicacious, sagacious, shrewd**). [182]

perennial, *adj.* lasting through many years, enduring, perpetual. [224]

perfunctory, *adj.* 1. done in a routine manner, as if merely to get finished; hasty: a *perfunctory* greeting (SAT synonyms: **cursory, superficial**). 2. showing little interest or enthusiasm, careless, halfhearted: a *perfunctory* effort (SAT synonyms: **apathetic, indifferent, listless**). [41, 189, 295]

peripheral, *adj.* on or pert. to the boundary, edge, or outer part of something; hence, not in the center of things, of minor concern: a *peripheral* issue that did not affect the outcome of the election. [103]

periphery, *n.* a boundary or the area just outside a boundary: the *periphery* of the campus. [4, 214, 278]

perjure, *v.* to make (oneself) guilty of lying, esp. while under an oath to tell the truth (as in a court of law). [146]

permutation, *n.* a thorough change in form, character, or condition; transformation, alteration. [109]

pernicious, *adj.* harmful, destructive (SAT synonym: **noxious**). **perniciously,** *adv.* [105]

persistent, *adj.* continuing in spite of difficulty or opposition, persevering: a *persistent* suitor (SAT synonym: **dogged, tenacious, undaunted**). [50]

perspicacious, *adj.* having a powerful and penetrating mind, quick to see and understand (SAT synonyms: **astute, discerning, insightful, keen, perceptive, sagacious, shrewd**). **perspicacity,** *n.* [107, 181, 265]

pertinent, *adj.* connected in some way to the matter at hand, to the point, appropriate (SAT synonyms: **germane, relevant**). [xvi, 125, 139, 168, 183, 265]

perturbation, *n.* agitation, disquiet, uneasiness. [42]

peruse, *v.* to read or examine closely and carefully: to *peruse* a real estate contract before signing it (SAT synonym: **scrutinize**). [ix, 11, 86, 139, 167, 176, 264]

pervade, *v.* to spread throughout, permeate: silence *pervaded* the room. [32, 63, 290]

perverse, *adj.* 1. improper, incorrect. 2. stubbornly contrary or wrongheaded. **perversity,** *n.* [155, 312]

pervert, *v.* to twist the meaning or character of (SAT synonym: **distort**). [109]

petrified, *adj.* hardened, stonelike. [29]

petty, *adj.* 1. of little importance, minor: a *petty* disagreement (SAT synonyms: **frivolous, insignificant, negligible, paltry, trivial**). 2. spiteful, small-minded, mean: *petty* criticism. [99, 160, 285, 286]

philanthropist, *n.* a person who contributes time and resources (esp. money) to help others. [46, 275, 280]

philistine, *n.* a narrow-minded person with ordinary tastes and ideas who has no interest in the arts or learning. [187]

phlegmatic, *adj.* not easily excited or moved to action, calm, unemotional. [66, 196]
—*Sluggish, listless, lethargic,* and *languid* suggest a lack of energy and a lack of desire to act. *Apathetic, dispassionate, impassive,* and *indifferent* suggest a lack of emotion, interest, or concern. *Phlegmatic* suggests a lack of both emotion and energy.

pious, *adj.* deeply religious, devout (SAT synonym: **reverent**). [224]

placid, *adj.* calm, peaceful, quiet, restful (SAT synonyms: **halcyon, serene, tranquil**). [40, 117, 260]

plausible, *adj.* seemingly true, honest, or reasonable; appearing worthy of belief or trust on first glance: a *plausible* excuse for arriving so late. [98, 103, 104, 201, 210, 225]

plenitude, *n.* a large number or great amount (SAT synonyms: **abundance, plethora, profusion**). [171]

plethora, *n.* an excessive amount or a very large number (SAT synonyms: **abundance, plenitude, profusion**). [61, 173, 188, 298, 303]

podium, *n.* a raised platform on which a public speaker or an orchestra conductor stands. [141]

poignant, *adj.* affecting the emotions, touching, intensely or painfully moving: a *poignant* reunion. [26, 82]

poised, *adj.* 1. self-assured, at ease, composed. 2. balanced, held steady. [40, 100, 102]

pompous, *adj.* puffed up with self-importance (SAT synonym: **pretentious**). [92, 101, 288]

ponderous, *adj.* 1. large and heavy, bulky. 2. dull, boring, labored. [6, 68, 95, 122, 194]

portly, *adj.* stout, heavyset, fat (SAT synonym: **rotund**; cf. **corpulent**). [92]

portray, *v.* 1. to describe in words. 2. to make a picture or likeness of (SAT synonym: **depict**). [103, 128, 198, 295]

posthumous, *adj.* occurring after a person's death: a *posthumous* award; the *posthumous* publication of an autobiography. **posthumously,** *adv.* [78, 266]

potent, *adj.* having a strong effect, powerful: a *potent* chemical. [271]

pragmatic, *adj.* practical as opposed to **theoretical**. [20]

precept, *n.* a rule for guiding conduct or action. [xiv, 9, 309]

precipitate, *v.* to bring about suddenly or sooner than expected: to *precipitate* an argument. [53, 306, 311]

preconceived, *adj.* formed in advance, as an opinion. [115]

predetermined, *adj.* decided in advance, determined beforehand. [35]

predilection, *n.* a preference, liking, tendency to favor. [35, 45, 308]

predominant, *adj.* in greater strength, influence, or number; most frequent or common (SAT synonyms: **prevailing, prevalent**). **predominantly,** *adj.* [102]

preeminent, *adj.* superior, outstanding, **notable** above all others. [65]

preliminary, *adj.* coming before or leading up to the main event, introductory, prefatory. [71, 175]

preposterous, *adj.* senseless, foolish, ridiculous (SAT synonyms: **absurd, farcical, ludicrous**). [73, 226]

prerequisite, *n.* something required as a qualification for something else: Freshman composition is a *prerequisite* for all upper-division English courses and for many other courses as well. [31]

prescient, *adj.* having knowledge of events before they occur, having foresight. [72]

prescribe, *v.* to give as an order or direction, lay down as a rule. [60]

prestigious, *adj.* having or giving fame or importance based on reputation or achievements; honored, distinguished (SAT synonym: **esteemed**). [2, 77]

pretentious, *adj.* 1. showy, making a flashy outward show to attract attention: a *pretentious* gift (SAT synonyms: **grandiose, ostentatious**). 2. making exaggerated or false claims (SAT synonyms: **arrogant, pompous**). [1, 85, 97, 305, 306]

prevail, *v.* to succeed, gain control, be victorious: to *prevail* over one's enemy. [156, 299]

prevailing, *adj.* widely accepted, most common or frequent (SAT synonyms: **predominant, prevalent**). [129]

prevalent, *adj.* common, generally practiced, occurring widely or frequently (SAT synonyms: **predominant, prevailing**). [98]

prevaricate, *v.* to lie, speak falsely, stray from the truth. [193, 287, 291]

primordial, *adj.* primitive, original, basic, elemental, primeval. [271, 297]

priority, *n.* 1. something first in importance or order: Balancing the budget is a top *priority* of the legislature. 2. the right of being first in importance, order, or rank: The most qualified applicant has *priority* over the others. [16, 70, 163]

problematic, *adj.* being or presenting a problem; questionable, difficult, unresolved. [109, 214, 246, 247]

procrastinate, *v.* to postpone taking action until a future time, esp. habitually. **procrastination,** *n.* [127, 274, 287]

procure, *v.* to get by some effort, secure, obtain, acquire: to *procure* water during a drought. [105, 271]

prodding, *n.* jabbing, poking, or goading with or as if with a prod (a pointed stick). [146]

prodigious, *adj.* 1. huge, enormous, monumental; extraordinary in size, extent, or degree. 2. marvelous, amazing, phenomenal. [45, 110, 155, 245, 294, 297]

proficient, *adj.* highly capable, expert, skilled (SAT synonyms: **adept, adroit, deft, dexterous**). [viii, 9, 69]

profound, *adj.* 1. deep. 2. having or demonstrating deep understanding or intelligence: *profound* ideas. 3. complete, absolute, unbroken: a *profound* silence. 4. sweeping, extensive: *profound* changes. 5. intensely felt: *profound* sadness. [13, 32, 50, 103, 129, 138, 143, 155, 255, 285, 286]

profusion, *n.* a large supply, great quantity or amount (SAT synonyms: **abundance, plenitude, plethora**). [28]

prognosis, *n.* a prediction, forecast, esp. about the course of a disease and the possibility of recovery. [19]

prolific, *adj.* highly productive or **fruitful**: a *prolific* artist; a *prolific* apple tree (SAT synonym: **fertile**; cf. **arable**). [109]

prominent, *adj.* 1. widely known, usu. favorably; important, distinguished (see synonym study below). 2. sticking out, projecting, noticeable: a *prominent* chin; a *prominent* feature on a map (SAT synonyms: **conspicuous, salient**). **prominence,** *n.* [9, 23, 31, 202, 267, 308]
—*Prominent, notable, eminent, renowned,* and *illustrious* all are used of persons who are well known and respected. *Prominent* and *notable* stress the relative importance of a person, suggesting that he or she stands out in comparison with others. *Eminent* stresses the superiority of the person's rank, achievement, or character. *Renowned* stresses the person's fame, suggesting that he or she is widely known. *Illustrious* stresses a highly distinguished reputation, esp. one based on brilliant achievement.

promulgate, *v.* to make known formally or officially, publish, circulate, proclaim, publicize. [101, 299, 307, 312]

prone, *adj.* stretched out face downward, prostrate. [149]

propensity, *n.* a natural tendency or inclination: to have a *propensity* for getting into trouble. [118]

prophetic, *adj.* of or pert. to a prophet (one who makes predictions) or to a prophecy (a prediction, esp. one that is divinely inspired): a *prophetic* dream. [76, 309]

propound, *v.* to present for consideration, suggest, propose: to *propound* an idea to a committee. [105]

prosaic, *adj.* unimaginative, boring, ordinary, dull: a *prosaic* existence (SAT synonyms: **commonplace, lackluster, mundane, pedestrian**). [7, 307, 312]

prosperity, *n.* wealth, good fortune, success. [201]

prosperous, *adj.* 1. successful, thriving. 2. wealthy, well-to-do (SAT synonym: **affluent**). [6, 36, 297]

protagonist, *n.* the leading character in a work of literature. [189, 287]

prototype, *n.* an original model on which later versions are based. [174]

protracted, *adj.* drawn out in time, prolonged, stretched out, lengthened. [6, 73, 138, 196, 251, 298, 303]

protruding, *adj.* sticking up or out, projecting. [250]

proverbial, *adj.* well-known because widely repeated; famous. [282]

provocative, *adj.* tending to arouse, as by making one curious, angry, or interested: a *provocative* laugh; a *provocative* reply. [69, 107]

prudent, *adj.* 1. characterized by cautious planning and sound, careful judgment (SAT synonyms: **circumspect, discreet**). 2. thrifty, spending or using wisely and carefully (SAT synonym: **frugal**). [89, 147, 192, 247]

prurient, *adj.* tending to have or causing lustful desires or thoughts. [32, 210]

pseudonym, *n.* a fictitious name assumed by a writer or other well-known person, usually to conceal his or her identity; pen name, alias: George Eliot is the *pseudonym* of Mary Ann Evans. [102, 106, 244, 290, 293]

pugilist, *n.* a fighter, boxer. **pugilistic**, *adj.* [25, 277, 290]

pungent, *adj.* sharp or biting to smell or taste: Indian cooking often features dishes with *pungent* spices. [84]

purloin, *v.* to steal, pilfer, take dishonestly, commit theft. [175, 241]

purport, *v.* to claim, often falsely: The article *purports* to show no **bias**. [101]

Q

quagmire, *n.* an area of swampy ground, a bog; hence, a situation difficult to get out of. [261]

quandary, *n.* a state of uncertainty about what to do; a perplexing or difficult situation, predicament, jam, fix, pickle: Her absence left them in a *quandary*. (SAT synonym: **dilemma**). [193]

querulous, *adj.* tending to find fault; complaining, peevish, or whiny. [50]

quiescent, *adj.* in a resting state, quiet, not active. [3, 21]

quizzical, *adj.* questioning, disbelieving, or puzzled: She listened to his story with a *quizzical* expression on her face. **quizzically**, *adv.* [218]

R

radical, *adj.* 1. of or relating to roots or origins, fundamental. 2. extreme, thoroughgoing: *radical* reforms (SAT synonym: **drastic**). **radically**, *adv.* [59, 97, 101, 174, 299, 304]

random, *adj.* 1. unplanned or unorganized. 2. lacking order, method, or purpose. **randomly**, *adv.* [xiv, 28, 84, 109, 144, 208, 240]

—*Random, haphazard, fortuitous,* and *desultory* all apply to that which is unplanned or accidental. *Random* suggests a lack of organization, pattern, or purpose. *Haphazard* suggests a careless leaving to chance. *Fortuitous* may be applied to chance events with good or bad outcomes; today it is often used of happy accidents. *Desultory* suggests an aimless shifting from one thing to another.

rash, *adj.* acting too quickly and without enough thought, reckless (SAT synonyms: **foolhardy, imprudent,** and see **impetuous**). [108, 262, 298]

rational, *adj.* founded on or guided by reason: a *rational* decision. **rationally,** *adv.* [144, 166, 177]

rationalist, *n.* one whose opinions or beliefs are based on reasoning. [105]

raucous, *adj.* disorderly, wild, rowdy: a *raucous* party (SAT synonyms: **boisterous, vociferous**). [213]

ravage, *n.* devastating damage, violent destruction: the *ravages* of wind and weather. [273]

rebut, *v.* to deny or disprove (an argument or claim) by offering opposing evidence or proof. **rebuttal,** *n.* [97, 104]

reciprocate, *v.* to return in equal measure: He invited her to dinner and she *reciprocated* by inviting him. [141]

reckoning, *n.* the settling of accounts; an accounting, as for something received or done. [264]

recluse, *n.* a person who lives alone, shut away from the outside world. [101, 287, 291]

reconcile, *v.* to bring into agreement, make consistent, harmonize: Every month he tries unsuccessfully to *reconcile* his bank statement. [100, 295, 300]

recount, *v.* to narrate, tell in detail, describe. [168]

rectify, *v.* to set right or adjust: to *rectify* an injustice. [116]

rectitude, *n.* rightness in principles and conduct; moral virtue. [200]

recuperate, *v.* to recover from illness or fatigue, regain health. [134]

refinement, *n.* 1. elegance of thought, feeling, manners, taste, or language. 2. improvement, polish. [108, 226]

reflective, *adj.* thoughtful (SAT synonym: **contemplative**). [54]

refute, *v.* to prove to be untrue or erroneous: *refute* a claim. [104, 188, 308]

regal, *adj.* kingly or queenly, majestic, fit for royalty. [31, 172, 187]

rejuvenated, *adj.* refilled with energy or youthfulness, made to seem new or fresh again. [271]

rejuvenating, *adj.* refreshing, restorative, giving new life and energy to (SAT synonym: **invigorating**). [126, 283]

relative, *adj.* considered in comparison to something else, comparative. **relatively,** *adj.* [103, 175, 278]

relent, *v.* to become more gentle, less severe, or more forgiving. [170]

relevant, *adj.* bearing upon the point or matter at hand; to the purpose (SAT synonyms: **germane, pertinent**). [x, 131, 142, 297]

relic, *n.* a surviving trace of a culture or age that no longer exists: a *relic* of the Dark Ages. [84, 253, 289]

reluctance, *n.* unwillingness, disinclination, lack of desire to act or become involved. **reluctant**, *adj.* **reluctantly**, *adv.* [153, 243, 263, 283, 296, 301]

reminiscent, *adj.* tending to awaken memory, suggestive of the past. [170, 286]

remonstrate, *v.* to argue with strong reasons against, plead in protest, present an objection. [246]

renegade, *adj.* disloyal, traitorous. [201]

renovate, *v.* to renew, make as good as new. **renovation**, *n.* [46, 281]

renown, *n.* fame, widespread reputation. [111, 266]

renowned, *adj.* famous, well-known, acclaimed (SAT synonyms: see **prominent**). [12, 130, 172, 299]

repression, *n.* the act or state of keeping something down or holding it in check, often by force: *repression* of free speech; *repression* of desires. [103, 288]

repressive, *adj.* tending or serving to keep something down or hold it in check, restrictive, authoritarian: a *repressive* government. [103, 295]

reprimand, *n.* a severe, often official, expression of disapproval; scolding, rebuke. [46, 124]

reproachful, *adj.* full of or expressing disapproval for a wrong or fault: a *reproachful* cluck. [54]

reprobate, *n.* a wicked, immoral person (SAT synonym: **scoundrel**). [277]

repugnant, *adj.* disgusting, repulsive, objectionable, repellent: The receding flood left a *repugnant* odor (SAT synonym: **offensive**). [29, 165, 306]

rescind, *v.* to repeal or cancel. [37]

resentment, *n.* ill will produced by a perceived insult or injury (SAT synonym: **indignation**). [54]

resilient, *adj.* recovering quickly, as from misfortune or illness. [166, 298]

resonant, *adj.* having a full and rich tone or sound (SAT synonym: **sonorous**). [51, 142, 251, 273]

resourceful, *adj.* clever and creative in solving problems or difficulties. [44, 78, 133, 169, 272, 296, 301]

restrain, *v.* to hold back. **restraining**, *n.* [260, 295, 301]

restraint, *n.* self-control, the act of holding back, the condition of being held back, or something that holds one back. [156]

retrospect, *n.* the consideration or **analysis** of past events or circumstances: In *retrospect,* we should have sold that stock at its peak last year. [156, 207]

revel, *v.* to take great pleasure in, enjoy intensely. [77, 243]

revelation, *n.* something made known or revealed, esp. something surprising. [274]

revere, *v.* to regard as **venerable**, treat with **reverence**. [201, 307]

reverence, *n.* a feeling of awe and respect often mingled with affection. **reverent**, *adj.* (SAT synonym: **pious**). **reverently**, *adv.* [106, 201, 258]

revitalize, *v.* to give new life and energy to, make **vital** again. [69, 243]

rhetoric, *n.* 1. the skillful and persuasive use of language. 2. overblown or intellectually empty language. **rhetorical**, *adj.* [90, 131, 265, 307]

ribald, *adj.* coarse or **vulgar** in the use of language: a *ribald* story. [53]

ridicule, *n.* speech or actions intended to create scornful laughter at someone or something (SAT synonym: **derision**). [101, 290, 293, 309]

ritual, *n.* a ceremonial act, formal procedure, or customary practice. [36, 168, 281]

robust, *adj.* strong, hearty, sturdy, firm, full of health (SAT synonym: **vigorous**). [141, 281, 294]

rotund, *adj.* round in shape, **notably** plump or chubby (SAT synonym: **portly**; cf. **corpulent**). [66]

rudiment, *n.* a simple, basic, elementary principle or fundamental skill. **rudimentary,** *adj.* [90, 97, 110, 176, 223]

rueful, *adj.* filled with sorrow, regret, or pity. **ruefully,** *adv.* [105, 246, 271]

ruminate, *v.* to chew on mentally, ponder, contemplate, meditate or reflect (SAT synonym: **muse**). [60, 73, 216]

ruthless, *adj.* showing no pity or **compassion**, cruel, merciless. [193]

S

sabotage, *v.* to deliberately hinder, obstruct, injure, destroy, etc. (SAT synonyms: **subvert, undermine**). [103, 275]

sagacious, *adj.* wise, exercising sound judgment (SAT synonyms: **astute, discerning, insightful, keen, perceptive, perspicacious, shrewd**). [107, 181, 242]

salient, *adj.* standing out, attracting attention, easily seen, noticeable (SAT synonyms: **conspicuous, prominent**). [66, 119, 290, 293]

sallow, *adj.* of a sickly, pale, yellowish color or complexion. [270]

salubrious, *adj.* favorable to health, healthful (SAT synonyms: see **wholesome**). [127]

salutary, *adj.* promoting a **beneficial** purpose or effect, good for one's health, producing an improvement, remedial, corrective. (SAT synonyms: see **wholesome**). [3, 77, 297]

sarcasm, *n.* the use of sharp, biting language to make fun of or wound. **sarcastic,** *adj.* (SAT synonym: **derisive**). **sarcastically,** *adv.* [187, 189, 271]
—*Sarcasm* and *irony* are related in meaning. *Sarcasm* refers to sharp, sneering language meant to hurt or insult. *Irony* suggests the use of more **subtle** language (spec. language that **implies** the opposite of what it **literally** says) to make fun of in a milder way.

satiate, *v.* to satisfy completely: The chocolates *satiated* our craving for sweets (cf. **surfeited**). [63]

satirical, *adj.* relating to the art of exposing human folly or vice with wit (SAT synonym: **ironic**). [229]

saunter, *v.* to walk in a leisurely way, stroll. [95]

savant, *n.* a person of great learning, scholar. [271]

savor, *v.* **literally,** to taste or smell with pleasure; figuratively, to enjoy, delight in, relish: to *savor* a delicious meal; to *savor* a victory (cf. **unsavory**). [104]

scatterbrained, *adj.* incapable of orderly thought, flighty. [178]

scintillating, *adj.* 1. **emitting** sparkles or twinkles of light, shining: *scintillating* fireflies. 2. lively, intelligent, clever, or witty: a *scintillating* discussion. [61, 210, 226, 298]

scope, *n.* range, the area covered. [70]

scoundrel, *n.* a dishonorable person, cad, villain (SAT synonym: **reprobate**). [269, 290]

scruple, *n.* a moral principle that **restrains** action. [155]

scrupulous, *adj.* precise and exacting (SAT synonyms: **conscientious, fastidious, meticulous, painstaking**). **scrupulously,** *adv.* [98, 120, 158]

scrutinize, *v.* to examine carefully and closely (SAT synonym: **peruse**). **scrutinizing,** *n.* [xi, 40, 78, 83, 130, 151, 157, 163, 188, 195, 214]

scurrilous, *adj.* coarse, indecent, or abusive: a *scurrilous* attack (SAT synonym: **vulgar**). [270]

secluded, *adj.* hidden, removed, sheltered, withdrawn: a *secluded* corner. **seclusion,** *n.* [102, 288]

sect, *n.* a group of people who share a particular **doctrine** or follow a particular leader, esp. a group that either forms a distinct unit within or has separated from a larger religious group. [174, 253]

seduce, *v.* 1. to lure or attract. 2. to lead into error. [105, 140, 286]

self-aggrandizement, *n.* the increase of one's own importance, position, or reputation. [156]

senile, *adj.* relating to or characteristic of old age, esp. showing a decline in mental abilities (cf. **dotard**). [29, 273, 276]

sentiment, *n.* a feeling, opinion. [103, 277]

sentimental, *adj.* expressing tender feelings, sometimes to excess. [1]

serene, *adj.* calm, quiet, peaceful, undisturbed (SAT synonyms: **halcyon, placid, tranquil**). [51, 225]

serenity, *n.* calmness, contentment, repose, tranquillity. [143, 165]

serpentine, *adj.* like a snake; hence, winding, curving, twisting (SAT synonym: **sinuous**). [250]

servile, *adj.* like a slave, fawning, submissive, lacking spirit (SAT synonyms: **obsequious, sycophantic**). [98, 129]

shard, *n.* a fragment of a brittle substance, esp. of broken pottery. [217, 287]

shrewd, *adj.* sharp or clever in practical matters, artful, cunning (SAT synonyms: **astute, discerning, insightful, keen, perceptive, perspicacious, sagacious**). **shrewdly,** *adv.* [56, 58, 65, 284]

shroud, *n.* something that covers, screens, or veils. [176]

shrouded, *adj.* shut off from sight or light, hidden, concealed: Her face was *shrouded* in shadows. [61]

shun, *v.* to keep away from deliberately, avoid consistently or habitually. [105, 310, 311]

simultaneous, *adj.* happening, existing, or operating at the same time. **simultaneously,** *adv.* [201, 228]

singular, *adj.* extraordinary, rare, remarkable, exceptional: a *singular* accomplishment. [100, 108, 272]

sinuous, *adj.* having curves or turns, wavy, winding, snakelike: a *sinuous* road (SAT synonym: **serpentine**). [216, 235]

skeptical, *adj.* 1. tending to question or doubt, disbelieving. 2. feeling or showing doubt or disbelief (SAT synonyms: **dubious, incredulous**). [18, 124, 146, 153, 210]

sluggish, *adj.* 1. lazy, dull, inactive, or lacking energy (SAT synonyms: see **phlegmatic**). 2. very slow-moving. [9, 149, 176, 196, 214, 297, 302]

smirk, *v.* to smile in a self-satisfied or artificial way; simper: He *smirked* when John gave the wrong answer. **smirk,** *n.* [79, 95, 259]

smug, *adj.* self-satisfied to an annoying or irritating degree: a *smug* attitude (SAT synonym: **complacent**). [276]

sojourn, *v.* to remain or live (in a place) for a while. [271]

sojourn, *n.* a temporary stay. [251]

solicitous, *adj.* concerned, worried, or anxious about someone or something: *solicitous* about her welfare. [162]

solitude, *n.* the state of being or living alone, seclusion. [46, 287, 291]

somber, *adj.* 1. dark, gloomy, grim, dreary, dismal: *somber* furnishings; a *somber* occasion (SAT synonyms: **austere, grave, staid**). 2. sad, unhappy: a *somber* feeling (SAT synonyms: **glum, melancholy**). [11, 43, 122, 295]

sonorous, *adj.* rich and full in sound: the *sonorous* beat of the timpani (SAT synonym: **resonant**). [51, 168, 269]

soothsayer, *n.* one who claims to be able to foretell the future; a seer. [271, 287, 291]

sophisticated, *adj.* 1. cultured and refined (a *sophisticated* group) or suited to the taste of cultured and refined people (a *sophisticated* drama). 2. knowing and worldly-wise: a *sophisticated* gentleman (SAT synonyms: **genteel, suave, urbane**). 3. complicated or highly developed: *sophisticated* electronic devices. **sophistication,** *n.* [31, 74, 100, 105, 111, 295, 301]

soporific, *adj.* inducing sleep; tending to dull the awareness. [178]

sordid, *adj.* 1. seedy, foul, wretched, squalid: *sordid* ghettos. 2. morally degraded, ignoble, base, vile: *sordid* deeds; *sordid* urges. [210, 295]

sparse, *adj.* of a few, scattered elements; not thick or dense: *sparse* vegetation; *sparse* attendance. **sparsely,** *adv.* [105, 150]

spartan, *adj.* rigorously self-disciplined and self-restrained in lifestyle; stern and strict (SAT synonyms: **ascetic, austere**). [281, 297, 302]

specificity, *n.* precision, definitiveness. [70]

specify, *v.* to state or list in detail, define, stipulate (SAT synonym: **enumerate**). [72, 312]

spectral, *adj.* spooky, eerie, otherworldly, like a specter (a ghost). [186]

speculate, *v.* to reason and form theories on the basis of inadequate or **inconclusive** evidence (SAT synonym: **surmise**). [98]

speculation, *n.* 1. the act or product of thinking or reasoning, esp. on the basis of incomplete or **inconclusive** evidence. 2. a supposition, educated guess (SAT synonyms: **conjecture, surmise**). 3. a financial investment with some risk. [97, 104, 114, 137, 173, 176, 199, 267]

speculator, *n.* a person who makes risky financial investments. [174]

spendthrift, *n.* someone who wastes money or spends it foolishly. [50]

spontaneous, *adj.* 1. occurring naturally or without practice or forethought: a *spontaneous* performance (SAT synonym: **impromptu**). 2. acting in **accordance** with one's own inner nature rather than with external forces, guided by instinct or impulse (SAT synonyms: **impulsive, involuntary**). [4, 25, 127, 218, 287]

spurious, *adj.* fake, fraudulent, counterfeit: a *spurious* painting; *spurious* testimony. [200, 299]

squabble, *n.* a noisy quarrel or argument, usu. over a small matter: The discussion turned into a silly, noisy *squabble* over details. [99]

squandering, *n.* using or spending foolishly and wastefully. [49]

stagnant, *adj.* inactive, not advancing or developing: a *stagnant* economy. [45]

staid, *adj.* proper, sober, dignified, conservative, strait-laced (SAT synonyms: **austere, grave, somber**). [7, 67]

stalwart, *adj.* of outstanding strength, sturdy (SAT synonym: **brawny**). [95, 276]

stately, *adj.* impressively formal and serious in style or proportions. [21, 64]

stature, *n.* height or level of achievement. [109]

status, *n.* 1. a stage of progress or development; condition: the *status* of the case. 2. relative position or rank: her *status* in the community. [70, 102]

staunch, *adj.* firm, loyal, true: many *staunch* supporters (SAT synonym: **steadfast**). [46, 296, 301]

steadfast, *adj.* faithful, constant, loyal, firm: *steadfast* in his determination (SAT synonym: **staunch**). [156]

stereotype, *n.* something that conforms to a fixed pattern, not allowing for individuality, esp. a mental image or a way of thinking about a person, thing, or event. **stereotyped,** *adj.* [229, 235]

stimulate, *v.* to excite to growth or greater action, rouse (SAT synonym: **galvanize**). **stimulating,** *adj.* [10, 61, 99, 139, 151]

stoic, *adj.* not affected by or showing emotions, esp. pain or distress; calm, unmoved (SAT synonyms: **dispassionate, impassive**). **stoically,** *adv.* [1, 276, 297, 302]

stratagem, *n.* a trick or scheme used to outwit an enemy, gain an advantage, or achieve a goal. [30, 290]

stratum (*pl.* **strata**), *n.* a level, layer, rank, or grade. [107, 108]

strident, *adj.* loud, noisy, grating, shrill (SAT synonyms: **discordant, dissonant**). [50, 117]

studious, *adj.* 1. concerned with study or learning. 2. earnest, purposeful, deliberate (SAT synonym: **diligent**). **studiously,** *adv.* [138, 273]

stupefaction, *n.* a state of stupidity, grogginess, or half-consciousness: After the feast, they sat around in a state of near *stupefaction.* [176]

suave, *adj.* smooth and courteous, polished and **poised** in social situations (SAT synonyms: **genteel, sophisticated, urbane**). [56]

subjective, *adj.* of or arising from a person's emotions, prejudices, or interests, not from external evidence; based on personal feelings or opinions (cf. **objective**). **subjectivity,** *n.* [xii, 115, 137]

subordinate, *adj.* occupying an inferior position, rank, or class; secondary, minor. [98]

subside, *v.* to become quiet or less active, settle down to a lower level. [77, 111]

substantiate, *v.* to support by proof or reliable evidence (SAT synonyms: **authenticate, confirm, corroborate, validate, verify**). **substantiated,** *adj.* [104, 137, 140, 246]

subterranean, *adj.* underground. [40, 249, 297, 302]

subtle, *adj.* 1. indirect, not obvious, difficult to see or understand: *subtle* changes. 2. delicate, refined, or faintly mysterious: a *subtle* smile. 3. sly, cunning: a *subtle* plot. **subtly,** *adv.* [viii, 104, 161, 174, 215, 229, 290, 299, 304, 313]

subtlety, *n.* a fine point, delicate distinction. [9]

subvert, *v.* to overturn or overthrow, destroy, ruin (SAT synonyms: **sabotage, undermine**). **subversive,** *adj.* [272, 299]

succinct, *adj.* expressed precisely and compactly, without wasted words (SAT synonyms: **concise, terse**). [xii, 137, 263, 307]

succumb, *v.* to yield or give in (as to an appeal or a superior force). [178, 185, 299, 304]

suffused, *adj.* spread through or over (as with light or color). [268]

sumptuous, *adj.* exceptionally rich and luxurious (SAT synonyms: **lavish, luxuriant, opulent**). [93, 234, 280]

supercilious, *adj.* looking down at or treating others in a proudly superior way (SAT synonyms: **arrogant, contemptuous, disdainful, haughty, imperious**). [56, 267]

superficial, *adj.* concerned only with the surface, with what is obvious or apparent; shallow, lacking in depth or substance (SAT synonyms: **cursory, perfunctory**). **superficially,** *adv.* [255, 281, 286, 294, 295, 300]

superlative, *adj.* excellent, of the greatest or highest quality: a *superlative* achievement. [93]

suppress, *v.* 1. to hold back or stifle. 2. to keep from becoming known (SAT synonym: **censor**). **suppressed,** *adj.* [18, 65, 103, 185]

surfeited, *adj.* overly, excessively, or nauseatingly full (cf. **satiate**). [127, 187]

surmise, *v.* to conclude based on scanty evidence, suppose, guess (SAT synonym: **speculate**). **surmise,** *n.* (SAT synonyms: **conjecture, speculation**). [129, 194, 226, 234]

surpass, *v.* to go beyond, transcend. [263]

surpassing, *adj.* superior. [69]

surreptitious, *adj.* secret and stealthy, not open or **conspicuous** (SAT synonyms: **clandestine, covert, devious, furtive**). **surreptitiousness,** *n.* [105, 146, 215, 235]

sustenance, *n.* food, nourishment. [250, 299, 304]

sycophant, *n.* someone who tries to win favor or gain advancement by flattering influential people; a self-seeking, fawning person (SAT synonym: **toady**). **sycophantic,** *adj.* (SAT synonyms: **obsequious, servile**). [73, 287]

symmetrical, *adj.* possessing **symmetry,** having balanced proportions. [4, 35]

symmetry, *n.* 1. a correspondence of parts (in size, shape, position, etc.) on opposite sides of a dividing line or plane. 2. beauty of form resulting from balanced and orderly proportions. [218, 288, 299]

synopsis, *n.* a condensed summary or statement outlining the main points (of a narrative, **treatise,** etc.). [53]

syntax, *n.* the way words are arranged to form phrases, clauses, and sentences: awkward, ungrammatical *syntax.* [110, 306]

synthesis, *n.* the combining of separate parts into a **coherent** whole or the whole formed in this way. [137]

T

tamper, *v.* to interfere or meddle with, esp. to damage or weaken: to *tamper* with a lock. [172]

tangential, *adj.* straying from or only slightly connected (to a subject). [182, 183, 290]

tangible, *adj.* capable of being touched, concrete, real, definite, actual. [149, 242, 299]

tantalizing, *adj.* intensely tempting, arousing great interest or desire for something that seems unreachable or unobtainable (SAT synonym: **alluring**). [146]

tardiness, *n.* lateness, the state of being delayed. [67]

tattered, *adj.* ragged, torn, shredded. [75]

taunt, *v.* to provoke, challenge, or make fun of in an insulting way. [213]

tawdry, *adj.* flashy and tasteless, cheap, showy (SAT synonyms: **garish, gaudy**). [215]

tedious, *adj.* tiresome and boring: a *tedious* assignment. [vii, viii, 34, 97, 289, 293]

telltale, *adj.* indicating or revealing something intended to be secret: a *telltale* remark. [89, 122]

tempestuous, *adj.* stormy, passionate, greatly agitated, like a tempest (a violent windstorm). [250, 287]

tenacious, *adj.* 1. holding or adhering firmly: a *tenacious* vine. 2. stubborn, perseverant (SAT synonym: **persistent**). [xv, 110, 122]

tentative, *adj.* hesitant, halting, uncertain, timid, halfhearted: a *tentative* answer; a *tentative* approach. **tentatively,** *adv.* [25, 57, 125, 133, 227, 257, 281, 306]

tenure, *n.* 1. the **status** assuring an employee a permanent position, esp. as a teacher. 2. the act, right, or manner of holding something (such as a teaching position) or the length of time something is held. [45, 165, 280]

terse, *adj.* brief and to the point: a *terse* manner of speaking (SAT synonyms: **concise, succinct**). [123, 149, 287]

theoretical, *adj.* of, pert. to, or based on (1) unsupported opinion or limited information or (2) a general set of principles or knowledge. **theoretically,** *adv.* [107]

thesis (*pl.* **theses**), *n.* 1. a position or proposition that is to be proved by argument. 2. a **dissertation** developed from original research, esp. one presented by a candidate for an academic degree. [65, 97, 100, 101, 104, 289]

threadbare, *adj.* so frayed that the threads show, old and worn out. [66, 90, 255]

throng, *n.* a host of people, crowd, multitude. [117, 237, 305, 310]

timorous, *adj.* fearful, hesitant, timid, lacking self-confidence. [138]

tirade, *n.* a prolonged and angry speech, harangue, diatribe. [275, 288]

toady, *n.* someone who flatters others hoping to gain favors, an **obsequious** follower, bootlicking servant (SAT synonym: **sycophant**). [276]

tome, *n.* a weighty, large, or scholarly book. [95, 171, 194, 256, 287]

torrid, *adj.* passionate, heated (SAT synonyms: **ardent, fervid**). [140]

toxic, *adj.* harmful, poisonous. [125, 289]

traditional, *adj.* 1. pert. to or following customs, beliefs, or practices that have been passed down from one generation to the next (SAT synonyms: **conventional, orthodox**). 2. done according to tradition (a long-established, inherited way of thinking or behaving). [4, 65, 102, 109, 171]

tranquil, *adj.* calm, quiet, peaceful (SAT synonyms: **halcyon, placid, serene**). [61, 271]

transcribe, *v.* 1. to make a handwritten or printed copy. 2. to translate or write out in the corresponding characters of another alphabet. **transcription,** *n.* [194, 195, 202, 203, 219, 239, 243, 246]

transgression, *n.* the violation of a command or law; a sin or offense. [278]

translucent, *adj.* allowing the passage of light but not a view of objects beyond. [157, 298]

traumatic, *adj.* causing serious physical injury or severe and long-lasting emotional shock. [106]

treatise, *n.* a systematic and usu. lengthy and scholarly discussion of a subject in writing: a *treatise* on modern poetry. [xii, 46, 101, 171]

trite, *adj.* worn-out, overused (SAT synonym: **hackneyed**). [200, 295]

trivial, *adj.* of small value or importance, not worth noticing: *trivial* differences; a *trivial* thought (SAT synonyms: **frivolous, insignificant, negligible, paltry, petty, superficial**). **trivialize,** *v.* [28, 285, 286, 299, 304]

troupe, *n.* a group of touring theatrical performers. [99, 244, 287, 291]

tumult, *n.* 1. great uproar or commotion. 2. a noisy or violent outburst. **tumultuous,** *adj.* [110, 250, 274, 288]

turret, *n.* a little tower, usu. at an angle of a larger structure. [35, 287, 291]

tyrannize, *v.* to rule with absolute, often **oppressive** power. [97]

U

ubiquitous, *adj.* existing everywhere at the same time, widespread: The cockroach, like the flea, is a *ubiquitous* creature. [110, 290, 293]

ultimate, *adj.* 1. final or concluding: their *ultimate* destination. 2. eventual: to hope for *ultimate* success. 3. greatest or highest possible: *ultimate* degree. **ultimately,** *adv.* [xvi, 129, 165]

unabridged, *adj.* complete, having nothing removed, or the most complete of its type: an *unabridged* novel; an *unabridged* dictionary (cf. **abridge**). [171, 205]

unanimous, *adj.* having the agreement of all: The plans received the group's *unanimous* approval; a *unanimous* vote. **unanimously,** *adv.* [279]

unblemished, *adj.* having no fault or flaw. [222]

uncanny, *adj.* strange, mysterious, eerie: an *uncanny* light in the old abandoned house. [185]

unconventional, *adj.* not bound by accepted custom or practice, not ordinary, not **conventional** (SAT synonym: **unorthodox**). [155]

undaunted, *adj.* fearless and determined, not discouraged or dismayed. [131]

undermine, *v.* to weaken or ruin slowly or in small degrees: The constant criticism *undermined* his self-confidence (SAT synonyms: **corrupt, debase, sabotage, subvert**). [276, 295]

underscore, *v.* to draw a line under; hence, to stress or emphasize. [98, 137]

understatement, *n.* a statement that is made less strongly than the facts would indicate or that exhibits intentional **restraint. understated,** *adj.* [5, 255, 293, 309, 314]

unenlightened, *adj.* ignorant, misinformed, not educated or **enlightened** (SAT synonym: **benighted**). [135, 266]

unethical, *adj.* immoral, not **ethical** (SAT synonyms: **corrupt, depraved**). [232, 246]

unfathomable, *adj.* unable to be understood completely, gotten to the bottom of, or **fathomed** (SAT synonym: **incomprehensible**). [295]

uniform, *adj.* identical or alike, unvarying, consistent. **uniformly,** *adv.* **uniformity,** *n.* [240, 298]

universal, *adj.* 1. including, covering, or involving all: a *universal* belief. 2. existing or operating everywhere: a *universal* need for shelter. [110, 290]

unkempt, *adj.* uncombed, messy, untidy. [27]

unorthodox, *adj.* not customary, not **orthodox** (SAT synonym: **unconventional**). [65, 307]

unprecedented, *adj.* without parallel or precedent (an earlier example or model to follow) (SAT synonym: **novel**). [108, 299, 304]

unremitting, *adj.* not letting up, constant. [108]

unrestrained, *adj.* unchecked, uncontrolled, not under **restraint.** [297, 302]

unsavory, *adj.* **literally,** disagreeable to taste or smell; figuratively, undesirable, objectionable, morally **offensive**: an *unsavory* reputation (cf. **savor**). [144]

unscathed, *adj.* unharmed, uninjured, undamaged: He escaped from the burning building completely *unscathed.* [278]

unsettling, *adj.* disturbing, causing uneasiness or confusion. [64, 151, 309]

unwieldy, *adj.* not easy to handle or manage, esp. because of size, weight, awkward shape, etc. [82, 212, 259]

upbraid, *v.* to criticize severely, rebuke: The team was *upbraided* for its un-sportsmanlike behavior (SAT synonym: **castigate**; cf. **admonish, censure**). [50]

upright, *adj.* honest, adhering to what is morally right or just (SAT synonyms: **conscientious, ethical, virtuous**). [164, 274]

urban, *adj.* in or pert. to a city. [4]

urbane, *adj.* extremely polite and polished in manner (SAT synonyms: **genteel, sophisticated, suave**). [65, 211]

usurp, *v.* to seize and hold by force or without proper right or authority. **usurping,** *adj.* [102, 270]

V

valedictory, *adj.* containing a farewell, of or relating to a leave-taking. [2]

valid, *adj.* 1. right, well-founded, reasonable, just: a *valid* argument. 2. legal, official: a *valid* passport. **validity,** *n.* [214, 245]

validate, *v.* 1. to make **valid**, prove right or true (SAT synonyms: **authenticate, confirm, corroborate, substantiate, verify**). 2. to make official. **validation,** *n.* [130, 289]

valor, *n.* bravery and determination in facing danger, esp. in war. **valorous,** *adj.* [197, 253]

vandalism, *n.* willful or **malicious** destruction of property: They suspected that the fires were the result of an act of *vandalism*. [248]

vanquish, *v.* to subdue, conquer, defeat, overcome: *vanquish* the foe. **vanquished,** *adj.* [253]

vantage point, *n.* a position from which one has a wide view. [235]

vehement, *adj.* 1. characterized by intense emotion or passion: a *vehement* accusation. 2. acting with great energy, violent. **vehemently,** *adv.* [150, 170, 213]

venerable, *adj.* 1. deserving respect because of age, character, achievements, etc.: a *venerable* poet. 2. impressive because of age: a *venerable* tradition. [12, 139, 216]

verbose, *adj.* overly wordy, long-winded, containing more words than needed (SAT synonym: **diffuse**). [1, 82, 97, 118, 307]

verify, *v.* to prove the truth or accuracy of (SAT synonyms: **authenticate, confirm, corroborate, substantiate, validate**). [157, 288]

veritable, *adj.* true, actual, not false or exaggerated: a *veritable* hero. [173, 274]

vernacular, *n.* the common, everyday spoken form of a language. **vernacular,** *adj.* [110, 307]

vexatious, *adj.* troubling, disturbing, annoying, irritating. [142]

vibrant, *adj.* filled with energy, lively: a *vibrant* performance (SAT synonym: **vivacious**). [143]

vigilant, *adj.* on the alert, watchful (SAT synonyms: **circumspect, wary**). [122, 135, 232, 278]

vigor, *n.* active physical or mental health, strength, force, energy, etc. (SAT synonym: **vitality**). [289]

vigorous, *adj.* full of healthy energy, energetic, strong, forceful (SAT synonyms: **robust, vibrant**). [93, 227, 273]

vilify, *v.* to abuse in speech or writing, say or write damaging or false things about, slander, defame. [101]

vindictive, *adj.* **motivated** by a desire for revenge, unforgiving and spiteful. [200, 290, 293]

violate, *v.* 1. to break or disregard: to *violate* a law. 2. to defile, desecrate, or disrespect: to *violate* a sanctuary. [151, 260]

virtually, *adv.* practically, almost but not quite, nearly. [101, 176]

virtuous, *adj.* possessing moral excellence, pure, righteous (SAT synonyms: **conscientious, ethical, upright**). [164, 266]

visceral, *adj.* of or pert. to the internal organs of the body, esp. the abdomen; hence, instinctive and **intuitive** rather than intellectual or **rational**. [110]

vital, *adj.* 1. characteristic of living beings or essential to maintaining life. 2. full of life and energy (SAT synonyms: **robust, vibrant, vigorous, vivacious**). 3. being of the utmost importance: a *vital* issue. [28, 152, 294]

vitality, *n.* 1. the capacity to live or go on living (SAT synonym: **animation**). 2. liveliness, pep (SAT synonym: **vigor**). [x, 24, 40, 111, 168, 299]

vivacious, *adj.* filled with life and spirit, lively, sprightly (SAT synonyms: **animated, robust, vibrant, vigorous**). [66, 155]

vivid, *adj.* 1. strong, bright, intense: a *vivid* hue. 2. colorful, brightly or intensely colored: *vivid* balloons. 3. producing clear, sharp images: a *vivid* description; a *vivid* memory. 4. having the appearance of life: a *vivid* portrait. [29, 57, 82, 121, 144, 151]

vociferous, *adj.* loud and noisy: a *vociferous* fan; *vociferous* complaints (SAT synonyms: **boisterous, raucous**). [213]

voluminous, *adj.* of great volume, number, or extent. [14, 42, 282]

voracious, *adj.* 1. exceedingly hungry, ravenous. 2. never getting enough of something: a *voracious* reader (SAT synonym: **insatiable**). **voraciously,** *adv.* [28, 127, 143, 285, 286, 289, 306]

vulgar, *adj.* 1. without **refinement** or taste, coarse, crass, crude, gross: *vulgar* gestures (SAT synonym: **scurrilous**). 2. of or pert. to the common or ordinary people: *Vulgar* Latin, as distinguished from the literary form of the language. **vulgarity,** *n.* [53, 105, 266, 307, 311]

vulnerable, *adj.* susceptible to being injured or wounded, open to attack, having insufficient defenses. **vulnerability,** *n.* [6, 74, 151, 161, 298]

W

wane, *v.* to fade away, diminish gradually. [120, 214]

wanton, *adj.* 1. mean or cruel without **motive** or provocation: a *wanton* killing. 2. immoral, lustful: a *wanton* look; *wanton* desires (SAT synonym: **depraved**). 3. careless, reckless: *wanton* disregard for the law. [210, 264, 279]

wary, *adj.* watchful and cautious, distrustful, leery (SAT synonyms: **circumspect, vigilant**). **warily,** *adv.* [9, 99]

wayward, *adj.* 1. willfully following one's own desires, disobedient, head-strong, contrary. 2. inconstant and unpredictable (SAT synonym: **capricious**). [104, 237]

weathered, *adj.* faded or altered by exposure to the weather. [213]

whim, *n.* an unpredictable and often sudden notion or fancy. [275]

wholesome, *adj.* promoting well-being, healthful, conducive to the development of the mind or character. [3, 126]

—*Wholesome, salubrious,* and *salutary* all mean good for one's health. *Wholesome* refers to that which benefits or builds up the body, mind, or spirit: a *wholesome* diet; *wholesome* recreation. *Salubrious* refers to that which promotes physical health: a *salubrious* climate. *Salutary* refers to that which has a corrective or remedial effect upon the health or general condition of someone or something: *salutary* advice; a *salutary* proposal.

winsome, *adj.* charming, agreeable, and pleasant in appearance or manner (SAT synonyms: **beguiling, captivating, engaging**). [57, 122, 290]

wizened, *adj.* shrunken, shriveled, wrinkled from aging: a *wizened* face. [61, 270]

wreak, *v.* to inflict or bring about. [2, 232]

writhe, *v.* to twist or turn, as in pain. **writhing,** *adj.* [212, 277]

Z

zeal, *n.* intense passion, enthusiasm, or devotion. [82, 297]

zealous, *adj.* filled with great passion and devotion, highly or excessively enthusiastic (SAT synonyms: **ardent, avid, fanatical, fervent**). [94, 108, 311]